CICERO

THE SECRETS
OF HIS
CORRESPONDENCE

VOLUME I

By the same author
DAILY LIFE IN ANCIENT ROME

JÉRÔME CARCOPINO

CICERO

THE SECRETS

OF HIS

CORRESPONDENCE

VOLUME ONE

NEW HAVEN

YALE UNIVERSITY PRESS

LES SECRETS DE LA CORRESPONDANCE DE CICÉRON
First published in France 1947

CICERO: THE SECRETS OF HIS CORRESPONDENCE
Translated by E. O. LORIMER and first published by
YALE UNIVERSITY PRESS
New Haven Connecticut
1951

TO MY WIFE

Printed in Great Britain by William Clowes and Sons, Limited
London and Beccles

CONTENTS OF VOLUME I

Contents of Volume I

PART II

TRANSLATOR'S NOTE

IN rendering the Latin of Cicero's *Letters*, I have of course worked with the seven volumes of the invaluable edition of Tyrrell and Purser open beside me. I have also found Shuckburgh's translation extremely useful in giving quick access to the context of passages quoted.

At need, I have gladly and gratefully adopted the renderings suggested by Tyrrell and Purser and Shuckburgh, but in the main I have preferred to work directly from the Latin, feeling that, since the quotations provide the authority for passages in the author's text, a strictly literal rendering, where possible, was to be preferred to more fluent or idiomatic English. It must be realised that the quotations from Cicero's letters made in the text and notes do not always follow the readings of the Tyrrell and Purser edition. All such quotations appear in this translation in the same form as in the original French edition of the book.

The Plutarch quotations I have taken from Dryden's edition revised by Arthur Hugh Clough (now available in Everyman's Library, Nos. 407–409). For the quotations from Horace and Lucretius I am indebted to the versions of the Loeb Classics: the former by Fairclough, the latter by W. H. D. Rouse.

Since the dates occurring in the text are all of the first century B.C. I have omitted the disturbing capitals "B.C." after each, but I have retained these in the notes, so that not even the most absent-minded reader should be misled.

I take this opportunity of warmly thanking the Librarian and staff of the London Library for their ever ready and helpful co-operation, and generous supply of books required for consultation.

E. O. LORIMER.

INTRODUCTION

1. THE PROBLEM, THE DATA, THE METHOD TO BE FOLLOWED

EVEN before he has finished the last page of the Introduction
to Gaston Boissier's *Cicero and his Friends*,[1] anyone who has
had the pleasure of reading it will realise that Cicero's
Letters are the finest document of Roman history, one of the finest
documents of all history.

From the artistic point of view they are brilliantly successful.
No other epoch, no other language can show memoirs or letters
which by the quality of their form can rival Cicero's Correspondence. It surpasses them all in the value and profusion of its material;
it eclipses them by the dazzling variety of gifts it combines, gifts
elsewhere found only in dispersion. Cicero's *Letters* are now as
clear and vivid as Voltaire's, now as picturesque and light-hearted
as Madame de Sévigné's, now as tantalising and enigmatic as
Mérimée's, now as bitter and corrosive as Saint-Simon's. At one
moment they skilfully exploit all the conscious devices of the orator
who seeks to bewitch public opinion far outside the circle of his
immediate audience; at another, the shock of some occurrence
gives them the more intimate appeal, the quiver of irrepressible
emotion, the inspiration of a first enthusiasm. They present us
with a masterpiece which is a perfect blend of every quality and
every style: narrative and portrait, argument and anecdote, maxim
and metaphor, invective and irony, seductive coquetry and stinging
sarcasm.

Lastly, and above all, the *Letters* are a mine of information whose
wealth overwhelms the miner. The Correspondence which we
possess comprises 931 letters[2] ranging from 68 to 43 B.C. In something under 19 months the pace increases to as many as three letters

---

[1] Gaston Boissier, *Cicéron et ses amis*, 14th ed., Paris, 1908, p. 2f.: " . . . Cicero's *Letters* plunge us into the very middle of events and permit us to follow
them day by day."

[2] According to Tyrrell and Purser's calculation. I shall systematically append
to my quotations the chronological references of their edition.

a week, giving us 222 letters between early Jan. 44 and July 28, 43, when they cease for ever. Nine-tenths of them are from the pen of Cicero himself, the remaining tenth are written by his correspondents.[1] In either case they introduce and bring on to the stage the men who played a decisive part in an era when a new world was coming to birth.

Whether it is a question of Cicero or Atticus, Cato or Brutus, Caesar or Pompey, Antony or Octavian, the *Letters* record the activity of each one, analyse his attitudes, feelings and motives, with a precision which increases as the dénouement draws near. Towards the close they let us follow from day to day, sometimes from hour to hour, the development of a crisis out of which there was destined ultimately to emerge the framework of the Roman Empire, tried and tested, to endure for centuries. From beginning to end the *Letters* arouse and sustain an interest worthy of the great drama whose incidents they record. There are no secret schemings which they do not reveal to us, no dark and complex souls which they fail to interpret, no *dramatis personae* whom they do not endow with the colour and movement of real life. So much is this so, that two thousand years after the curtain has fallen on this vast tragi-comedy, participants and actors seem still to be alive: we seem to see their gestures, to hear their words, to participate in their conspiracies and their struggles, to outwit their cunning; we share their joys and hopes, their fears and their anger. They are rescued from oblivion and from death, and continue to evoke the illusion of a present reality and a contemporary existence.[2]

Be this as it may, the more Cicero's Correspondence strips off the mystery surrounding the long-distant and stirring era whose vicissitudes it recalls, and whose protagonists it brings again to life, the more the mystery thickens which shrouds the question of the appearance of the *Letters*. The more keenly we welcome their amazing resurrection, the more it irritates us to know so little of the accompanying circumstances. The greater our surprise at the extent, the variety, the virulence of Cicero's *Letters*, the greater grows our longing to know when and why and how they came to be

[1] According to Tyrrell and Purser's inventory (VII, pp. 165–7) there are only 118 letters not from Cicero's hand. These are divided unequally between the *Familiares*, the copies annexed to Cicero's letters to Atticus, and the seven replies from Brutus in the collection which bears his name.

[2] We might say of all of them what Quintus Cicero wrote to his brother: "I saw you completely in your letter"—*te totum in litteris vidi*—*Ad Fam.* XVI, 16, 2 (927 T.P.).

in our possession. In proportion as they enable us to learn more secrets, to penetrate further into the recesses of men's hearts and the underlying springs of their desires, the greater grows our need to understand the reason why this formidable mass of confidential information has been flung down before us for our curiosity to feed on. Since Cicero himself did not publish them in his lifetime, we should like to be able to name those responsible for a posthumous publication whose indiscretions awaken down the centuries echoes of whispered scandal and of violent explosion.

Whether we like it or not, this question cannot be evaded; it dominates the history to which the *Letters* lend new life. Unfortunately the Ancients have given no explicit answer,[1] and the replies of the Moderns,[2] whose common sense too often seems to have deserted them, are vitiated by an over-detailed erudition; for a century their answers have been mutually at war, and present us only with the discouraging contradictions of their futile conjectures. It would be over-fastidious to draw up a list of their hypotheses as a prelude to the present study, but it is all the more important to enunciate the principles which must most certainly govern research into the question. The critics of the nineteenth and twentieth centuries necessarily invoked these same principles, even where they neglected to apply them or applied them only to draw false conclusions.

First, since every valid method proceeds from the known to the unknown, we must not begin, as people usually do,[3] by trying to reconstruct a necessarily imaginary picture of volumes of letters which are believed to have been lost, and losing ourselves in hypotheses about the texts we presume to be missing. Let us, rather,

---

[1] Only Cornelius Nepos, in a passage to which I shall later revert (below, II, p. 495), has spoken, in terms that have been again and again discussed, of the preparation—but not of the publication—of the collection *Ad Atticum*.

[2] From Drumann (1846) to Nake (1861) and from Boissier (1863) to Karl Büchner in Volume VIIA of the *Realenzyklopädie Pauly-Wissowa* (published in 1941), cols. 1192–1235.

[3] From Boissier to Büchner everyone has hitherto taken for granted that Cicero's Correspondence included at least 39 books over and above the 36 that we possess; and each has exercised his ingenuity in linking with these supposedly lost volumes—either as a "selection" or as an appendix—the 16 books which we call *Ad Familiares*. I shall later recur to these discussions (II, p. 530f.) and the evidence on which they are based. I hope to prove that many letters are missing from the volumes we have, and that for many complex reasons; but that the books which are believed to have disappeared are in reality merely being confused with the letters missing from the existing books. It is only the vagueness of the Ancients' classification which accounts for their having been thought to be distinct.

3

Introduction

start by seeking answers from those we have in hand. Next, we must not expend our efforts in lengthy discussion of the date to be assigned to ancient allusions to the contents of the *Letters*. Such references testify to the diffusion of the Correspondence, but not to the moment at which this diffusion began. The actual date of the publication cannot logically be deduced from these references unless, by the most unlikely chance, the first allusion to the *Letters* had happened to coincide with their first appearance. It is preferable to try to discover from the tenor of the *Letters* themselves firstly the period at which public curiosity would most eagerly have welcomed the opportunity of reading them, and secondly the cause which their publication at that particular moment happened to serve.

2. THE CORRESPONDENCE WAS PUBLISHED FOR POLITICAL PURPOSES

If it were suddenly announced that all Cicero's works with one single exception were condemned to perish, the world would immediately and unanimously vote for saving the Correspondence: the scholars, for the sake of its documentary value; men of letters, for the talent Cicero reveals in it, the range of matter and the ease of style, which surpass those of even the most eloquent of his speeches and the most musical of his discourses. Like Voltaire's Letters, Cicero's are the most complete and vital expression of their author's self.[1] None the less, we cannot easily be persuaded that the *Letters* were brought into the light of day in order to magnify the oratorical renown of the man of Arpinum and through the magic of his name to popularise a form of rhetoric which had from time to time been used by several Greek philosophers of the fourth century B.C.—Plato, Aristotle and Epicurus, for example— for the edification of their disciples.[2] Even in Greek it was not until after the battle of Actium (31 B.C.) that a theory of the art of letter-writing was formulated. It is attributed to a certain Demetrios, wrongly confused with Demetrios of Phalerum.[3]

[1] See above, p. 2, note 2.
[2] In the opposite but mistaken sense see Peter's book *Der Brief in der römischen Literatur*, Leipzig, 1901, and, following Peter, Lafaye's article in the *Journal des Savants*, 1905, p. 319f.
[3] The treatise which opens the collection of the *Epistolographi graeci* is written by a rhetorician a little later than Dionysius of Halicarnassus (cf. Christ, *Griech. Lit.*, p. 512), who came to Rome only about 30 B.C. (cf. ibid. p. 637).

Introduction

It was not till still later, almost a century after Cicero's death, that "letters"—very different, however, from his—were recognised as a distinct branch of Latin literature. This recognition was due no doubt to a desire on the one hand to follow the example of Greece and on the other to renew the "literary" success which had been achieved, unsought, by Cicero's Correspondence.[1] First came the moral letters which Seneca addressed to Lucilius[2] towards the middle of the first century A.D.; then the secular letters of Pliny the Younger at the beginning of the second century; lastly, in the latter half of the second century, the boringly learned letters of the ex-Consul Fronto, with their laboured intimacy. Fronto would seem to have been the first to acclaim Cicero's Correspondence as the model of perfection—*epistulis Ciceronis nihil est perfectius*[3] and the last to draw real inspiration from them. His editor conceived that they were modelled on Cicero; and there is no denying that the deliberate attempt to follow Cicero's example begot a literary posterity, however bastardised and belated we may think it to be.

From this point of view Cicero's Correspondence, which ultimately gave birth to imitations, had neither immediate nor remote ancestry. Until its appearance no Roman had ever dreamt of winning by his letters the applause of men of taste. He had seen his letters only as an additional means of maintaining his rank and influence in the City. If the Romans piously preserved letters in rolls (*capsae*) in their reception room (*tablinum*),[4] this was merely a tribute to the ancestors who had written them, and the intention was proudly to display them[5] to visitors who called. Such letters were items in their archives, titles of nobility which perpetuated from generation to generation the greatness of the family. If they decided to circulate them, it was only in order to extend more

[1] If we accept the date I suggest (cf. below, II, p. 511) for the editions of Cicero's *Letters* in the course of 33 B.C., we are immediately struck by the synchronisation, within a few years, of this sensational publication and the first attempt, some ten or fifteen years later, to codify the rules of letter-writing.

[2] On the date of Seneca's letters to Lucilius, see E. Albertini, *La composition dans les ouvrages philosophiques de Sénèque*, Paris, 1923, p. 43f.

[3] Fronto (to Marcus Aurelius), p. 107 Naber: *Omnes Ciceronis epistulas legendas esse censeo mea sententia, vel magis quam orationes eius. Epistulis Ciceronis nihil est perfectius.*

[4] Cf. Cicero, *Brutus*, XVI, 61: . . . *familiae* . . . *quasi ornamenta ac monumenta servabant*; and Pliny, *H.N.*, XXXV, 2: . . . *tablina codicibus implebantur et monumentis rerum in magistratu gestarum.*

[5] See Cicero's letter *Ad Atticum*, XIII, 6, 4 (617 T.P.), in which he refers to the letters that Spurius Mummius had written from Corinth, and which his descendants used to read aloud to anyone who could be induced to listen.

widely the influence of their house. Held in reserve, such letters nourished the family pride; if published, the family ambition. They bore in themselves no relation to literature. When they had been written, they had been composed not for literary reading circles but for the Forum, so they were addressed not to the cultured man for his enjoyment, but to the citizen to secure his allegiance and his vote. Going backwards in time till we finally come to Cicero himself, letters continued to furnish the political masters of the day with the instruments of their power, and to provide munitions for the party battle.

The oldest letters of which we have any trace[1] and to which Cicero,[2] the Elder Pliny[3] and Festus[4] all in turn refer, and which Priscian was still consulting[5] in the sixth century, are those of Cato the Censor, who died in 149 B.C. One of these was written to the Consul Popilius,[6] the others to his own son. At first sight they appear to defy the rule and bear a distant resemblance to chapters of a didactic work. They are all, in fact, concerned with the education of young men. In writing to Popilius, Cato expounds the principles which he is teaching his son. In writing to the son he would seem to spare the youth no precept of any sort, whether relating to hygiene or military discipline or international law. But we must not be misled by appearances. These were open letters directed to a wider public than the recipients. In them Cato was characteristically preaching at his fellow-countrymen and inflicting on them the lessons of which he thought they stood in need, taking care to illustrate each with edifying pictures of himself. The eternal sermoniser found the Curiae and the Rostra too restricted a pulpit for his moralisings, and under cover of his friends and of his only son, he used his letters to give publicity to his preaching, which he expected would work miracles in strengthening his authority and prolonging the series of his electoral successes.[7]

---

[1] There is no need to deal with the official letters addressed by Scipio Africanus and Scipio Nasica to the kings (Polybius, X, 9, 3 and Plut. *Aem. Paul.* XV, 4). No fragment of these survived in Cicero's day (*De Off.* III, 1, 4).

[2] Cicero (*De Off.* I, 11, 36 and 37).

[3] Pliny, *H.N.* VII, 171 and XXIX, 14.

[4] Festus, p. 154 and 242 M. I omit Aulus Gellius, whose witness is disputed.

[5] Priscian, *Gr. L.* (Keil), II, p. 377, 5: *Cato in epistula ad filium.*

[6] Forgotten by Schanz-Hosius, but expressly referred to by Cicero (*De Off.* I, 11, 36: *Cato ad Popilium scripsit ut . . .*). The purpose of this letter is the same as that of the *epistula ad M. filium* quoted in the following paragraph.

[7] According to the mutually corroborative statements of Plutarch (*Cato Mai.* XX, 14), the Elder Seneca (*Controv.* I, *Praef.* 9), and Pliny (*H.N.* XXIX, 27), an oracular note was struck in Cato's pronouncements.

Introduction

Some fifteen years after the death of Cato the Censor, Caius Gracchus had sent and dedicated to his friend M. Pomponius a document—*scriptum*[1]—which Plutarch calls a small book,[2] but which seems to have been in fact simply an open letter,[3] like Cato's. No fragment of this has come down to us.[4] From the only paragraph of it which Cicero, the Elder Pliny and Plutarch[5] have all summarised—and their summaries agree—it would seem that the document in question was an apologia. This told a little story that has been more often quoted than understood: the story of two serpents, one male and one female, which Tiberius Gracchus, the Censor, was supposed to have found one morning in his house, at a time when Cornelia his wife was carrying her husband's child Caius. Disturbed by this unusual discovery and the omen evidently implied, the father of the Gracchi consulted the augurs. They were quick to enlighten him. For the safety of the family one of the two serpents must be destroyed and the other saved. If the female is saved the *pater familias* will perish before long; if the male, it is the wife who will be doomed. Confronted by a similar dilemma, Admetus had basely allowed Alcestis to sacrifice herself in his stead. The noble opponent of Hannibal, Antiochus and the Celtiberians offered his life for his consort. "In that case," said he to the augurs, "slay the serpent whose life is linked with mine, for Cornelia is young and may once again become a mother."[6] They obeyed his orders: the female serpent was spared; soon after, Tiberius Gracchus died at the age of fifty-four, and Cornelia, who was still under forty[7] and whose life had been fortunately preserved by the death of the male serpent, bore the last and most famous of her children. It was obviously Caius Gracchus's intention in his letter to Pomponius to popularise this story that men might marvel at the heroism which crowned his father's life and at the same time at the supernatural circumstances that attended his own birth.

Coming down to slightly later times, we find that during the last

---

1 Cicero, *De Div.* I, 18, 36: *scriptum reliquit.*
2 Plutarch, *Ti. Gr.* VIII, 5.
3 *De Div.* II, 29, 62: *C. Gracchus ad M. Pomponium scripsit.* Cf. Schanz-Hosius, I, p. 204.
4 The heirs of the said Pomponius were able to show it to Pliny 200 years later (Pliny, *H.N.* XIII, 83).
5 See notes 1 and 3 above and note 6 below.
6 Pliny, *H.N.* VII, 122: *Immo vero, inquit, meum necate ; Cornelia enim iuvenis est et parere adhuc potest.*
7 With reference to these facts, see my book *Autour des Gracques*, pp. 67-8 and 79-80.

Introduction

years of the Republic the letters which the Romans wrote, far from changing their aim, consistently maintained it, even at need by fraudulent means. In the years when the aristocratic Senate was using every available weapon against its democratic enemies and they similarly against the Senate; at the time of Opimius's opposition (120–119 B.C.); later during the wars of Marius and his supporters (88–82), and finally during the agitations that surrounded agrarian reform, that legacy of the Gracchi which Julius Caesar exploited for his own ends in 63–59, letters were found circulating in Rome which Cornelia, mourning the murder of her elder son, was supposed to have written from her restless retreat at Misenum to her younger son, Caius Gracchus.[1]

After Cardinali's exhaustive study of such fragments of these letters as have been preserved no one, I think, can perversely maintain that they are genuine.[2] This barefaced fraud betrays its real nature. These letters were in fact forgeries perpetrated in their own interest by the factions engaged in the struggle for power. These factions saw in the historic figures of the Gracchi only symbols, venerated or abhorred, of their own aspirations or their own resentment, and they unashamedly exploited them in the service of their warring passions. There were oligarchs so blinded by hate that they concocted accusatory letters not only against the Gracchi but against their mother, letters in which between the lines Cornelia confessed her share in the murder of Scipio Aemilianus, as if she were prepared to get rid of this great man by a crime rather than see him repeal her sons' laws and repudiate her daughter.[3] Another letter was forged in 121 in which Cornelia was supposed to encourage Caius to sedition, telling him that she was sending him a body of armed men disguised as harvesters.[4] This was going too far, and the forged letters gave rise to counter-forgeries, refuting or weakening the others and breathing the loftiest sentiments. In one of these Cornelia was supposed to have impressed on Caius that the pursuit of vengeance against an enemy must cease at the point where there arises danger of injury to the Republic.[5] In another, since she did not seem to have convinced him, she expressed her grief and indignation with a vehemence worthy of her.[6]

---

[1] See my book *Autour des Gracques*, pp. 105–107.
[2] Cardinali, *Studi Graccani*, Genoa, 1912, pp. 6–14.
[3] Appian, *B.C.* I, 28, 83; cf. my book *Autour des Gracques*, p. 101.
[4] Plut. *C. Gr.* XIII, 1; cf. *Autour des Gracques*, p. 106.
[5] Cf. Peter, *H.R.F.*, p. 222, 16.   [6] Cf. Peter, *H.R.F.*, p. 222, 16.

Introduction

These apocryphal letters[1] give each other the lie, and yet the same causes brought them forth. Whether flattering or defamatory, they blaze with the burning hostility of the parties. It is true that Cicero took these letters seriously as genuine, admired their style and thought he heard in them the true voice and accent of the Gracchi.[2] It was only retrospectively that anyone thought of according them this praise.[3] At the time their authors had no desire to see them collected in an anthology. Their bogus compositions had no other aim and no other virtue than to nourish the sensational arguments of the savage political war that raged between the nobles and the plebs, the *optimates* and the *populares*, who were fighting each other with passionate fanaticism.

A little later, better was to come. During Cicero's lifetime there appeared the letters which Sallust wrote to Julius Caesar in 49 and 46 to express his hopes and prayers concerning administration, justice and the reduction of the power of money. The dictator was all the more inclined to grant these prayers in that they anticipated his own intentions. Sallust neither desired nor suggested any changes in the government other than those which Caesar had long since been intending to effect, and Caesar was not sorry to see public opinion being prepared to favour them.

The two letters of Sallust which we read today have provoked long controversies amongst the learned. Some scholars accept the manuscripts just as they stand, and this seems confirmed by the appositeness of their allusions. Others dwell on the somewhat surprising superscription: "To the Aged Caesar"—*ad Caesarem senem*—and on the fact that the second bears a date earlier than the letter which is traditionally considered the older. This latter school considers the letters as declamatory speeches elaborated in some school of rhetoric under the Principate of Augustus. It makes, however, very little difference whether they were in fact composed or merely endorsed by Sallust. At worst, the rhetoricians of the next generation after his could conceive their exercises only within the framework, on the canvas, and in accordance with the matter which reality supplied. It is therefore clear that these "letters" reveal both the manner and the tenor of the command-productions of Caesar's writers.[4] Directly or indirectly they show the mental

1 Collectors, of course, still possessed the originals under the Empire (cf. Pliny, *H.N.* XIII, 83).
2 Cic. *Brutus*, LVIII, 211.   3 Still repeated by Quintilian, *Inst. Or.* I, 1, 6.
4 See my *César* (3), p. 981.

fodder on which Caesar wished to feed men's minds and the recipes according to which he wanted to prepare public opinion. He enlisted third parties—duly coached by himself—to prompt the public to make such suggestions as he wished to hear, and to condense for them the various items of the programme which he was secretly intending to carry out. His "ministers of the pen" naturally adopted the form and tone of a letter, since a brief and lively letter, when freely distributed to all comers, seemed to take each individual into his confidence and was the most effective kind of propaganda.

"Propaganda", modern though the word may be, is the term most suitable to the purpose of the letters the Romans circulated amongst themselves in the last century of their Republic. There was not in those days the clear distinction, which printing later introduced, between a letter and a book. The two differed only by the number of copies which the copyists put into circulation, more in the one case, fewer in the other. So the letter, provided only that it was copied and recopied, easily passed muster as a kind of book of small size and limited circulation. The fact that it was short happily reduced delay in passing it on, and its feigned note of intimacy increased its influence. As Gaston Boissier[1] has well said, the letter served as a substitute for the still non-existent newspaper. After Julius Caesar had in 59 by a stroke of genius invented —and ten years later monopolised—it in the form of the *Acta Diurna*, which he instituted and captured, the letters filled its gaps,[2] corrected its bias and brought life into its official dullness. The better known the authors were, the more the letters were in demand. The merely curious passed them from hand to hand in order to catch the eagerly sought news on the wing, and the politicians seized on them to learn the very newest reasons by which they could justify their conduct. Full as they were of news, of grievances and of justifications, the letters carried the fever of the Forum out into Italy and the Empire. No wonder that in Cicero's day they had become the statesman's favourite weapon to defend his cause, to reassure his friends and to lay his enemies low.

Let us be content here to quote a few proofs. In 49 at the beginning of the civil war between Caesar and the *Patres*, it was by means of publicly exchanged letters that Domitius Ahenobarbus and Pompey hurled each at the other's head the accusation

---

[1] See *Cicéron et ses amis*, p. 2f.　　　　[2] Cf. my *César* (3), pp. 719, 983.

of having been responsible for the check to the senatorial army at Corfinium.[1] Before war had actually broken out, Pompey placarded a letter everywhere in which he tried to lay the blame for the coming conflict on Caesar's intransigeance.[2] As for Cicero, he used his fluency in letter-writing for similar purposes at every stage of his career. We have abundant indications of the anxious care which Cicero devoted on many occasions—long before any collection of his Correspondence was made—to seeing that some of his letters got the benefit of timely publicity. In 62 he despatched to Pompey in Asia an inordinately long letter—*instar voluminis*[3]—which consisted of an extravagant eulogy of Pompey's consulship,[4] and he took great pains to see that copies of this were left lying about pretty well everywhere. We do not today possess this letter; but it had immediately reached so large a circle of readers in Rome that when Cicero was delivering his speech *Pro Sulla* in the same year, he was obliged to re-expound its meaning and comment on its terms.[5] The memory of this letter was so slow to die that in his defence *Pro Plancio* in 54 he was driven to advert to it again, and stress the value of the service which, as he claimed, it had rendered to the Republic.[6]

In 60 he re-despatched to his brother Quintus in Ephesus a letter[7] as well-balanced as an oration, as fully developed as a treatise,[8] which makes sense only if we compare the text with the circumstances in which it was composed and if several copies of it were at once distributed.

His brother Quintus had just been invested as Propraetor with

---

[1] *Ad Att.* VIII, 12B (325, T.P.); 12C (329, T.P.); 12D (330 T.P.), between Feb. 15 and 21, 49 B.C.

[2] *Ad Att.* VIII, 9, 2 (340 T.P.) from Formiae, Feb. 25, 49 B.C.; *Ille ipse [Pompeius] ad eumdem [Caesarem] scribens in publico proposuit epistulam illam in qua est: pro tuis rebus gestis amplissimis.* . . .

[3] Schol. Bob. p. 270 Or.: *Epistulam non mediocrem ad instar voluminis Pompeio in Asiam de rebus suis in consulatu gestis miserat Cicero* . . . This letter bears no relation to the note preserved *Ad Fam.* V, 7 (13 T.P.).

[4] Cic. *Pro Sulla*, XXIV, 67: . . . *de meis rebus gestis et de summa republica.* Cicero here speaks as head of the government.

[5] Readings of it were given in public; cf. ibid.: . . . *epistulam meam saepe recitas;* and the prosecution quoted it against the accused.

[6] Cic. *Pro Plancio*, XXXIV, 85: . . . *quas ego [litteras] reipublicae video prodesse potuisse.*

[7] *Ad Q. Fr.* I, 1 (12 T.P.).

[8] This letter is also *voluminis instar scripta;* it consists of not less than 46 paragraphs divided into 16 chapters and it now occupies 20 printed pages of Tyrrell and Purser's edition, I, 2, pp. 121–40. Cf. René Pichon, "Le but de Cicéron dans la première lettre à Quintus," *Revue de Philologie*, XXXIV, 1910, p. 140.

the governorship of the province of Asia, and Cicero wrote him this letter ostensibly to remind him of the duties pertaining to his office and to draw up for him a masterly sketch of the framework of an ideal administration. The writer continued, however, as usual, to hold himself up to the admiration of his colleagues in the Senate, while at the same time predisposing them to prolong Quintus's tenure of the *imperium* with which they had invested him for one year. Quintus in fact retained his post for three consecutive years, until 58, without arousing either complaint in Ephesus or opposition in the City[1] at home.

In 56 during the tension accompanying the conference of the First Triumvirate at Lucca, Cicero was driven into taking a back seat. He sought to console himself for his present eclipse by recalling the glories of his past, and to re-awaken in others the memory—to which he himself was ever keenly alive—of his wonderful years as Consul. In the peaceful atmosphere of his retreat at Arpinum, he composed an urgent and fastidiously worded letter to the historian Lucius Lucceius. It is a little masterpiece of graceful eloquence, of humorous learning and of grave cajolery.[2] He tells his friend of a burning desire which he had not dared to express to him in conversation, but which he can confide to a letter since it "cannot blush"—*epistula enim non erubescit*.[3] Since Lucceius is engaged in putting the last touches to his account of the War of the Allies and the civil discords which followed, he begs him to put all other work aside and give his attention to the conspiracy of Catiline. Every word and phrase of this message was weighed and polished so as to gratify and persuade Lucceius.

Cicero was well pleased with the result, but as he had made so much play with his erudition and his wit, and had moreover in skilful asides contrived to slip in praises of his own consulship, he would have been heartbroken if L. Lucceius had been the only person to detect its allusions and enjoy its charm. So, for fear that others should miss the pleasure, he wrote another letter, this time to Atticus, and despatched it from Arpinum the very same day, or at most a couple of days later. He suggested that Atticus should call on Lucceius and get permission to divulge "the letter which I

---

[1] Cf. Drumann-Groebe, VI, p. 641.
[2] *Ad Fam.* V, 12 (109 T.P.).
[3] *Ad Fam.* V, 1; cf. how it goes on: *ardeo . . . cupiditate incredibili*, etc.

wrote to Lucceius to induce him to record my history. It is a really beautiful letter."[1]

Finally, Cicero, who had been watching with the gravest anxiety the gathering of clouds which seemed to presage a fresh civil war, wrote on Feb. 25, 49, to Caesar from Formiae, begging him to save the country from this terrible disaster by consenting to a reconciliation with Pompey.[2] He was anxious that this letter should not remain a secret, and his wishes were more than gratified. While Cicero himself distributed a large number of copies to his friends, Caesar for his part, finding the letter lavish in compliments to him, hastened to have it read by his partisans. In writing to Atticus Cicero was presently able, somewhat naively, to congratulate himself on so satisfying a result: "What you tell me about the distribution of my letter to Caesar is not calculated to displease me. I had had many copies of it made myself."[3]

We cannot doubt that many other letters of his had similar good fortune, so many, indeed, that when he was once again toying with the idea, after Caesar's death, of returning some day to the Bar, he suddenly accepted his publisher's suggestion to bring together in one work a collection of his letters. He could thus commemorate the doings he was proudest of and at the same time display his inexhaustible spirits and vitality. This would contribute more than anything to increase his prestige in the provisionally re-born Republic. Writing on July 9, 44, from Puteoli he discussed the question with Atticus. "So far no collection of my letters exists; but Tiro has some seventy of them, and some that you have must be taken too. I shall have to look at them carefully again myself and correct them; and after that they can be published: *mearum epistularum nulla est συναγωγή, sed habet Tiro instar septuaginta. Et quidem sunt a te quaedam sumendae. Eas ego oportet perspiciam, corrigam; tum denique edentur.*[4]

There has been much discussion, and assuredly useless discussion,[5] about this vital sentence. The meaning is in fact perfectly clear and of the greatest importance. It shows that "the first person who thought of collecting" not "*the* letters of Cicero",

[1] *Ad Att.* IV, 6, 4 (110 T.P.): *Epistulam, Lucceio quam misi, qua meas res ut scribat rogo, fac ut ab eo sumas—valde bella est.*
[2] *Ad Att.* VIII, 9, 1 (340 T.P.).
[3] *Ad Att.* VIII, 9, 1 (340 T.P.): *Epistulam meam quod pervulgatam scribis esse, non fero moleste. Quin etiam ipse multis dedi describendam. . . .*
[4] *Ad Att.* XVI, 5, 5 (770 T.P.).
[5] Cf. below, II, pp. 485f.

Introduction

as Gaston Boissier has pointed out in a dissertation[1] of his too often overlooked, but *some* letters of Cicero, "was Cicero himself". At the same time it makes it clear that while he had at last made up his mind to contemplate a collection of his letters, he always refused to think of it as other than a limited and carefully chosen selection. This would have consisted of a minimum of seventy and a maximum of a hundred or so,[2] all cautiously chosen, carefully revised and expurgated without scruple. The "collection" Cicero speaks of would never have been anything but a tendentious selection, skilfully calculated to enhance the author's glory.

In its present form, however, Cicero's Correspondence includes letters other than his, and it takes up in somewhat disorderly fashion[3] a volume ten times as large. It therefore bears no relation to the plan—dangerous enough despite its self-imposed limitation —to which Cicero had reluctantly consented fifteen months before his death. It is not enough to say that his original intention was not carried out. To put it plainly, a new collection was substituted for the one he had planned, a new collection made in a different spirit and for totally different propaganda purposes.

3. POLITICS EXCLUDE THE IDEA OF PUBLICATION UNDER AUGUSTUS

How can we define the significance and the scope of this publication, and how consequently determine its date?

Gaston Boissier, who was the first in France to devote his attention to these questions, and did so with rare acuteness, has sought to explain the appearance of the Correspondence as we possess it, at once by the survival of old political passions and by the rise of a new literary fashion. He therefore places its date midway between the events which it records and the first signs amongst the Romans of letter-writing as a literary art. It would then have served to refresh the memories of survivors of the preceding generation and at the same time have quickened the following generation's taste for a form of literature whose success was to be sealed by Seneca. But Boissier's position is less of a judicious mean than of an unstable compromise; it is in fact so difficult to maintain

---

[1] Gaston Boissier, *Recherches sur la manière dont furent recueillies et publiées les lettres de Cicéron.* Paris, 1863, p. 8.

[2] Including such letters as Cicero proposed to get back from Atticus in addition to the seventy.

[3] Cf. below, II, pp. 504–7.

this position that in order to defend it he has surreptitiously shifted the landmarks.

In his paper of 1863[1] he fixes on the period following "the battle of Actium".[2] Two years later, in *Cicero and his Friends*,[3] though he repeats the formula "after the battle of Actium", he no longer attaches the same importance to it, and he places the date twenty years later, "towards the middle of the reign of Augustus".[4] In support of his first opinion he invoked "the universal lassitude" on which Augustus "was fain to rely to accustom people without a jar to the new régime".[5] In favour of the second view he asserts that Augustus was at first "mistrustful" because his position was insufficiently secure, and that towards the end "he became mistrustful again when he found he was losing popular favour". In the course "of a reign which begins by the proscribing of men, and ends by the burning of books", it was only in the interval between these two outbursts of excess that Cicero's Correspondence could have been published.[6] In their discreet opposition these two sets of reasoning are equally ingenious and equally unconvincing, because both run counter to historic probability.

From the moment that Augustus, the conqueror at Actium, made it his aim to rule as master over a pacified world, he would have shaken his own authority and endangered his work if he had lightheartedly rekindled the last embers of the Civil War, still smouldering beneath their ashes. Once he had become all-powerful, he could not possibly have dreamt of putting within reach of the Romans the still unpublished letters of Cicero, since in the exercise of his imperial authority he had already forbidden the entry into his own palace of the works of Cicero published long since. Boissier makes play with the homage which "in a day of outspoken remorse" the Emperor paid to the man whose murder he had arranged: "He was an eloquent man, yes, eloquent, and he loved his country."[7] But Boissier is careful not to call our attention to the circumstances which led Augustus to pronounce these words of tepid praise. He had just surprised one of his grandsons buried in the reading of a *volumen* of Cicero's, and the boy's first gesture

[1] G. Boissier, *Recherches* . . ., p. 35.
[2] The battle of Actium was fought on Sept. 2, 31 B.C.
[3] *Cicéron et ses amis.*
[4] G. Boissier, *Cicéron et ses amis*, p. 410. This carries us down to 10 B.C.
[5] Boissier, *Recherches* . . . , p. 35.
[6] Boissier, *Cicéron et ses amis*, p. 82.   [7] Plutarch, *Cic.* XLIX, 2.

on his grandfather's approach was to conceal the roll under his toga,[1] so fearful was he of provoking the Emperor's wrath by having guiltily transgressed the interdict which pursued even into the grave the great man whom the Triumvirs[2] had proscribed. The grandfather's words were intended to reassure the lad.

The truth is that neither as Octavian nor as Augustus had he ever relented towards Cicero. Immediately after the proscriptions, the Triumvir permitted Asinius Pollio in his speech for Lamia[3] to insinuate that Cicero, feeling himself at bay, had sought to save his head by proposing to Antony to retract his *Philippics* and write a refutation, which if necessary he would read in person before the People's Assembly.[4]

Some years later he permitted, nay, encouraged the rhetorician Didymus, who was living in Rome during the struggle of Cicero against Mark Antony, and who died shortly after 27,[5] to write a diatribe in six books against Cicero's policy. Four centuries later Ammianus Marcellinus compared this to the distant baying of a dog who scents the approach of a lion.[6]

Later, when Augustus had become sole master of the world, his hatred slept, but never died. He preferred silence to open attack, and when silence was impossible he assumed a sort of sentimental pitying contempt which saw no good in Cicero save his oratory. The poets of his time were sure of pleasing him provided their verses omitted all reference to Cicero.[7] To avoid giving him offence,

---

[1] Plutarch, *Cic.* XLIX, 2.

[2] Plutarch does not tell us which of Julia's sons this was. Both were quite young: Caius Caesar was born in 20 B.C. and Lucius Caesar in 17 B.C. This is of little importance; the anecdote must lie between 12 B.C. and 7 B.C., that is, in the middle of the reign; and this is enough to invalidate Boissier's theory. Finally, concerning this passage in Plutarch, see Pierre Grenade, "Remarques sur la théorie cicéronienne dite du principat," in the *Mélanges de l'École française de Rome*, LVII, 1940, p. 39.

[3] For the date see Groebe, *P.W.* II, c. 1594.

[4] Pollio *ap.* Seneca the Elder, *Suas.* VI, 15: *Itaque nunquam per Ciceronem mora fuit, quin eiuraret suas, quas cupidissime effuderat, orationes in Antonium: multiplicesque numero et accuratius scriptas illis contrarius edere ac vel ipse palam pro contione recitare pollicebatur.*

[5] Suidas, s.v. *Didymus*; cf. *P.W.* V, c. 445.

[6] Amm. Marc. XXII, 16: *Tullium reprehendit ut . . . frementem leonem putredulis vocibus canus catulus longius circumlatrans.*

[7] The name of Cicero is never mentioned in the works of Horace, Propertius, Tibullus or Ovid. It is also absent from the *Aeneid*, though we may think we recognise him under the name of Drances, the weak and envious but eloquent speaker (*Aen.* XI, 340–41), or appearing anonymously as the incestuous father . . . *hic thalamum invasit natae vetitosque hymenaeos (Aen.* VI, 623). These suggestions are made by Frank Olivier, *Deux Études sur Virgile*, Lausanne, 1930, and I accept his interpretation (*Revue historique*, 1931, 166, p. 333).

the historians, who could not avoid mentioning Cicero in their writings, showed unscrupulous ingenuity in not assigning too creditable a role to the man whom the Emperor had proscribed. Asinius Pollio, in his *History*, written before 23[1], cut short his praise of Cicero's eloquence under the pretext that "it is super-fluous to praise the ability and industry of a man whose numerous and remarkable works ensure his immortality";[2] and he attributes to Cicero's lack of courage and restraint the evils he had suffered.[3] More admiration for Cicero than in fact he ever effectively dis-played is commonly attributed to Livy.[4] In the 120th book of his history, which undoubtedly appeared shortly before the death of Augustus,[5] he shows himself, however, neither less skilful in his phrasing nor more generous in his judgment. He pays homage to Cicero's gifts and merit, but like Pollio refrains from enumer-ating them, because forsooth "to praise them worthily a man would need to be himself endowed with them."[6] He recognises the dignified resignation shown by the victim of the Triumvirs,[7] but cautiously qualifies his tribute by the remark that death was the only one of his misfortunes that he met like a man.[8] He throws on Mark Antony and his soldiers the blame for the senseless cruelties which accompanied the murder,[9] but has the effrontery to find extenuating circumstances, remarking with sinister irony that to put a man of sixty-three to death is not putting a premature end to his life.[10] He even justifies the murder with the specious plea: "it seems the less undeserved when we reflect that he was struck

[1] On the question of this date see Schanz-Hosius, II, p. 28.
[2] Pollio, *ap.* Seneca the Elder, *Suas.* VI, 24: *Huius ergo viri tot tantisque operibus mansuris in omne aevum praedicare de ingenio atque industria supervacuum est.*
[3] Pollio, *ap.* Seneca the Elder, *Suas.* VI, 24: *Utinam moderatius secundas res et fortius adversas ferre potuisset!*
[4] Cf. Schanz-Hosius, I, p. 545: *Von grosser Zuneigung für Cicero war Livius beseelt und spricht in warmen Ausdrücken von ihm.* "Tepid" would be nearer the mark than "warm".
[5] According to the *epitomator*, Book 121 seems to have been the first to be published after the death of Augustus.
[6] Livy, *ap.* Seneca the Elder, *Suas.* VI, 22: . . . *in cuius laudes exsequendas Cicerone laudatore opus fuerit.* Cf. Livy's letter to his son, quoted by Quintilian, IX, 1, 39: . . . *legendos Demosthenem atque Ciceronem.*
[7] Livy, *ap.* Seneca the Elder, *Suas.* VI, 17: . . . *ipsum deponi lecticam et quietos pati quod sors iniqua cogeret iussisse.*
[8] Livy, *ap.* Seneca the Elder, *Suas.* VI, 22: . . . *omnium adversorum nihil ut viro dignum erat tulit praeter mortem.*
[9] Livy, *ap.* Seneca the Elder, *Suas.* VI, 17: . . . *nec id satis stolidae crudelitati militum fuit,* etc.
[10] Livy, *ap.* Seneca the Elder, *Suas.* VI, 22: *Vixit tres et sexaginta annos, ut, si vis afuisset, ne inmatura quidem mors videri possit.*

down with no more cruelty than he would himself have shown to his enemy if he had been victorious."[1] There is nothing here to make us honour Livy for his ardent devotion to Cicero's memory. Extracts from Livy's earlier books are lacking; we have only summaries, but these show no more genuine appreciation. The historian was of course unable to pass in silence over the skilful part Cicero played in defeating the intrigues of Catiline,[2] or over the enthusiastic welcome Italy offered him on his return from exile.[3] But he would seem to have approved his banishment as perfectly justified,[4] while he glosses over the intense and extremely effective vigour shown by Cicero in 44 and 43.[5] Quite gratuitously he inserts in Book 120 a long discussion of Cicero's behaviour, inglorious if not worse, at the battle of Pharsalia: "Cicero did not leave the camp, no man could possibly have been less born for war."[6] In no single passage has Livy sought to bring back into public favour the memory of a man who was to the last an object of dislike to his imperial patron. This silent hostility of Augustus was so strong that it survived in the hearts of his relatives, to such a point that Livia, who was his intimate confidant, discouraged the future Emperor Claudius when studying history in his youth from having anything to do with the period of Cicero's fall. No one who claimed to remain faithful to the prejudices and dislikes of the founder of the dynasty was allowed to speak freely or truthfully about Cicero.[7]

Of all the periods we have to choose from, it is therefore clear that the reign of Augustus is the last to which we have any right to attribute the publication of Cicero's Correspondence. If the aim of publication was political, this date is too late; if the object was

[1] Livy, *ap.* Seneca the Elder, *Suas.* VI, 22: . . . *quae [mors] vere aestimanti minus indigna videri potuit, quod a victore inimico nihil crudelius passus erat quam quod eiusdem fortunae compos victor fecisset.*

[2] Livy, *Per.* 102: . . . *ea coniuratio industria M. Tulli Ciceronis eruta est.*

[3] Livy, *Per.* 104: *M. Cicero . . . ingenti gaudio senatus ac totius Italiae ab exilio reductus est.*

[4] Livy, *Per.* 103: *M. Cicero . . . quod indemnatos cives necavisset in exilium missus est.*

[5] There is no mention of his name in *Per.* 117, 118 or 119.

[6] Livy, *Per.* 120: . . . *apud Pharsaliam . . . Cicero in castris remansit, vir nihil minus quam ad bella natus.*

[7] Suetonius, *Claud.* XLI, 1: *Initium autem sumpsit historiae [Claudius] post caedem Caesaris dictatoris, sed et transiit ad inferiora tempora coeptique a pace civili, cum sentiret neque vere neque libere sibi de superioribus tradendi potestatem relictam, correptus saepe et a matre [Antonia] et ab avia [Livia].* In A.D. 25 under Tiberius, Cremutius Cordus was persecuted and driven to suicide by Sejanus because he had called Cassius the last of the Romans. Cf. Schanz-Hosius, II, p. 643.

Introduction

merely to satisfy justified and really disinterested curiosity, it is too early. Without even mentioning the theory which Gaston Boissier, with some hesitation, twice recurred to, modern critics tend nowadays for the most part to assign it to the time of Tiberius, Claudius, or even Nero, a century after Cicero's death.[1]

4. LITERARY CRITICISM EXCLUDES THE IDEA OF PUBLICATION AFTER TIBERIUS

The critics have thus leapt forward at a bound to the extreme limit imposed by the evidence of the texts. We cannot in fact place the collection *Ad Familiares* later than Tiberius (died A.D. 37) or the collection *Ad Atticum* later than the time of Nero (A.D. 54–68). There is a decisive reason: the Elder Seneca in his *Suasoriae*, which were composed in about A.D. 38, refers his readers to a phrase which Caius Cassius wrote to Cicero, and which we find in fact written by his pen in the *Ad Familiares*[2]; and the younger Seneca in a letter to Lucilius written about A.D. 63[3] refers to a passage in a letter to Atticus which we find exactly word for word in *Ad Atticum*.[4]

It is only by an error of judgment as frequent as it is blameworthy, which I have already exposed,[5] that anyone can contend that the earliest quotations from any work provide a certain clue to the date of its appearance. The scholars who have been victims of this gross illusion naturally deny that they have fallen into the trap, and they subsequently make the wildest efforts to convince us that, at least in the particular case in question, the synchronism

[1] The latest of the scholars who have tackled the problem writes in 1943 without turning a hair: ... *der Briefwechsel (mit Atticus) ist etwa* 100 *Jahre nicht bekannt gewesen* (Büchner, *P.W.* VII A, c. 1213). The same note is struck by his immediate predecessors, especially Ed. Meyer, *Caesars Monarchie* (2), Stuttgart, 1922, p. 610.
[2] Sen. *Suasoriae* I, 5, 5: *Eleganter in C. Cassi epistola quadam ad M. Ciceronem missa: multum iocatur de stultitia Cn. Pompei adulescentis . . . deinde ait: Nos quidem illum deridemus sed timeo ne ille nos gladio* ἀντιμυκτηρίσῃ. Cf. Cic. *Ad Fam.* XV, 19, 4 (542 T.P.): *Scis Gnaeus quam sit fatuus . . . scis quam se semper a nobis derisum putet: vereor ne nos rustice gladio velit* ἀντιμυκτηρίσαι. Though made from memory, the quotation is immediately recognisable.
[3] Cf. E. Albertini, op. cit., p. 49.
[4] Sen. *Ep.* 97, 4: *Ipsa ponam verba Ciceronis quia res fidem excedit, Ciceronis epistularum ad Atticum I: arcessivit ad se, promisit, intercessit,* etc.—a literal reproduction of Cic. *Ad Att.* I, 16, 5 (22 T.P.). Moreover one could add further comparisons: an allusion of Sen. *Ep.* 118, 2 to Cic. *Ad Att.* I, 12, 1 (17 T.P.), and yet another textual reference of Sen. *Ep.* 118, 1: *. . . nec faciam quod Cicero facere Atticum iubet ut etiam, quod in buccam venerit scribat,* to Cicero *Ad Att.* I, 12, 4 (17 T.P.): *Si rem nullam habebis, quod in buccam venerit, scribito.*
[5] See above, p. 3.

Introduction

which they have assumed between the date of such and such allusions and that of the collections to which they refer is justified, quite apart from the postulate which they protest they have not taken for granted. They do not hesitate to adduce, as independent of any such postulate, all sorts of reasons that have influenced them: in writings immediately preceding the period which they assign to our collections they have detected traces of statements which these collections refute, and which therefore could not have been made if the collections had already appeared; they proceed to eliminate, not without difficulty, all earlier allusions; finally they abandon themselves to historical and juridical arguments which, if they were well founded, would serve to create a strong presumption in favour of their thesis.

Nowadays this collection of incongruous arguments is accepted everywhere as law.[1] At the risk of overweighting my exposition, I am therefore driven to examine them one by one in order to clear the ground, once and for all, of the misapprehensions which encumber it.

Let us begin with the two documents whose supposed divergences from Cicero's Correspondence are taken to imply that its publication was subsequent to them. Both of these come from the Commentary which Asconius made between A.D. 54 and 57 on the speeches of Cicero.[2]

The first of these texts relates to the chapter of *Pro Milone* in which Cicero denounces the series of criminal assaults committed by Clodius over a long period of years. He shows us Clodius directing the dagger at him on at least two separate occasions: "after a long interval (of quiet) Clodius has again turned this dagger against me; recently, as you know, he nearly slew me near the *Regia*": *haec [sica] eadem, longo intervallo, conversa rursus est in me; nuper quidem, ut scitis, me ad Regiam paene confecit.*[3]

Asconius seems to have had no difficulty in giving a circumstantial account of the various armed assaults of which Clodius had been guilty in the time when, protected first by his tribuneship and

---

[1] From Schanz in Germany it passed to L. A. Constans in France (edition of *Lettres de Cicéron*, I, p. 11); to Rose in Britain (*Handbook of Latin Literature*, London, 1936, p. 194); to Terzaghi in Italy (cf. *Storia della Lett. latina*, Turin, 1935, p. 236).

[2] This date seems fixed by a phrase of the Commentary which implies both the death of Claudius (died 54) and the survival of his former colleague in the consulship, Caecina Largus (died 57). Cf. Schanz-Hosius, p. 732.

[3] Cic. *Pro Mil.* XIV, 37.

then by the power of Caesar, he had engineered the banishment of
Cicero (58) and obstructed his return (57).[1] These attacks were
present to everybody's mind and the scholiast rightly laid less
stress on the best known.[2] But when he came to the last of them he
was pulled up short; at least he had to make enquiries. "I think,"
he writes, "that it happened one day during the consulship of
Domitius and Messalla (53) and before the year in which Cicero
delivered his speech for Milo (52).[3] There was a regular battle that
day between the gangs of (two of) the candidates for the consulship:
Hypsaeus and Milo. What makes me think that Cicero was alluding
to this attack and the danger he ran is the place where he locates
it, for it is indisputable that it occurred in the Sacred Way on to
which the *Regia* opens, and that each of the candidates was
accompanied by his supporter: Milo by Cicero, and Hypsaeus by
Clodius."[4]

No one could possibly be more methodical or more consci-
entious. Yet, instead of being grateful to Asconius for his scruples,
Leo, followed by Schanz, attributes them to lack of knowledge.[5] In
connection with the commentator's momentary perplexity, it is
the fashion to transcribe Cicero's letter to Atticus which ought
immediately to have dispelled his doubts. Here is the passage:
"On 11th November, as I was going down the Sacred Way,
Clodius and his gang flung themselves on us. Cries, stones,
clubs, swords, all took us unawares. We took refuge in the vesti-
bule of Tettius Damio. The men who were with me were able
easily to bar the way to the rascals. I could myself have had the
fellow cut down. But I'm tired of surgery, I'd rather stick to a
doctor's dieting": *ante diem tertium Idus Novembr(es), cum Sacra
via descenderem, insecutus est me cum suis. Clamor, lapides, fustes,*

[1] See my *César* (3), pp. 765–71.
[2] Cf. Asconius, p. 47 Or.: . . . *manifestum est pertinere ad id tempus quo post
rogationem a Clodio in eum promulgatam urbe cessit.* Here follow details of the
unsuccessful attack on Pompey and the ambush on the Appian Way into which
Marcus Papirius fell.
[3] The street incidents are definitely assigned to the last months of 53 B.C.
(my *César* (3), p. 837). Clodius was killed on Jan. 1, 52 B.C. (ibid., p. 837). Milo's
trial took place from April 5 to 8, 52 B.C. (ibid., p. 840).
[4] Asconius, p. 48 Or.: *Videtur mihi loqui de eo die, quo consulibus Domitio et
Messala, qui praecesserant eum annum cum haec oratio dicta est, inter candidatorum
Hypsaei et Milonis operas pugnatum est. . . . De cuius caede et periculo suo ut putem
loqui eum facit et locus pugnae (nam in Sacra via traditur commissa in qua est
Regia) et quod adsidue simul erant cum candidatis suffragatores, Milonis Cicero,
Hypsaei Clodius.*
[5] Leo, *Miscella Ciceroniana*, Göttingen, 1892, quoted by Schanz in Schanz-
Hosius, I, p. 480.

*gladii, haec improvisa omnia. Discessimus in vestibulum Tettii Dami-
onis. Qui erant mecum, facile operas aditu prohibuerunt. Ipse occidi
potuit. Sed ego diaeta curare incipio, chirurgiae taedet.*[1]

The comparison is at first sight tempting, and one is inclined to
suspect that the scholiast may have had access to the letter to
Atticus which suggested the collation of the passages to Leo and
to Schanz. But on reflection it is clear that there is a hitch in this
and that Asconius, when he decided to reject it, was wiser and
better-informed than these modern scholars. The affray referred
to in *Pro Milone* is certainly not the same as the one described in
the letter to Atticus. In the latter, Cicero had Clodius at his mercy.
In the former, Clodius very nearly succeeded in murdering Cicero.
Besides, though both took place in the Sacred Way which passes
through the Forum they clearly occurred in two quite different
sections of its length. The letter describes the attack as taking place
on the slope down from the Palatine where Cicero's own quarters
were; this would therefore have been close to the spot where the
Via Sacra crossed the *Clivus Palatinus* on the slope of the *Velia*,
where later the Arch of Titus[2] was erected, and immediately
adjacent to the house of Tettius Damio—of whom we know
nothing further[3]—which was probably one of a group of houses
built between the top of the *Velia* and the *Atrium Vestae*. The
attack alluded to in the speech took place some sixty or seventy
yards further north at a definitely lower level, in the neighbourhood, not of a private dwelling-house, but of the *Regia*,[4] the official
residence of the Pontifex Maximus.

Lastly, the chronological data do not tally. The attack recorded
in the *Pro Milone* could not have occurred more than a few months
before the speech was made, for in this speech of April 8, 52,
Cicero speaks of it as having taken place "recently"—*nuper*.[5]
On the other hand the date of the attack described in the letter
to Atticus is fixed by the letter itself as Nov. 11, 57, namely five
years earlier. This leaves exactly that "long interval" between the

---

[1] *Ad Att.* IV, 3, 3 (92 T.P.).
[2] Platner-Ashby, *Top. Dict.*, p. 124.
[3] Platner-Ashby, *Top. Dict.*, p. 191.
[4] On the excavations of the buildings of many different ages, which covered the
Velia, cf. Huelsen-Carcopino, *Le Forum romain*, p. 251; on the *Regia* cf. ibid.,
pp. 191–5.
[5] This conforms completely with the report of the end of 53 B.C. concerning
the battles which took place in November and December of that year between
the rival gangs of Clodius and Milo; cf. my *César* (3), p. 837 and above, p. 21.

Introduction

two which is mentioned in the opening words of the *Pro Milone*.[1] There is therefore no possible identity between the quite recent attack on which Cicero seized for his speech and the other attack an account of which he had previously written to Atticus. This being so, it is natural that Asconius did not appeal to the letter to throw light on the speech. Whatever his reason, it did not spring from ignorance of Cicero's correspondence with Atticus. On the contrary, it can better be explained by his exact knowledge of the circumstances. There was, moreover, no need for the scholiast to inform his pupils of the tragically notorious disorders which had drenched Rome in blood between 58 and 56, while his knowledge of the obscure attack of 53 threw no light on the point which puzzled him when explaining the *Pro Milone*.

Now let us turn to the notes which Asconius made on Cicero's speech *In Toga Candida*. They have been misunderstood in exactly the same way as those on the *Pro Milone*, and in the same way they bear witness against the modern scholars who have mistakenly invoked them in support of a thesis which is as inconsistent as it is generally accepted.

From the fragments of it which still survive, we can guess at the contents of the speech which Cicero, clad in the white toga of a candidate, delivered in 64 for the consular elections of 63, whence its name *Oratio in Toga Candida*. It was a vehement protest against the *intercessio* lodged by the Tribune Quintus Murcius Orestinus against the *senatus consultum* which, the "Fathers" had flattered themselves, by increasing the penalties for bribery, was to dam the flood of electoral corruption, shamelessly loosed by Cicero's opponents, Caius Antonius and Lucius Sergius Catilina. Cicero approached the real matter of his speech only after indulging in a flow of invective, so savage as to challenge credulity, so violent as to border on vulgarity. His protest gave him the opportunity thus to discredit his two competitors and drive them out of public favour by the weight of a sudden, last-minute attack.

Caius Antonius, his future colleague, was abused in this speech as a brigand, a gladiator and a circus charioteer, and Catiline as an adulterer, a prevaricator, an assassin and a desecrator of temples.[2] Hearing the roar of this torrent of savage insults, Asconius was

[1] Cf. Cic. *Pro Mil.* XIV, 37: . . . *haec* [*sica*] *eadem longo intervallo conversa rursus est in me*; see above, p. 20.
[2] See my *César* (3), p. 661.

23

suddenly inclined to doubt, in spite of the statement of Fenestella, that Cicero had consented only the year before (65) to undertake the defence of Catiline in the trial for extortion which had been instituted against him on his return from the Propraetorship of Africa. With the connivance of the prosecutor, Clodius, he had by the iniquity of unworthy judges[1] been acquitted without a stain on his character, in flagrant defiance of weighty evidence. With great deliberation Asconius justifies his scepticism thus: "According to Fenestella's contention Catiline was defended by Cicero before the *Quaestio de repetundis*. For my part I am inclined to doubt this, partly from the very text of the *Oratio in Toga Candida*, especially because it contains no mention of the matter, whereas Cicero could easily have made play with the fact to discredit a rival who had shown such scandalous ingratitude towards him."[2] This reasoning of Asconius is faultless. But if we were to believe Buecheler[3] and Schanz,[4] the scholiast would have had no need to reason at all, nor to be satisfied with the mere probability his reasoning yielded; he would have been able to ascertain the truth from the first page of Cicero's correspondence with Atticus and could have spared himself the trouble and uncertainty of reasoning.

In the first lines of the first letter of Book I Cicero sends his friend, then in Athens, the list of possible candidates in 65 for the consular elections of 64. He includes Catiline's name, using the most damning language about this man committed for trial on charges of extortion. "If the judges decide that black is white," he writes, "this man will certainly be a candidate": *Catilina, si iudicatum erit meridie non lucere, certus erit competitor.*[5] This phrase implies so strong a conviction of Catiline's guilt that the contempt with which it is laden seems to exclude the possibility that Cicero even thought of defending him, still more it refutes Fenestella's assertion that he had actually done so. No one dreams of taking up a case the injustice of which he has openly proclaimed. This testimony of Cicero himself confirms so fully the timid disbelief of

[1] See my *César* (3), p. 656.
[2] Asconius, p. 85 Or.: *Defensus est Catilina, ut Fenestella tradit, a M. Cicerone. Quod ego ut addubitem haec ipsa Ciceronis oratio facit, maxime quod is nullam mentionem rei habet, cum potuerit invidiam facere competitori tam turpiter adversus se coeunti.*
[3] Buecheler, *Rheinisches Museum*, XXXIV, 1879, p. 352.
[4] Schanz-Hosius, I, p. 480.
[5] *Ad Att.* I, 1, 1 (10 T.P.), before July 25, 65 B.C.

Asconius that the Moderns hold that nothing could have prevented the scholiast from making use of it but the fact that when he was editing his notes this decisive document was not available to him. In other words, the correspondence of Cicero with Atticus had not yet seen the light in A.D. 54–7. This conclusion goes far beyond what the premisses warrant. It would nevertheless be plausible enough if on turning over the next page of the Correspondence we did not come upon a sentence which expressly states the exact opposite of what the earlier seemed to imply.

This time Cicero writes: "We are now thinking of taking up the defence of Catiline, our competitor. We have got the judges whom we wanted, with the complete acquiescence of the prosecutor.[1] If Catiline is acquitted, I hope he will join us more closely in the matter of the candidature. If things turn out otherwise we shall bear it philosophically": *Hoc tempore Catilinam competitorem nostrum defendere cogitamus. Iudices habemus quos voluimus, summa accusatoris voluntate. Spero, si absolutus erit, coniunctiorem illum nobis fore in ratione petitionis. Sin aliter acciderit, humaniter feremus.*[2] We have scarcely read this second letter through before the impression which the first letter created has vanished. The assumption that Asconius failed to make use of either letter because he knew neither of them immediately becomes less probable than the theory that he passes them over in silence because their contradictions proved too embarrassing. In Letter I Cicero expresses equal indignation at Catiline's proved extortions and at the judges' possible betrayal of justice. In Letter II he cynically takes Catiline's part, and views the whole situation only in the light of its effect on his electoral manoeuvrings. Nothing, however, in his later letters reveals whether the hopes he so frankly expresses in this second letter were or were not translated into fact. We can therefore understand that Asconius preferred to confine the discussion to the *Oratio in Toga Candida.* Assuredly not because he had failed to read the two letters, but rather because he was, like everyone else, long since familiar with them, and had interpreted them more accurately than others had. As for Fenestella and his belief that Cicero had contemplated defending Catiline, a belief which Asconius rejected, it is highly probable that this historian was also

[1] It was at Caesar's instigation that P. Clodius was treating Catiline with tactful consideration, after having cited him before the *quaestio repetundarum.*
[2] *Ad Att.* I, 2, 1 (11 T.P.), after July 25, 65 B.C.

Introduction

aware of both letters; but, being of a less cautious disposition than Asconius, he reasonably enough assumed that the second letter to Atticus cancelled the first, since it was written a few days later. He would seem to have been as flexible-minded as Cicero himself, and thus wrongly accepted Cicero's momentary impulse as an accomplished fact. To sum up: if we ask the direct and simple question: "Did Cicero in fact undertake the defence of Catiline in 65? Yes or No?" we find that Fenestella and Asconius took opposite sides. Fenestella replies with an unqualified affirmative and Asconius with a gentle negative.

How can we deduce from this whether either of them was or was not acquainted with the two letters, since these letters yield no answer to the vital question? Logically, the probability seems to be that Asconius deliberately turned a blind eye to a correspondence which provided no clear answer to the question at issue; and that Fenestella, having read the letters too hastily and superficially, thought at first that he had found the answer in them.[1] Instead of proving that Cicero's letters to Atticus were not yet published at the time when Asconius drew up his Commentary, this Commentary itself invites us to assume that both Asconius and Fenestella had used them: Asconius, to put them voluntarily aside in a case on which for him they threw no light[2]; Fenestella, to go beyond the text of the letters and hastily misinterpret their meaning.[3]

Now, if this hypothesis is as well-founded as it is natural, it will at once lead us to date the publication of Cicero's Correspondence considerably earlier. The date of Fenestella's death is a matter of dispute: St. Jerome places it in a year corresponding to A.D. 19,[4] while the Elder Pliny postpones it to the end of the reign of Tiberius (A.D. 37);[5] but Pliny himself compels us to place the composition of his *Annals* in the last years of Augustus[6] and consequently the appearance of the *Letters* nearly half a century earlier, certainly before the beginning of Augustus's reign—for

---

[1] This conjecture is the more plausible because Asconius has not told us on what Fenestella based his belief, and it is easy to see how he may have drawn it from a precipitate reading of the second letter of Book I.

[2] In fact, they pose the problem without solving it.

[3] It is fair to acknowledge that this is the opinion of isolated, but well-inspired scholars, in particular Wirz, *Festgaben für Büdinger*, Innsbruck, 1898, p. 114; and Reitzenstein, *Festschrift für Vahlen*, Berlin, 1900, p. 422 (cf. Schanz-Hosius, I, p. 480).

[4] St. Jerome, *Chron.*, Abr. 2035.

[5] Pliny the Elder, *H.N.* XXXIII, 146: . . . *novissimo Tiberii principatu.*

[6] Pliny, *H.N.* VIII, 195. See a résumé of the question in Schanz-Hosius, II, pp. 595–6.

it is inconceivable that they can have been published during that Emperor's rule.[1]

This conclusion may be considered rash. But the hypothesis on which it rests will presently be seen to be corroborated by many allusions to Cicero's Correspondence made about the beginning of our era, allusions which the champions of a more belated publication are hard put to it to explain away.

Let us leave aside the harmony that has been observed between *Periocha* 115 of Livy[2] and Letter 12 of the Fourth Book of *Ad Familiares*,[3] in their two accounts of the murder of Marcus Marcellus, Consul of the year 51, who was exiled in 48, took refuge in Mitylene, and was pardoned by Caesar in 46. At the Piraeus, on his way back to Rome he fell under the dagger of one of his clients, P. Magius Cilo. His death was announced to Cicero in Athens on the morrow of the murder by Servius Sulpicius on May 31, 45. Since Livy died in A.D. 17[4] only three years after Augustus, into whose reign the monumental *Roman History* falls, the resemblance between these two passages would be conclusive if it was the result of a borrowing by the historian from Cicero's Correspondence.[5] But it is not, for it is impossible to be certain of any filiation[6] on account of the lamentable condition of the text of the *Periochae*

---

[1] See above, p. 15f.

[2] Livy, *Per.* 115: "At the request of the Senate, Caesar granted the ex-Consul M. Marcellus permission to return. But Marcellus was not able to enjoy this favour, for he was murdered in Athens by a client of his, Cn. Magius"—[*Caesar*] *M. Marcello consulari, senatu rogante, reditum concessit. Quo beneficio Marcellus frui non potuit, a Cn. Magio cliente suo Athenis occisus.*

[3] *Ad Fam.* IV, 12, 2 (613 T.P.): "P. Postumius came to me and informed me that our colleague, M. Marcellus, was stabbed after dinner with a dagger by P. Magius Cilo and received two wounds, one in the stomach, the other in the head behind the ear: it was hoped, however, that he might live: Magius later killed himself. . . . So I warned the doctors, and immediately set forth myself at dawn. I was not far from the Piraeus when I was met by a servant boy of Acedinus, who brought a note which said that Marcellus had died a little before daybreak"—*P. Postumius . . . ad me venit et mihi nuntiavit M. Marcellum, collegam nostrum, post cenae tempus, a P. Magio Cilone pugione percussum esse et duo vulnera accepisse, unum stomacho alterum in capite secundum aurem : sperari tamen eum vivere posse : Magium se ipsum interfecisse postea. . . . Itaque medicos coegi et e vestigio eo sum profectus prima luce. Cum non longe a Piraeo abessem, puer Acedini obviam mihi venit cum codicillis in quibus erat scriptum, paullo ante lucem diem suam obisse.*

[4] St. Jerome, *Chron.* Abr. 2033: *Livius historiographus Patavi moritur.* The first 120 Books were published in the lifetime of Augustus (Liv. *Per.* 121).

[5] The filiation may be supported by the co-existence of a version rejected by Livy, according to which Magius is represented as having been actuated by a consuming jealousy, and having wanted to kill Caesar (Val. Max. IX, 11, 4).

[6] The fact that the P. Magius of *Ad Fam.* has become Cn. Magius in the *Periochae* would exclude the theory of filiation only if we were armed against the blunders of copyists.

and the mutilation undergone by Livy's Book 115 in the workshop of his abbreviator. In any case, before accepting any responsibility, we should need to be sure that the resemblance was not simply due to the reality of the facts which were naturally common to the two narratives.

To detect the source of this resemblance in the Correspondence of Cicero, let us on the other hand recall the anecdote which Valerius Maximus stole from it to enrich his *Memorabilia* and the striking quotations Quintilian took from Domitius Marsus.

The anecdote about the actor Diphilus which Valerius Maximus has recorded is nothing but a re-hash of a letter of Cicero's to Atticus. A comparison of the two passages puts this beyond doubt. Here is what Valerius Maximus says: "The tragic actor Diphilus was taking part in the *Ludi Apollinares*. When in the course of his acting he came to the lines containing the words: 'Thou art great through our unhappiness' he stretched out his hands in the direction of Pompey as he declaimed them. More than once the audience encored him, and each time he unhesitatingly repeated the gesture accusing Pompey of excessive and intolerable power. He displayed the same insolence also in another line: 'The time will come when thou wilt bitterly regret this valour'."[1]

Let me now quote the words from Cicero's Letters to Atticus which deal with the same episode: "At the *Ludi Apollinares* the tragic actor Diphilus made an insolent attack against our Pompey. He was made to repeat a thousand times: 'Thou art the Great through our unhappiness.' To the clamour of the whole theatre he declaimed: 'The time will come when thou wilt bitterly regret this same valour'":

> *Ludis Apollinaribus Diphilus tragoedus in nostrum Pompeium petulanter invectus est,*
> "*Nostra miseria tu es Magnus*"
> *millies coactus est dicere,*
> "*Eamdem virtutem istam veniet tempus cum graviter gemes*"
> *totius theatri clamore dixit.*[2]

---

[1] Val. Max., VI, 2, 9: *Diphilus tragoedus, cum Apollinaribus ludis inter actum ad eum versum venisset, in quo haec sententia continetur "miseria nostra magnus es", directis in Pompeium Magnum manibus pronuntiavit revocatusque aliquotiens a populo sine ulla cunctatione nimiae illum et intolerabilis potentiae reum gestu perseveranter egit. Eadem petulantia usus est in ea quoque parte: "virtutem istam veniet tempus cum graviter gemes".*

[2] *Ad Att.* II, 19, 3 (46 T.P.)

Introduction

The resemblance between the two passages is glaringly obvious, at once betraying direct imitation. It may perhaps be objected that here, just as above, it is a question of fact and that once the fact is admitted the narrative follows as, so to speak, a necessary consequence.

The two cases are, however, not parallel. Following on the memorable session of the Senate whose resolutions it practically defeated, the murder of ex-Consul M. Marcellus was a resounding event which created a stir in the political circles of the time, an event to which Livy half a century later still devoted one or more chapters of his Book 115. The gestures and demonstrations which accompanied the play-acting of Diphilus at the Games of 59 belong to the gossip-monger rather than to the historian. They are one of the minor incidents of city life which, if only out of courtesy to Pompey, the Consul Caesar would carefully have refrained from mentioning in the *Acta Diurna*,[1] and which will have served only for a day as subject-matter for talk or letter-writing. Above all, there is a textual identity between the two versions that we possess of the episode. The only things in Cicero's letter to Atticus which Valerius Maximus has altered are the quotations. In the first he changes *nostra miseria* into *miseria nostra* and he omits the opening word *eamdem* in the second. He develops the idea contained in the colourful expression *invectus est in* by picturing the actor's hands stretched out accusingly towards Pompey, and on the other hand he has reduced the "thousand" encores which Cicero in jealous delight had accorded to Diphilus. Perhaps he intended by these trifling modifications to make the text his own, though he was copying it rather than drawing inspiration from it. Nevertheless, in spite of this tentative independence, his plagiarising of Cicero is obvious. He follows the exact order of Cicero's letter from the opening mention of the *Ludi Apollinares* to the line of the final quotation. He makes use of the very words, for though he does not avail himself of the adverb *petulanter* to describe the actor's insolence, the adverb haunts him when he adopts the noun *petulantia* to provide the same shade of meaning, and he also describes the actor as *tragoedus*. There is no need to labour the point. In composing at leisure this paragraph of his *Memorabilia* Valerius Maximus never took his eyes off the page, vibrant with the noises

[1] If the *Acta*, which were started in that same year, had already begun to appear.

29

Introduction

of the theatre, which we read today in Cicero's letter to Atticus: manner and matter, he lifted it entire.

We observe exactly the same thing with Domitius Marsus. This writer was also most certainly in a position to draw from the same well as Valerius Maximus, and as we shall see he did not neglect his opportunity. His treatise *De Urbanitate* is not entirely lost. Quintilian did not in fact confine himself to summarising for us the tenor of this work. He reproduced in addition the essential points of the chapter in which Marsus justifies his classifications by sheltering behind Cicero's authority. "Not to understate the opinion of Marsus," writes Quintilian, "this most learned man distinguishes three types of serious *urbanitas*: the respectful, the insulting and the intermediate. As an example of the respectful type he quotes Cicero's words to Caesar in his speech in defence of Q. Ligarius: "You, Caesar, are not wont to forget anything save your wrongs." As an example of the insulting type he adduces what Cicero wrote to Atticus about Pompey and Caesar: "I have one man I would fly from and none whom I would follow." As an example of the intermediate type, which he also calls *apophtheg-matic*, he takes this phrase of Cicero's: "Death cannot be grievous for a brave man, nor untimely for one who has been a Consul, nor sad for a man of wisdom . . ."[1]

Except for a slight inversion, we can find the second of Marsus's quotations word for word in exactly the place where he said he found it, namely in a letter of Cicero to Atticus: *Ego vero quem fugiam habeo, quem sequar non habeo.*[2]

You will say that the reason is clear. We simply take note of this flagrant borrowing and recognise that when Domitius Marsus was working on his *De Urbanitate* he had the opportunity of examining at his leisure Cicero's Correspondence with Atticus. This, however, is a conclusion which the Moderns usually refuse to accept. We should be amazed at such obstinacy were it not that all too often the most ill-founded theories are the very ones which persist longest, and did we not know from experience that the upholders

---

[1] Quintilian, *Inst. Or.* VI, 3, 108: *Nec tamen iudicium Marsi, hominis eruditissimi, subtraham, seria [urbanitas] partitur in tria genera: honorificum, contumeliosum, medium. Et honorifici ponit exemplum Ciceronis pro Q. Ligario apud Caesarem qui "nihil soles oblivisci nisi iniurias"; et contumeliosi quod Attico scripsit de Pompeio et Caesare: "habeo quem fugiam, quem sequar non habeo"; et medii quod ἀποφθεγματικὸν vocat et est ita cum dixit: "neque gravem mortem accidere viro forti posse nec immaturam consulari neque miseram sapienti . . ."*
[2] *Ad Att.* VIII, 7, 2 (338 T.P.).

of such theories are fertile in subtle arguments to avoid accepting anything which would compel them to revise their prejudices. In this case they lay stress on the change in the position of the verb *habeo*: the original of the letter to Atticus says *quem fugiam habeo* and Marsus writes *habeo quem fugiam*; and this suffices for them triumphantly to prove their case. They maintain, despite the express reference of Marsus, that he had not had recourse to the letter itself. They hastily support this theory by a supplementary hypothesis, gratuitously assuming that Marsus had culled this admirable Ciceronian phrase, this *sententia*—which is repeated by Plutarch[1] and Macrobius[2]—from a collection of Cicero's best sayings, made by his former secretary Tiro, who had private access to the Correspondence of his master before it was published.[3]

I am, I confess, more than a little disconcerted by a type of dialectic where an hypothesis assumes a dogmatic air of certainty and distorts—apparently without noticing it—every element of reality, round which it skirts without attempting to penetrate it. This collection of Cicero's sayings? But Macrobius, who based a whole chapter of his *Saturnalia*[4] on this very collection, has quoted with perfect accuracy the phrase in the letter to Atticus on which this discussion turns.[5] Tiro? Assuredly his master's correspondence would have few secrets from him. But what proof have we that he ever made such a collection? Quintilian is the only person who attributes one to him by name, and Quintilian is careful to warn us that this is a rumour only and that he has no intention of guaranteeing its truth.[6]

Above all, it is clear from the context of Domitius Marsus that the disparity, which has been used as a challenge to his good faith,

---

[1] Plutarch, *Reg. et Imp. Apophth.* 205C.

[2] Macrobius, *Sat.* II, 3, 6: *Cuius [Ciceronis] de eo [Pompeio] dicta ferebantur. Ego vero quem fugiam habeo, quem sequar non habeo.* Another collection had been made by Trebonius in Spain in 47 B.C.: *Ad Fam.* XV, 21, 2 (450 T.P.).

[3] Finally see Büchner, *P.W.* VII A, c. 1214: *Die veränderte Form, in der es bei Quintilian gegenüber der Fassung in den Atticusbriefen steht, beweist dass Domitius Marsus das Wort aus der Apophthegmensammlung hatte.*

[4] Compare the text of Macrobius, *Sat.* II, 3, 6 (quoted above, note 2) with the text of *Sat.* II, 1, 12: *liberti eius libros, quos is De Iocis patroni composuit*, etc.

[5] Not only with *habeo* in the same position but also with the *Ego vero* of the letter (cf. above, p. 30).

[6] Quintilian, *Inst. Or.* VI, 3, 5: *libertus eius Tiro, aut alius quisquis fuit, qui tres hac de re libros edidit.* Quintilian's uncertainty about the authorship is easily understood if the publication of these three books of *Ioci* seemed to him to have taken place after Tiro's death in 4 B.C. Cf. Groebe, *P.W.* VIIA (1943), c. 1325.

Introduction

has no significance whatever. It is no more than the liberty he
always allowed himself towards his authors when trusting his
memory for a quotation. There is not one of the three quotations
which he uses to illustrate his theory which is not in a greater or
less degree somewhat inexact. All his remembered quotations, not
having been collated with his *volumina*, have become slightly
damaged in transit. In the *Pro Ligario* we read *qui oblivisci nihil
soles* and not, as he quotes, *qui nihil soles oblivisci*—namely two
transpositions in a phrase of four words.[1] In the fourth Catiline
oration, which was too famous to require a reference, he trusted
his memory and committed not only another transposition—*viro
forti* for *forti viro*, which is the reading of the manuscripts—but
also a blunder by adopting the indirect construction and sub-
stituting *gravem mortem* for the original *turpis mors*.[2] What then?
It will certainly not occur to anyone to deny, on account of these
peccadilloes, that Domitius Marsus had read the text of the *Pro
Ligario*, which appeared in 45,[3] or the text of the Catiline Orations,[4] which were published as early as 60, and since he has
treated these famous documents in precisely the same way as
Cicero's *Letters to Atticus*, it follows that the Correspondence had
its place beside them in his library and that with full knowledge he
made use of it as of them.

5. THE CORRESPONDENCE WAS PUBLISHED UNDER OCTAVIAN

Let us make an end of this long controversy. The allusions to
Cicero's *Letters* which we have just quoted, the one from Valerius
Maximus and the other from Domitius Marsus—the second of
which can boast an authenticity and a significance equal to
Seneca's[5] quotations—bring us back to the point where we left
the *Commentaries* of Asconius and the dispute between this scholiast
and Fenestella. We may carp at the *Memorabilia* of Valerius Maximus, whose curses against Sejanus—possibly a later addition at
the time of a re-issue—seem to point to their composition at the
end of Tiberius's reign,[6] while the extravagant flatteries of Tiberius

[1] Cic. *Pro Lig.* XII, 35: . . . *qui oblivisci nihil soles, nisi iniurias.*
[2] Cic. *Cat.* IV, 2, 3: . . . *nam neque turpis mors forti viro potest occidere, neque immatura consulari nec misera sapienti.*
[3] *Ad Att.* XIII, 19, 2 (631 T.P.): *Ligarianam, ut video, praeclare auctoritas tua commendavit [apud Caesarem].* The date of this letter is June 29, 45 B.C.
[4] *Ad Att.* II, 1, 3 (27 T.P.). I do not believe in an interpolation.
[5] Cf. above, p. 19.　　　　　　　[6] Cf. Schanz-Hosius, II, p. 588.

which the Dedication contains would place it rather at the beginning; and a mediaeval note expressly assigns it to the year A.D. 19.[1]
Domitius Marsus, however, who was a member of the circle round
Maecenas,[2] and who was already dead when Ovid—who himself
died in A.D. 18—was versifying his laments in the *Epistulae ex
Ponto*,[3] most unquestionably wrote his *De Urbanitate* under Augustus. It necessarily follows that the Cicero Correspondence to which
he alludes in that work had already in Augustus's day become
public property, while it cannot possibly have been published
during the Principate of Augustus (30 B.C. to A.D. 14). In other
words, the quotation borrowed by Domitius Marsus is by itself
sufficient to assign the publication of Cicero's *Letters* to the earlier
period, that of the Triumvirate (43–31). This is also the only period
which satisfies all historical considerations.

Taking first the consideration of literary history. Contrary to
first appearances and to the opinion of the majority of scholars,
these considerations lead us away from rather than towards the
time of Seneca. It was not until a century later that Fronto praised
Cicero's *Letters* to the skies as an incomparable model.[4] In Nero's
day they enjoyed no such reputation. In seeking to acclimatise in
Rome the art of letter-writing adopted by the Greek philosophers,[5]
what we might call the art of writing witty and intellectual letters,
Seneca did not hesitate to exalt it by contrasting it with the coarse
materialism of Cicero's *Letters*. "It was agreed," he reminds
Lucilius, "that your letters should be the first; you would write
to me, and I reply to you. But I shan't make difficulties. I know
you can be trusted. I shall make a beginning, but I shall not
follow the advice that Cicero—that most discursive fellow—gave
to Atticus, to write just whatever came into his head even when he
had nothing to say. I shall never run short of subject-matter, even
if I pass over all the things which fill Cicero's letters: who is
making heavy weather as a candidate, who is fighting with his
own forces and who with other people's; who is basing his election
campaign on Caesar's favour, who on Pompey's, and who on his
money-chest, and how close-fisted is the money-lender Caecilius.
. . . It is better to discuss one's own misfortunes than those of

[1] Matthew of Westminster, quoted by Schanz-Hosius, II, p. 589: . . . *anno
divinae Incarnationis XIX Valerius historiographus Romanorum dicta descripsit et
facta.*
[2] Cf. Schanz-Hosius, II, p. 174.
[3] Ovid, *Pont.* IV, 16, 5.

[4] See above, p. 5.
[5] See above, p. 4.

others, to analyse oneself, to see for how many things one is a candidate and not to canvass for votes. In this, my Lucilius, lies dignity, in this, security, in this, freedom: to compete for nothing and to keep right away from Fortune's hustings."[1]

Hearken to this lofty homily on disinterestedness. It is a profession of literary faith. Seneca appears fully conscious of his originality as a writer. He here lays claim to an innovation wholly to his honour, the type of moral instruction by correspondence which he achieved in his letters to Lucilius. He here renounces all kinship with Cicero's correspondence. Cicero's genius impresses him less than the lack of edification repels him. His pitiless criticism reduces his pseudo-precursor to the base level of tatlers, gossip-mongers and idle chatterers. He withholds from Cicero not only all respect as a philosopher but, what is more, all intellectual interest in his writings.

This page of Seneca, too often overlooked, clearly negatives the idea—which we have already rejected on general grounds[2]—that Cicero's *Letters* were at this date an instrument of literary propaganda. Further, it proves that the hour of their use as political propaganda was long since passed.

It is to err on the side of over-ingenuousness to postpone the date of their publication to the days of Claudius or Nero, on the ground that they would have provoked protest if published earlier; and to contend that it was necessary to wait to bring them out until everyone whom they might hit on the raw or deeply offend was dead.[3] No one can fail to see that too long a delay, while it might avoid arousing the annoyance of a small, delicately placed minority, would incur the risk of meeting nothing but indifference among the far greater number of the general public. In their anxiety to wound no one, the editors would have bored everybody. By the time the last survivors of the revolutionary epoch, into

[1] Seneca, *Ep.* 118, 1–3: *Convenerat quidem, ut tua priora essent, tu scriberes, ego rescriberem. Sed non ero difficilis : bene credi tibi scio. Itaque in antecessum dabo nec faciam quod Cicero, vir disertissimus, facere Atticum iubet, ut etiam si rem nullam habebit quod in buccam venerit scribat. Nunquam potest deesse quod scribam ut omnia illa quae Ciceronis implent epistulas transeam : quis candidatus laboret ; quis alienis, quis suis viribus pugnet ; quis consulatum fiducia Caesaris, quis Pompei, quis arcae petat, quam durus sit foenerator Caecilius. . . . Sua satius est mala quam aliena tractare, se excutere et videre quam multarum rerum candidatus sit et non suffragari. Hoc est, mi Lucili, egregium, hoc securum, hoc liberum nihil petere et tota fortunae comitia transire.*
[2] Cf. above, p. 33.
[3] Rose, *Handbook of Latin Literature*, London, 1936, p. 194: "When the persons who might have taken offence . . . were all dead."

which we are plunged by Cicero's *Letters*, had perished, there would have been no readers remaining capable of understanding them without learned research. To avoid the inconveniences of their earlier publication all reason for publishing them at all would have been lost.

Thus one after another we see all avenues of escape closed to us. Whichever way we turn, we are driven back to history, from which Cicero's *Letters* are inseparable. They carry us back several generations, to the men who witnessed the intrigues of which they are woven and to the political convulsions they portray, back to the Triumvirate which followed Cicero's death, to the days when the fires that burn in them were not yet extinguished, fires at whose lingering sparks the new masters of the hour could still rekindle the strife by which their victory was won.

Let us not forget that the victory of "Augustus" had been won by Octavian. Having become Augustus, appeased by his victory and by the omnipotence it had brought him, his sole task was now to reconcile his subjects amongst themselves, and to impose silence about the events and the champions of the civil wars. The violent, cunning and implacable[1] man who had been Octavian had a powerful interest in seizing against his political enemies the terrible weapon which Cicero's correspondence placed suddenly at his service. It would later have embarrassed him as sovereign ruler in his work of peaceful reconstruction.[2] While he was still aspiring to power, it had helped him to achieve it. It would then contribute to rally to his side, and against Mark Antony, not only the partisans of his adoptive father Julius Caesar, but also the wavering senators who were still hesitating to embrace his cause, despite the hatred of his foe with which the *Philippics* had recently inspired them, because that cause had in their eyes been stained by a cruel consent to the proscription of Cicero in 43 when the Triumvirate was coming into being.

---

[1] Sen. *De Clem.* VII, 1, observes that the mildness of Augustus began only with his Principate; ibid. 3, he recalls that it was he who at Antony's instigation issued the Edict of Proscription; ibid. IX, 1, he repeats that his moderation began only *post mare Actiacum Romano cruore infectum . . . post Perusinas aras et proscriptiones*; ibid. 2, he calls Augustus's clemency a "tired cruelty," *lassam crudelitatem.* Later, Suetonius, *Aug.* reports horrible acts of cruelty committed by him as Triumvir: the refusal of burial to the proscribed (Chap. XIII); the refusal of mercy to the people of Perugia (Chap. XV); above all, his harshness, more savage than that of his colleagues, at the time of the proscriptions: . . . *inceptam [proscriptionem] utroque [collegae] acerbius exercuit* (Chap. XXVII, 1).

[2] Cf. above, pp. 16–18.

35

Introduction

The tragedy of Dec. 7, 43,[1] had involved the authors of the proscription in an inescapable dilemma: either the slaying of Cicero, a noble figure of the last days of Republican Rome, had simply been a murder, and Octavian, who had signed his death-warrant, was just a criminal; or else it had been an act of justice, in which case the victim's character must be sufficiently blackened to throw on him the ignominy of the crime. Octavian cleared himself by publishing the dead man's shame. At the height of the struggle for supreme power the Correspondence made it possible for him not only to discredit those of his still-living enemies whom the *Letters* had torn to pieces, but to overwhelm Cicero himself under the irrefutable accusations, evidence for which he had unguardedly amassed in them.

The cry of paradox will assuredly be raised. I shall have no difficulty in justifying my opinion in the pages which follow, but to begin with I shall have against it the unanimity of the critics; those who, like Boissier, persuade themselves that "the thing which gained from the publication of Cicero's *Letters* was the fame of the writer," and that "once you have read them, you can never again forget this gentle and witty figure, so likable, so humane, so attractive even in his weaknesses"[2]; and those who deny that Julius Caesar's son could ever have authorised the publication of documents in which his adoptive father was so odiously mishandled.[3] But both schools are certainly wrong.

It is true, as we shall presently see, that in his *Letters* Cicero had railed against and outraged Julius Caesar. These insults, however, secretly poured out at the very moment when Cicero was soliciting Caesar's favours, enjoying his kindness and overwhelming him with courtly flattery, are powerless to tarnish the halo which encircled the head of the great man in his apotheosis. They serve only to besmirch the writer, base enough to play so infamous a double game, and they recoil, like a boomerang, to smite the man who uttered them. As for Cicero's memory, we have seen that he himself was the first to fear that it would suffer if the *Letters* were published in their entirety; he never contemplated allowing them to appear otherwise than in a very careful selection, chosen after the most mature reflection and delicately retouched.[4]

In a sudden flash of lucid thinking Boissier momentarily aban-

[1] Cf. Drumann-Groebe, VI, pp. 325–6.
[2] Boissier, *Cicéron et ses amis*, pp. 412–13.
[3] Schanz-Hosius, I, p. 480.
[4] Cf. above, p. 13.

dons his conventional optimism and is forced to confess that "some day a curious commentator will study these over-frank confessions and make use of them to draw a portrait of the imprudent man who made them, such as will horrify posterity."[1]

Meantime, as Octavian intended, the portrait roused the indignation of contemporaries, and Cicero's indiscreet revelations needed no commentator to destroy in his fellow-citizens' eyes whatever remained of his reputation as a statesman and to stamp his name with ineffaceable dishonour.[2]

[1] Boissier, *Cicéron et ses amis*, p. 20. At the very moment when Boissier was writing the "curious commentator" had made his appearance in the person of Drumann. The greater number of the heads of the indictment which Drumann has drawn up against Cicero are drawn directly from the Correspondence. Cf. Drumann-Groebe, VI, p. 329f.

[2] I developed this subject in Feb. 1940 in a lecture which the American Academy in Rome did me the honour of requesting, and orally in a course of lectures at the *École normale supérieure* in 1942–3.

CICERO VERSUS CICERO

PART I

THE MAN AS REVEALED IN HIS LETTERS

AFTER the death of Augustus, the Emperor Claudius made use of his knowledge and learning to restore Cicero's memory[1] to honour; and under the Empire, writers in general treated Cicero with respectful sympathy. Only twice, it would seem, was he the object of concerted attacks, and these attacks were so heavily charged with hate and fury that in the eyes of history they have missed their mark.[2] One was the invective which a rhetorician of Augustus's day put forth under the name of the historian Sallust;[3] the other a speech which Dio Cassius fathered on Fufius Calenus, as if the ex-Consul had delivered it at the session of the Senate which was held on Jan. 1, 43.[4] This third-century historian had in fact himself composed it, basing it on lampoons of the same period and written in the same spirit as the Pseudo-Sallust.[5]

We must, however, resign ourselves to the unexpected fact that —apart from the coarse vulgarity of their language—these anti-Cicero pamphlets—wherever we are in a position to verify their distressing contents—allege nothing which is not to be found in Cicero's Correspondence, and which is to be found nowhere else, as if, on the evidence of Cicero himself and of his friends, the *Letters* had drawn up the most implacable and the least suspect

[1] Freed from the trammels of Augustus (see above, p. 18) Claudius would seem to have made it his duty to regain for Cicero the ear of the Roman public (Suet. *Claud.* XLI, 3). But in the literary field the Elder Seneca (*Controv.* I, Pr. 6) and Velleius Paterculus (II, 66, 5) had both begun under Tiberius to extol Cicero's memory.

[2] They must not be believed unless corroborated elsewhere. Even Drumann observes this rule.

[3] Sall., *In M. Tullium Ciceronem Declamatio*. I am convinced that we have here merely a school exercise. On this point, see the last stage of this controversy in Schanz-Hosius, I, p. 372.

[4] Dio Cass., XLVI, 1–28. Dio displays malevolence elsewhere: a proof that despite Claudius's efforts to rehabilitate Cicero, official history remained, under the Empire, hostile to the enemy of its founder. See in particular Dio Cass., XXXVI, 41; XXXVII, 33 and 42; XXXVIII, 9, 12 and 15; XL, 54 and 55.

[5] On this speech of Calenus as reconstituted by Dio Cassius cf. Münzer in *P.W.* VII, c. 206.

indictment against him.[1] Without this evidence we might indeed believe in his virtues, on the subject of which Plutarch—following perhaps Tiro's biography of his master—was never tired of expatiating[2] in terms of praise. Without it, we might preserve the right, if not to pay quite so much admiration to his political genius as his speeches seek to inspire in us, at least to look on him as a great statesman whom Fate ultimately betrayed, a man whose actions were guided by those moral principles and political maxims immortalised in his orations and his writings, a man who deserved a better fate than the sorrows and sufferings which befell him.

The Correspondence, however, throws the ugly side of Cicero's character into sharp relief; it displays the inconsistencies and treacheries of his conduct, which was neither straightforward nor courageous nor disinterested. As we turn these pages whose outspokenness borders on cynicism, our enthusiasm is quenched, our illusions take flight. The politician revealed in them is so odious that his misfortunes appear as the due punishment of unpardonable faults, into which he was plunged by the miscalculations of a mind too self-centred to be clear-sighted, and by the misguided manoeuvres of a will too infirm to rise above the crises amid which his generation were engaged in strife. As regards his private life Cicero's correspondence strips him of every rag of respectability, sparing him no vice or eccentricity; it covers him with ridicule where it does not cover him with infamy.

That, you may well say, is a severe judgment which could not be upheld without a stately array of proofs. Alas! Proofs abound in the *Letters*. Our difficulty will be not to find proofs, but to select the most striking from among them, and duly to distribute among the main chapters of Cicero's life the mass of those we choose.

---

[1] Asconius, *In Mil.* 38, p. 49 *Or.*: . . . *legimus apud Tironem, libertum Ciceronis, in libro IV de vita eius.* On the use of these books, of which there were at least four, cf. Plutarch, *Cic.* XLI, 1 and XLIX, 1. Other texts cited by Groebe, *P.W.* VIIA, c. 1322. There was also a biography by Cornelius Nepos (Aul. Gell. XV, 28, 1). Neither of these would have been written too long after Cicero's death, and, taking the respective ages of Nepos and Tiro, I should place both immediately after the amnesty granted in 39 B.C. to Cicero's son (cf. below II, p. 489).

[2] Cf. below, pp. 43, 127, 149, etc.

Chapter I

CICERO'S FORTUNE AND WAY OF LIFE

1. THE LAND-OWNER

THE *Letters* prove that Cicero, contrary to Plutarch's statement, had in a few years amassed a considerable fortune.[1] If only from the imperfect inventory of his real estate which they allow us to draw up, we must certainly reckon him amongst the great Roman capitalists of his day, though not of course the equal of powerful personages like Pompey and Crassus, each of whom could raise legions from his own demesnes[2] and maintain them at his own expense.

From his father Cicero had inherited a property at his birthplace of Arpinum and a house in Rome.[3] He retained the former, but resigned the house to his brother Quintus[4] in Dec. 62, when he moved from the *Carinae* quarter,[5] where it was situated, and decided to buy himself a luxurious mansion (*domus*) on the aristocratic Palatine Hill.[6] Over-indulgent Plutarch attributes this move to the most generous of motives. If we are to believe him, Cicero— devoted advocate that he was—moved to the Palatine in the interest and for the convenience of his clients[7]: he would then be nearer them. This suggestion, however, can imply only that Cicero had lost his wits and his sense of values or, alternatively, that he intended in future to undertake the defence only of the great, his aristocratic neighbours on the Palatine. Cicero had, as it happens and as he confessed to Atticus, nothing else in mind than to gratify his own snobbery and increase his social prestige: *ad aliquam*

---

[1] Plut. *Cic.*, VII, 2; cf. below, p. 55, note 2.
[2] Cf. my *Histoire romaine*, I, 2, p. 445, and II, 3, p. 561.
[3] Cf. André Lichtenberger, *De Ciceronis Re Privata*, Paris, 1895, p. 3.
[4] Plut. *Cic.* VIII, 3.
[5] *Ad Q. Fr.* II, 3, 7 (102 T.P.): [*domum*] *tuam in Carinis.* Feb. 56 B.C.
[6] *In Palatio* (Cic. *De Domo*, XXXIX, 103 and XLIV, 116).
[7] Plut. *Cic.* VIII, 3.

dignitatem pervenire.[1] By changing his dwelling he rose in the social scale. As a New Man who had attained consular rank, he was puffed up with pride at acquiring a house which had belonged to the plutocrat M. Licinius Crassus—*quod de Crasso domum emissem*[2]—and thus getting a footing in the citadel of the Aristocracy.[3] This was no small matter. Crassus, who had no great love for Cicero[4] and knew all about prices, insisted on a cash payment of three and a half million sesterces—*emi eam ipsam domum HS* $|\overline{XXXV}|$.[5] Reckoning merely by weight, this would be equal to the same number of Poincaré francs[6]—a pretty penny for Cicero to have disgorged for one residence in Rome.[7]

Plutarch mentions no other, but the *Letters*—making good his perhaps unconscious omissions—compel us to add several *insulae* (blocks of flats for letting, we might perhaps call them), advantageously situated near the centre of the City. One of these *insulae* was built in the Argiletum, another on the Aventine, a third near the Chapel of the Goddess Strenia at the top of the Sacred Way. The rents from the two former brought him an annual income of between 80,000 and 100,000 sesterces,[8] say 80,000 to 100,000

---

[1] *Ad Att.* I, 13, 5 (19 T.P.). Jan. 26, 61 B.C.

[2] *Ad Fam.* V, 6, 2 (16 T.P.). Dec. 62 B.C. Letter to P. Sestius.

[3] It is curious that this information is common to Cicero's *Letters* and to the Pseudo-Sallust attack, 2: . . . [*domum*] *comparasti quae Crassi fuit.* Finally on the question of Cicero's *domus* see the note in the Platner-Ashby *Topographical Dictionary.*

[4] That this feeling was mutual is shown by the *Letters*: cf. *Ad Att.* IV, 13, 2 (130 T.P.) . . . *o hominem nequam*; and *Ad Fam.* XIV, 2, 2 (79 T.P.): *Crassum metuo.*

[5] *Ad Fam.* V, 6, 2 (16 T.P.), Dec. 62 B.C.

[6] I shall here repeat what I said in 1942 in the third edition of my *César*, p. 1077: "In quoting sums stated in the ancient texts in *denarii* or *sestertii*, I have given their French equivalent in francs, worked out on a basis of equal weights. I did not feel bound to alter this in my second edition, nor do I now in my third. Any attempt to keep pace with successive devaluations leaves the historian breathless, and though at the date at which I write these lines the Poincaré franc is nothing but a bitter memory to us Frenchmen, I have retained it for my equations since it had approximately the same value as the *sestertius* of Republican Rome." [At present-day (1950) values, the equivalent might be something like eight times this.—ED.]

[7] On the morrow of Cicero's exile, in 57 B.C., Clodius burnt his house to the ground. On Cicero's return the Senate voted him an indemnity of two million sestertii. (*Ad Att.* IV, 2, 5 (91 T.P.): . . . *nobis superficiem aedium consules de consilii sententia, aestimarunt sestertium viciens.*)

[8] *Ad Att.* XII, 32, 2 (568 T.P.): *Accommodet* [*Cicero filius*] *ad mercedes Argileti et Aventini;* cf. ibid. XV, 17, 1 (749 T.P.): *Quod scribis tibi deesse HS* $\overline{C}$ *quae Ciceroni curata sint, velim ab Erote quaeras, ubi sit merces insularum;* ibid. XVI, 1, 5 (769 T.P.): *fructum insularum . . . hunc ex Kal. April(es) ad HS LXXX accommodetur.*

Poincaré francs. The third cannot have been much less in importance than the other two, since the owner in one of his letters advises Atticus to reduce the number of its windows by one-eighth.[1]

This certainly does not exhaust the list of *insulae* owned by Cicero, even if we reject as too corrupt the manuscript passage in which Cicero would seem to have commissioned Atticus to see that he secured for him a block of flats whose seller, Caerellia, had raised the sale-price to 380,000 sesterces.[2] We seem justified in at least doubling the value of his properties in Rome, since in 56 he boasts to his brother Quintus that he had several builders' yards all working for him at the same time, some constructing new buildings on three different sites and others in other places busy on the repair of old buildings: *tribus locis aedifico, reliqua reconcinno*[3].

Now, Cicero owned more landed property outside Rome than in the City itself. Naturally, it is not Plutarch who tells us this. According to him, Cicero merely possessed "one fine estate at Arpinum, a small one near Naples, and another, also a small one, at Pompeii."[4] But there stands the Correspondence to challenge the tendentious statements of accommodating biographers and to trace Cicero's journeys along the roads of Latium and Campania as he moved from one to another of his estates, like Perrault's Marquis de Carabas. From the *Letters* we learn not of three but of eight country-houses or *villae*, to which we must add another ten or so of rest-houses or *deversoria*.[5] For Cicero, one of the New Rich, made it a point of honour to adopt the extravagant habits and pleasant luxuries of the old nobility. He was determined to have an embarrassingly wide choice of pleasure and health resorts of his own, like those where the aristocratic Roman could, according to the season, find repose from the worries of the City. Like the

[1] *Ad Att.* XV, 26, 4 (763 T.P.): . . . *octavam partem luminarium ad Streniae memineris.*

[2] *Ad Att.* XV, 26, 4 (763 T.P.): . . . *quod Caerellea vidiris mancipio dare ad eam summam quae sub praecone fuit maxima : id opinor esse* CCCLXXX.

[3] *Ad Q. Fr.* II, 4, 3 (105 T.P.). It is improbable that in this letter, written from Rome, we need take into account reconstructions and repairs carried out at Cicero's order in his *villae* in Latium and Campania. The contrary view is held—wrongly, I think—by Drumann, cf. Drumann-Groebe, VI, p. 340, note 13, and p. 342, note 12.

[4] Plut. *Cic.* VIII, 2.

[5] *Deversoria* or *deversoriola*: on the meaning of these words cf. André Lichtenberger, op. cit., p. 10. On Cicero's houses and *villas* see Laurand, *Cicéron* (3), Paris, 1939, p. 85f.

aristocrats, Cicero planned his own little rest-houses with suitable distances between them, so arranged, in stages as it were, that however far they were from each other or from Rome, he would never need when travelling to solicit the humiliating hospitality of an innkeeper.[1]

Only one of all his estates came to him by inheritance, his demesne at Arpinum. According to Plutarch, it was the most extensive.[2] It was not the most happily situated, but it yielded the best return. It was surrounded by developed agricultural lands which Cicero's father had formerly superintended himself.[3] The son, however, now leased them out to local farmers on contracts which, as he tells Atticus, he was periodically obliged to discuss with his tenants in person: "I have to go to Arpinum. For there is work to be done in arranging about my little farms"—*Mihi Arpinum eundum est. Nam et opus est constitui a nobis illa praediola.*[4] Little though he lingered there, he found the house and the simple form of life which had been good enough for his parents, too rude and shabby for the visits of an ex-Consul. As early as 61 we find him toying with plans for adding rockeries and embellishments such as his correspondent Atticus had ingeniously introduced in the Amaltheum of his mansion in Epirus: *velim ad me scribas cuius modi sit ἀμαλθεῖον tuum, quo ornatu, qua τοποθεσίᾳ : lubet mihi facere in Arpinati.*[5]

In a letter of 59 Cicero does not hesitate to speak of it by the lines in which Ulysses evokes for Alcinous the picture of the little island[6] which was his home:

A rugged isle, but a good nurse of noble youths; and for myself I can see nought beside sweeter than a man's own country.[7]

Seven years later,[8] he repeats the comparison in his dialogue *De Legibus*, in which the speakers discourse at the foot of Marius's

[1] Cf. André Lichtenberger, op. cit., loc. cit.
[2] Cf. above, p. 45, note 4.
[3] Cic. *De Lege Agraria*, III, 2, 8: . . . *paternus avitusque fundus Arpinas.*
[4] *Ad Att.*, XIII, 9, 2 (623 T.P.).
[5] *Ad Att.*, I, 16, 18 (22 T.P.). On Atticus's artificial grotto, the Amaltheum, and on *topothesia* in general, see the Index to P. Grimal's excellent thesis, *L'art des jardins*, etc., Paris, 1943, and the passages to which he refers. On the Arpinas, the site of which must be sought near the island formed by the Fibrenus before it flows into the Liris, cf. Cotard, "Un voyage à Arpinum," *Les Humanités*, VI, 1933-4, pp. 100–104.
[6] Homer, *Odyssey*, IX, 27–8.
[7] [The English translation is Butcher and Lang's.—E. O. L.] These two lines follow immediately on the passage already quoted in *Ad Att.* II, 11, 2 (39 T.P.); cf. below, p. 47, note 3.
[8] On the date of *De Legibus*, cf. Schanz-Hosius, I, pp. 498–9.

oak, in front of Arpinum[1]: "Know that this is the very place where I was born. There is in it something, I know not what, that lingers in my heart and senses, which makes this spot delight me perhaps most of all, as indeed it is written that the wisest of men rejected immortality that he might see Ithaca once more."[2] Let us not be taken in by the emotion which Cicero, for the benefit of the public at large, mingled with his reminiscences. In the above-quoted letter—which was written not from Arpinum but from Formiae—he makes it quite clear to Atticus that the stay which he is going to be compelled to make in the home of his ancestors is not going to be so pleasant that he would want to prolong it more than necessary, or invite his friends to come and share it: "I want to remain here at Formiae until May 6. If you do not come here before that date perhaps I shall see you in Rome. For why invite you to Arpinum? . . ."[3] Cicero's preferences can be read between these last lines. In spite of all the enlargements and transformations he had carried out in his ancestral *villa*, Cicero preferred whenever possible those other places which he had bought elsewhere as he grew richer and richer, and which he had arranged to his liking.

The most famous of all his properties is the one which the *Tusculan Disputations* were to immortalise. We ought really to speak of it in the plural rather than the singular. It is clear from the Correspondence that in successive annexations he soon contrived at Tusculum to merge three estates into one. The first of these, which must have been of some considerable size, for it had recently been reckoned by the dictator Sulla as one of his demesnes,[4] was bought when Cicero first attained the rank of a Curule Magistrate. As early as the end of 68, when he had reached the Aedileship, he asks Atticus, who was still in Athens, to help him to furnish it: "Please do as you propose in your letter and buy anything you think would be suitable for my place at Tusculum as well as the things I commissioned you to get—always provided it is not too

---

[1] Cic. *De Leg.* I, 1, 1.
[2] Cic. *De Leg.* II, 1, 3: *Hoc ipso in loco me scito esse natum. Qua re inest nescio quid et latet in animo ac sensu meo, quo me plus hic locus fortasse delectet, si quidem etiam ille sapientissimus vir, Ithacam ut videret, immortalitatem scribitur repudiasse.*
[3] *Ad Att.* II, 11, 2 (39 T.P.). Atticus, as a matter of fact, preferred Arpinum. *Ad Att.* II, 16, 4 (43 T.P.): *Te in Arpinati videbimus et hospitio agresti accipiemus, quoniam maritimum hoc contempsisti;* but we can hardly read much enthusiasm for Arpinum into Cicero's phrase "rural hospitality."
[4] Pliny, *H.N.* XXII, 12: *Sulla dictator in villa sua Tusculana quae fuit postea Ciceronis.*

47

much trouble. For this is the only place where I can get thoroughly rested from all my vexations and toils."[1] A few weeks later, in Jan. 67, he reverts to the pleasure which he gets from it: "I am so much delighted by my *Tusculanum* that I am never contented till I get there."[2] This style of happy contentment was not destined to last. Imposing and magnificent as we picture it, the *villa* which had been good enough for Sulla was soon not sufficiently grand for our ex-Consul; and Cicero could not resist the temptation of combining with it the neighbouring estates. First, after the death of the Senator Catulus he took over his estate,[3] which had been sold to Vettius, and which Cicero must have bought either the day before or the day after the murder of that base intriguer in 59.[4] He did not succeed in doing so without arousing the jealousy of the rival purchasers, whom he outbid, and about whose bitterness he was still complaining to Atticus three years later.[5] Next he acquired the property of Culleo, on which in 56 he had set his heart. The auction, of which he writes to his brother Quintus in Sardinia, does not seem to have attracted other bidders.[6]

There is some doubt about the exact position of Cicero's *Tusculanum*. But it matters little whether we locate it on the Hill of Broom (*Colle delle Ginestre*) between Frascati and Grottaferrata on the Ruffinella, where Lucien Bonaparte took refuge with his broodings in the nineteenth century, or nearer the ruins of the ancient city of Tusculum, on the lower slopes of the Alban Hills. In either case we may picture Cicero's Tusculan property as one of generous extent, impressive and delightful views, welcome shade, and the flowing waters of one of the great seignorial manors such as since Renaissance times have been the characteristic glory of the Frascati landscape. Only, whereas the princes of Rome today content themselves with their one country seat, Tusculum soon was for

---

[1] *Ad Att.* I, 5, 7 (1 T.P.): *Quae tibi mandavi et quae tu intelleges convenire nostro Tusculano, velim, ut scribis, cures, quod sine molestia tua facere poteris. Nam nos ex omnibus molestiis et laboribus uno illo in loco conquiescimus.*

[2] *Ad Att.* I, 6, 2 (2 T.P.): *Nos Tusculano ita delectamur ut nobismet ipsis tum denique, cum illo venimus, placeamus.*

[3] Cf. my *César* (3), p. 707; Catulus died in 61 B.C.

[4] On this date and the circumstances, cf. my *César* (3), p. 737.

[5] *Ad Att.* IV, 5, 2 (108 T.P.): *Et ii subringentur qui villam me moleste ferunt habere, quae Catuli fuerat, a Vettio me emisse non cogitant.* Cicero would seem to imply that Vettius was alive. In which case the sale must have taken place in 60 or 59 B.C.

[6] *Ad Q. Fr.* II, 2, 1 (100 T.P.): *Culleonis auctio facta est. Tusculano emptor nemo fuit. Si condicio valde bona fuerit, fortassis non omittam.*

Cicero only one of half a dozen *villae*, which shared his attentions and where he liked to spend his leisure.

In 66 he had taken up his residence on the actual sea coast at Vindicium,[1] in a country house two-thirds of the way between Caieta—which he speaks of in the earliest of his letters to Atticus[2] —and Formiae, whence he later gave this the name of the *Formianum*.[3] In 60 a double purchase: two new *villae* make their simultaneous appearance in his *Letters*. One was at Antium,[4] of which he later said that he knew "nothing quieter, nothing cooler, nothing more agreeable."[5] The other was at Pompeii at the foot of Vesuvius; this was his *Pompeianum*, from which we hear of his returning to Rome in May 60[6] and to which he used hastily to fly to escape the boring callers of the City and to hide himself from importunate visitors.[7]

No sooner had he breathed the air of Campania than he longed for the famous beaches where the aristocrats of Rome— from Pompey to Varro, from Brutus to L. Marcius Philippus, step-father of Octavius[8]—were wont to congregate. After his triumphant return from exile he settled himself in the very heart

[1] An excellent seaside resort, well sheltered by the promontory of Caieta (the modern Gaeta), and dominated by the tomb of L. Munatius Plancus, now converted into a naval signalling-station. The identification of the *Formianum* with the Villa Rufino (two kilometres from Formiae) is at best doubtful (Schmidt, "Ciceros Villen" in the *Neue Jahrbücher für Phil. und Päd.* 1899, III, p. 350).

[2] *Ad Att.* I, 4, 3 (9 T.P.): *Caietam . . . ornabo.*

[3] So called already in the above letter, ibid.: *In Formiano sunt, quo ego nunc proficisci cogitabam.* The *Formianum* recurs notably in *Ad Att.* IV, 2, 5 and 7 (91 T.P.) and II, 13, 1 (40 T.P.).

[4] *Ad Att.* II, 4, 1 (27 T.P.): *. . . eunti mihi Antium,* June 60 B.C.

[5] *Ad Att.* IV, 8A, 1 (112 T.P.): *. . . nihil quietius, nihil alsius, nihil amoenius.* He adds: "You must know that Antium is the Roman Buthrotum as yours is the Corcyraean Buthrotum"—*Hoc scito Antium Buthrotum esse Romae ut Corcyrae illud tuum.* Since we know the importance of Atticus's Buthrotum property, this comparison seems to exclude the possibility that Cicero's *villa* at Antium was identical with the house he owned inside the city, whose existence we infer from a passage in the same letter in which he informs Atticus that he has not been able to find a building for him out in the open country and that it is doubtful whether he will be able to find a house for sale in the town near to his (Cicero's) own— *aedificati tibi in agris nihil reperio. In oppido est quiddam, de quo est dubium, sitne venale, ac proximum quidem nostris aedibus.* These *aedes* may be the *domus* which Cicero parted with to Lepidus in 45 B.C. (cf. below, p. 51, note 2).

[6] *Ad Att.* I, 20, 1 (26 T.P.): *. . . cum e Pompeiano me Romam recepissem* (May 60 B.C.).

[7] *Ad Att.* XV, 13, 6 (795 T.P.): *. . . ego in Pompeianum properabam . . . inter-pellatores illic minus molesti;* XVI, 11, 6 (799 T.P.): *me non abdidi in Pompeianum.*

[8] On Philippus cf. *Ad Att.* XIII, 52, 1 (679 T.P.); XIV, 11, 2 (714 T.P.). On Brutus cf. ibid. XII, 36, 2 (578 T.P.); on Pompey cf. p. 50, note 4 below. It is only in the case of Varro that Drumann-Groebe, VI, p. 343, notes 10–12, has drawn his references from a philosophic treatise (*Acad. Post.* I, 1) and not from the *Letters*.

of his region, blessed alike by sea and sky, at the gates of Baiae, on the shore of the Lucrine Lake dominated by the acropolis of Cumae.[1] Having selected a site, he set about getting his future *Cumanum* built for himself. It was still incomplete in April 56; the main body of the house was still open to every wind, yet Cicero was already enjoying it[2] though he excused himself from offering hospitality to an invalid guest.[3] Next year he was able to entertain the great Pompey, whose first visit pleased him so much that he was tempted to repeat it the following spring.[4]

Another man might have been satisfied. But there was no limit to Cicero's ambition. He rounded off his *Cumanum* by acquiring a small adjacent estate.[5] He then had the good fortune to inherit from Cluvius in 44 a luxurious *villa* lying between Baiae and Naples in the Bay of Puteoli.[6] This became his *Puteolanum*, of which he asserted one day that there was nothing lovelier: *non hoc loco quicquam pulchrius*.[7]

In the long run, however, at certain painful moments in his life, he grew weary of so much wealth, but he never had the courage to give it up. The more he multiplied his purchases of land in fashionable places, the more, no doubt, it seemed to him that the City with its tiresome people pursued him even into the country, and it was natural that he should try to escape. In his own way he is rather like the Kings of France, who sought refuge from the pomp of Versailles in their Marly and their Trianons. Yet we do not see him setting out more often to seek the rustic peace of his property

[1] *Ad Q. Fr.* II, 5, 4 (106 T.P.): *Cogitabam . . . aspicere Cumanum.*

[2] Cf. above, note 1. His enjoyment steadily increased; cf. *Ad Q. Fr.* II, 12, 1 (139 T.P.): *Ego me in Cumano . . . oblectabam.* 54 B.C.

[3] *Ad Q. Fr.* II, 8, 2 (123 T.P.): *hominem infirmum in villam apertam ac ne rudem quidem etiam nunc invitare nolui.* As regards the date, I prefer Schmidt's interpretation (op. cit., loc. cit., p. 480, note 4) to Tyrrell and Purser's.

[4] *Ad Att.* IV, 10, 2 (121 T.P.): *Pompeius in Cumanum Parilibus venit*; ibid. 9, 1 (122 T.P.): *. . . venit etiam ad me in Cumanum* [*Pompeius*]. According to Tyrrell and Purser, the two visits were one and the same, for the Parilian feast of April 21, 55 B.C. According to Schmidt (op. cit., loc. cit.) the second visit, which from the context took place on April 27, six days later, must be assigned to the following year.

[5] *Ad Att.* XIV, 13, 5 (718 T.P.): *Scribis esse rumores me ad lacum quod habeo venditurum; minusculam vero villam Quinto traditurum* (April 26, 44 B.C.). From the plural *rumores* we gather that at least two rumours were current; so there must have been two *villae* by the Lake, a large and a small one (*minusculam*).

[6] *Ad Att.* XIV, 9, 1 (712 T.P.): *Primum vehementer Cluviana delectant* (letter of April 18, 44 B.C., from Puteoli). On the question of this inheritance, cf. below, p. 107f., and Schmidt, op. cit., loc. cit., pp. 342 and 487.

[7] *Ad Att.* XV, 13A, 6 (795 T.P.). This *villa* was so beautiful that the Emperor Hadrian was buried there (*H.A., Hadr.* XXV, 7: *sepultus est in villa Ciceroniana Puteolis*).

at Arpinum. Nor yet, as some have thought,[1] seeking to rid himself
of his fashionable *villas*.[2] On the contrary. When he felt the urgent
need for quiet retirement on the death of his daughter Tullia, he
sought these in acquiring a supplementary retreat not less pleasant
than his others, but more isolated. In 45 he bought the lonely
wooded island[3] by the coastal river Astura, where it flows into the
sea near the little town of the same name.[4] It lies between the
Mons Circeius and Antium, a view of which lay on his new
horizon.

Let us sum up: three *villae* merged in one at Tusculum; two
others, similarly merged, at Cumae; one *villa*, not used so much
for residence as for letting, at Arpinum; one at Astura, one at
Antium, one at Formiae, one at Puteoli, and finally one—the most
southerly of all—at Pompeii. According as we reckon the several
purchases made or the composite estates created, that gives us a
maximum of eleven *villae* or a minimum of eight. These were
progressively added to his real properties in Rome. Meanwhile we
must not forget the various rest-houses, or *deversoria*, which he
arranged for himself at convenient intervals, the free use of which
enabled him to travel at ease between one and another of his
estates,[5] thus avoiding the hateful promiscuity of inns or the danger
of taxing friends who might live along his route. It was only with
the greatest reluctance that he availed himself of such hospitality,
as for instance whenever he had to halt at Terracina.

Apart from one in this neighbourhood which he had coveted—

---

[1] Especially Lichtenberger, op. cit., p. 15.

[2] From *Ad Att.* XIII, 47B, 1 (654 T.P.) it is clear that Lepidus had bought in
July 45 B.C. the house that Cicero owned at Antium (see above, p. 49, note 6):
*Lepidus ad me heri vesperi litteras misit Antio : nam ibi erat : habet enim domum
quam nos vendidimus*, Letter of July 30, 45 B.C., from Astura. This leaves still
undecided the question whether the *domus* situated in the built-up area of Antium
is to be identified with the *villa* or was distinct from it. Whatever we may think
on this point, Cicero never gave up any of his *villae* properly so called.

[3] Pliny, *H.N.* III, 57; Plut. *Cic.* XLVII, 1.

[4] *Ad Att.* XII, 13, 1 (545 T.P.): *Me haec solitudo . . . stimulat*. March 7,
45 B.C.; 15 (547 T.P.): *In hac solitudine careo omnium colloquio, cumque mane me
in silvam abstraxi densam et asperam, non exeo inde ante vesperum* (March 9,
45 B.C.); 19, 1 (552 T.P.): *Est hic quidem locus amoenus et in mari ipso, qui et
Antio et Circeiis aspici possit*. March 14, 45 B.C. Within a few days Cicero is
again thinking more of *amoenitas* than of solitude.

[5] Cf. above, p. 45. Two passages in the *Letters* throw light on the advantages
of these *deversoria*; the one is quoted in the following note, the other is Cic. *Ad
Att.* VII, 5, 3 (296 T.P.): "I shall not go (from Formiae) to Tusculum this
time. It is a roundabout way for those coming to meet me and has other dis-
advantages"—*Ego in Tusculanum nihil sane hoc tempore. Devium est* τοῖς
ἀπαντῶσιν *et habet alia* δύσχρηστα (50 B.C.).

the opportunity to acquire which he lost by the carelessness of the freedman charged with making the purchase for him[1]—his *Letters* enable us to identify most of these halting-places which he provided for himself as a precaution against the fatigues of travel and the vicissitudes of the road. There was the one at Lanuvium[2] on a farm in the Solonium, a fertile plain which stretched towards the sea in the direction of Ostia[3]; one at Anagnia between Rome and Arpinum[4]; the two at Sinuessa (Mondragone)[5] and Minturnae[6] on the frontier between Latium and the Campania; one at Frusino between Arpinum and the Campanian coast.[7] Others, whose position has been forgotten, lay on ground which had been sold to him in one place or another, whether by the Praetor C. Memmius or the Tribune Sextus Atilius Serranus[8] or Canuleius.[9] In short he had succeeded in equipping nine *deversoria* to serve his eight estates, and many of them almost equalled the importance of a

---

[1] *Ad Fam.* VII, 23, 3 (126 T.P.): *Ista quidem summa ego multo libentius emerim deversorium Terracinae, ne semper hospiti molestus sim. Omnino liberti mei video esse culpam, cui plane res certas mandaram.*

[2] The halting-place acquired as early as 60 B.C. (see following note) was more especially used between Astura and Tusculum. *Ad Att.* XII, 44, 3 (590 T.P.), May 13, 45 B.C.; XIII, 26, 2 (591 T.P.), May 14, 45 B.C.; XIII, 34, 1 (647 T.P.): *. . . vitandi enim caloris causa Lanuvii tris horas acquieveram.* July 26, 45 B.C. The sybaritism of the millionaire who has a relay-station where he can enjoy his siesta!

[3] *Ad Att.* II, 3, 3 (29 T.P.): *. . . ire in Solonium.* The letter is of 60 B.C. On the *Solonium* cf. *P.W.* IIIA, c. 982.

[4] This would seem to have been acquired between April 56 B.C. and Nov. 46 B.C. as we gather from comparing the two following quotations:
   (a) *Ad Q. Fr.* II, 5, 4 (106 T.P.): *. . . eo die apud T. Titium in Anagnino manerem.* April 8, 56 B.C.
   (b) *Ad Att.* XII, 1, 1 (505 T.P.): *. . . eo die cogitabam in Anagnino, postero autem in Tusculano . . .* From Arpinum 9th day of the Kalends of Dec. 46 B.C.

[5] *Ad Att.* XIV, 8, 1 (710 T.P.): *. . . accepi in diversoriolo Sinuessano tuas litteras;* XV, 1B, 1 (731 T.P.): *. . . exiens e Puteolano deverteram in Cumanum. Mansi eo die in Sinuessano atque inde postridie Arpinum proficiscens, hanc epistolam exaravi.* These letters are dated April 15 and May 18 of 44 B.C. respectively. See similar expressions, *in Sinuessanum, de Sinuessano,* in the letters dated respectively Nov. 8 and 10, 44 B.C., *Ad Att.* XVI, 10, 1 (801 T.P.) and 13A, 1 (802 T.P.).

[6] *Ad Att.* XV, 2. 1 (732 T.P.), May 13, 44 B.C.: *E Sinuessano proficiscens in Vesciano accepi tuas litteras.* Like Quintus Cicero's *Arcanum,* the *Vescianum* was a suburb of Minturnae; it belonged to the elder brother, *Ad Q. Fr.* II, 5, 4 (106 T.P.).

[7] *Ad Att.* XI, 4, 1 (413 T.P.): *De Frusinati si modo fruituri sumus . . .* (Nov. 46 B.C.); and 13, 4 (428 T.P.): *De fundo Frusinati redimendo . . . in eadem sum voluntate.*

[8] *Ad Att.* V, 1, 2 (184 T.P.): *. . . et sunt aliquot satisdationes secundum mancipium veluti Me(mm)ianorum praediorum vel Atilianorum* (51 B.C.).

[9] *Ad Att.* X, 5, 3 (384 T.P.): *. . . emere de Canuleio deversorium illud posse.* April 16, 49 B.C.

villa and deserved the title: his *Anagninum*, his *Sinuessanum*, his *Frusinas*.[1]

These incontrovertible statistics leave far behind the modest little balance sheet faked up, rather than seriously calculated, by Plutarch. They suggest that we may safely estimate at some ten million[2] the fortune in landed property of which Cicero was in possession at the close of his life.

The calculation is relatively easy to make. If the rents from two of his blocks of flats in Rome brought him in 100,000 sesterces and if we count that this represents a capital of ten times that sum, his three urban *insulae* would have been worth a million and a half.[3] Then we have seen that his mansion on the Palatine cost him three and a half million. We thus arrive at a total of five million for his real property in the City.[4]

His country properties were obviously on a similar scale. His *Letters* give us thirty to forty thousand sesterces as the price of a *deversorium*.[5] His nine *deversoria* therefore represent in round numbers four hundred thousand sesterces.

Though the *Letters* give us no figures for any of the *villae*, they give us material for comparison which indirectly supplies this lack. From the financial point of view, the most important of Cicero's country properties was that of Arpinum, because of the connected farms.[6] Without much margin of error we may divide the estates which were simply pleasure resorts into two series: first those in fashionable neighbourhoods frequented by society, where prices were naturally enhanced: these were his *Tusculanum*, his *Cumanum* and his *Puteolanum*; secondly those that were less oppressively famous, though still attractive and coveted: these were the *Formianum*, the *Pompeianum* and the *villae* of Antium and Astura.

[1] Cf. above, p. 52, notes, 4, 5 and 7.

[2] Namely 10 million sesterces and the same number of Poincaré francs. [Ramsay-Lanciani's *Roman Antiquities* in 1901 reckoned one million sesterces as approximately equal to £8,333 6s. 8d.—E. O. L.]

[3] Cf. above, pp. 44–5. The rate of interest is here over-estimated. From Billeter's studies in his *Geschichte des Zinsfusses im griechisch-römischen Altertum*, Leipzig, 1898, it appears that capital in Rome brought in on an average 5 per cent. Cicero's three *insulae* may well have been worth three million rather than a million and a half.

[4] Cf. above, p. 44.

[5] *Ad Att.* X, 5, 3 (384 T.P.): *Cum enim mihi Philotimus dixisset se HS L̄ emere de Canuleio deversorium illud posse, minoris etiam empturum, si Vettienum rogassem, rogavi . . . promisit: ad me nuper se HS X̄X̄X̄ emisse, ut scriberem cui vellem addici, diem pecuniae Id. Novembr(es) esse.*

[6] Cf. above, p. 46, and Lichtenberger, op. cit., p. 11.

Now it happens that by good fortune Cicero's correspondence has preserved a valuable indication of the approximate value of the components of each series. From the *Letters* we learn that when in 57 the Senate through the consuls voted compensation for the damage to Cicero's properties that had followed his exile, he was granted half a million for his *Tusculanum* and a quarter of a million for his *Formianum*. As he complained of the ungenerous nature of these indemnities: *valde illiberaliter*[1]—and as we also know that he received only two millions for his house on the Palatine which had cost him three and a half, it is legitimate to calculate the basic value of his *villae* on the same principle: namely *Tusculanum* 750,000 sesterces and *Formianum* 375,000.[2]

We can then use these figures to give us an average value for the estates of the two series. We are therefore justified in reckoning the three *villae* of the first category as worth two and a half million and the four of the second as one and a half. Remembering that the *Arpinas* equalled, if it did not exceed, *Tusculanum* in value, it is reasonable to conclude that the total value of Cicero's country estates was at least equal to the five million of his City properties.

Even in the unlikely event of the *Letters* not having omitted any single one of his possessions, they justify us in assuming that Cicero's assets in real estate totalled more, rather than less, than ten million. This sum is the more impressive when we remember that it takes no account of the immense sums that he spent on "furnishing" his mansion in Rome and his *villae* in Italy. We must remember too that with the exception of the *Arpinas* and the city *insulae*, all this immovable property was unproductive[3]; and finally that, with the certain exception of the *Arpinas* and the probable exception of the Roman *insulae*, he had paid for them all out of his own pocket. Such large investments of capital, made without the smallest hope of profit, but solely for pleasure, are eloquent of the

[1] *Ad Att.* IV, 2, 5 (91 T.P.): *Nobis superficiem aedium consules de consilii sententia aestimarunt HS viciens: cetera valde illiberaliter: Tusculanam villam quingentis milibus, Formianum HS ducentis quinquaginta milibus* (57 B.C.).

[2] I believe that these calculations are actually far below the mark, when I see Cicero, in treaty for the purchase of the gardens of Silius, proposing to defray the cost with 600,000 sesterces of ready cash which he has by him, plus a further 600,000 owed to him by Hermogenes, which he is trying to recover. Cf. *Ad Att.* XII, 25, 1 (561 T.P.) and below, p. 58.

[3] What Cicero himself called "voluptuary" property, admitting that not everybody was enamoured of it. Cf. *Ad Att.* XII, 25, 1 (561 T.P.): *Voluptuarias enim possessiones nolet Silius.* March 21, 45 B.C.

resources of his treasury and the lordly style of living indulged in by our "New Man".[1]

2. THE FINANCIER

In the course of studying the *Letters*, how often is the reader dazzled by his wealth! How many pages there are where his hands seem full of money! The further we read the more we feel that even advancing years instead of assuaging seem rather to have over-stimulated the passion—from which Plutarch would fain exonerate him[2]—which money, to judge from his Correspondence, always inspired in him. He liked to keep at hand enormous quantities of ready cash which he carried with him on his journeyings. One day in 45, for instance, he writes to Atticus that amid the loneliness of Astura he took the trouble to empty out his drawers and make an inventory of their contents, and he announces quite simply, as it were a matter of course, "I see that I have 600,000 sesterces by me"—*et domi video esse HS $\overline{DC}$.*[3]

Larger sums of money he naturally deposited with his bankers, the chief of whom, as everyone knows, was Atticus.[4] To Cicero it was the most natural thing in the world to open a large account with a tax-gathering firm by one large payment of 2,200,000 sesterces.[5] Nor did he let the sums that fell to him lie idle. He is indefatigable in urging his confidential men of business to find remunerative employment for them and firmly to remind the borrowers to whom they have been lent when their payments are due. The names of many of these debtors recur in the Correspondence.[6] There was his brother Quintus, for one, who was little less extravagant than Cicero himself[7]; there was the great

---

[1] Laurand, *Cicéron* (3), p. 100, is well justified in heading one of his sections: "Cicero was rich." If we add to his patrimony the value of his real property and the total of the legacies he harvested (20 millions: cf. below, p. 101) he possessed a fortune three times as great as that which Nepos credits to Atticus, who was one of the great capitalists of his time. Nepos, *Att.* V and XIV, 2 (cf. below, II, pp. 433, 437 and 453).

[2] Plut. *Cic.* VII, 2.

[3] *Ad Att.* XII, 25, 1 (561 T.P.). From Astura, March 21, 45 B.C.

[4] Cf. below, pp. 66, 154, etc.

[5] *Ad Fam.* V, 20, 9 (302 T.P.): *Simul cogitare debes me omnem pecuniam quae ad me . . . pervenisset, Ephesi ad publicanos deposuisse: id fuisse HS $\overline{XXII}$.* Letter of mid-Jan, 49 B.C. to Mescinius Rufus. Cf. below, p. 124.

[6] See the list drawn up from the Correspondence by Drumann-Groebe, VI, p. 348. To this may be added the name of Lepta, for instance, cf. *Ad Att.* X, 11, 2 (396 T.P.).

[7] *Ad Att.* XV, 20, 4 (752 T.P.): *. . . in eam diem* (Nov. 1, 44 B.C.) *cadere nummos qui a Quinto debentur . . .* Letter written from Tusculum between June 17 and 20, 44 B.C.

Pompey, who in 49 borrowed more than a million from him at one time[1]; and, if we are to believe the letters of 45, there was Faberius,[2] the personal secretary of Julius Caesar—the exact amount of whose indebtedness the *Letters* unfortunately do not anywhere work out.

Services of this kind can scarcely be refused to members of the family, and a politician may feel constrained to offer them at a favourable moment to some great man of the day[3] in order to enlist his goodwill, but we need not be surprised to find that in such cases Cicero reaped but a poor reward. The *Letters* do not tell us whether he ever succeeded in getting his money back from Faberius in spite of all the applications he made for it,[4] and it is a safe guess that Pompey was murdered in Egypt without having had time to repay his debt.[5] We consequently find Cicero usually preferring less speculative transactions and seeking his borrowers in every stratum of society, having regard only to their solvency. So we find amongst them, beside a certain Papia,[6] a woman otherwise unknown to fame, one Funisulanus, a man of modest rank but admirably well-to-do,[7] a Flaminius Flamma, for whom L. Munatius Plancus stood guarantor,[8] young men from families of very various social standing whose debts were covered by their fathers' fortunes. There was young Axius, for instance, for whom

[1] This appears from a comparison of the Letter *Ad Fam.* V, 20, 9 (302 T.P.), quoted p. 55, note 5, with the letters *Ad Att.* XI, 1, 2 (406 T.P.): 2, 3 (407 T.P.); and 13, 4 (428 T.P.), written in 48 B.C. On the details of this transaction cf. below, pp. 66–7 and 124.

[2] Cf. below, p. 57, note 6. On this Faberius see Appian, *B.C.* III, 5, 16.

[3] In connection with this loan to Pompey, Cicero later admitted: "I lent Pompey the money I had at my disposal at a time when this seemed to me a wise action"—*si quas habuimus facultates, eas Pompeio tum, cum id videbamur sapienter facere, detulimus. Ad Att.* XI, 13, 4 (428 T.P.), from Brundisium, April 47 B.C.

[4] His repeated efforts to recover this debt will be found in twelve letters to which Drumann-Groebe refers, VI, p. 348, note 2; cf. below, p. 57.

[5] The hypothesis that he did repay is excluded (cf. Drumann-Groebe, VI, p. 347); but it is not impossible that Cicero tried to recover his money after the battle of Pharsalia, when the property of the defeated Pompey had been confiscated by Caesar. If this was so, the loan to Faberius was perhaps not unconnected with Cicero's desire to induce Caesar to repay the money due. At all periods of history financiers have been driven to rob Peter in order to pay Paul.

[6] *Ad Fam.* XVI, 24, 2 (806 T.P.): . . . *appellabis etiam Papiam*, Letter to Tiro, mid-Nov. 44 B.C.

[7] *Ad Att.* X, 15, 1 (401 T.P.): *Adhuc non satisfaciebat* [*Funisulanus*] . . . *nec habetur locuples. Nunc ait se daturum* . . . From Cumae, May 12, 49 B.C.

[8] Cf. below, p. 58. The guarantee of Plancus is invoked in *Ad Att.* XII, 52, 1 (599 T.P.). From Tusculum, May 21, 45 B.C.

his father the financier[1] was surety, and Hermogenes, whose father Aesopus was the great tragic actor of the day.[2]

As Cicero's aim was to employ his capital to advantage, any loan which was sound was good enough for him, and the amounts which he was prepared to lend varied greatly. In the case of Axius, for instance, the loan was a trifling one of 13,000 sesterces.[3] With Hermogenes, on the other hand, it was a question of 600,000[4]; and it is probable that the sums lent to Funisulanus[5] and to Faberius[6] reached somewhere about the same figure. In any case, Cicero was accustomed without turning a hair to bank repayments of this size, like the 580,000 sesterces which he casually mentions in the first letter to Atticus from his governorship of Cilicia.[7]

Anyhow, whether the sums lent were large or small, Cicero exacted a profitable rate of interest, a minimum of at least 6 per cent.,[8] and displayed the same keenness to recover what was due to him whenever he required it. He complains that a capitalist like Axius should make "bad times" an excuse for not paying on the agreed date a trifling debt of his son's.[9]

[1] Cf. below, and p. 59.

[2] Cf. below, pp. 165–6. On this identification see *Ad Att.* XI, 15, 3 (430 T.P.), XII, 25, 1 (561 T.P.) and 31, 2 (569 T.P.), and Horace *Sat.* II, 3, 39. On this person cf. below, II, p. 529. Other borrowers' names occur in the Correspondence: members of Cicero's household, like his scribe and freedman Tullius (*Ad Att.* XIII, 22, 4 (635 T.P.), July 4, 45 B.C.; XV, 26, 4 (763 T.P.), July 2, 44 B.C.; 29, 1 (768 T.P.), July 6, 44 B.C.); middle-class Italians, like Aufidius of Tusculum (*Ad Fam.* XVI, 19 (655 T.P.), beginning of Aug. 45 B.C.), and Minucius of Tarentum (*Ad Att.* XI, 14, 3 (429 T.P.), May 47 B.C., and 15, 2 (430 T.P.), May 14, 47 B.C.); nobles like Cocceius (Nerva?) and L. Scribonius Libo, father-in-law of Sextus Pompeius (*Ad Att.* XII, 13, 2 (545 T.P.), March 7, 45 B.C.; 19, 2 (552 T.P.), March 14, 45 B.C.; and particularly 18, 3 (549 T.P.), March 11, 45 B.C.): *Cocceius vide ne frustretur; nam Libo quod pollicitur, ut Eros* (Atticus's accountant) *scribit, non incertum puto.*

[3] Cf. below, note 9. A loan of 30,000 sesterces to Minucius, *Ad Att.* XI, 14, 3 (429 T.P.), of which only 12,000 was repaid, *Ad Att.* XI, 15, 2 (430 T.P.).

[4] Cf. below, p. 58, note 2.

[5] *Ad Att.* X, 15, 1 (401 T.P.): . . . *debet autem [Funisulanus] mihi multos nummos.*

[6] If we may judge from Cicero's insistence, see especially *Ad Att.* XII, 25, 1 (561 T.P.): . . . *dum a Faberio vel ab aliquo, qui Faberio debet, repraesentabimus.* From Astura, March 21, 45 B.C.; XII, 31, 2 (569 T.P.): *Si enim Faberianum venderem.* From Astura, March 29, 45 B.C.; he has now got to the point of wanting to hasten matters by negotiating the loan: XIII, 27, 2 (603 T.P.), May 25, 45 B.C., *Quidquid erit in Faberio ponamus;* and below, p. 58, note 2.

[7] *Ad Att.* VI, 1, 19 (252 T.P.): *Quod de . . . solutione HS $\overline{XXDC}$ scribis,* 50 B.C.

[8] This is the rate of interest agreed to by his freedman Tullius, *Ad Att.* XV, 29, 1 (768 T.P.): *De Tulliano semisse . . .*

[9] *Ad Att.* X, 11, 2 (396 T.P.): *Si mihi Q. Axius in hac mea fuga HS $\overline{XIII}$ non reddit quae dedi eius filio mutua, et utitur excusatione temporis.* From Cumae, May 4, 49 B.C.

In Nov. 44 he charges his freedman Tiro to give no grace to Flaminius Flamma: "If you cannot extract the whole sum from Flamma, get at least some fraction of it from him and see in particular that interest be paid on the Kalends of January"—*a Flamma si non potes omne, partem aliquam velim extorqueas, in primisque, ut expedita sit pensio K(alendis) Ian(uariis).*[1] The year before he had begged Atticus to bring enough pressure on Hermogenes to make him pay back his 600,000 sesterces—*HS $\overline{DC}$ exprimes ab Hermogene.*[2] The better to infect Atticus with his own impatience to compel Faberius at last to repay his debt, he launches at him three imperatives at once: "In regard to Faberius, drive, urge, make an end!"—*De Faberio urge, insta, perfice!*[3]

The harshness towards his debtors which the *Letters* reveal[4] is to this extent excusable that he rarely displays it unless he is himself confronted by urgent expenditure[5] or hard put to it to appease the pack of creditors who all his life were yapping at his heels.

In 62, just after his famous consulship, this victor over the Catiline conspirators jests about his financial embarrassments in a letter to Sestius; but he jests in the spirit of Figaro, who used to make merry, not to be compelled to weep, over the folly of mankind: "Know now that I am so much in debt that I would be fain to join a conspiracy if anyone would have me; but some, filled with hate, exclude me and obviously fear the suppresser of conspiracy, and some do not trust me and suspect some treachery from me, and they cannot believe that a man can lack money who has just rescued the money-lenders from danger."[6]

[1] *Ad Fam.* XVI, 24, 1 (806 T.P.). To Tiro, mid-Nov. 44 B.C.

[2] *Ad Att.* XII, 25, 1 (561 T.P.). March 21, 45 B.C.

[3] *Ad Att.* XIII, 32, 1 (610 T.P.). From Tusculum May 29, 45 B.C. Perhaps Caesar ultimately released Faberius if, according to the somewhat plausible conjecture of J.-V. Le Clerc, it was really Caesar himself who, under the pseudonym of Meton, reorganiser of the Greek calendar, is alluded to in the letter of May 20, 45 B.C., in which Cicero suggests to Atticus to wait before paying Caerellia until he is clear about the attitude of Meton and Faberius: . . . *dum de Metone et de Faberio sciamus: Ad Att.* XII, 51, 3 (598 T.P.).

[4] See also, for instance, the letter of July 4, 45 B.C., in which Cicero congratulates Atticus on the writs he has served on the recalcitrant debtors: *Attributos quod appellas, valde probo. Ad Att.* XIII, 22, 4 (635 T.P.).

[5] To pay for Astura, for instance: *Ad Att.* XII, 13, 2 (545 T.P.): *Cocceium velim appelles. Quod enim dixerat non facit. Ego autem volo aliquod emere latibulum et perfugium doloris mei.* From Astura, March 7, 45 B.C.

[6] *Ad Fam.* V, 6, 2 (16 T.P.): *Nunc me scito tantum habere aeris alieni ut cupiam coniurare, si quisquam recipiat, sed partim odio inducti me excludunt et aperte vindicem coniurationis oderunt, partim non credunt et a me insidias metuunt nec putant ei nummos deesse posse qui ex obsidione feneratores exemerit.*

Cicero's Fortune and Way of Life

Cicero began to wonder in 61 to what bankers he could fly for assistance: Considius? Axius? Selicius?—*opinor, ad Considium, Axium, Selicium confugiendum est.*[1] He was still short of funds when the sentence of exile overtook him in 58. If he did not suffer unduly in Macedonia, where he took refuge, that was because kind-hearted people of means, C. Ateius Capito,[2] Atticus,[3] Plancius[4] advanced him money, and Atticus in addition subscribed towards the maintenance of his household.[5] On his return he at once resumed his improvident ways, and though he had drawn large indemnities by way of reparation, his affairs were in such disorder[6] that he was forced to apply once more to the bankers, and was much gratified by the generous credits granted him by Vestorius[7] in 56. It was not till seven years later that he reimbursed Vestorius, in May 49.[8]

A few months later, during the Civil War, when after innumerable hesitations he decided to rejoin Pompey's camp, he was completely "cleaned out" and uttered anguished and pathetic appeals for help.[9] He succeeded in reaching Epirus thanks only to a viaticum of 70,000 sesterces with which the affection of Atticus had supplied him, a gift which also served to supply an outfit of new clothes to replenish his wardrobe.[10] When he had deserted the defeated side after Pharsalia, we note that, however his political line might vary, the state of his finances remained the same. No sooner had he disembarked at Brundisium than we hear him—March 8, 47—worrying about how he was to repay Cn. Sallustius, brother of

---

[1] *Ad Att.* I, 12, 1 (17 T.P.).

[2] *Ad Fam.* XIII, 29, 2 (457 T.P.), written at the beginning of 46 B.C.: *C. Ateio Capitone utor familiarissime . . . In omne genere honorum et laborum meorum etiam res familiaris Capitonis praesto fuit et paruit et temporibus et fortunae meae.*

[3] *Ad Att.* III, 20, 2 (78 T.P.): *. . . facultates tuas ad meam salutem polliceris*; cf. ibid. 11, 2 (68 T.P.).

[4] *Ad Att.* III, 22, 1 (81 T.P.): *Me adhuc Plancius liberalitate sua retinet . . .*

[5] *Ad Att.* III, 5 (60 T.P.) and 9, 3 (65 T.P.): *Terentia tibi saepe agit gratias.* He admits that, thanks to all this co-operation: *nihil amplius opus est. Ad Q. Fr.* I, 3, 7 (66 T.P.).

[6] *Ad Att.* IV, 1, 8 (90 T.P.): *. . . in re familiari valde sumus . . . perturbati.* Sept. 57 B.C.

[7] *Ad Att.* IV, 6, 4 (110 T.P.): *[Vestorius] valde . . . est in me liberalis.*

[8] *Ad Att.* X, 13, 2 (399 T.P.): *Vestorio reddidi,* May 7, 49 B.C.

[9] *Ad Att.* XI, 1, 2 (406 T.P.): *Te etiam atque etiam oro ut me totum tuendum suscipias*; ibid. 2, 2 (407 T.P.): *Per omnes deos te obtestor ut totam rem suscipias.* These two letters are dated from Epirus, Jan. and Feb. 48 B.C. respectively.

[10] *Ad Att.* XI, 2, 4 (407 T.P.): *A tuis et nummorum accepi HS LXX et vestimentorum quod opus fuit.* From Epirus, Feb. 5, 48 B.C. Cf. ibid. 13, 4 (428 T.P.): *. . . itaque tum et a tuo vilico sumpsimus et aliunde mutuati sumus,* April, 47 B.C.

P. Sallustius, the 30,000 sesterces he had borrowed from him, and which were already three-quarters spent.[1]

In 45 he was reduced to begging from women. From Ovia, the widow of C. Lollius, he received 100,000 sesterces[2] at one stroke, and he also drew on his old friend Caerellia.[3] The truth is that Cicero held his dignity cheap when either his desires or his creditors had him by the throat. What is alarming in his *Letters* is not so much the urgent, breathless repetition of his demands, as the conscienceless irresponsibility with which he accepted from every quarter the money he wanted, and ignored every promise which it would be inconvenient to fulfil. This inertia was perhaps never more woefully displayed than in his borrowings from Caerellia and Julius Caesar.

If we are to believe the scandal, a belated echo of which reaches us in the apocryphal[4] if not bogus speech attributed to Fufius Calenus, Caerellia was a former mistress of Cicero's, whom he in his sixties continued to court when she herself was over seventy.[5] His letters, however, seem to belie these slanderous rumours.[6] In the first place in his *Letters* he speaks highly—with no trace of embarrassment—of Caerellia to P. Servilius Isauricus, the ex-Consul and friend of Caesar, who became Proconsul in Asia in 46. Cicero had spoken about her to him before Servilius left Rome to take over his governorship, and he returned to the charge in a letter which he expressly sent after Servilius to his province. He reminds Servilius that he had already warmly recommended the lady to him, and he ends by assuring the new ruler of Asia that any services he renders to Caerellia will be most gratifying to Cicero.[7]

He offers only one reason for his interest: Caerellia is a friend of

---

[1] *Ad Att.* XI, 11, 2 (426 T.P.): *P. Sallustio curanda sunt HS $\overline{XXX}$ quae accepi a Cn. Sallustio . . . Ipsum iam prope consumptum est.* From Brundisium, March 8, 47 B.C.

[2] *Ad Att.* XII, 21, 4 (557 T.P.): *Oviae C. Lolli curanda sunt HS $\overline{C}$.* From Astura, March 17, 45 B.C. The repayment of this was long delayed. Ibid. XII, 24, 1 (560 T.P.); 30, 2 (567 T.P.). It was still outstanding in July 45 B.C. Ibid. XIII, 22, 4 (635 T.P.).

[3] See below, pp. 60–2.

[4] Cf. above, p. 41.

[5] Fufius Calenus in Cass. Dio XLVI, 18, 4.

[6] Judging by what remains of them and by the suppression of the letters to Caerellia in the canonical edition of the Correspondence, as I shall later show. (See below, II, p. 544, note 3.)

[7] *Ad Fam.* XIII, 72, 1 (511 T.P.): *Commendavi tibi praesens . . .* (2): *sic velim existimes quibuscumque rebus Caerelliae benigne feceris mihi te gratissimum esse facturum.*

his: *necessaria mea*.[1] Obviously there was no need for him to make excuses for this friendship, since no one in Servilius's entourage would dream of suspecting in it any taint of gallantry. Nor is there any shadow of evidence for such a thing. For when serious rifts showed themselves almost immediately after the wedding and threatened to destroy the happiness of Cicero's second marriage, it was to Caerellia that the young wife Publilia and her family turned as mediatrix to try to smooth away the difficulties. And Caerellia intervened without embarrassment and without insistence—and equally without success—to dissuade Cicero from seeking a divorce for the second time.[2] The bond between Caerellia and Cicero, though behind their backs scandal-mongers may have made merry over it, was not love, but love of philosophy.[3] Cicero rejoiced to find in her an admirer whose ability gave him as much pleasure as her enthusiasm. Caerellia was so much enthralled by the master's teaching that she ventured in person to raid the "bookshop" of Atticus, and with the connivance of some of the copyists, whom she had bribed, she secured a copy of *De Finibus Bonorum et Malorum* before Cicero had authorised its publication.[4]

Their relations were based on a common foundation of literary vanity and worldly snobbery, and nothing more. The text of the *Letters* of Cicero which have been preserved to us completely excludes every element of passion. But at the same time it vexatiously introduces an element of materialism. It represents Caerellia as endowed with more than a love of science and philosophy, and it was in an effort to maintain intact her landed properties, which extended into Asia, that Cicero had spoken and written to Servilius.[5] So, though he did not extract financial advantage from a romantic affection, we cannot deny that he succeeded in turning into cash the enthusiasm kindled by his culture and talents in the

---

[1] *Ad Fam.* XIII, 72, 1 (511 T.P.): *Caerelliae necessariae meae rem . . . commendavi tibi.*
[2] *Ad Att.* XIV, 19, 4 (725 T.P.): *Huc enim Caerellia missa ab istis [Publilia et Publilio] est legata ad me;* XV, 1A, 4 (730 T.P.): *Caerelliae vero facile satisfeci, nec valde laborare mihi visa est, et, si illa, ego certe non laborarem.* May 17, 44 B.C.
[3] On Caerellia see Tyrrell and Purser, IV, p. lxxi.
[4] *Ad Att.* XIII, 21, 5 (632 T.P.): *Mirifice Caerellia studio videlicet philosophiae flagrans describit a tuis: istos ipsos de Finibus habet.* June 30 or July 1, 45 B.C.; 22, 3 (635 T.P.): *Ego et librarios tuos culpa libero neque te accuso, et tamen aliud quiddam ad te scripseram, Caerelliam quaedam habere (quae nisi a te habere) non potuerit.* July 4, 45 B.C.
[5] *Ad Fam.* XIII, 72, 1 (511 T.P.): *Caerelliae . . . rem nomina possessiones Asiaticas commendavi tibi praesens . . . Caerelliae procuratores scripserunt.*

breast of this inordinately wealthy blue-stocking. As soon as he learned of it, Atticus condemned this somewhat scandalous blend of philosophic and financial speculations. To forestall the jests which would be rained on a philosopher so practical-minded as to exploit the radiance of his ideas amongst his women friends, he summoned Tiro to him. He did not mince his words. He told the secretary bluntly that if his master attached any value to preserving his dignity, he must repay immediately this indecent loan: *debere non esse dignitatis* . . .[1] Cicero was incapable of understanding or feeling the position. When he received this reproof he was content to go on temporising and to postpone the redemption of his debt to Caerellia until he himself had collected repayments due at some rather doubtful and distant future dates.[2]

To go back ten years, the story of the debt he contracted towards Julius Caesar is equally unedifying. No sooner had the vote of the people, engineered by Vatinius, invested Caesar with the government of both Cisalpine and Transalpine Gaul than the future dictator began to see the possibility of realising his dreams, thanks to the two sources of actual and potential power he had just secured. Today he had the soldiers, tomorrow he would have the wealth accruing from the booty their swords would bring him. Foreseeing the vast riches that this would put at his disposal, he formed a plan of wholesale corruption that would smooth his path towards the fulfilment of his ambition. With the product of his victories he would rain down on the plebs such largesse as would bring him irresistible popularity. At the same time, judiciously calculated assistance to certain individuals of the governing aristocracy would undermine the united resistance which they ought to offer him.

He was well informed about the actual position of the men who conducted the government, the state of their fortunes and the degree of their venality. Dangerously clear-sighted as he was, he showed himself impartially generous to his supporters, whose zeal he would fan into fresh flame, and to his opponents, whose hostility he would disarm. He would thus ultimately stifle under his favours the Patricians, whom his policy ought to have terrified, but who would be too vulnerable to his insidious advances long to retain their liberty of action. Cicero, who well gauged the span of Caesar's

[1] *Ad Att.* XII, 51, 3 (598 T.P.): *De Caerellia, quid tibi placeret Tiro mihi narravit: debere non esse dignitatis meae* . . . May 20, 45 B.C.
[2] *Ad Att.* XII, 51, 3 (598 T.P.): *Sustinenda tamen, si tibi videbitur, solutio est nominis Caerelliani, dum et de Metone et de Faberio sciamus.*

wings, ought to have been the last to fall a prey to the seducer.[1] On the contrary, he was one of the first to snap at the bait. In 54, when his brother Quintus was chosen as one of the Legati of the Proconsul of the Two Gauls and thus shared personally in the spoils of conquest, Cicero indirectly took advantage of the opportunity to dip unblushingly into the conqueror's purse. In one of his letters to Lentulus he announces the honour which Caesar has done to Quintus[2] in choosing him as a Legate, and in the same passage he speaks of the advantages he will enjoy through his brother's influence with the Proconsul: "I have the benefit as if they were my own, of all his power, which is very great, and of his riches, which, as you know, are immense."[3]

Cicero's letters of 51 lift a corner of the veil: amongst other advantages he received a loan of 800,000 sesterces at the rate of $2\frac{1}{4}$ per cent., less than half the normal rate of interest.[4] Just before setting out to take up his proconsulship in Cilicia,[5] he felt for the first time in the mood to repay Caesar the capital sum of 800,000 sesterces, along with 20,000 sesterces interest which was outstanding.[6] But he went no further. On returning to Italy at the close of 50 Cicero was no better off; he was still looking round for money-lenders to free him from embarrassments. In 51 he had begged Atticus to sound Oppius on the subject, but Oppius declined.[7] In Dec. 50, when the first low rumblings of imminent civil war began to be heard and he was still in doubt as to the line to take in the coming conflict, he seemed to endorse the prudent advice of Atticus and be prepared to preserve his political independence by making—as his friend suggested—full restitution and

[1] On the intentions of the future Dictator, see my *César* (3), p. 735f.
[2] *Ad Fam.* I, 9, 21 (153 T.P.): *Quintus frater meus est legatus Caesaris.*
[3] *Ad Fam.* I, 9, 21 (153 T.P.): *Itaque eius [Caesaris] omni et gratia, quae summa est, et opibus, quas intellegis esse maximas, sic fruor ut meis.*
[4] Cicero himself made loans at 6 per cent. to his own freedman, Tullius the Scribe. Cf. above, p. 57, note 2.
[5] Drumann-Groebe, VI, p. 157, has been able from the Correspondence to date Cicero's leaving for Cilicia as May 22, 51 B.C., and his return to Brundisium and then to Rome as Nov. 24, 50 B.C., and Jan. 4, 49 B.C.
[6] *Ad Att.* V, 5, 2 (188 T.P.): . . . *antequam proficiscare, utique explicatum sit illud de HS $\overline{XX}$ et $\overline{DCCC}$* . . .; 9, 2 (195 T.P.): *Quales res nostras Romae reliqueris, maxime de $\overline{XX}$ et $\overline{DCCC}$, cura ut sciamus.*
[7] *Ad Att.* V, 1, 2 and 4, 3 (184 T.P. and 187 T.P.): *De Oppio bene curasti quod ei de $\overline{DCCC}$ exposuisti.* In the following letter he had veered somewhat in the direction of Atticus, who, being his adviser, ought in Cicero's opinion to do the paying; ibid. 5, 2 (188 T.P.): *Hoc velim . . . ut quod auctore te velle coepi adiutore adsequar*; cf. ibid. 10, 4 (198 T.P.).

thus emancipating himself.[1] But the plan came to nothing, or, if you prefer, Cicero was only humbugging, for even in these critical moments he would neither attempt to reduce his expenditure, nor to sell off any of his property. His only idea was to pay Caesar with his right hand sums which with his left he tried to raise from Caelius, that is to say from one of Caesar's agents.[2] Not for a moment did he hesitate, or blush at stooping to expedients which sorely strained the affection of Atticus, who found them nauseating.

On the eve of a struggle in which the Romans were destined to tear each other to pieces, these expedients condemned him either to embrace a cause he detested, out of gratitude to the man in whom that cause was incarnate, or to betray that cause by opposing it in disregard of obligations incurred towards its leader. His vanity strove in vain to put his correspondents on a false scent, by audaciously inverting the roles and pretending it was Caesar whom he had attached to his own fortunes by accepting his generosity.[3] The truth which emerges from the Correspondence is that in this matter Cicero, who wanted to avoid limitations on his expenditure—which he dreaded more than anything—and who feared having to forgo the empty pomp of the triumph he was then claiming, which would involve him in enormous financial sacrifices, turned a deaf ear to the voice of honour.[4]

We need feel no surprise: other letters prove that when the choice confronted him he preferred to infringe the most elementary rules of honest dealing rather than deny himself or curtail his expenses.

Two examples suffice to expose his shame. The first falls in the period when his brother Quintus was governing Asia—with no little reluctance, as we know. It will be remembered that when Quintus was appointed Propraetor at the beginning of 61 he was anxious to return to Italy the moment his term of office expired in 60. Cicero, however, frustrated his brother's wishes by using his

[1] See the text above quoted (dating from 51 B.C.) and compare this text of 50 B.C.: *Solvamus, inquis.* Cic. *Ad Att.* VII, 3, 11 (294 T.P.). On the close connection between this loan and the work on the *Forum Iulium*, cf. the contrary view of André Lichtenberger, op. cit., p. 79, and below, p. 115f.

[2] *Ad Att.* VII, 3, 11 (294 T.P.): *Age, a Caelio mutuabimus.* See Boissier's vivid chapter on M. Caelius Rufus, *Cicéron et ses amis*, pp. 166–219.

[3] *Ad Fam.* I, 9, 21 (153 T.P.): *Ut ego eum [Caesarem] mihi devinctum putarem.*

[4] *Ad Att.* VII, 8, 5 (299 T.P.): *Mihi autem illud molestissimum est, quod solvendi sunt nummi et instrumentum triumphi eo conferendum.* End of Dec. 50 B.C.

influence with the Senate to get his tour of duty extended by the prorogation which Quintus feared and which postponed his return till 59.[1] As we have already seen, the didactic letter which opens Book I of the collection *Ad Quintum Fratrem* had one aim only: to draw a superb portrait of the ideal governor, on which Quintus would certainly model himself, thus justifying a measure that was in itself exceptional and even more disappointing to his probable successors, whose promotion was thus delayed, than to Quintus himself. At the very beginning of this profession of faith Cicero admits that he is to blame for his brother's being retained, against his will, in the propraetorship of Asia,[2] and he boldly assumes the responsibility for a measure prompted only by cogent considerations of public interest: solicitude for the allies of the Roman people, desire to check the encroachments of certain traders, and the legitimate ambition to see the glory of their name enhanced by the services his brother would render the country.[3] His language has in sooth a touch of pride and dignity.

How regrettable it is that a more confidential and less studiously elaborated letter should strike a discordant note in this concert of lofty reasoning, and rouse in the reader's mind the ugly suspicion that someone had something to gain by the prorogation of Quintus! As Propraetor Quintus had in fact the right to draw from the public Treasury the sums allocated by decree of the Senate for the expenses of running the province, the expenditure essential to the dignity and prestige of his post.[4] To simplify the transfer of remittances, Quintus had given authority to his brother to draw the money for him and use it as he thought best. It is not without shame for a great man that we read the staggering confession, written in his own hand under the shock of his own exile, and learn that while Cicero had duly drawn and banked the allowances due to his brother, he had wittingly omitted to keep them in trust for him or remit them to him: "It is just in that matter I am so painfully conscious what a crime I have committed in uselessly

---

[1] On Quintus Cicero's government of Asia, cf. Drumann-Groebe, VI, p. 639f., and above, pp. 11–12.

[2] Cic. *Ad Q. Fr.* I, 1, 2 (30 T.P.): *Facta est enim mea culpa, contra quam tu mecum et proficiscens et per litteras egeras, ut priore anno non succederetur.*

[3] Cic. *Ad Q. Fr.* I, 1, 2 (30 T.P.): *Quod ego dum saluti sociorum consulo, dum inpudentiae non nullorum negotiatorum resisto, dum nostram gloriam tua virtute augeri expecto* (letter of 60 B.C.).

[4] Mommsen: *Römisches Staatsrecht und Römisches Strafrecht.* Fr. trans., *Droit publique*, I, p. 336f.

squandering the sums I accepted from the Treasury in your name"—*Qua in re ipsa video miser et sentio quid sceleris admiserim, cum . . . ego acceptam ex aerario pecuniam tuo nomine frustra dissiparim.*[1]

Quintus probably forgave his exiled brother in consideration of his distress,[2] but Cicero's misfortune of 58 cannot excuse acts committed at least a year earlier. The fact remains that in a perfectly normal time he let his need for money drive him into committing, at his brother's expense, what we should now call malversation of funds or breach of trust.

Ten years later he would have acted even worse towards his friend Atticus, if Atticus had not mastered better than anyone else has ever done the art of being no man's dupe. This is the story. In Jan. 48 Cicero landed in Epirus to rally Pompey's legions at the last moment. He was there overtaken by bad news about the shocking state of his affairs, which news Atticus had been obliged to send him by the hand of Anteros. Cicero replied at once. He is deeply pained to learn of the deficit which is shown by the accounts, but he flatters himself with the hope that some helpful steps will be taken by Atticus to put matters straight. "I count on your friendship. I beg and implore you to come to my aid." How could Atticus resist his prayer? There is no risk involved in granting it, for Cicero has 2,200,000 sesterces in *cistophori*, the beautiful coinage of Asia, with the Ephesus bankers, and to clear off all Cicero's debts at once Atticus can draw bills of exchange on this bank deposit.[3]

Now if Atticus had rashly yielded to Cicero's urgency he would have been the victim of his own good nature. For two or three weeks later, in a letter dated Feb. 5 which would have reached Rome not more than a fortnight later, Cicero is obliged to confess that this deposit no longer exists. In the interval between his two letters it had been divided into two halves; one of these had been placed at Pompey's disposal by the firm of tax-gatherers who were his bankers, and he had himself withdrawn the balance to put it in

---

[1] *Ad Q. Fr.* I, 3, 7 (66 T.P.). From Thessalonica in 58 B.C.

[2] Cicero later indemnified Quintus by sending him to act as his deputy in the Sardinian *Legatio*, which Pompey conferred on him in 56 B.C.; cf. Drumann-Groebe, VI, p. 648, and the references there given in notes 9, 10 and 11 (all taken from the Correspondence).

[3] *Ad Att.* XI, 1, 1 (406 T.P.): *Idque ut facias te obtestor atque obsecro . . . (2) Ego in cistophoro in Asia habeo ad HS bis et viciens. Huius pecuniae permutatione fidem vestrum facile tuebere . . .* Jan. 48 B.C.

a safe place which he did not specify more clearly.[1] There is no fear that Atticus had not, with his customary prudence, postponed the payments he had been so urgently requested to make. Whether he had made them or no, Cicero's manoeuvre is no less fraudulent, and it would nowadays incur the penalties which our Penal Codes prescribe for the uttering of worthless cheques.

3. THE PRODIGAL

Considering the imposing total of his bank accounts, the extensive money transactions in which he was habitually engaged, the immense wealth represented by his landed properties, the inventory and the value of which we have deduced from a study of his Correspondence, we are driven to ask how it came about that Cicero fell not only into that state of chronic impecuniosity but also into those indelicate irregularities to which his *Letters* bear witness.

In moments of sincerity and distress he asked himself this question. Faced by the yawning gulf of his debts he uttered in 48 a cry of grief and alarm. As he confessed to Atticus, he felt his position the more bitter because his conscience was not at rest. On two occasions he beat his breast and admitted that he had been at fault, and once at least he blamed himself also for carelessness.[2] The negligence was sufficiently obvious. Amid the distractions of his public life, under the weight of the professional cases which he undertook to plead and the insatiable desire to pursue his studies, it is easy to understand that he could not find the time to devote to his private affairs the attention that they would have required. We are almost tempted to forgive this great intellectual genius for preferring philosophic reflection and literary creation to the meticulous overhauling of his accounts. But Cicero was wealthy enough to delegate to his staff so necessary and exacting a job. He had retainers in plenty, and amongst them was his slave Tiro, whom he had manumitted in 53,[3] a man sufficiently devoted, intelligent and

---

[1] *Ad Att.* XI, 2, 3 (407 T.P.): *Ex ea pecunia quae FUIT in Asia, partem dimidiam fere exegi. Tutius videbatur fore ubi est quam apud publicanos.* Feb. 5, 48 B.C. With reference to the money released to Pompey, cf. above, p. 56, and Cic. *Ad Att.* XI, 13, 4 (428 T.P.): . . . *facultates* . . . *Pompeio detulimus.* April 47 B.C.

[2] *Ad Att.* XI, 11, 2 (426 T.P.): *Quarum rerum eo gravior est dolor quo culpa maior;* and 2, 2 (407 T.P.): . . . *per omnes deos te obtestor, ut totam rem suscipias et illam miseram mea culpa et neglegentia tueare* . . . The first letter quoted is the second in date, March 8, 47 B.C., the second quoted is Feb. 5, 48 B.C.

[3] Cf. Drumann-Groebe, VI, p. 357: according to the letter of April 28, 53 B.C.

honest to have been entrusted with the work.[1] Cicero had in fact accorded him wide powers of administration and left him the greatest freedom of initiative in these matters. It was Tiro's business to recover overdue debts,[2] to keep an eye on the balance between assets and liabilities,[3] and in embarrassing circumstances to devise solutions and carry them into effect. As Cicero told him in 44, Tiro was in all matters of arithmetic what the Greeks used proverbially to call "the stem and the stern" of his master, or what the Hebrew would describe as "the law and the prophets": the confidential man of business who was relied on to reduce chaos to order: *ut rationes nostras explicaret.*[4] In other words, it was up to Tiro to find a way out.

We have not Tiro's reply. Perhaps we may risk a guess. There are limits to the application of System D.[5] Hampered by his master's instructions, he may have been unable to work the desired miracle. When he got orders to spend the last penny or was confronted with a new bill, no ingenuity could rescue him from the dilemma: either he must protest it and plead for respite or he must meet the situation by negotiating another loan. In a small way, Tiro's position with Cicero was as delicate in face of the impossible demands of his master as Colbert's with Louis XIV. In all times the most brilliant qualities of a faithful steward are used up if employed in the service of a spendthrift, and if the prodigal has his way, the end sooner or later is bankruptcy.

Extravagance was Cicero's greatest crime. When he blames himself for negligence, he is confessing to a secondary, venial fault. He forgets the chief, the radical one, which he would never admit, and of which he would never cure himself: the crime of always spending and never counting the cost.

From this point of view, his life, as reflected in his *Letters*, was one long contradiction of the teaching and preaching of his works.

[1] *Ad Fam.* XVI, 1, 3 (285 T.P.): . . . *de tuis innumerabilibus in me officiis*; 4, 3 (288 T.P.): . . . *innumerabilia tua sunt in me officia, domestica, forensia, in re privata, in publica*; 15, 1 (925 T.P.): *ingenium tuum, quod ego maximi facio.*

[2] *Ad Fam.* XVI, 24, 2 (806 T.P.): . . . *appellabis etiam Papiam.* Nov. 44 B.C.

[3] *Ad Fam.* XVI, 24, 1 (806 T.P.): *A Flamma, si non potes omne, partem aliquam velim extorqueas, in primisque, ut expedita sit pensio K(alendas) Ian(uarias).*

[4] *Ad Fam.* XVI, 24, 1 (806 T.P.): *Mihi prora et puppis, ut Graecorum proverbium est, fuit a me tui dimittendi, ut rationes nostras explicares.* On the liberty of initiative left to Tiro, cf. *Ad Fam.* XVI, 19 (655 T.P.): *De Aufidiano nomine nihil te hortor, scio tibi curae esse.* Aug. 45 B.C.

[5] ["System D," as the author kindly informs me, was a slang term, born of the 1914 war, covering every sort of irregular expedient adopted to meet inconvenient or unpleasant situations.—E. O. L.]

His philosophical treatises are starred with maxims in strict conformity with the traditional ethics of the Roman people, and would not have disgraced the great Stoic, Cato. "O immortal gods, men do not understand how large an income thrift brings in."[1] And again: "One should take good care of one's property, for it is disgraceful to allow it to melt away."[2] But let us read through his *Letters*: this disgrace is there amply displayed, along with the unbridled lust for luxury which explains it.

There was no refinement of luxury, however costly, which he would deny himself if it could add to the beauty or the enjoyment of his life. Unfortunately for his purse, his tastes as a man of letters and an artist led him always to covet the most expensive things.

First of all, he loved books and filled his houses with them. At Tusculum his library, well stocked with the philosophers, took up a whole wing of the main dwelling-house[3]; at Antium the library was so amply filled[4] that he needed a specialist librarian to classify the books;[5] at Pompeii and Cumae he had assembled in 54 all the authorities he needed to document the treatise, *De Republica*,[6] which he was writing. Swollen by all the Greek manuscripts which Atticus got copied for him in Athens,[7] his collection of volumes grew so large that a catalogue became indispensable, and in 45 he bade Tiro draw one up.[8] In a day when each book was more or less a bibliophile's treasure, many of these manuscripts cost him fabulous sums of money. Some of them reached so high a price that once—it is true that this was before his consulship—Cicero had to beg Atticus to stop sending any more manuscripts for fear he would

---

[1] Cic. *Par.*, VI, 3, 49: *O di immortales, non intellegunt homines quam magnum vectigal sit parsimonia.*
[2] Cic. *De Off.* II, 18, 64: *Habenda ratio est rei familiaris, quam quidem dilabi sinere flagitiosum est.*
[3] *Ad Att.* II, 2, 2 (28 T.P.): Πελληνάιων *in manibus tenebam et hercule magnum acervum Dicaearchi mihi ante pedes exstruxeram,* cf. *De Div.* II, 38: . . . *in bibliotheca, quae in Lycio est, adsedimus.* 60 B.C.
[4] *Ad Att.* II, 6, 1 (33 T.P.): . . . *libris me delecto, quorum habeo Antio festivam copiam.* 59 B.C.
[5] The Greek grammarian Tyrannio; cf. Cic. *Ad Att.* IV, 4B, 1 (107 T.P.); 8A, 2 (112 T.P.); *Postea vero quam Tyrannio mihi libros disposuit, mens addita videtur meis aedibus.* 56 B.C.
[6] *Ad Q. Fr.* II, 12, 1 (139 T.P.): *Ego me in Cumano et Pompeiano* . . . *oblectabam; scribebam illa quae* πολιτικά, *dixeram spissum sane opus et operosum.* 54 B.C.
[7] As early as 68 B.C. Cicero was writing to Atticus (*Ad Att.* I, 7, 1 (3 T.P.)): . . . *velim cogites, id quod mihi pollicitus es, quemamodum bibliothecam nobis conficere possis.*
[8] *Ad Fam.* XVI, 20 (693 T.P.): . . . *libros compone indicem, cum Metrodoro lubebit.* End of 45 B.C.

not be able to foot the bill.[1] There is no doubt that this passion for books often destroyed the balance of his budget. Still, it would be unfair not to forgive Cicero a passion inspired by the noblest and most profound sense of vocation, thanks to which he plundered the fairest flowers of Greek thought to make that Latin honey in whose clear and quiet sweetness the humanism of the West has for centuries been steeped.[2]

His passion for works of art, gardens and building was equally intense and even more costly. In indulging it without restraint he was taking a more fashionable line; and it is probable that social snobbery played as large a part in this compelling infatuation as any love of beauty for its own sake. Heaven knows that, in extolling the conduct of wise men, he railed violently enough against the folly of those who took undue delight in statues, pictures, chased silver-ware and Corinthian bronzes.[3] His philosophy was for others' consumption. For himself he light-heartedly gave way to the weaknesses he condemned. His *Letters* are full of undisciplined cravings for all the lovely things with which he was never tired of adorning his houses. The earliest letters he wrote to Atticus in Athens were full of recommendations on this subject and of orders of this kind.

Towards the end of Nov. 68 he announced to his friend in one brief line the death of his cousin, which had occurred on the 23rd of the month,[4] and he adds immediately: "That is what I had to tell you. Now, if you can find some specimens of art worthy of the place you wot of (that is the Tusculanum) do not fail to secure them."[5] When he received Atticus's reply some weeks later, he reverts to his cousin's death and the grief it caused him and also to his previous request: "Take pains, as you say, about the things I ordered which you think will be suitable for my 'Tusculanum,' at least if you can do so without too much trouble."[6] A month had

---

[1] *Ad Att.* I, 4, 3 (9 T.P.): *Libros tuos conserva et noli desperare eos me meos facere posse.* 66 B.C. On Atticus as a supplier of books, cf. below, II, p. 467f.

[2] Cf. my *César* (3), p. 1018.

[3] Cic. *Par.* V, 2, 36: . . . *in pari stultitia sunt quos signa, quos tabulae, quos caelatum argentum, quos Corinthia opera . . . nimio opere delectant.*

[4] *Ad Att.* I, 6, 2 (2 T.P.): . . . *Frater nobis decessit ad IIII Kal. Decembres.* This letter is the second in Tyrrell and Purser's edition and the MSS. write *pater.* But I have adopted the emendation and interpretation of L. A. Constans. He considers this the earliest letter of all and puts it first in his edition.

[5] *Ad Att.* I, 6, 2 (2 T.P.): *Haec habebam fere quae te scire vellem. Tu velim, si qua ornamenta γυμνασιώδη reperire poteris, quae loci sint eius quem tu non ignoras, ne praetermittas. Nos Tusculano ita delectamur . . .*

[6] *Ad Att.* I, 5, 7 (1 T.P.): *Quae tibi mandavi et quae tu intelleges convenire nostro Tusculano velim, ut scribis, cures, quod sine molestia facere poteris.*

gone by and Atticus had reported the success of his mission. Without delay Cicero informed him that on Feb. 11, 67 he would hand over to his friend's business agent the sum of 20,400 sesterces, the cost of the reported purchases, and he begged that they should be despatched immediately.[1] No sooner had he made this payment than he presumed on it to urge Atticus to hasten the despatch of the articles he had been kind enough to describe and to procure more for him: "I have arranged for the payment to L. Cincius (the man of business before referred to) of 20,400 sesterces for the Megarian marble statues of which you wrote me. Your statues of Hermes of Pentelic marble with the bronze heads about which you told me, give me immense pleasure in anticipation. I should like you to send them and the statues, and the other things which may seem to suit the place and my wishes and your own good taste; send in particular as quickly as possible as many things as seem suitable for a gymnasium and a *xystus*."[2]

Some weeks passed. Nothing had yet arrived in Italy. Cicero could no longer control his impatience: "I am eagerly awaiting the statues of Megarian marble and the figures of Hermes you told me about. Do not hesitate to send me anything of this sort you may have that seems to you worthy of my Academy and have faith in my bank balance."[3] Having paid one bill, Cicero immediately ordered more items, and did not hesitate to repeat: "I should like you to ship as soon as you conveniently can my Megarian statues and the figures of Hermeracles. . . . Further I commission you to get me some bas-reliefs which I can insert in the stucco wall of my anteroom, and two embossed well-covers."[4] When he still saw nothing coming he took up his pen again a few days later and harped once more on the old string: "I should like you to send, at

---

[1] *Ad Att.* I, 7, 1 (3 T.P.): *L. Cincio HS $\overline{XX}CD$ constitui me curaturum Idibus Febr(uariis). Tu velim ea quae nobis emisse te et parasse scribis, des operam ut quam primum habeamus.*

[2] *Ad Att.* I, 8, 2 (4 T.P.): *L. Cincio HS CCIↃↃ CCIↃↃ CCCC pro signis Megaricis, ut tu ad me scripseras, curavi. Hermae tui Pentelici cum capitibus aeneis, de quibus ad me scripsisti, iam nunc me admodum delectant. Qua re velim et eos et signa et cetera quae tibi eius loci et nostri studii et tuae elegantiae esse videbuntur quam plurima quam primumque mittas et maxime, quae tibi gymnasii xystique videbuntur esse.* Feb. 67 B.C.

[3] *Ad Att.* I, 9, 2 (4 T.P.): *Signa Megarica et hermas de quibus ad me scripsisti vehementer exspecto. Quidquid eiusdem generis habebis, dignum Academia quod videbitur, ne dubitaris mittere et arcae nostrae confidito.*

[4] *Ad Att.* I, 10, 3 (6 T.P.): *. . . signa nostra et Hermeraclas . . . cum commodissime poteris, velim imponas . . . Praeterea typos tibi mando, quos in tectorio atrioli possim includere, et putealia sigillata duo.* L. A. Constans dates this letter between April and July 67 B.C.

the earliest possible moment, the things you have bought for my (Tusculan) Academy."[1] At last the cargo with the arrival of which he had been obsessed reached the Italian coast. His joy and his gratitude to Atticus overflowed: "The statues you have secured for me have been unloaded at Caieta. I have not seen them, for I have not been able to leave Rome. I have sent someone to pay the freight. I love you dearly."[2] Cicero's delight stirred Atticus up and increased his promptitude; he announced the despatch of another consignment. This redoubled Cicero's pleasure and quickened his greed: "What you write me about Hermathena is welcome news. It is an ornament appropriate to my Academy, because Hermes is the usual decoration of all Academies, and Minerva is peculiarly suited to this *gymnasium* of mine. So I should like you, as you suggest, to adorn the place with other ornaments too, the more the better."[3] After he had received and seen and touched this Hermathena he wrote exultantly: "Your Hermathena is my delight. It is so happily placed that the whole gymnasium seems like an offering to the goddess. I love you greatly. . . ."[4]

Thus, from 68 to 65 there is scarcely a letter of Cicero's which is not a-quiver with his cravings as an amateur of art. During this period he was elected Praetor—in 67. He entered on the office in 66. With the prestige it brought him, he contributed by his speech *Pro Lege Manilia* to invest Pompey with an extraordinary command which was destined ultimately to undermine the senatorial Republic and pave the way to individual dictatorship. During this

[1] *Ad Att.* I, 11, 3 (7 T.P.): . . . *Tu velim, quae Academiae nostrae parasti, quam primum mittas.* July–Aug. 67 B.C.

[2] *Ad Att.* I, 3, 2 (8 T.P.): *Signa quae nobis curasti ea sunt ad Caietam exposita. Nos ea non vidimus : neque enim exeundi Roma potestas nobis fuit. Misimus qui pro vectura solveret. Te multum amamus* . . . First half of 67 B.C.; cf. 4, 3 (9 T.P.): . . . *signa . . . nondum vidi. In Formiano sunt, quo ego proficisci cogitabam. Illa omnia in Tusculanum deportabo.* Beginning of 66 B.C.

[3] *Ad Att.* I, 4, 3 (9 T.P.): *Quod ad me de Hermathena scribis per mihi gratum. Est ornamentum Academiae proprium meae, quod et Hermes commune omnium et Minerva singulare est insigne eius gymnasii. Quare velim, ut scribis, ceteris quoque rebus quam plurimis eum locum ornes.*

[4] *Ad Att.* I, 1, 5 (10 T.P.): *Hermathena tua valde me delectat et posita ita belle est ut totum gymnasium (eius) ἀνάθημα esse videatur. Multum te amamus.* Summer, 65 B.C. On the condition of the text consult the various editions. I have adopted the emendation of Klotz rather than the suppression of *eliu* suggested by L. A. Constans. The meaning is not in doubt and proves that the Hermathena and the Hermeracles were not double busts (Hermes back to back with Athena and Heracles), but busts of Athena and Heracles mounted on pedestals shaped in the form of Hermes. On these works of art which some people identify with some pieces in the Ludovisi Collection, see L. A. Constans, *Rev. de Phil.* 1931, pp. 224–30.

period too he lost his first cousin[1] and acquired an infant son.[2] But in his *Letters* of these days political events and the incidents òf private life hold little or no place. All his interest is centred on the art collections which he had asked Atticus to make for him in Greece. There is certainly something rather disarming in the eagerness he puts into increasing the number of his treasures, in his impatience at the delays caused by distance and the difficulties of transport, in the joy with which he finally unpacks the longed-for cases. We must also give him credit for the scruples with which he strives to force his desires to keep in some relation to his resources, and the prudence which makes him postpone to better days his plan to extend to his *villa* at Formiae the improvements and embellishments which are transforming his Tusculanum.[3] But these admirable sentiments suffer occasional eclipse and we see peeping out those faults which were subsequently to become more serious: a dangerous inclination to imagine that anything that pleased him was a good bargain,[4] and to go on increasing his orders; a reprehensible tendency to value artistic pieces less for their intrinsic beauty than for the function he wished them to fulfil in producing the general effect his vanity was aiming at, the contribution they would make to the atmosphere he wished to create to envelop, or rather enhance, his personality: a gymnasium which was to be an Academy[5] or a Lyceum[6]; in fact to increase the prestige and fame he hoped to gain from their possession.

The genuine art-lover of genuine preferences chooses his treasured specimens at leisure and with care, and affectionately hoards them. Cicero, who in his Verrine orations[7] had sneered at the art-lover, was an upstart in the role. He wrote Atticus a blank cheque to make a selection for him, indifferent to the quality, if not to the number, of the specimens chosen. He raves about them with his eyes shut and shouts his wishes and rejoicings from the housetops

---

[1] Cf. above, p. 70, note 4.
[2] *Ad Att.* I, 2, 1 (11 T.P.): . . . *filiolo me auctum scito salva Terentia.* 65 B.C.
[3] *Ad Att.* I, 4, 3 (9 T.P.): *Caietam, si quando abundare coepero, ornabo.* On a first instalment of 20,400 sesterces, cf. above, p. 71.
[4] *Ad Att.* I, 3, 2 (8 T.P.): *Te multum amamus quod ea abs te diligenter parvoque curata sunt.* In other words, 20,400 sesterces is only a trifle!
[5] *Ad Att.* I, 11, 3 (7 T.P.): *Tu velim, quae Academiae nostrae parasti, quam primum mittas*; cf. above, p. 72, note 1.
[6] *De Div.* I, 5, 8: . . . *in Tusculano* . . . *Lyceum superiori gymnasio nomen est*; cf. above, p. 70, note 4.
[7] *Verr.* II, IV, 3, 5.

so effectively that his sudden and spectacular infatuation was not slow to arouse jealous mockery. He whimpered about this as early as 67, in a letter to Atticus: "I am so enthusiastic about all this that I deserve your help and, perhaps, the reproach of others"—*in eo genere sic studio efferimur ut abs te adiuvandi, ab aliis prope reprehendendi simus.*[1]

Ten years later he offers a fair target to these same critics. He is just as enthusiastic as ever, if not more so. The number of his orders increases; instead of Hermes and busts he now wants full-length statues[2] and pictures by master painters.[3] He has changed his purchasing agent and entrusted to Fadius Gallus the task earlier confided to Atticus; he has altered neither the nature nor the urgency of his demands.[4] He continues to order, regardless of cost, which is often beyond his means, and to clinch bargains which he thinks too expensive. He says he is prepared to re-sell at a loss to Damasippus or anyone else any specimens he does not like which Fadius Gallus had chosen[5]—as Atticus used to do—independently and on his own sole responsibility.[6] When he rejects the statue of Mars[7] and the group of Bacchantes which Gallus had bought for him, it is not that he questions their style or their beauty, but only because he feels that the dancers and the God of War are out of tune with the intellectual life whose peace is to pervade his *villae*, and with the atmosphere of the Greek *gymnasia* which is to surround the porticoes of his Tusculanum.[8]

In other words, his artistic taste was governed not by considera-

---

[1] *Ad Att.* I, 8, 2 (5 T.P.). This is Letter No. 4 in L. A. Constans's edition.

[2] Cf. below, note 7.

[3] *Ad Fam.* VII, 23, 3 (126 T.P.): *Ea [exhedria] volebam tabellis ornare : etenim, si quid generis istius modi me delectat, pictura delectat.* This letter is dated 55 B.C. by Tyrrell and Purser, later by L. A. Constans.

[4] *Ad Fam.* VII, 23, 1 (126 T.P.): *Sed essent, mi Galle, omnia facilia, si et ea mercatus esses quae ego desiderabam, et ad eam summam quam volueram. Ac tamen ista ipsa, quae te emisse scribis, non solum rata mihi erunt, sed etiam grata . . . (2) quanti ego genus omnino signorum omnium non aestimo, tanti ista quattuor aut quinque sumpsisti.*

[5] *Ad Fam.* VII, 23, 2 (126 T.P.): *Velim maneat Damasippus in sententia : prorsus enim ex istis emptionibus nullam desidero . . . (3) Si . . . Damasippus in sententia non manebit, aliquem Pseudodamasippum vel cum iactura reperiemus.*

[6] *Ad Fam.* VII, 23, 1 (126 T.P.): *plane enim intellego te non modo studio, sed etiam amore usum quae te delectarint, hominem, ut ego semper iudicavi in omni iudicio elegantissimum, quia me digna putaris, coemisse.*

[7] *Ad Fam.* VII, 23, 2 (126 T.P.): *Bacchis vero ubi est apud me locus? . . . Martis vero signum quo mihi pacis auctori?*

[8] *Ad Fam.* VII, 23, 2 (126 T.P.): *Ea enim signa ego emere soleo, quae ad similitudinem gymnasiorum exornent mihi in palaestra locum.*

tions of style or school,[1] but by the mental picture he had created of his dwellings and the flattering light that they would throw on him. His interest in a work of art lay not in the expression it gave to the soul of the creative artist, but in the credit it would reflect on Cicero. Statues and pictures were for him in one sense symbols of his own mind, projections of his own personality. In another, less noble, sense, he felt towards his pictures and his statues as he did towards the *trapezophorum* which Fadius Gallus had slipped into his consignment,[2] or as he felt towards the immense quantities of silver which he possessed, like those of Louis XIV during the War of the Spanish Succession, or Marcus Aurelius at the time of the invasion of the Quadi and Marcomanni. He was prepared to put his silver up to auction when he was hard driven in 47, and also his round table of citrus wood valued at half a million.[3] There was no need for his *Letters* to mention this table, for it was celebrated in the City and throughout the whole Roman world,[4] and more than three centuries after Cicero's death the price it had cost him still haunted Tertullian.[5] All these things were merely tokens of his wealth, proofs of his distinction and of his refined taste, the glorious trappings of that luxury and ease which were indispensable to him, and in which he took more and more pleasure as he advanced in age. He was less an artist in love with perfect form than a voluptuary for whom art crowned his pride and heightened his daily pleasure.

[1] Two passages of the letter to Fadius, *Ad Fam.* VII, 23, 2 (126 T.P.), deserve to be borne in mind and contrasted with the impression of a *Cicéron artiste* which E. Bertrand (Grenoble, 1890) has derived and supported by numerous quotations from Cicero's orations and treatises. The first proves that Cicero was only secondarily interested in the beauty of the works of art he was buying: *At pulchellae sunt* (the *Bacchae*, which he did not want). *Novi optime et saepe vidi. Nominatim tibi signa mihi nota mandassem, si probassem*; the second that he attaches no importance to works of art in themselves: . . . *quanti ego genus omnino signorum omnium non aestimo, tanti ista quattuor aut quinque sumpsisti.* Another case of illusions created by his other works and shattered by his Correspondence!

[2] *Ad Fam.* VII, 23, 3 (126 T.P.): *Quod tibi destinaras trapezophorum, si te delectat, habebis: sin autem sententiam mutasti, ego habebo scilicet.* Note incidentally this detachment of the great man to whom one purchase more or less is of no account.

[3] *Ad Att.* XI, 25, 3 (436 T.P.): *Te oro, ut in perditis rebus, si quid cogi, confici potest, quod sit in tuto, ex argento atque satis multa ex supellectile, des operam.* Cf. ibid. 24, 3 (441 T.P.): *Scripseras, ut HS $\overline{XII}$ permutaret, tantum esse reliquum de argento.*

[4] Pliny, *N.H.* XIII, 91: . . . *confines Mauri, quibus plurima arbor citri et mensarum insania, quas feminae viris contra margaritas regerunt. Exstat hodie M. Ciceroni in illa paupertate, et quod magis mirum est, illo aevo empta HS $\overline{D}$.*

[5] Tertullian, *De Pallio*, 5: *M. Tullius quingentis milibus nummum orbem citri emit.*

Cicero's Fortune and Way of Life

4. THE LOVER OF LUXURY

In face of public opinion which admired him and listened to his words, Cicero affected to despise comfort, luxury and the softer side of life. In his *De Finibus*, for instance, he grandiloquently denies that either the structure of man's body or the admirable nature of man's intelligence show enjoyment to be the sole purpose for which he was born.[1] In the *De Officiis* he preaches that it is base for a man to abandon himself to enervating luxury and to live in sensual delight.[2] From his *Letters*, however, it is clear that he was far from heeding his own teaching. We see him eschewing inconvenience and suffering, to the point of modifying the most important political decisions rather than take the risk of being sea-sick.[3] We see him yielding to the most foolish temptations, with regard to one of which he blandly writes to Atticus: "Make this your own job, and do not judge what the state of my private affairs would demand, a thing about which I care not, but consider what I desire."[4] He loved the luxuries, the superfluities which he found so necessary, and sought so eagerly that on another occasion he calmly wrote to his friend: "Whatever it costs, a thing is cheap if you need it."[5]

It is true that both these passages refer to the passionate desire that suddenly overcame him to acquire some beautiful gardens on the bank of the Tiber in which he could erect a shrine—a *heroum*—in memory of his beloved daughter Tullia. And, so far, all the extravagances we have seen him commit have been in connection with houses, books, statues and pictures—all of them things of the spirit. But Cicero was capable of extravagance on a lower plane, and there was no material gratification which he despised. Coming back from exile he breathed a sigh of relief, observing that he would now be able to live a more liberal life than before; that was his ideal.[6] But this ideal was not so lofty as the word "liberal"

---

[1] Cic. *De Fin.*, II, 13, 41: . . . *nec figura corporis nec ratio excellens ingenii humani significat ad unam hanc rem natum hominem, ut frueretur voluptatibus.*

[2] Cic. *De Off.* I, 30, 106: . . . *intellegemus, quam sit turpe diffluere luxuria, et delicate ac molliter vivere.*

[3] Cf. the texts of the Correspondence quoted in this sense by Drumann-Groebe, VI, p. 429. It was fear of sea-sickness which prevented his evading the Triumvirs' assassins (Plut. *Cic.* XLVII, 7).

[4] *Ad Att.* XII, 22, 3 (558 T.P.): *Habe tuum negotium, nec quid res mea familiaris postulet, quam ego non curo, sed quid velim existima.* March 18, 45 B.C.

[5] *Ad Att.* XII, 23, 3 (559 T.P.): *Sed quanti quanti, bene emitur quod necesse est.* March 19, 45 B.C.

[6] *Ad Q. Fr.* II, 4, 3 (105 T.P.): *Vivo paullo liberalius quam solebam.* End March 56 B.C.

might lead us to suppose. The word had not in his day the same connotation as in ours. It meant only that Cicero hoped to preserve his rank while enjoying his ease, for he was as much attached to the one as the other. From the number and excellence of his servants we must admit that he had no difficulty in achieving the double aim of his somewhat peculiar "liberalism". Thanks to the *Letters* we can draw up statistics about his slaves and his expert freedmen.[1] Apart from Tiro, who was not only his head-steward but his confidential secretary, they name twenty-six retainers. Two of them, Dionysius and Sositheus, were readers; four of them, Chrysippus, Hilarus, Laurea and Spintharus, were secretaries; and two were physicians, Alexio and Metrodorus.[2]

From the number of these specialists, we can conjecture the horde of subordinates at his command. There must have been hundreds of non-specialised servants who hummed round him. Cicero had organised his domestic affairs on a princely footing. He was thus able to delegate to members of his household the less important and more wearisome affairs of daily life, and also to lap himself round with all the delicate little attentions and services that ministered to his physical pleasure and comfort.[3]

He was always irreproachably turned out in the most refined style. If we are to believe the heavy-footed sarcasms of the faked speech of Fufius Calenus: "he used more oil than wine",[4] draped himself in a toga that reached to his heels, and threw over it a dark cloak like a lady's,[5] while he shed all round him the smell of the perfumes with which his artistically combed white hair was dressed.[6] It is possible that the pamphleteer's account is somewhat

---

[1] Drumann-Groebe, VI, pp. 353–6.

[2] On Chrysippus cf. *Ad Att.* VII, 2, 8 (293 T.P.); 5, 3 (296 T.P.); *Ad Q. Fr.* III, 4, 5 (152 T.P.); and 6, 6 (155 T.P.). On Sositheus cf. *Ad Att.* I, 12, 4 (17 T.P.): *anagnostes noster Sositheus*; on Hilarus cf. *Ad Att.* XIII, 19, 1 (631 T.P.): *Hilarus librarius*; on Dionysius cf. *Ad Fam.* V, 9, 2 (639 T.P.): *anagnostes*, and XIII, 77, 3 (638 T.P.); on Laurea, *scriba meus*, cf. *Ad Fam.* V, 20, 1 (302 T.P.) and *Ad Att.* XIII, 22, 4 (635 T.P.); on Spintharus, cf. *Ad Att.* XIII, 25, 3 (642 T.P.); on Alexio, cf. *Ad Att.* XV, 1, 1 (730 T.P.) and 2, 4 (732 T.P.); on Metrodorus, cf. *Ad Fam.* XVI, 14, 1 (924 T.P.) and 20 (693 T.P.); *Ad Att.* XV, 1, 2 (731 T.P.). For a more complete list of names see the Indexes of Orelli and of Tyrrell and Purser's edition, Vol. VII.

[3] Add to the human livestock, the pack-animals and draft-animals with which Cicero was so well provided that in 45 B.C. he bids Atticus levy, from amongst those that are to spare, whatever beasts his son will need for the journey to Athens: *Ad Att.* XII, 32, 2 (568 T.P.): *Iumento certe Athenis nihil opus est. Quibus autem in via utatur, domi sunt plura quam opus erat, quod etiam tu animadvertes.*

[4] Dio. Cass. XLVI, 18, 1f.

[5] Dio. Cass. XLVI, 18, 1f.   [6] Dio. Cass. XLVI, 18, 1f.

exaggerated. But we may notice that in his *De Officiis* the philosopher is more indulgent to a man's toilette than to other luxuries. A man must not indulge in the coquetry which is permissible in a woman; his mien must be one of manly dignity,[1] but he must not display an unworthy, rustic carelessness in his dress.[2] In the *Letters*, where he is not posing in front of a looking-glass, we find nothing explicit to corroborate the details over which Fufius Calenus made merry at his expense. They do, however, reveal a certain preoccupation with clothes, if only in the letter which shows him preparing to join Pompey's army in 48 and taking the precaution of supplying himself with ample changes of costly clothing.[3]

This justifies us in assuming that the abusive pamphlets which ridiculed his dandyism were only caricaturing one of the features which his teaching but not his practice repudiated, and which every passer-by in Rome could bear witness to. The *Letters* do, on the other hand, convict him of having lingered more than a philosopher ought to do over the pleasures of the table; not only those pleasures where good food is the pretext, rather than the purpose, of the gathering, where intellectual conversation flourishes in friendly interchanges round the table[4]; but quite frankly the material pleasure in the delicious viands which it offered and the noble wines which mingled in the goblets. Without the *Letters* we should never suspect Cicero of having been either gourmand or gourmet. The Pseudo-Sallust, it is true, declaims against his insatiable appetite: *gula immensa*.[5] But we should have been justified in writing off this isolated imputation if we could have pinned our faith to the virtuous maxims enunciated in his later days—perhaps Molière had these in mind when he makes Harpagon say that a man must eat

---

[1] Cic. *De Off.* I, 36, 130: . . . *venustatem muliebrem ducere debemus, dignitatem virilem.*

[2] Cic. *De Off.* I, 36, 130: *Adhibenda praeterea munditia tantum quae fugiat agrestem et inhumanam neglegentiam.* It is true that Cicero specifies: *munditia non odiosa neque exquisita nimis*, and that he adds: *eadem ratio est habenda vestitus, in quo, sicut in plerisque rebus, mediocritas optima est.*

[3] *Ad Att.* XI, 2, 4 (407 T.P.); cf. above, p. 59. This outfit was sufficiently sumptuous and costly to be weighed verbally against a debt of 60,000 sesterces.

[4] Cf. amongst other examples, *Ad Fam.* VII, 22 (761 T.P.), to Trebatius: *Inluseras heri inter scyphos quod dixeram controversiam esse, possetne heres, quod furtum antea factum esset, furti recte agere*; and IX, 25, 2 (246 T.P.): *in iis controversiis quas habeo cum tuis combibonibus Epicuriis* (letter to L. Papirius Paetus, Feb. 50 B.C.). The same *cenae* with Atticus: *Ad Att.* XII, 4, 2 (469 T.P.): . . . *scribam quod tui convivae non modo libenter sed etiam aequo animo legere possint*, etc. Cf. below, p. 81 and II, p. 478.

[5] Ps.-Sal. *In Cic.* 3.

to live, not live to eat[1]—or to the boast, derisively attributed to him by Fufius Calenus, that he never drank anything but water at his evening meal so as to be able to work better at night on his discourses[2]; or if we could believe in the tribute which Plutarch retrospectively paid to his frugality and asceticism. According to his biographer: "It was rare for him to sit down to table before sunset, less because he was too busy than because he had to remember the delicacy of his digestion. He took great pains to take care of his bodily health, underwent daily a regular course of massage and outdoor exercise and thus succeeded in strengthening his constitution."[3] Unfortunately the *Letters* are there to dim the glowing colours of this flattering picture.

It may well be that Cicero did not dine till after sunset,[4] but he frequently lingered feasting with his boon companions[5] till far into the night. He left the feast not feeling too steady, for this water-drinker tells Trebatius, with whom over his wine—*inter pocula*—he had discussed a thorny question of law the night before, that he got home very late "having well drunk"—*bene potus seroque redieram*.[6] So this great personage could drink like a man, and eat even better, neatly evading the sumptuary laws which threatened to curb his appetite:[7] the ancient Licinian Law about which he grumbled to M. Fadius Gallus, the recent law of Julius Caesar[8] which he made fun of to amuse L. Papirius Paetus.

The first of these two letters wittily lays at the door of the surly law-giver all the blame for an attack of dysentery which came on after a meal compounded strictly according to regulations, but nevertheless very ample, and to which he had done too much honour. "When our gourmets try," he says, "to bring to honour various earth-grown foods which are exempt from the law, they flavour up mushrooms, potherbs and vegetables of every sort

[1] *De Sen.* XI, 36: *Tantum cibi et potionis adhibendum, ut reficiantur vires, non opprimantur.*
[2] Dio. Cass. XLVI, 18, 5.
[3] Plut. *Cic.* VIII, 2.
[4] Though the *Letters* show exceptions to this rule: *Ad Fam.* IX, 26 (479 T.P.): *Accubueram hora nona.* Aug. 46 B.C. At the summer solstice "the ninth hour" would have been between 2.31 p.m. and 3.46 p.m. It is hard to believe that a month and a half later the sun would have set at the time Cicero sat down to table. Cf. my *Daily Life in Ancient Rome*, Eng. trans., 1941, p. 263f.
[5] *Combibones*: *Ad. Fam.* IX, 25, 3 (246 T.P.); cf. above, p. 78, note 4.
[6] *Ad Fam.* VII, 22 (761 T.P.), June 44 B.C.
[7] On the sumptuary law passed in 104 B.C. by Publius Licinius Crassus, cf. my book *Des Gracques à Sulla* (2), p. 332.
[8] Cf. my *César* (3), p. 907.

in such a way that nothing could be more delicious. When I fell on these at Lentulus's augural dinner (ten days ago) I was seized with a diarrhoea so violent that it has only today begun to abate, and I who had had no difficulty in abstaining from oysters and murenas was taken in by beets and mallows. Henceforth I shall beware."[1] Well and good, but the second letter, written eleven years later, shows that Cicero had lost sight of this lesson. Just as in 57, he rails in 46 against the restrictions designed to check over-luxurious catering. He speaks with irony of the new prohibitions with which Julius Caesar has re-enforced earlier *plebiscita*, and he makes no attempt to hide his intention of evading them, at need in the very way that had previously proved so disastrous. Without the flutter of an eyebrow, he writes to L. Papirius Paetus: "As soon as ever he [i.e. Julius Caesar] has gone, I shall betake myself to your mushrooms."[2]

Good dinners interest him greatly, and he explains to his correspondent, about the same time, how and why he foregathers at Tusculum with the two epicures, Hirtius and Dolabella: "I have Hirtius and Dolabella, these masters of dining, as my students of speaking. For I think you will have heard—if haply all the news reaches you—that they come to me to declaim and I go to them to dine."[3] A little while after, he hears that gout-stricken Paetus is suffering from a fresh attack of his complaint, the penalty probably of a too generous diet. None the less he asks himself informally to dinner. In the note he sends him, it is true that he represents himself as "the least greedy of guests and a foe to elaborate dinners"— *hospitem cum minime edacem tum inimicum cenis sumptuariis*. But that was only a courteous phrase to excuse his indiscretion, for he ill conceals the pleasure he expects from being entertained by a friend whose cook he opines will not be suffering from gout—*non enim arbitror cocum etiam te arthriticum habere.*[4] We shall see too how proudly he boasts in the following year to Atticus of having

[1] *Ad Fam.* VII, 26, 2 (94 T.P.): *Ea [lex sumptuaria] mihi fraudi fuit. Nam dum volunt isti lauti terra nata, quae lege excepta sunt, in honorem adducere, fungos, helvellas, herbas omnes ita condiunt, ut nihil possit esse suavius. In eas cum incidissem in cena augurali apud Lentulum tanta me διάρροια adripuit, ut hodie primum coepisse consistere. Ita ego qui me ostreis et muraenis facile abstinebam, a beta et a malva deceptus sum. Posthac igitur erimus cautiores.* 57 B.C.
[2] *Ad Fam.* IX, 15, 5 (481 T.P.), Sept. 46 B.C.
[3] *Ad Fam.* IX, 16, 7 (472 T.P.): *Hirtium ego et Dolabellam dicendi discipulos habeo, cenandi magistros. Puto enim te audisse, si forte ad vos omnia perferuntur, illos apud me declamitare, me apud illos cenitare.* July 46 B.C.
[4] *Ad Fam.* IX, 23 (504 T.P.).

entertained Caesar "extremely sumptuously and splendidly" in his *villa* at Cumae—*opipare sane et apparate*.[1]

Nor is this all. If he dislikes long voyages, it is not only because of sea-sickness[2]; it is very probably because of the wretched cooking to which he was exposed on the journey. When he sailed by short stages to his distant province of Cilicia, he was happily surprised to be able to enjoy delicious food provided at Corcyra (Corfu) and the Sybota Islands by the agents of Atticus. As he writes to their master, they invited him to "banquets worthy of the Salii,"[3] or, as the French would phrase it, to "feasts worthy of canons". Even in times of blackest crisis Cicero was obsessed by the craving for good fare. In Feb. 43, when Italy was being again laid waste by civil war, delicate though his letter is, we are taken aback to find him teasing L. Papirius Paetus on his having suddenly cut himself off from all feasting: "I am distressed that you have given up going out to dinner; you are depriving yourself of much pleasure and enjoyment. For indeed I am afraid that you will ultimately lose the customs and ways you used to have and forget the art of making little suppers. Even when you had good examples to follow, you did not make very good progress; what will you do now I wonder? Do you see how by philosophising I am trying to bring you back to dine? But if you love me do not think that because I write in jest I have thrown off all anxiety for the Republic. Be persuaded, my Paetus, that day and night I do nothing, and think of nothing, but that my fellow-countrymen shall be unharmed and free."[4]

Despite these final words, what is left of all the puritan maxims of Cicero and Plutarch's eulogies of his abstemiousness? Not much, we must admit. And though the *Letters* do not go the full length of the Pseudo-Sallust pamphlet, they at least explain how it came to be written. The man whom it crudely accuses of gluttony was

---

[1] *Ad Att.* XIII, 52, 1 (679 T.P.). Dec. 45 B.C.; cf. below, II, pp. 292–3.

[2] Cf. above, p. 76.

[3] *Ad Att.* V, 9, 1 (195 T.P.): *Actium venimus a.d. XVII Kal. Quinct.; cum quidem et Corcyrae et Sybotis muneribus tuis, quae et Areus et meus amicus Euty-chides opipare et* φιλοπροσηνέστατα *nobis congesserant epulati essemus Saliarem in modum.* Second half of June 51 B.C.

[4] *Ad Fam.* IX, 24, 2 (820 T.P.): *Te ad cenas itare desisse moleste fero; magna enim te delectatione et voluptate privasti. Deinde etiam vereor . . . ne nescio quid illud quod solebas, dediscas et obliviscare cenulas facere. Nam si tum, cum habebas quos imitarere, non multum proficiebas, quid nunc te facturum putem?* (3) *Vides, ut te philosophando revocare coner ad cenas?* (4) *Sed cave, si me amas, existimes me, quod iocosius scribam, abiecisse curam reipublicae. Sic tibi, mi Paete, persuade, me dies et noctes nihil aliud agere, nihil curare, nisi ut mei cives salvi liberique sint.*

not wholly innocent of that vice, and the invectives of the pamphlet have only exaggerated a fault. At best, the *gula immensa* against which it declaims was a very refined palate, too refined for the pose Cicero tried to assume, too refined to fit into the picture of the wise man, which he liked to paint of himself.

Let us now turn to the question of women. The *Letters* suggest no liaison, not even with Caerellia.[1] They give no hint of scandal. This reflects the opinion of his bitterest enemies. Being unable to convict him of open adultery or to discover a mistress whom he kept,[2] they have been reduced in their blind hatred to the expedient of mud-slinging, making the most monstrous and absurd accusations of incest with his daughter Tullia,[3] of pederasty with his professor of rhetoric M. Pupius Piso,[4] and then with his favourite slave, Tiro.[5] His letters make no mention of Piso, but are full of contempt for Piso's son, who by Pompey's favour was made Consul in 61.[6] Of his own daughter, Cicero speaks with the fond affection of a father,[7] and of Tiro with the friendship and esteem

---

[1] Plutarch, *Cic.* XXIX, 3 and XXX, 4, is the only writer to suggest that Clodia had aroused Terentia's jealousy, but he is careful not to adduce any serious justification for such jealousy.

[2] Cf. above, p. 6of.

[3] Dio. Cass. XXXVI, 18, 6. Ps.-Sall. *In Cic.* 2: . . . *filia matris paelex tibi iucundior atque obsequentior quam parenti par est.* Frank Olivier, in the memorandum of his quoted above, p. 16, note 7, has expressed the opinion that, as a gloss of Donatus suggests, line 623 of Book VI of the *Aeneid* refers to this alleged incest. (Servius, *Ad Aen.* VI, 623: *hic thalamum invasit natae vetitosque hymenaeos.* —*Thyestes unde Aegisthus natus, idem Cinyras : nam quod Donatus dicit nefas est credi dictum esse de Tullio.*)

[4] Ps.-Sall. *In Cic.* 1: . . . *scilicet istam immoderatam eloquentiam apud M. Pisonem non pudicitiae iactura perdidicisti. Itaque minime mirandum est quod eam flagitiose venditas, quam turpissime parasti.*

[5] Pliny the Younger, *Ep.* VII, 4, 3–6, reading in his Laurentine villa of the comparison drawn by Asinius Gallus between his father Pollio and Cicero, hit on a smutty epigram supposedly hurled by Cicero at Tiro—*incidit epigramma Ciceronis in Tironem suum.* The meaning, if not the paternity, of this epigram— probably composed by Asinius Gallus to support Pollio's lies—is clear: it is a naughty variation of Pliny's on the original theme. He composed it after his siesta:

> *Lascivium inveni lusum Ciceronis . . .*
> *Nam queritur quod fraude mala frustratus amantem*
> *Paucula cenato sibi debita savia Tiro*
> *Tempore nocturno subtraxerit . . .*

[6] *Ad Att.* I, 13, 2 (19 T.P.): *Consul ipse parvo animo et pravo . . . facie magis quam facetiis ridiculus . . . ;* 14, 6 (20 T.P.): *ille alter [consul] uno vitio minus vitiosus quod iners, quod somni plenus, quod imperitus . . . ;* 16, 8 (22 T.P.): *Pisonem consulem nulla in re consistere umquam sum passus . . . ;* 18, 3 (24 T.P.): *Consul est impositus is nobis, quem nemo praeter nos philosophos aspicere sine suspirio posset :* etc., etc.

[7] See Tyrrell and Purser's Index, VII, p. 108.

which the trusty devotion of this model servant fully deserved.[1] Thus Cicero's own *Letters*—especially if my theory is accepted that the intention of publishing them was to blacken his memory—are enough to sweep away the infamous imputations, which leave him stainless and disgrace none but his contemptible detractors: the authors of the bogus discourse of Fufius Calenus and of the *declamatio* of the Pseudo-Sallust and Asinius Gallus, who grafted his falsehoods on to the libels of Asinius Pollio. At the same time, the *Letters* obliterate the halo of sanctity with which Plutarch,[2] more even than Cicero himself, has surrounded his character.

In these matters Cicero has not tried to impose on us. Good Roman as he was, of peasant stock, he never dramatised nor wrote poetically about love. He was indulgent towards weaknesses of the flesh, and condemned debauchery only because of its disastrous consequences. In his *De Officiis* he would check licence at the point where it threatens to impair the vigour which a man needs if he is to fulfil in manly wise the duties that fall to him in peace and war. He grants due place to enjoyment, provided those who enjoy themselves do so in moderation and preserve appearances.[3]

In the *Tusculan Disputations* he considers outbursts of passion disgraceful, but he would not deny the joy which Venus grants her worshippers where passion is calm and quiet.[4] He expresses himself with even more frankness in *Pro Caelio*. Like a middle-class Parisian before the dramas of Dumas *fils*, he is willing to see a youth sow his wild oats, turn aside a while from the straight paths of virtue, "desert and derelict, abandoned to copse and jungle"; he would not see him cut off from all relaxations; he admits that at times lust and desire may win the victory over reason, but they should be indulged within the bounds of moderation. Morals demand only that a man should respect his neighbour, not waste his patrimony, not put himself at the money-lender's mercy, not

---

[1] See in particular *Ad Fam.* XVI, 4, 4 (288 T.P.): *Sic habeto, mi Tiro, neminem esse qui me amet quin idem te amet.*

[2] Plut. *Cic.* II, V, VII; and remember that this optimistic view tallies with Cicero's *Pro Cael.* XIX, 46.

[3] Cic. *De Off.* I, 34, 122: . . . *maxime haec aetas a libidinibus arcenda est . . . ut . . . et eorum in bellicis et in civilibus officiis vigeat industria. Atque etiam cum relaxare animos et dare se iucunditati volent, caveant intemperantiam, meminerint verecundiae.*

[4] Cic. *Tusc.* IV, 32, 68: . . . *ut turpes sunt, qui ecferunt se laetitia tum, cum fruuntur Veneris voluptatibus, sic flagitiosi, qui eas inflammato animo concupiscunt.*

attack the home or the good name of another.[1] He forbids dishonourable approach to young girls or married women, but would by no means prevent a man's enjoying himself with courtesans, provided they are not too flashy or too expensive. Like the majority of his contemporaries—and as might indeed be expected in a society which had not yet been reached by the Gospel—he ignores the question of chastity, and advises in sexual relations only the self-discipline required by family considerations and regard for the proprieties. He is not preaching morals, but merely laying down rules for practical use. Naturally then, being indulgent to others, he does not appear in his *Letters* more exacting towards himself than towards them.

Drumann and Groebe, hostile though they are, taking account of the Correspondence, give one of their chapters the heading *Reinheit der Sitten*: "Purity of Cicero's Morals". The two passages which they quote in support seem at first sight to prove them right.[2] Both are taken from letters to L. Papirius Paetus. In the one Cicero prides himself on consistently following Plato's example: "I observe and shall observe—as is my wont—the self-restraint of Plato"; *ego servo et servabo—sic enim adsuevi—Platonis verecundiam*.[3] In the other, he recalls that gay living had never attracted him when he was young, still less now that he is old—*me vero nihil istorum ne iuvenem quidem movit umquam, ne nunc senem*.[4] We can only applaud these sentiments; they are in themselves exemplary.

The context of these quotations, however, robs them of their edifying effect. In the first we note that the Platonic *verecundia* of which he boasts refers not to conduct but to language; and, further, that Cicero gives a definition of it which radically alters it: "I like the restraint or rather the freedom of his speech"—*amo verecundiam vel potius libertatem loquendi*.[5] Finally, the letter in which these phrases occur is one mainly of jesting mood, daring rather than restrained, in which Cicero in his gayest manner displays a

---

[1] Cic. *Pro Cael.* XVIII, 42: *Ergo haec deserta via et inculta atque interclusa iam frondibus et virgultis relinquatur; detur aliqui ludus aetati; sit adolescentia liberior; non omnia voluptatibus denegentur; . . . vincet aliquando cupiditas voluptasque rationem dummodo illa in hoc genere praescriptio moderatioque teneatur; pareat iuventus pudicitiae suae ne spoliet alienam, ne effundat patrimonium, ne faenore trucidetur, ne incurrat in alterius domum atque famam.* These are also the morals of Horace, *Sat.* I, 2.

[2] Drumann-Groebe, VI, p. 366.

[3] *Ad Fam.* IX, 22, 5 (633 T.P.).   [4] *Ad Fam.* IX, 26, 2 (479 T.P.).

[5] *Ad Fam.* IX, 22, 1 (633 T.P.). [See, however, Tyrrell and Purser's notes on the whole of this letter.—E. O. L.]

master's skill in the use of double meanings and innuendos, suggesting the most indelicate ideas while appearing not to have them in mind and skating over the thin ice of obscenity without even damping his feet. "A most admirable lute-player taught Socrates to play the lute; he was called '*Connus*'[1]: do you see anything obscene in that? If we say there are 'three of us' (*terni*) there is no harm in that; but when we say 'two of us' (*bini*) that is obscene. At least, it embarrasses the Greeks [in Greek *binei* means: he sleeps with her]. Therefore there is nothing in a word. . . . 'Rue' and 'mint' are both quite harmless: I am allowed to use the diminutive of 'rue' (*rutula*), but the diminutive of 'mint' is not permitted [*mentula* means penis] . . ." and so on. No one could more neatly evade the reticence he is pretending to observe, nor more artfully shelter his dubious jokes behind a respectful tribute to Plato.

As for the other letter to Paetus, it is bad luck for Cicero that he chose to insert into this letter in particular his disclaimer of any inclination to gallantry, just after he had been retailing in somewhat softened form his ribald recollections of an evening spent in all-too-merry company. "I have just taken my place at table at three o'clock and am jotting down a copy of my letter to you on my tablets. 'Where were you?' you ask. I was dining with Volumnius Eutrapelus. Atticus lay on the couch above me and Verrius below, both of them acquaintances of yours. . . . Listen to the rest. Below Eutrapelus Cytheris was lying. 'Was Cicero then in this company,' you say, 'Cicero whom the Greeks gazed on and whose name was in their mouths?' No, I swear to you, I did not expect her to be there. But Aristippus the well-known follower of Socrates was unashamed when he was taunted with Laïs's having captured him. 'I have her,' he said, 'not she me.' It sounds better in Greek: translate it if you will."[2]

[1] *Ad Fam.* IX, 22, 3 (633 T.P.): *Socraten fidibus docuit nobilissimus fidicen; is Connus vocitatus est : num id obscenum putas? Cum loquimur terni, nihil flagitii dicimus : at cum bini, obscenum est. Graecis quidem inquies. Nihil est ergo in verbo. . . . Ruta et menta recte utrumque : volo mentam pusillam ita appellare, ut rutulam, non licet.*

[2] *Ad Fam.* IX, 26, 1–2 (479 T.P.) Summer of 46 B.C.: *Accubueram hora nona, cum ad te harum exemplum in codicillis exaravi. Dices, ubi? Apud Volumnium Eutrapelum et quidem supra me Atticus, infra Verrius, familiares tui . . . Audi reliqua. Infra Eutrapelum Cytheris accubuit. In eo igitur, inquis, convivio Cicero ille quem aspectabant,* "*cuius ob os Graii ora obvertebant sua?*" *Non, mehercule, suspicatus sum illam adfore : sed tamen ne Aristippus quidem ille Socraticus erubuit, cum esset obiectum habere eum Laïda. Habeo, inquit, non habeor. Graece hoc melius : tu si voles interpretabere.*

It was after this little fling that Cicero voices his distaste for gallantries and adds the remark, which Drumann and Groebe so much approve, about the indifference he felt towards women's charms. As I read it, he was airily revealing the embarrassment he felt over the situation in which he had become involved. Having lightheartedly accepted the invitation to dine, he would gladly have been excused from sharing an entertainment vulgarised by the presence of Cytheris.

Cytheris was an actress of mimes who had a very bad reputation in the City. In comparing her with the courtesan Laïs, Cicero knew his own feelings towards this theatre prostitute, whom he had never spared elsewhere. Three years earlier in a letter to Atticus, he vented his indignation over the effrontery of Mark Antony, who had had the impudence to ride through the streets of Rome in an open litter with this woman at his side, as if she were a second wife. This litter was followed by seven others packed with their male and female friends.[1] Two years later, writing to Atticus to convince him of Antony's warlike intentions and the Consul's threat that "no man shall live who is not on the side of the victor," he did not speak of his enemy by name, he indicated him by the intentionally damning phrase "that fellow of Cytheris's"—*hic Cytherius*.[2] So Cicero did not feel proud of having figured at a dinner-party alongside this notorious character, and was anxious to let Paetus understand that if he had anticipated her presence, he would probably have declined his host's invitation: *non, mehercule, suspicatus sum illam adfore*.[3] But he tells us all about it, and his libertinism is aggravated in this case by hypocrisy. For he had every right to expect to find Cytheris at Volumnius's table since it is to him we owe two pieces of information which together might well have made him suspicious: Volumnius had been a companion of Mark Antony's debauches[4]; and it was Volumnius who had started up Cytheris—whom he had recently manumitted—when in 45 she accompanied Antony, then Tribune of the Plebs, on his visits to the towns of Italy. There she was greeted by the local

---

[1] *Ad. Att.* X, 10, 5 (395 T.P.): *Hic tamen "Cytherius" Cytherida secum lectica aperta portat, alteram uxorem : septem praeterea coniunctae lecticae amicarum sunt an amicorum.* May 3, 49 B.C. The last words are intended to indicate the catamites of Antony or the lesbians of his mistress, or both.

[2] *Ad Att.* XV, 22 (755 T.P.): *Hic autem noster Cytherius nisi victorem neminem victurum.* June 22 or 23, 44 B.C.

[3] See above, p. 85, note 2.

[4] Cic. *Phil.* XIII, 2, 3: *Additi Antoni conlusores et sodales Eutrapelum* . . .

officials not under the stage name she had adopted, but under her official name of Volumnia.[1]

The truth is that in dining with Volumnius, Cicero was necessarily exposing himself to the risk of meeting the beautiful freedwoman there, and that—barring the fear of scandal—this risk did not deter him. When the deed was done, he sought to ward off the scandal. At the moment, he thought only of his pleasure. As he confesses, he loved elegant dinner parties. In his days of prosperity they refreshed him after the cares of the day; in the days of eclipse they consoled him, as he implies, for his servitude.[2] Here, he would from time to time sink lament and complaint in his jesting and laughter: *convivio delector . . . ibi . . . gemitum in risus maximos transfero*.[3] Here he would vent his feelings about current politics.

When he had spent part of the day in reading and writing, he devoted the rest of it to the care of his physical health: *corpori omne tempus datur*[4]; and indeed redoubled his thought for it. It is better to die of indigestion in Rome than of starvation anywhere else: *satius est hic cruditate quam istic fame*.[5] His cook tries to copy the recipes of the gourmets.[6] He becomes something of a connoisseur himself, and is no longer content with sausages and olives.[7] He does full justice to the menu and brings an honest hunger to the initial egg while keeping a keen appetite for the later course of roast veal.[8] He now pitches his tent among his enemies the Epicureans—*in Epicuri nos adversarii nostri castra coniecimus*[9]—or rather he has joined the ranks of those who relish good living: *fama ad te de mea lautitia veniet*.[10]

---

[1] Cic. *Phil.* II, 24, 58: . . . *vehebatur in essedo trib(unus) pl(ebis) lictores laureati antecedebant, inter quos aperta lectica mima portabatur quam ex oppidis municipales homines honesti ob viam necessarie prodeuntes, non noto illo et mimico nomine sed Volumniam consalutabant.* Cf. the gloss of Servius, *Ad Ecl.* X, 2 on the name Lycoris under which our Cytheris was masquerading at the time of her love affair with Gallus: *liberta Volumnii et meretrix.*

[2] *Ad Fam.* IX, 26, 1 (479 T.P.): *Miraris tam exhilaratam esse servitutem nostram.*

[3] *Ad Fam.* IX, 26, 2 (479 T.P.).   [4] *Ad Fam.* IX, 20, 3 (475 T.P.). Aug. 46 B.C.

[5] *Ad Fam.* IX, 18, 4 (473 T.P.). July 46 B.C.

[6] *Ad Fam.* IX, 20, 2 (475 T.P.): *Sed vide audaciam : etiam Hirtio cenam dedi, sine pavone tamen, in ea cocus meus praeter ius fervens nihil potuit imitari.*

[7] *Ad Fam.* IX, 16, 8 (472 T.P.): *Neque est quod in promulside spei ponas aliquid, quam totam sustuli. Solebam enim antea debilitari oleis et Lucanicis tuis.* July 46 B.C.; cf. ibid. 18, 3 (473 T.P.) in contradiction of the passage quoted above, note 6, he writes: *plures iam pavones confeci quam tu pullos columbinos.*

[8] *Ad Fam.* IX, 20, 1 (475 T.P.): *Integram famem ad ovum adfero ; itaque usque ad assum vitulinum opera perducitur.*

[9] *Ad Fam.* IX, 20, 1 (475 T.P.).

[10] *Ad Fam.* IX, 16, 8 (472 T.P.). He is treated as a debauchee in Dio Cass. XLVI, 18, 5.

Cicero's Fortune and Way of Life

Cicero sees two advantages in this pleasant and luxurious life. It gratifies his sensual appetite and at the same time flatters his vanity by putting him on the same social footing as the high society of Rome. Having rivalled the cream of the nobility by the luxury of his *villae*, the rarity of his collections, the grandeur of his domestic arrangements and equipment, the elegance of his wardrobe, he shared with guests his pleasures, his entertainments, his refined cookery, and even the company of the professional courtesans who were in fashion. He believed that he thus raised himself in public estimation, and in his own, above the general level, and that his modest bourgeois origin would be forgotten in all this new-born glamour.

Chapter II

GREED AND UNSCRUPULOUSNESS

I. AN EXPENSIVE LAWYER

CICERO needed a great deal of money, and ever more money, for this life of a great lord, and we have already seen that at the time of his death he was still considered immensely wealthy, despite the burden of his debts.[1] Since he was not born a multi-millionaire[2] we are entitled to ask how he came by these riches.[3] The question touches his honour. His enemies in their libels saw only tainted sources for his wealth. According to them, he had exploited and unworthily ground down his compatriots and valued his wives solely for their dowries. Far from refuting these insinuations, we are forced to confess that the *Letters* provide overwhelming evidence for his cupidity.

In the first place we must tot up the professional earnings which he amassed in the course of his career. Cicero was, first and foremost, a pleader; he even tied with Hortensius for first place among the law orators of his day.[4] For this reason he was able to command enormous sums, proportioned both to his fame and the importance of the cases he took up.[5] It is true that the Cincian Law of 204 forbade any pleader to accept fee or gift for his services, and that this law had never been abrogated.[6] But the pleaders of Ancient

---

[1] Cf. above, p. 43.
[2] Cf. above, p. 54. The fact is emphasised by Dio Cass. XXXVIII, 20, 3.
[3] Where does the money come from? asks Ps.-Sall. *In Cic.* 4: . . . *redde rationem, quantum patrimonii acceperis, quid tibi litibus accreverit . . . aut, si retices, cui dubium potest esse, quin opulentiam istam ex sanguine et visceribus civium paraveris?*
[4] Plut. *Cic.* V, 3.
[5] Cases are quoted in which pleaders during the first century of the Empire demanded 400,000 sesterces for a single case (Tac. *Ann.* XI, 5).
[6] On the *Lex Cincia* cf. Cic. *De Sen.* IV, 10; *De Or.* II, 71, 286; Liv. XXXIV, 4, 9; and Festus, p. 143 M. The law was confirmed—perhaps with reduced penalties—under Augustus (Dio Cass. LIV, 18, 3); it was later restored in its primitive severity (Tac. *Ann.* XIII, 42).

Rome in the last century of the Republic were accustomed to receive payment for their good offices in an indirect or clandestine way, just as in France today, though French law forbids an advocate to accept a fee, no one is shocked by the fact that his client pays him what is known as a "provision".[1] Did Cicero abide by the strict letter of the Cincian Law? Or did he prefer to follow the current custom? That is the question. His apologists, like Plutarch, describe him as remaining obstinately faithful to the strict observance of a rule which most people—foremost among them Hortensius—vied with each other in evading.[2] His detractors on the other hand, the Pseudo-Sallust and the author of the alleged speech of Fufius Calenus inserted by Dio Cassius in his History, represent him as the very type of the venal pleader—*patronus mercenarius*[3]—whose rapacity is insatiable—*manus rapacissimae*[4]— who goes a-hunting law-suits and puts them up like so many birds, shamelessly battening on other men's misfortunes.[5]

Once again: the Correspondence will decide between these contradictory opinions. The *Letters* show Cicero taking equal care on the one hand not to seem to contravene the law, and on the other to extract the maximum advantage from his labours whether in defence or prosecution.[6] Formally, therefore, his *Letters* belie the imputations of the pamphleteers, but fundamentally they cut the ground from under Plutarch's pious statements. On the evidence of the *Letters* Cicero's respect for the Cincian Law consists in his skill in glossing over or concealing his violations of it.

Once at least, in a letter of 60 to Atticus, then living in Epirus, Cicero expressly refers to the *Lex Cincia*, and the passage is too suggestive not to reproduce it in full: "Now to get back to my own business: L. Papirius Paetus, a good man and an admirer of mine, has given me the books which Servius Claudius left. Since your friend Cincius tells me that I am allowed under the Cincian Law to accept them, I have said that I would willingly receive them if he (Paetus) brought them." This last sentence implies a condition, but it is only a stylistic formula. Cicero knew that the books of Servius Claudius were in Greece, and he was well aware of the difficulties of despatching them. He was far too keen on getting

---

[1] Cf. the text of the *Ann.* XI, 5, quoted p. 89, note 5.
[2] Plut. *Cic.* VIII, 1.   [3] Ps.-Sall. *In Cic.* 5.   [4] Ps.-Sall. *In Cic.* 5.
[5] Dio Cass. XLVI, 6, 1; cf. p. 89, note 3.
[6] It is common knowledge that in Ancient Rome the duties now assigned to the Public Prosecutor fell on what we should now call the plaintiff's lawyer.

them to make any stipulation. He therefore hastens to add—as if
he had forgotten to say it: "Now, if you love me and trust my love
for you, try to ensure, through your friends, clients, guests and
even your freedmen and slaves, that not even a single page be lost:
for I am eagerly interested in the Greek books which I suspect he
left, and in the Latin ones which I know he left."[1] To make sure
that his meaning was understood, he repeats it more explicitly:
"This gift of his is placed in your care. If you love me, see to it
that the books are preserved and forwarded to me. Nothing could
be more welcome. . . . I shall think of this as a little present from
you. . . ."[2]

We must not let ourselves be taken in by the graceful tone of
these affectionate words: a substratum of hypocrisy underlies
them. Cicero had taken Hortensius severely to task in 70 for having
accepted an ivory sphinx[3] from Verres as the price of his legal
advice. He is now himself committing the same breach of etiquette
in welcoming this gift of books from Paetus, but he is doing his
best to make it seem excusable by drawing fine distinctions which
merely betray an uneasy conscience. In the secret hope of mini-
mising the lapse from rectitude he underestimates the value of the
gift he is receiving. This is highly unconvincing and hardly fair to
Paetus: the gift—*munus*—has now become only "a little present"
—*munusculum*—and he devalues it still further by diverting to
Atticus, who is acting only as intermediary, the gratitude due to
the donor. Looked at in this light, the gift seems neatly to slip
through the meshes of the law. To widen them a little more
Cicero shelters himself behind a witty but fantastic interpretation
of the Cincian Law. It forbade the acceptance of either fees or
gifts—*de donis et muneribus*[4]—*ne cui liceret munus accipere*[5]—and

[1] *Ad Att.* I, 20, 7 (26 T.P.): *Nunc, ut ad rem meam redeam, L. Papirius Paetus,
vir bonus amatorque noster, mihi libros eos quos Ser. Claudius reliquit donavit.
Cum mihi per legem Cinciam licere capere Cincius amicus tuus diceret, libenter dixi
me accepturum si attulisset. Nunc si me amas, si tu a me amari scis, enitere per
amicos, clientes, hospites, libertos denique ac servos tuos ut scida ne qua depereat:
nam et Graecis iis libris quos suspicor et Latinis quos scio illum reliquisse mihi
vehementer opus est.* Mid-May 60 B.C.
[2] *Ad Att.* II, 1, 12 (27 T.P.): *Paetus, ut antea ad te scripsi, omnes libros quos
frater suus reliquisset mihi donavit. Hoc illius munus in tua diligentia positum est.
Si me amas, cura ut conserventur et ad me perferantur. Hoc mihi nihil potest esse
gratius; et cum Graecos tum vero Latinos diligenter ut conserves velim. Tuum esse
hoc munusculum putabo.* Mid-June 60 B.C.
[3] On this sphinx, cf. Plut. *Cic.* VII, 7.
[4] Cic. *De Sen.* IV, 10; cf. *De Or.* II, 71, 286.
[5] Festus, s.v. *muneralis lex*, p. 143 M.

this prohibition was directed impartially against all whose services had not been rendered free and gratis—*adversus eos qui pretio causas oravissent*.[1] So a Cincius living in 60, even if he were a direct descendant of the Tribune M. Cincius Alimentus who had got the Cincian Law passed a century and a half before, had no authority to modify its application at his own caprice.[2] Why not recognise the obvious? Caught in the very act, and unable to deny his misdemeanour, Cicero tried from time to time to disarm the just criticism to which his reprehensible conduct had exposed him. His excuses are so thin that they still embarrass his admirers, who are driven, like L. A. Constans, to suggest that Paetus was under no obligation to him for professional services as pleader, and that possibly this whole passage is written in jest.[3] But it is this hypothesis which cannot be taken seriously. We need only read the perfectly clear text of the letter to be convinced that Cicero alludes to the Cincian Law only because he was consciously infringing it, while seeking to persuade others that he was acting in accordance with it.

If he was so prudent as not to admit, even in an intimate and confidential letter, the distorted interpretation he was putting on the law, we can imagine the precautions he took elsewhere to conceal from the public his recourse to questionable practices, general though they were, which might expose him to the attack of enemies ready to invoke against him the severe penalties of a dormant but still existing law.[4] His conduct, moreover, was in such glaring contrast to the uncompromising principles he was wont to proclaim in the Forum that if once it became known he would immediately lose the favour of the electoral *comitia*. The fact is that in this trifling matter of the library of Servius Claudius which Paetus was presenting to him, we see revealed the ulterior motives of a pleader who was seeking to reap two incompatible rewards at the same time: the material benefit of handsome gifts unofficially accepted by him, as by the greater number of his fellows, in the

[1] Tac. *Ann.* XIII, 42.
[2] The Cincius of 60 B.C. was an intermediary between Atticus and Cicero. Cf. *Ad Att.* I, 20, 1 (26 T.P.).
[3] See Constans's edition, I, p. 286.
[4] I think these penalties probably took the form of fines or indemnities eight times the amount of the sums illegally accepted. For under a decision of Augustus infractions of this law carried a penalty of four times. When the Senators in Nero's day wished to increase it, they thought there was nothing better than simply to revert to the original text of the *Lex Cincia*. Cf. Dio Cass. LIV, 18, 3 and Tac. *Ann.* XIII, 42, and above, p. 89.

teeth of official regulations, and the moral prestige attaching to his ostentatious refusal of such gifts and his assumed disinterestedness.

Disinterested? Why, even in his treatise on public duty, *De Officiis*, Cicero thought it only natural that a pleader should be excused from being disinterested. "If it is a question of giving help, which of us," he asks ingenuously, "would not take up the case of a successful and powerful man, in preference to the case of a most excellent man without means? For as a rule we are more inclined to work with a will for the man whose reward seems likely to be prompter and speedier."[1] Since Cicero in a moral treatise so cheerfully takes the side of normal experience and shows so much indulgence for others' practice, it would be extraordinary if he were less indulgent to himself in the exercise of his profession. Inwardly convinced that he was justly entitled to payment for his talents and his trouble, the fact is that he never ceased secretly to expect it, and under his breath to demand it, despite the existing law, though in certain cases he was prepared to agree to deferred payment or to use the windfall for advantageous Exchange transactions.

At the beginning of his career, his successes at the Bar were useful in building up his political future. If they did not always bring in the large sums his clients would gladly have offered, that was because while his reputation was still in the making he coveted distinction more than money. In 70 he stepped forward on behalf of the oppressed Sicilians against Verres, their oppressor. The next year, during his Aedileship, they sent him as a tangible token of their gratitude a cargo of grain. Instead of keeping it for himself, he handed it over to the public store-houses for division amongst those of the Roman Plebs who were in need of relief. Plutarch, to whom we owe this anecdote, is astounded at this generosity.[2] We do not need to share Plutarch's admiration. For the satisfaction Cicero derived is too obvious to be ignored. One of his duties as Aedile was to see to the supply of provisions for the City; he could not have annexed a whole cargo of grain for himself without raising a scandal and lowering himself in the public eye. On the other hand, in contributing it to the public store he was sure to win the favour of the mob, and this is the manoeuvre which, after

---

[1] Cic. *De Off.* II, 20, 69: *Quis est tandem qui inopis et optimi viri causae non anteponat in opera danda gratiam fortunati et potentis? A quo enim expeditior et celerior remuneratio fore videtur, in eum fere voluntas nostra propensior.*

[2] Plut. *Cic.* VIII, 2.

securing the consent of his Sicilian clients, he brilliantly carried out. It was most successful. For, eighteen months later, at the height of his popularity, he was unanimously elected Praetor.[1] Disinterestedness had nothing to do with his action. Cicero did not decline the payment in kind on which he and the Sicilians had agreed. He simply sowed his corn in the electoral soil, where it brought forth admirable fruit. We have here a living example of one of the characteristics of his over-skilful foresight, which as certain passages—hitherto overlooked—in the Correspondence prove, was soon to become a regular feature of his political tactics.

We find the same principle too in some incidental paragraphs of a document which has been preserved for us in the Transalpine Manuscripts of the *Epistulae ad Familiares*.[2] Lengthy though the text is, consisting of no less than fourteen chapters, and despite the fact that it has a coherent unity of subject indicated by the sub-title under which it is commonly referred to—*Commentariolum Petitionis*: Brief Essay on the Duties of a Candidate—this Hand-book of Electioneering is only a letter like those others addressed *Ad Familiares*. This letter was written in 64 by Quintus to his brother—*Quintus Marco fratri salutem dicit*—as the polling for the Consular elections drew near, in which Cicero was a candidate. As I have elsewhere suggested, it seems not improbable that the addressee collaborated in its composition.[3] Its aim was to divert and entertain the brothers during the fatigue and slavery of the campaign, while ostensibly offering to pilot the candidate through the reefs, and ultimately ensure his success in standing for the Presidency of the Roman Republic. The various sections of the letter, systematically arranged, attempt with alarming frankness and humorous gravity to arm the candidate with every weapon, honourable or dishonourable, with all the electioneering tricks, recognised or unmentionable, which might prove decisive in the skilled fencing match of the *comitia*. The fact that these cynical counsels, exchanged confidentially between brothers under cover of their intimacy, with the shame their duplicities imply,[4] should

---

[1] Cic. *In Toga Candida*, 5: . . . *propter dilationem comitiorum ter praetor primus centuriis cunctis renuntiatus sum*; other texts quoted by Drumann-Groebe, V, p. 377.
[2] Cf. the edition of L. A. Constans, I, p. 18.   [3] Cf. my *César* (3), p. 660.
[4] *Comm. Pet.* I, 1 (12 T.P.): *Quamquam plurimum natura valet, tamen videtur in paucorum mensium negotio posse simulatio naturam vincere.*

have been exposed to the public gaze, ought long ago to have revealed the deadly poison which the publishers of the Correspondence, to which we owe our knowledge, were deliberately circulating. Be that as it may, we find amongst these counsels a goodly place accorded to those which permit Cicero to reap, at the right moment and without risk, the reward of his exertions as pleader.

The candidate is invited to treat his clients in the modern sense of the word, as "clients" in the Roman sense, that is to say as persons bound to offer their patron all such services as his dignity and interest require. In the first place, since "a numerous following when going down daily (to the Forum) contributes greatly to dignity and reputation",[1] the candidate must not hesitate to insist that those whom he has defended and who owe him their safety and their acquittal should accompany him.[2] Let him demand this from them point blank, since thanks to him the one has saved his business, another his honour, another his life and all his wealth, and that at no cost, and as there may be no future opportunity to show their gratitude, let them repay now by serving him as his escort.[3]

These recommendations of Quintus imply, of course, that these are cases where Cicero had levied no fee from the accused whom he had defended or the parties whose legal quarrels he had adjusted. But it is, at the same time, abundantly clear that this omission had been carefully calculated and that while his services as their pleader had not been financially costly for them, neither had they been free of obligation. So long as his eyes were fixed on his immediate goal, the consulship, he was willing to defer and transmute his demands. But he did not fail to keep a careful account, and he was fully determined, in one way or another, to exact his due.

If we were still inclined to doubt his intention in this matter, another passage in the *Commentariolum Petitionis* would suffice to

---

[1] *Comm. Pet.* IX, 36 (12 T.P.): *Magnam adfert opinionem, magnam dignitatem cotidiana in deducendo frequentia.*

[2] *Comm. Pet.* IX, 38 (12 T.P.): *Praeterea magnam adfert laudem et summam dignitatem, si ii tecum erunt qui a te defensi et qui per te servati ac iudiciis liberati sunt.*

[3] *Comm. Pet.* IX, 38 (12 T.P.): *Haec tu plane ab his postulato ut, quoniam nulla impensa per te alii rem, alii honestatem, alii salutem ac fortunas omnes obtinuerint, nec aliud ullum tempus futurum sit, ubi tibi referre gratiam possint, hoc te officio remunerentur.*

convince us of it. It reminds us in fact that with an eye to future elections for official posts Cicero was careful, before granting his services to anyone who sought them, to ensure the future co-operation of the new client, and to make his conditions so explicit that when the moment came for the fulfilment of the promise no one could possibly evade the obligation. Try as he might to avoid keeping his promise, the client was helpless; it was necessary only to remind him of the conditions he had taken on himself and promised in the presence of their friends as witnesses.[1] The victim was trapped and compelled to play the part allotted to him by his benefactor. And though "you were never in any way unpleasantly pressing to anyone" it is a simple thing "to let people understand that you have been holding in reserve for this very moment all the things that you think they owe you."[2] It would be difficult to be more clear and open in indicating discreetly that Cicero's apparent disinterestedness at one time was only a long-term investment which he would in due course realise in full, the repayment taking the form of votes and helpful canvassing.

When once he had attained the supreme honour of the consulship and commanded enhanced authority and increased influence—if not greater oratorical skill—why should we suppose that Cicero suddenly began generously to give those services for nothing which he had formerly rendered only for very definite considerations? He had neither changed his way nor lessened his demands. He continued to come to an agreement in advance with his clients on the remuneration (*munus*) which was to be the condition of his services. As he now had, however, all the votes he wanted, his pleadings were henceforward to be paid in cash.

The Roman pleaders had a large choice of methods by which they could collect the fees which the Cincian Law was supposed to forbid their receiving. The simplest, and probably the most usual, was quietly to pass from hand to hand either the sum agreed on with the client or the gift considered its equivalent in value: the ivory sphinx, for instance, which Verres had offered to Hortensius,[3] the cargo of grain which the Sicilians sent to Cicero,[4]

---

[1] *Comm. Pet.* V, 19 (12 T.P.): *Horum in causis ad te deferendis quid tibi eorum sodales receperint et confirmarint scio. Nam interfui . . .*

[2] *Comm. Pet.* V, 20 (12 T.P.): *Fac ut plane iis omnibus quos devinctos tenes discriptum ac dispositum suum cuique munus sit. Et quemadmodum nemini illorum molestus nulla in re umquam fuisti, sic cura ut intellegant omnia te quae ab illis tibi deberi putaris ad hoc tempus reservasse.*

[3] Cf. above, p. 91.   [4] Cf. above, pp. 93–4.

the library of Greek and Latin manuscripts which Servius Claudius had bequeathed to L. Papirius Paetus and which Paetus hastened to pass on to Cicero to liquidate his debt to him.[1] Whatever form the payment took, it could be made only in the most absolute secrecy. Unless he were to make a spectacular refusal and thus advertise, without proving, his entire innocence, the pleader was therefore bound to keep silence, even in intimate letters—which might go astray in transit. It was only in quite exceptional circumstances—and one swallow does not make a summer—that Cicero was emboldened to risk taking Atticus into his confidence, for without his friend's co-operation he could not hope to receive intact the generous gift of Paetus.[2] In giving Atticus the news about it Cicero carefully underestimated its value, while unblushingly protesting that he was scrupulously obeying the legal regulations.

There remained at least two other ways in which a pleader could openly accept the fee that rewarded his labour, by obliterating all connection between the payment and the reason of the payment: by loan or by legacy. Cicero's letters show that he was expert in employing both methods.

The loan saved the pleader's face, for, far from appearing to be his client's creditor, he became his debtor. The device was specious. At best, it was only a paper transaction; at worst, if the loan were negotiated at a low rate of interest or if it were repayable only at a distant date, it might prove highly profitable, for the sum borrowed might advantageously be reinvested, and the larger it was the more lucrative this would be. 'The man grows rich who pays his debts'—so says the proverb. The pleaders of Rome had learnt how to grow rich by contracting debts towards their clients. At least once in his life Cicero took a lesson from their experience in order to acquire what was perhaps the most princely item of his real property: his mansion on the Palatine.[3] Crassus was asking three and a half million sesterces from the purchaser and Cicero had not a farthing by him. Fortunately for him, the year of the sale, 62, saw the conclusion of the Catiline affair. This had brought in its train an avalanche of prosecutions and criminal suits. Everyone was denouncing his personal enemies as having been accessory to the conspiracy and exposing them to public obloquy. L. Torquatus in particular attacked P. Cornelius Sulla, nephew of the dictator Sulla. No one doubted Sulla's complicity, but his birth,

[1] Cf. above, p. 90.   [2] Cf. above, p. 91.   [3] Cf. above, pp. 43-4.

his wealth and his roguery had hitherto protected him. Cicero held all the threads of the conspiracy in his fingers, and a word from him could put an immediate end to this artificial immunity. People were stupefied to see the ex-Consul appear at the bar of the court not as witness for the prosecution but as defending counsel for the accused. The prosecution forthwith collapsed; and Sulla, who had been in danger of exile and the confiscation of his property, was acquitted.[1] In the teeth of all probability, he owed his safety to the man who ought to have ensured his condemnation. The truth is—and the rumour of it soon got about—that Sulla had bought over Cicero.

This is the version given by Aulus Gellius: "When Cicero wanted to buy a house on the Palatine and had not at the moment the necessary money he secretly accepted a loan of two million sesterces from P. Sulla, who at that time was being prosecuted."[2] We have all the less reason to doubt this since, though the *Letters* do not breathe a word of the loan, they do imply it. Sulla's acquittal dates from the second half of 62.[3] Now in the second half of Nov. 62 Cicero, not without some reserve, mentioned to P. Sestius: "I have bought this very house [the house of Crassus] for three and a half million sesterces; know therefore that I am so much in debt that I would fain join in a conspiracy if anyone would have me."[4] A month later he writes banteringly to Atticus: "What news have I to write you? What indeed? The Consul Messalla has bought Autronius's house for 3,300,000 sesterces. What has that to do with me, you ask? This; that this purchase proves that I bought to advantage and people will begin to understand that it was legitimate to use the money of my friends so as to attain some degree of dignity for myself."[5]

How much light these partial confessions throw on the informa-

---

[1] On these facts see Drumann-Groebe, II, p. 439f.; Ed. Meyer, op. cit., pp. 21, 31, etc.

[2] Aulus Gellius, *N.A.* XII, 12, 2: *Cum emere vellet in Palatio domum et pecuniam in praesens non haberet, a P. Sulla, qui tum reus erat, mutua sestertium viciens tacite accepit.*

[3] Cf. Laurand, *Cicéron*, p. 36.

[4] *Ad Fam.* V, 6, 2 (16 T.P.): . . . *emi eam ipsam domum [de Crasso] HS* $\overline{|XXXV|}$ *; itaque nunc me scito tantum habere aeris alieni, ut cupiam coniurare, si quisquam recipiat.*

[5] *Ad Att.* I, 13, 6 (19 T.P.): *Novi tibi quidnam scribam? Quid etiam? Messalla consul Autronianam domum emit HS* $\overline{|XXXIII|}$. *Quid id ad me, inquies? Tantum, quod ea emptione et nos bene emisse iudicati sumus et homines intellegere coeperunt licere amicorum facultatibus in emendo ad dignitatem aliquam pervenire.* Letter dated VI Kal. Febr. viz. Jan. 25, 61 B.C.

tion supplied us by Aulus Gellius! Cicero did not join the conspiracy with the idea of which he was toying. He contented himself with doing a deal with one of the conspirators who, having been detected, flung himself into Cicero's arms. The fiery orator of the Catiline Orations, who without speechifying had promptly put Cethegus, Lentulus and their gang to death, drew on their accomplice Sulla for two million. To put a good face on the transaction, he actually includes him in the number of his "friends". But from a pleader's point of view Sulla was only a client, from whom Cicero had commandeered financial assistance. The loan, the size of which had been agreed on beforehand, was probably a loan in name only; for while congratulating himself on having pulled off such a fine stroke of business Cicero does not speak of borrowing, but only of having drawn on other folks' resources (*facultatibus*); he is giving no thought to dividends to be paid nor to ultimate reimbursement. Later letters, which as we have seen[1] are full of apprehension about the falling due of much smaller sums, have no mention of the payment of either principal or interest to Sulla. As for the complaisant lender, the *Letters* pay no more heed to him than if he had given up the ghost the day after.[2] When he really did die—in 45—the cynical malevolence of the obituary references the *Letters* were prompt to make, comes as a surprise. "The public was much excited about P. Sulla's death, before this was certainly known. Now they have ceased to inquire how he perished. It is enough for them to be sure that he is dead. As for me, I bear the knowledge cheerfully: I am only afraid that Caesar's auctions may flag."[3] And again: "Here we have heard . . . that P. Sulla . . . is dead: some say he was killed by robbers, some that he died of indigestion; the populace doesn't care, since they know for certain that he is cremated. You in your wisdom will bear the knowledge cheerfully . . . They think Caesar will feel it grievous, fearing that his auctions may fall off: Mindius the victualler and Attius the unguent-seller will greatly rejoice to have lost a rival

[1] Cf. above, pp. 59–60.
[2] Such allusions as occur are casual and incidental: in connection with the suit against Gabinius in 54 B.C. *Ad Q. Fr.* III, 3, 2 (151 T.P.) and *Ad Att.* IV, 18, 3 (154 T.P.); regarding his comings and goings in 47 B.C. *Ad Att.* XI, 21, 2 (445 T.P.) and 22, 2 (446 T.P.). Sulla was buying up confiscated properties at derisory prices; cf. the two notes following.
[3] *Ad Fam.* IX, 10, 3 (537 T.P.): *Te tamen hoc scire volo vehementer populum sollicitum fuisse de P. Sullae morte, ante quam certum scierit. Nunc quaerere desierunt, quo modo perierit. Satis putant se scire, quod sciunt. Ego ceteroqui animo aequo fero: unum vereor ne hasta Caesaris refrixerit.* To Dolabella, Jan. 45 B.C.

bidder."[1] These ugly remarks about a dead man are somewhat shocking. They would be inexcusable if P. Sulla had really been a friend of Cicero's. The one thing that excuses them is that the "friendship" was purely fictitious, a mere password, the expedient of a day to cover the all-too-profitable relations he had had with the accused, whom he had so improperly saved from conviction. It is the same type of friendship as his Correspondence and his speeches feign him to have felt towards the numerous testators who bequeathed him the whole or part of their estate in recompense for his earlier professional services.

A very remarkable feature of the Roman law of inheritance was the freedom left to every citizen to leave his property by will to persons outside his family, and even to disinherit his kith and kin to increase the bequest to an outsider.[2] This freedom was exercised during the last century of the Republic all the more widely and all the more frequently that the number of the unmarried was increasing and the birthrate among married couples was falling, so that it was more and more often possible for a testator to make use of this prerogative without disinheriting anyone. In the lifetime of Cicero it became the fashion amongst the nobles and the wealthy to summon the whole crowd of their acquaintances when they were going to seal their will. These people came as the necessary witnesses whose presence was essential to the validity of the will, and also as the probable beneficiaries under the secretly drawn terms of the document, their presence giving a hint of its tenor and contents. When a man was invited to seal and sign the outside of the tablets on the inside of which the testator had inscribed his wishes—without, however, allowing the witness to read them—this was understood as a mark of confidence and esteem, even if the testator did not cherish all the flattering feelings towards his guest that he hoped to convey. It was also a silent indication that the witness's name was amongst the list of legatees—even though a later codicil were to cancel it.

These politenesses were at times undoubtedly superficial and these promises evasive. Cicero admits as much in a letter to Atticus:

---

[1] *Ad Fam.* XV, 17, 2 (541 T.P.): *Nos hic . . . P. Sullam . . . mortuum habebamus: alii a latronibus, alii cruditate dicebant; populus non curabat, combustum enim esse constabat. Hoc tu pro tua sapientia feres aequo animo . . . Caesarem putabant moleste laturum, verentem ne hasta refrixisset: Mindius macellarius et Attius pigmentarius valde gaudebant se adversarium perdidisse.* To Cassius, same date.

[2] Cf. Giffard, *Précis du Droit romain* (3), Paris, 1938, I, p. 438f.

"There would seem to be good reason for your having been invited to the sealing of their will. They want us to think (that their intentions are kindly). I don't know why they should not really be so. What does it matter to us?"[1] Feigned indifference! He and his like would have been sorely grieved if they had not had their fair share of invitations to the will-makings going on around them. To have been excluded would have been a slight, for in those days a man's prestige hung on the possession of wealthy friends, and legacies bore witness to such friendships. When Mark Antony in 44 ventured to taunt Cicero with having received less than his due share of such bequests, Cicero was not slow to bridle up and vigorously protest: "You have denied that bequests have been made to me," he says in the *Second Philippic*;[2] "would that the reproach were justified! Then I should have more friends and relations still living. But how did you get this idea into your head? For I have in all received and accepted more than twenty million sesterces from legacies." How Cicero enjoyed the music of his ringing coins and the pleasure of dinning into Antony's ears the fact that he owes them to the uncounted number of benefactors who had spontaneously thus shown the deep affection and respect they felt for him! What a contrast to Antony! For Antony laid hands on the patrimonies of unknown men, the assets of people whom he compelled to disinherit their sons and nephews in his favour. Hardly were they dead ere he greedily pocketed the fortunes of people who had never laid eyes on him, and of whom he could not have said whether they were white or black.[3] Cicero proudly draws a comparison between the nobility of his own conduct and Antony's base intrigues. None but a friend has ever made Cicero his heir; while rejoicing in a welcome legacy Cicero's heart is wrung with sorrow for the loss of a friend.[4] In this respect, Cicero confesses, Antony's lot is the happier. This moving phrase breaking the invective of

[1] *Ad Att.* XIV, 3, 2 (705 T.P.): *Ad obsignandum tu adhibitus non sine causa videris. Volunt enim nos ita putare. Nescio cur non animo quoque sentiant. Sed quid haec ad nos?*

[2] Cic. *Phil.* II, 16, 40: *Hereditates mihi negasti venire. Utinam hoc tuum verum crimen esset! Plures amici mei et necessarii viverent. Sed qui istuc tibi venit in mentem? Ego enim amplius sestertium ducentiens acceptum hereditatibus rettuli.*

[3] Cic. *Phil.* II, 16, 41: *Te, is quem tu vidisti nunquam . . . fecit heredem. Et quidem vide, quam te amarit is, qui albus aterve fuerit ignoras. Fratris filium praeteriit . . . quem palam heredem factitarat, ne nominat quidem: te quem nunquam viderat fecit heredem . . .*

[4] Cic. *Phil.* II, 16, 40: *Quamquam in hoc genere fateor feliciorem esse te. Me nemo nisi amicus fecit heredem, ut cum illo commodo, si quod erat, animi quidam dolor iungeretur.*

Greed and Unscrupulousness

the *Philippics*, quivers with touching emotion. We are within an
ace of feeling pity for the unhappy orator who was fated to suffer
this bitter grief so frequently when a will was opened under which
he benefited. We pull ourselves together, however, when we take
a look at his Correspondence. We can count on our fingers the
tears he shed over the testators whose decease opportunely replenished his bank account. Amongst all the testators of whom he
was a legatee—an impatient rather than a mourning legatee—very
few indeed, to judge by the tone of his *Letters*, can truly be called
his friends.

The fair name of friend may certainly be justly applied to the
Stoic Diodotus, who died in 59 leaving his fortune to Cicero. Later,
writing to Caesar to commend to his favour a certain Apollonius,
who had been a friend of the dead man's, Cicero devotes a few lines
to praise of Diodotus's immense learning, and speaks of him as one
whom he had known since childhood and the companion of his
studies.[1] Yet in writing to Atticus, the day after Diodotus's death,
he wastes no words in expressing sorrow, but announces the two
pieces of news—the death and the legacy—as drily as an indifferent
stranger and as exactly as a man of business: "Diodotus is dead:
what he has left me may amount to 100,000 sesterces."[2]

We might also at a pinch extend the title of friend to that
Precius[3] to whom Cicero in 54 recommended Trebatius and who,
four years later, died leaving Cicero his heir. Two letters to Atticus
and one to Terentia in the autumn of 51 pay much the same tribute
to his memory. But in all three Cicero has tiresomely combined the
usual financial preoccupations with his expression of somewhat
conventional sorrow. In all three he is torn between regrets and
fears: regrets at having lost someone he was fond of; fears—which
outweigh the regrets—lest his wife's steward, Philotimus, should

[1] *Ad Fam.* XIII, 16, 4 (544 T.P.): *Nam domi meae cum Diodoto Stoico, homine,
meo iudicio, eruditissimo, multum a puero fuit.* It seems highly probable that Diodotus was a freedman of Cicero's who naturally drew up his will in his ex-
master's favour. The same was probably the case with Demonicus, mentioned in
Ad Att. XV, 3, 2 (733 T.P.) and certainly of the physician Alexio, *Ad Att.* XV,
2, 4 (732 T.P.). Both letters date from the second half of May 44 B.C. The list of
legacies which fell to Cicero, and which I have tried to complete, will be found
in Lichtenberger, op. cit., pp. 48–51, and in Drumann-Groebe, VI, pp. 331–3.

[2] *Ad Att.* II, 20, 6 (47 T.P.): *Diodotus mortuus est. Reliquit nobis HS fortasse C.*
Oct. 59 B.C. I adopt the only plausible emendation of the text: that of L. A.
Constans.

[3] *Ad Fam.* VII, 8, 2 (140 T.P.): *Quod scribis de illo Preciano iureconsulto, ego
te ei non desino commendare; scribit enim ipse mihi te sibi gratias agere debere.*
To Trebatius, 54 B.C.

mix himself up in the affair of the legacy, which was no concern of his. Hence the repetition to Atticus of his remarks in which sentiment is oddly blended with practical instructions: "It has been in truth a great grief to me—for I loved the man; see to it that that fellow (Philotimus) does not lay so much as a finger on the legacy of Precius, small as it is. . . .[1] First of all, and it is on this account that anxiety is added to my sorrow, but whatever the size of the legacy may be, I do not want it to be mixed up with the transactions which he (Philotimus) is dealing with for me."[2] At the same time Cicero sent similar instructions from the Piraeus to his wife, Terentia: "As regards the legacy from Precius—which is a matter of great grief to me, for indeed I loved him well—I should wish you to attend to this matter: if the auction should take place before my arrival let our business be looked after by Pomponius (Atticus), or if he is unable, then by our trusty Camillus."[3]

As Cicero was on his way home from his province of Cilicia, he was met in Greece by the news of Precius's death and the legacy left him by his friend. From that moment he was obsessed by the thought of possible interference by Philotimus and how to forestall it. As he confesses, this great anxiety immediately blended with his grief and presently drove his sorrow into the background. Nevertheless, it seems a little over-realistic to confine the expression of his affection for Precius, which his words imply—and which is readily explained by his friend's culture, tastes and profession, for he was a learned lawyer—to a brief parenthesis.[4] But it would be unfair to grudge Cicero his anxiety. The case of Precius, however, stands alone. Everywhere else in the Correspondence, when Cicero touches on the question of his legacies he either omits to refer to any friendship existing between the testator and himself, the heir, or by a wilful indiscretion he hints at relations between them of quite a different type which were obviously incompatible with friendship.

---

[1] *Ad Att.* VI, 9, 2 (282 T.P.): *Hanc, quae mehercule mihi magno dolori est— dilexi enim hominem—procura, quantulacumque est, Precianam hereditatem prorsus ille [Philotimus] ne attingat.* From the Piraeus, Oct. 15, 50 B.C.

[2] *Ad Att.* VII, 1, 9 (284 T.P.): *Hoc primum, quo accessit cura dolori meo, sed hoc tamen quidquid est, Precianum cum iis rationibus quas ille meas tractat, admisceri nolo.*

[3] *Ad Fam.* XIV, 5, 2 (283 T.P.): *De hereditate Preciana, quae quidem mihi magno dolori est, valde enim illum amavi, sed hoc velim cures : si auctio ante meum adventum fiet, ut Pomponius, aut, si is minus poterit, Camillus noster negotium curet.*

[4] *Ad Fam.* VII, 8, 2 (140 T.P.): *Quod scribis de illo Preciano iureconsulto, ego te ei non desino commendare,* etc. To Trebatius, 54 B.C., quoted above, p. 102, note 3.

Greed and Unscrupulousness

There cannot surely have existed any friendship between Cicero and those testators whom he does not even bother to name in writing to his agents when instructing them to see that the bequest is handed over. In 52 for instance, he was in conflict with the co-heirs under a will the maker of which he does not even name. He would like to take possession as soon as possible. The other heirs would prefer to wait before sending his share to him, until they have been able to sell to advantage one of the farm-properties of which the inheritance consists, the need to divide which has made adjudication necessary. Cicero had been informed that M. Marius was prepared to quote a sum in defect of which the co-heirs refused to compromise. He noted the offer and naively added: ". . . Now that I know your price I shall put up a sham bidder rather than let it go at less than that."[1] It is easy to see that he would naturally not give the honour of a name to the man of straw he was here thinking of as a sham bidder. But it is hard to account for the indifference shown by his preserving complete silence about the person whose posthumous generosity he was about to "realise".

In 48 a similar silence causes us even more surprise. Atticus had sent him to Epirus the news of a fresh bequest which had fallen to him. He advises Atticus by return of courier that he has completed without a moment's delay the necessary formalities of acceptance (*cretio*) which will permit Atticus to collect it for him.[2] The sum involved must have been considerable, since this man of affairs—who was good at arithmetic—reckoned that it would suffice to re-establish Cicero's credit and reputation: *ut scribis, ista hereditas fidem et famam meam tueri potest.*[3] Amid the relief and pleasure which this providential windfall has brought him, he finds it superfluous to spare a word of gratitude towards or even of regret for the testator to whom he owes it, and whose very name is unknown to us. No doubt Cicero was at least better acquainted with him than was Mark Antony with the deceased persons whose inheritances Cicero condemns him for extorting.[4] From his *Letters*, however, we should scarcely guess it, and no one can imagine that these deceased persons, whose wills invited him to share the wealth

---

[1] *Ad Fam.* VII, 2, 1 (182 T.P.): *Nunc, quoniam tuum pretium novi, illicitatorem potius ponam quam illud minoris veneat.* To M. Marius, 52 B.C.

[2] *Ad Att.* XI, 2, 1 (407 T.P.): *Litteras tuas accepi pridie Non(as) Febr(uarias); eoque ipso die ex testamento crevi hereditatem.* Feb. 5, 48 B.C.

[3] *Ad Att.* XI, 2, 1 (407 T.P.).   [4] Cf. above, p. 101.

they left and whose identity he shrouds, by way of gratitude, in a contemptuous anonymity, had been properly speaking "friends" of his.

Nor can we count as among his "friends" the obscure individual whom he denotes by the *cognomen* only—Felix—and who in 54 played on him the scurvy trick of dying and bequeathing only a share of his fortune to Cicero, an amount far smaller than Cicero had expected. Even if it is true that this miscalculation was due, as Cicero writes to Quintus, to the carelessness of a secretary[1] and not to the wishes of Felix, it is certain that the heir, partly disappointed in his hopes, wished the careless testator to the devil.[2] Cicero certainly did not treat Felix as a friend, and we are entitled to wonder whether the expected legacy—so cruelly diminished, as it turned out—was not in fact a deferred fee previously agreed upon between the aforementioned Felix and his pleader.[3]

To tell the truth, the same question arises in the case of most of the testators who made Cicero their heir between 58 and 44; their having done so is no proof that they had either won or reciprocated his friendship. There was Lucius Nostius, for instance—who died in 58?—a figure who is known to us only through his freedman and residuary legatee, Zoilus, who, following no doubt in his master's footsteps, had set out to trade in Asia, travelling under the protection of his co-heir, Cicero.[4] Then there was Galeo (who died in 47), a man of whom we know nothing but the name, and whom Cicero must himself have lost sight of, since he merely supposes, but is not sure, that he is his sole heir.[5]

Fufidius (died 47), a Roman *eques*,[6] was another of these "friends". Of him we know only that in 54 Cicero had bought an estate from him for 100,000 sesterces on behalf of his brother Quintus; it was situated in the neighbourhood of Arpinum, and

---

[1] *Ad Q. Fr.* III, 9, 8 (160 T.P.): . . . *eas* [*tabulas*] *vero—lapsus est* [*Felix*] *per errorem et suum et Sicurae servi—non obsignavit, quas noluit eas obsignavit.*

[2] *Ad Q. Fr.* III, 9, 8 (160 T.P.): Ἀλλ' οἰμωζέτω! *Nos modo valeamus* . . .

[3] There is a trace of a still bitterer disappointment. *Ad Att.* XV, 3, 2 (733 T.P.); *Calvae testamentum cognovi, hominis turpis ac sordidi.* This "vile and infamous" fellow Calva would seem to have substituted a will in which Cicero was not mentioned for the will which he had promised—and pretended—to execute in his favour.

[4] *Ad Fam.* XIII, 46 (921 T.P.): Letter recommending L. Nostius Zoilus to the kind offices of Appuleius, at that time Proquaestor of Asia: *coheres meus, heres autem patroni sui.* Possibly 58 B.C.

[5] *Ad Att.* XI, 12, 4 (427 T.P.): from Brundisium, March 8, 47 B.C.

[6] His son was also an *Eques Romanus*: *Ad Fam.* XIII, 11, 1 (452 T.P.), to Brutus 46 B.C. Cf. the letter following; both are letters of recommendation.

pleasant with abundant shade and flowing water.[1] Cicero felt so little affection for Brinnius (died 45) that he was anxious to avoid a meeting with his co-heirs—tiresome men and dishonest he thought them[2]—and he almost immediately got rid of the small farm which had been allotted to him as his share.[3]

We have no knowledge of any of these people apart from Cicero's correspondence; and his references to them are so brief that they remain featureless. They have no ancestry, no fame, nor do they play any political role. At best they belong to the comfortable middle classes who were quietly enriching themselves by working the soil of Italy, or by financially exploiting the distant provinces. We cannot imagine Cicero's having had other than business relations with men so undistinguished. This is, I admit, a pure conjecture. It is, however, irresistibly suggested by the slight glimpse allowed us of their modest silhouette, and strengthened by the details—grudgingly enough supplied—concerning those other testators who, like them, made bequests to Cicero, of whose position and activity the *Letters* tell: Titus Pinnius, Cluvius, and Cicero's excellent "friend" Manius Curius.

Titus Pinnius died in 51, having made Cicero his second heir.[4] His son was naturally the first heir.[5] Normally, this is equivalent to saying that Pinnius had diverted one-fourth of his fortune to Cicero, leaving three-fourths to his own son.[6]

[1] Cic. *Ad Q. Fr.* III, 1, 3 (148 T.P.): . . . *fundum quem tibi proximis nundinis Arpini de Fufidio HS C emeramus. Ego locum aestate umbrosiorem vidi numquam, permultis locis aquam profluentem et eam uberem.* Cicero shows no trace of concern about his inheritance from the owner except a haste to realise it. *Ad Att.* XI, 13, 3 (428 T.P.); 14, 3 (429 T.P.); 15, 4 (430 T.P.). All these letters 47 B.C.

[2] The reason for a meeting was the necessity for the division of the property. *Ad Att.* XIII, 12, 4 (626 T.P.): *De Brinniana auctione accepi . . . litteras . . .* etc. June 23, 45 B.C. The co-heirs would have liked to see him before the auction arranged for July 13. He begs Atticus to dissuade them from coming to bother him at Arpinum: *Ad Att.* XIII, 14, 1 (627, T.P. 3): *id ego plane nolo.* There will still be plenty of time if they meet him on July 6 at Tusculum. (Letter dated June 25, 45 B.C.) Before leaving Arpinum for this interview he hopes that Atticus will be able also to be present, for without Atticus's shrewdness to aid him he is afraid of being outwitted by their cunning. *Ad Att.* XIII, 22, 4 (635 T.P.): *Utinam tu quoque eadem die! . . . Etenim coheredes: a quibus sine tua opprimi malitia . . .* July 4, 45 B.C.

[3] The property was of no great size; cf. *Ad Att.* XIII, 14, 1 (627, T.P. 3): *Hereditas tanti non est.* The sale on July 13 released the property, and the *fundus Brinnanius* that fell to Cicero's share had been sold by him before August 22, 45 B.C.; cf. *Ad Att.* XIII, 50, 2 (667 T.P.).

[4] *Ad Fam.* XIII, 61 (233 T.P.): . . . *me . . . secundum heredem . . . instituerit.* 51 B.C.

[5] *Ad Fam.* XIII, 61 (233 T.P.). At the same time Cicero was made the son's guardian.

[6] According to the formula quoted below, p. 109, note 1,

Greed and Unscrupulousness

Cicero accordingly writes to Publius Silius Nerva, Propraetor of Bithynia, urging him, now that the father is dead, to induce the city of Nicaea to repay to the surviving son and heir the eight millions which Pinnius had lent the town.[1] Thus we see the second heir bringing to bear all the influence at his command on the Governor in whose province lay the town of Nicaea, to ensure that the first heir should recover at the earliest possible moment one of those gigantic loans which Roman bankers were in the habit of granting to provincial borrowers.[2] When drawing up his last will and testament it is not unlikely that T. Pinnius was mindful of the dual service Cicero had at times rendered him, first by his oratorical gifts and legal knowledge and secondly by his great personal influence. However that may be, he was very shrewd in thus linking the fortunes of his son to those of so powerful a personage, and sacrificing a fraction of his wealth to safeguard the bulk of it. No one can doubt that his relations with Cicero were excellent.[3] They may not have been based on an intimate friendship of man to man, but they certainly were securely founded on a close identity of business interest.

The letters telling of the bequest received from Cluvius may fairly bear a similar interpretation. In 45 Cluvius, a banker of Puteoli, left Cicero a charming property which he possessed in that town,[4] which represented an annual income of about 100,000 sesterces. More sensitive to and more preoccupied with the delights of his new estate than with the generosity of his benefactor, Cicero omits to dwell on the virtues of the man to whom he owed the joy of his new inheritance. He never wearies of singing its praises, calculating its value, and even working out the occasional outlays it involved.[5] Yet six years before he had written: "Cluvius of Puteoli is devoted to me and is indeed one of my intimates."[6]

---

[1] *Ad Fam.* XIII, 62 (233 T.P.): *Eius filio . . . pecuniam Nicaeenses grandem debent ad HS octogiens.*

[2] Cf. below, II, p. 346f., the story of loans made by Brutus.

[3] Confirmed by the opening words of the letter indicated in note 1 above: *T. Pinnio familiarissime me usum esse scire te arbitror.*

[4] Cf. above, p. 50.

[5] *Ad Att.* XIV, 9, 1 (712 T.P.): *Primum vehementer me Cluviana delectant.* April 18, 44 B.C.; 10, 3 (713 T.P.): *Quod quaeris iamne ad centena Cluvianum adventare videtur, Scilicet primo anno $\overline{LXXX}$ detersimus.* April 19, 44 B.C.; 11, 2 (714 T.P.): *De Cluviano . . . res ad centena perducitur. Ruina rem non fecit deteriorem; haud scio an etiam fructuosiorem.* April 21, 44 B.C.

[6] *Ad Fam.* XIII, 56, 1 (231 T.P.): *Cluvius Puteolanus valde me observat, valdeque est mihi familiaris.* 51 B.C.; cf. the expression of confidence in him, ibid. VI, 2, 3 (256 T.P.). 50 B.C.

Greed and Unscrupulousness

This is a handsome tribute. Note, however, the purpose of the letter and the person to whom it is addressed! Quintus Minucius Thermus was Propraetor of Asia, and Cicero wanted him to use his powers as Governor to support Cluvius's claims against persons in his province. Cluvius had lent a certain sum on mortgage to Philocles of Alabanda. It was due for repayment and had not yet been paid.[1] There were loans also outstanding in Heraclea Salbace and in Bargylia in Caria which he had failed to recover.[2] Lastly, the town of Mylasa had borrowed moneys from his firm and was now becoming forgetful of the terms attaching to the loan. He would like to see the debtor community give some proof of good faith, such as sending some *ecdici* from Mylasa to Italy. When he had recently been passing through Ephesus on his way to take up the proconsulship of his province of Cilicia, he had succeeded in getting a promise that these should be sent. Without their presence it would be impossible to reach agreement between the parties.[3] On each of these points Cicero makes the claims of Cluvius his own, and tries to enlist the assistance of his correspondent. This makes his letter to Minucius Thermus very instructive. It shows that he was so completely up to date in the Asiatic affairs of the Puteoli bank that he could enumerate them by heart; and so deeply concerned for their success that he subordinated his imperial tasks to the private interests of Cluvius, though the responsibilities of the proconsular office with which he had just been invested ought to have caused him to forget his private files and consecrate himself entirely to his official duties. Comparing this letter of recommendation with the will that later followed we can clearly see that Cicero could have acquired this amount of knowledge and displayed this degree of zeal only by virtue of being the legal adviser of Cluvius. The intimacy between the two men was obviously that of lawyer and client.

---

[1] *Ad Fam.* XIII, 56, 2 (231 T.P.): *Philocles Alabandensis ὑποθήκας Cluvio dedit* . . .

[2] *Ad Fam.* XIII, 56, 2 (231 T.P.): *Praeterea Heracleotae et Bargylietae, qui item debent, aut pecuniam solvant aut fructibus suis satis faciant.* The provincials of Caunos are added: ibid. 3: *Caunii praeterea debent* . . . At the close of the paragraph Cicero gives the impression that Pompey had an interest in the recovery of these loans.

[3] Mylasa and Alabanda; *Ad Fam.* XIII, 56, 1 (231 T.P.) *Μυλασεῖς et ᾽Αλαβανδεῖς pecuniam Cluvio debent. Dixerat mihi Euthydemus, cum Ephesi essem, se curaturum ut ecdicti a Mylasinis Romam mitterentur. Id factum non est. Legatos audio missos esse, sed malo ecdicos ut aliquid confici possit. Qua re peto a te ut eos et iubeas ecdicos Romam mittere.*

Greed and Unscrupulousness

Finally, it is unquestionable that it was ties of this nature which existed between Cicero and Manius Curius, a Roman money-lender living in Patras. We do not know the date of this man's death, nor even whether he predeceased Cicero or not. We cannot therefore be sure that the will he drew up in 50 ever became operative. That, however, is immaterial; it is the testator's intentions which concern us, and they were full of benevolence towards Atticus and Cicero: towards Atticus, whom Curius had made heir to three-quarters of his fortune, towards Cicero, who was to inherit the remaining quarter.[1] The letters are full of Cicero's protestations of friendship for Curius. Their mutual affection was guaranteed by the affection of Atticus, their common friend,[2] and sealed by the hospitality shown to Cicero by Curius in his home in Patras; so generous was it that Cicero might have thought he was in his own house at home.[3] There was between them a constant interchange not only of letters, which we possess, but of services great and small.[4] Each strove to outdo the other in courteous kindness.[5] This is surely more than enough to prove the genuine mutual friendship existing between Curius of Patras and the Consul Cicero? I should not dream of denying it; but at the same time I contend that it was based on their collaboration in business. In the letter of recommendation which Cicero wrote in 46 in favour of Curius to Servius Sulpicius Rufus, Governor of Achaia, he speaks warmly of their business relationship and points out that it is of long standing and began on the first day that Curius made his appearance in the Forum: *amicitia pervetus mihi cum eo est, ut primum in forum venit, instituta . . .*[6] Since Curius, running his banking business in Patras—*M' Curius qui Patris negotiatur*[7]—was neither a pleader nor a lawyer nor a candidate for magisterial office

---

[1] *Ad Att.* VII, 2, 3 (293 T.P.): *Fecit (Curius) palam te [heredem] ex libella, me ex teruncio.* Nov. 50 B.C. The preceding lines contain a lively tribute to M. Curius: *Curius autem ipse sensit quam tu velles se a me diligi et eo sum admodum delectatus . . .*

[2] *Ad Fam.* XIII, 17, 1 (512 T.P.): . . . *maximum vinculum . . . quod est Attici nostri (Curius) familiarissimus.* On this letter of 46 B.C. see below, notes 6 and 7.

[3] *Ad Fam.* XIII, 17, 1 (512 T.P.): . . . *et Patris . . . domus eius tota mihi patuit.*

[4] Letters from Cicero to Curius: *Ad Fam.* VII, 28 (477 T.P.): 30 (694 T.P.); 31 (697 T.P.), dated respectively 46, 45 and 44 B.C.; from Curius to Cicero, 29 (677 T.P.), 45 B.C.

[5] *Ad Fam.* VII, 31, 1 (697 T.P.): . . . *reliquum est ut officiis certemus inter nos.*

[6] *Ad Fam.* XIII, 17, 1 (512 T.P.), 46 B.C.

[7] *Ad Fam.* XIII, 17, 1 (512 T.P.).

Greed and Unscrupulousness

in Rome, this phrase is either meaningless or it implies that Curius appeared in the Forum as a plaintiff and that from the first he chose Cicero to plead for him. This old friend was in fact one of the earliest and one of the most faithful of Cicero's clients. The fact was well known and Cicero had no reason to conceal it, inasmuch as Curius was still living, his will had not been opened and the tenor of it could be guessed only by the small handful of witnesses who in Patras had been present at the sealing.[1] There was thus no question of the *Lex Cincia* coming into play.

The case is conclusive. Even with Curius, whom at first sight we might have thought specially privileged, the friendship for Cicero of those testators who made him their heir was only a more or less spontaneous form of gratitude displayed by his clients of the Forum. Notwithstanding his eloquent disclaimers in the *Philippics*[2] Cicero's correspondence shows that his conduct was no loftier than that of other contemporary pleaders. By stipulating for a place to be reserved for him in his client's will, he evaded the law's veto on accepting a fee or a gift. The bequests which fell to him, or were promised, were intended to pay—with a time-lag which was compensated for by their greater value—the debt owed him by the litigants whose cases he had conducted, or whom he had professionally advised, or for whom he had exerted his influence, who could not meet their obligation directly or openly[3] without infringing the law and exposing him to its penalties.[4]

2. A MAGISTRATE ON THE MAKE

Whether they came to him as gifts masquerading as loans or in the form of testamentary bequests, the moneys that Cicero acquired as pleader had an underhand flavour about them and were tainted by illegality. But in his own eyes, in the eyes of his peers, and in our own they were certainly legitimate. The moral law is satisfied

---

[1] *Ad Att.* VII, 2, 3 (293 T.P.): *Eius testamentum deporto duorum Ciceronum signis obsignatum cohortisque praetoriae.* From Brundisium, 50 B.C. The text is corrupt. I adopt the reading of Tyrrell and Purser.

[2] Cf. above, p. 101.

[3] To meet the overwhelming case against Cicero which the above-indicated letter provides, the pro-Cicero critics, from Bosius to J.-V. Le Clerc, have made the most of the corruption of the text and would have us believe that it conceals a jest. Curius and Cicero were playing at will-making for fun! Cf. J.-V. Le Clerc, XXII, p. 441. The text is easily emended and is crystal-clear. Cicero regarded the will seriously enough to take it after it had been sealed, put it with his kit and carry it off to Rome.

[4] Cf. above, pp. 89–90.

that work done deserves reward. It was perfectly normal for Cicero to want more tangible compensation for his ability and his exertions than the joy an orator feels when giving rein to his genius and eloquence.[1] His only error was obstinately to deny this justified desire and, while behaving like other men, to pose as a bright incarnate exception to the venality of the Roman Bar. His correspondence gives him the lie. All in all, however, this fault is far less grave than when love of lucre tempted him to add to his professional income by taking illicit and regrettable advantage from tampering with the regular course of trials in which he was engaged or to make money out of his political influence or his official position. Without his *Letters*, the historian would be hard put to it seriously to formulate such charges against him, but they emerge from his Correspondence with startling and damning clarity. His reputation for integrity cannot stand up to the distressing evidence against his memory which the *Letters* insidiously supply.

He had undertaken the defence of Milo, the murderer of Clodius. In the quiet of his study he had made of this speech a masterpiece. But, face to face with the members of the jury and the military array with which Pompey had surrounded them, he had delivered it without skill or warmth or force, and had been unable to save his client from sentence of death. This was passed on April 8, 52, by a majority of 38 to 13. Next day Milo fled into exile at Marseilles, and his goods were confiscated.[2] A syndicate was immediately formed to buy them up wholesale and retail them profitably at leisure. It is painful to find Cicero exploiting the fate which he had failed to avert from Milo, but to our horror we find in his correspondence that he did in fact do so. He was, as usual, hard up and was just preparing to set out for Cilicia to take up his post as Governor. In order to procure more funds, he did not hesitate to carve himself a slice from the condemned man's remains, and to insinuate himself into the company that was liquidating the assets, concealing himself for the purpose behind the figure of Philotimus, a freedman of his wife Terentia! The step was too hasty and too blatant. As soon as people detected the presence in the syndicate of this man of straw, they raised a cry of scandal. Cicero was

---

[1] *Ad Att.* IV, 16, 10 (154 T.P.): . . . *dicendi laborem delectatione oratoria consolor.*
[2] Cf. my *César* (3), p. 840.

proudly setting off on his journey as Proconsul when he was over-taken by the indignant protests the discovery had immediately aroused. From Brundisium he felt the urge to write to Atticus in June 51 and offer the outline of an apologia: "I have heard from Rome that my good Milo has written complaining of the wrong I have done him in that Philotimus is one of the joint buyers of his property."[1] He did not attempt to deny the fact. He ex-plained that the step had been taken on the advice of a certain Caius Duronius "whom I knew to be a most intimate friend of Milo's and a most honourable man."[2] The intention was to prevent some evilly intentioned buyer "from robbing Milo of the large number of slaves whom he had taken with him into exile"[3]; fur-ther, to secure the fortune of Fausta—daughter of Sulla and wife of Milo—who had not followed her husband to Marseilles.[4] Lastly, of course nothing should be done against Milo's wishes, nothing could make up for offending him.[5] What now, was to be done? If Milo continued to write complaining letters to his friends, if Fausta shared her husband's feelings, why then Philotimus—"as I personally told him and as he promised me"—must give up any dealings in Milo's property against Milo's will.[6] But were things so grave as all this? Possibly the affair was exaggerated. Atticus must kindly judge, and take such measures as seemed consonant with "my good faith, my name and my interests . . ."[7]

A shilly-shallying explanation if there ever was one, full of after-thoughts and equivocations.

Cicero had no sooner despatched this lame message to Atticus than he received a painfully explicit one from the young Caelius. Caelius did not mince his words. He expressed the hope that the freedman Philotimus would reduce his activities as liquidator and would as honourably as possible give satisfaction to the absent

[1] *Ad Att.* V, 8, 2 (193 T.P.): *Roma acceperam litteras Milonem meum queri per litteras iniuriam meam, quod Philotimus socius esset in bonis suis.*
[2] *Ad Att.* V, 8, 2 (193 T.P.): *Id ego ita fieri volui de C. Duronii sententia, quem et amicissimum Miloni perspexeram et talem virum qualem tu iudicas cognoram.*
[3] *Ad Att.* V, 8, 2 (193 T.P.): . . . *ne illum malus emptor . . . mancipiis, quae permulta secum habet spoliaret.*
[4] *Ad Att.* V, 8, 2 (193 T.P.): . . . *deinde, ut Faustae, cui cautum ille esse voluisset, ratum esset.*
[5] *Ad Att.* V, 8, 2 (193 T.P.): . . . *invito Milone . . . Nihil nobis fuerat tanti.*
[6] *Ad Att.* V, 8, 3 (193 T.P.): *Si ille queritur, si scribit ad amicos, si idem Fausta vult, Philotimus, ut ei coram dixeram mihique ille receperat, ne sit invito Milone in bonis.*
[7] *Ad Att.* V, 8, 3 (193 T.P.): *Si haec leviora sunt, tu iudicabis . . . statues, ut ex fide, fama, reque mea videbitur.*

Greed and Unscrupulousness

Milo and his relatives. Cicero's reputation would be saved in proportion to the zeal and good faith of Philotimus—*ut et Philotimus quam honestissime Miloni absenti eiusque necessariis satis faceret et secundum eius fidem et sedulitatem existimatio tua conservaretur.*[1] Obviously, in the eyes of Caelius, of all in Rome who knew about the matter, Philotimus had been injuring the interests of Milo, and was well known to be merely an understudy for Cicero.

We cannot, in truth, dispute Cicero's participation in the scramble for spoil which followed on Milo's fall and exile. Under cover of Philotimus's name it was he who was buying up his old client's title-deeds and was anxious to re-sell them. He had scarcely arrived in Athens before he was getting worried about them, and was enquiring from Atticus about their fate.[2] It was he who in an underhand way was organising the sale of the exiled man's properties and thus basely enriching himself at his expense. We do not know the total of the sums involved, but they must have been pretty considerable to judge by the appreciable balance left.[3] The fact is that Atticus had in the meantime taken action and, ably supported by Caelius, had succeeded in putting a timely brake on the insatiable greed of the nominal liquidator; to such good purpose indeed, that Philotimus, by an opportune modification of his methods, had soothed the irate partisans of Milo, lulled the suspicions of public opinion and successfully carried out the delicate task with which Cicero for his own sake had charged him. To complete the tale, the miserable collusion of the ex-Consul and the freedman resulted in the end in a bargaining bout between them. Philotimus was not the kind of man obligingly to work for nothing; and Cicero had a tussle with him before making him disgorge his share. Cicero's letters to Atticus keep us abreast of this preposterous epilogue. Cicero was not only furiously angry, but thoroughly ashamed of the mess he had got into, and in writing about it indulged in an unusual amount of precautionary mystery-mongering. For fear of the prejudice against him which would arise if the affair were to be rumoured in Rome, he ventured to write to his friend in enigmas only.[4] The moment he got really to grips with

---

[1] *Ad Fam.* VIII, 3, 2 (197 T.P.). June 51 B.C.
[2] *Ad Att.* V, 10, 4 (198 T.P.): . . . *nec hercule umquam tam diu ignarus rerum mearum fui. Quid . . . de Milonis nominibus actum sit?*
[3] Cf. below, p. 114.
[4] *Ad Att.* VI, 7, 1 (270 T.P.): *Bis ad te antea scripsi de re mea familiari, si modo tibi redditae litterae sunt, graece ἐν αἰνιγμοῖς.* From Tarsus, July 50 B.C.

the subject he suddenly abandoned the Latin he was using and substituted Greek, replacing proper names by periphrases for still greater security.

In a letter from Tarsus, dated June 5, 50, he wrote: "I shall wind up with a mystery. Your wit will divine what it is all about. Judging from some remarks which my wife's freedman casually dropped the other day—you know the fellow I mean [we may safely guess it was Philotimus]—I gather that he has cooked his accounts in the matter of selling the goods of the Crotonian tyrannicide."[1] This "tyrannicide" can be none other than the murderer of the tyrant Clodius, Milo, who was named after the famous athlete of Crotona. In another letter despatched three weeks later from Tarsus, disregarding the ridicule with which he was covering himself, he repeated: "Above all don't overlook the passage (in Greek) in my last letter. My wife's freedman seemed to me, by ever and anon stammering and showing confusion in his interviews and talks, to have done a bit of cooking of the accounts in the matter of the sale of the Crotonian's assets. Try with your usual shrewdness to discover the truth. For your guidance, here are some further details. On leaving the City of the Seven Hills he delivered to Camillus an account of two debts, amounting to 24 and 48 *minae*, and he set himself down as accountable for 24 *minae* from the sale of the Crotonian's estate[2] . . . He came to me to reconnoitre and with some little hope; when he saw it was all up, he went away without any explanation, adding

'I yield, 'twere shame to tarry long',

and he reproached me with the hackneyed proverb 'needs must'."[3]

So the proud Proconsul of Cilicia found himself at odds with the freedman Philotimus over 24 *minae*, that is for 24,000 sesterces resulting from the auction forced on Milo, and this little comedy probably ended much like the famous farce of Maître Patelin. Set a thief to catch a thief. Cicero had hoped to gamble with the secret complicity of Philotimus and to sweep up the crumbs of Milo's fortune; and Philotimus on his side was gambling on the fact that Cicero was both legally and morally estopped from openly

[1] *Ad Att.* VI, 4, 3 (268 T.P.): *Illud praeterea* μυστικώτερον *ad te scribam, tu sagacius odorabere.* . . .
[2] *Ad Att.* VI, 5, 1–2 (269 T.P.). The text is anything but brilliantly lucid.
[3] *Ad Att.* VI, 5, 2 (269 T.P.): The quotation is from Homer, *Iliad* II, 298, the proverb from Plato, *Gorg.* 499 C.

claiming his due[1] and pocketing the whole or part of the ungodly gain.

It is impossible to feel much sympathy for Cicero's having been more or less the dupe of this contemptible intrigue, and having stooped in vain to fish in troubled waters. Even if his professional conscience was silent, surely his honour should have forbidden "dear Milo's" unsuccessful defender to have anything to do with the oppressive sales that followed his unfortunate client's condemnation.

The case is aggravated by the fact that the general situation[2] makes it probable that before thus contravening the most elementary decencies, Cicero had taken refuge under the protection of the then almighty Pompey. Having disposed of Clodius by the dagger of Milo and of Milo by the sentence which followed Cicero's disastrous defence, Pompey had a definite interest in putting the speediest possible end to the lawsuit he had engineered. He was at that time absolute master in Rome and could at will hasten the execution of the sentence he had dictated. Everything points to his having pressed for the speedy sale of the confiscated property and having encouraged Cicero—though it were only by tacit understanding—to take a hand in seeing this through. There could have been no more effective way of compromising his man while taking care to attach him to himself. If this were the case, Cicero crowned his evil action by linking it up with a regular bargaining match of undue influences at the expense of Milo's fortune.

This hypothesis is the more plausible in that this is not the first instance of Cicero's having lent himself to transactions of this type. If it is not proven—though probable—that Pompey had paid him in 52 for his connivance in the Milo affair, his correspondence proves that in 54 he had most definitely, and most paradoxically, exploited financially the alliance he had just concluded with Julius Caesar. In a letter written from Rome to Atticus in Epirus in the early days of July in that year we read these amazing lines: "Caesar's friends, myself and Oppius—burst with rage if you like—have thought little of spending 60 million on the work, about which you used to be so enthusiastic, of opening up the Forum and extending it right up to the Hall of Liberty. We shall make a

---

[1] Hence Cicero's advice, *Ad Att.* VI, 7, 1 (T.P.) 270: *Scilicet nihil est movendum . . .*
[2] See my *César* (3), pp. 839–41.

most glorious job of it. For we are also going to make marble
cloisters in the Campus Martius for the *Comitia Tributa* and we
shall surround it all with a lofty covered colonnade of 1000 paces.
At the same time we shall join the *Villa Publica* to the new work.
You will say: 'What good will all that building be to me?' But why
need I trouble myself about that?"[1]

The news is unexpected, but unmistakably clear. As a dealer in
land and as a contractor, Cicero had accepted from Caesar the
commission—which he will share with Oppius—to proceed with
such friendly expropriations of privately owned property as were
necessary to carry out the plans from which there was to result that
marvel of architecture whose stately ruins have been revealed by
recent excavations: the *Forum Iulii*, Caesar's Forum.[2] The necessary funds were to be supplied by Julius Caesar himself, then
Proconsul of the two Gauls. Cicero was enchanted both by having
been chosen for the undertaking and by the beauty of the work in
which he was to share. At first, hearing the proud and boastful
tone of his voice, we might think that he was preoccupied solely
by his own glory as he shoulders this responsible and heavy task.
On reflection, however, we are compelled to attribute other
thoughts to him. Not only because of the last phrase—'Why need
I trouble myself about that?'—whose casual cynicism jars with
the enthusiasm of the opening. But most of all because of the brief
parenthesis which intervenes between the estimated cost and the
hopes based thereon, and which I purposely omitted above: "60
million: you could not come to terms with the private owners for
less"—*cum privatis non poterat transigi minore pecunia.*[3] This
rouses a suspicion that Cicero was prompted by motives of which
he did not wish to speak. When he thus anticipated the criticism of
people disturbed by the vastness of the sums placed at his disposal,
we can well believe that they considered his estimate excessive,
and were challenging the open or secret profit which the contractors would pocket for themselves. It is difficult *a priori* to

[1] *Ad Att.* IV, 16, 8 [17,7] (144 T.P. = 140 C.): *Caesaris amici—me dico et Oppium,
disrumparis licet—in monumentum illud quod tu tollere laudibus solebas ut forum
laxaremus et usque ad atrium Libertatis explicaremus contempsimus sexcenties HS
. . .; efficiemus rem gloriosissimam: nam in Campo Martio saepta tributis comitiis
marmorea sumus et tecta facturi eaque cingemus excelsa porticu, ut mille passuum
conficiatur; simul adiungetur huic operi villa etiam publica. Dices: "Quid mihi
hoc monumentum proderit?"—At quid id laboramus?*
[2] See my *César* (3), pp. 1008–10.
[3] *Ad Att.* IV, 16, 8 (144 T.P.): This parenthesis occurs in the quotation,
above, note 1, where its omission is indicated.

believe that Cicero would so lightheartedly have plunged into the long labyrinth of negotiations, discussions and painful transactions with innumerable private individuals merely for the sake of Julius Caesar's lovely eyes, or that just for the reflected glory which Caesar's collaborators would enjoy he would so gaily have tackled a job that promised so many headaches and heart-burnings. Commentators on the above letter have not raised the question, but it raises itself. We should dearly like to know what immediate profit Cicero foresaw for himself in the business, apart from the glory he counted on in the future: *efficiemus rem gloriosissimam.*[1]

André Lichtenberger justifiably rejects the idea that Caesar could have imposed such a heavy burden on Cicero without offering him some reward for his services.[2] He suggests some connection between this formidable undertaking and the loan of 800,000 sesterces which we know was made by Caesar to Cicero.[3] This is an ingenious theory, but it is refuted by the silence of the texts and by the discrepancy of dates. In the whole of the Correspondence there is not a line to hint that the loan from Caesar bore any relation to the unusual task with which he had burdened Cicero. And the dates, far from linking the two episodes, definitely dissociate them. The loan of 800,000 sesterces was made in Feb. 54,[4] and not until July of that year[5] did Cicero breathe a word of his taking part in the vast schemes for the *Forum Iulium.*

Surely the best explanation is also the simplest, namely that the expropriations would themselves yield remuneration enough to men who, within the limits laid down for them, would be able to persuade the private owners, one by one, to accept terms agreeable to both parties.[6] Caesar had placed at the disposal of his two contractors a total credit of 60 millions. Provided that they did not exceed this sum, it was up to them to conduct the necessary negotiations as seemed best. So long as the required result was arrived at and the programme satisfactorily carried out, without exceeding the estimate, it was only fair that the surplus should be theirs. It was ere long an open secret in Rome that for the *Forum*

---

[1] *Ad Att.* IV, 16, 8 (144 T.P.).   [2] A. Lichtenberger, op. cit., p. 79.
[3] Cf. above, pp. 62–4.
[4] Cf. *Ad Q. Fr.* II, 10, 4 and 5 (133 T.P. = 132 C.). L. A. Constans assigns this letter to Feb. 12, 54 B.C.
[5] This is the date of *Ad Att.* IV, 16 (144 T.P. = 140 C.).
[6] On the absence in Roman Law of any powers of expropriation for works of public utility, with reference to the *Forum Iulium*, see my *César* (3), p. 1009, note 246.

Iulium the purchase of land alone had cost Caesar 40 million more than he had expected. This figure of 100 million—which was later confirmed by the Elder Pliny[1] and by Suetonius,[2] for by 46 it was notorious—set alongside the 60 million which Cicero quoted, not without some uneasiness and an attempt to excuse it, in his letter to Atticus, puts Cicero in an awkward light. In his capacity of a "dealer in landed property" he does not seem to have had much luck—unless, indeed, he had too much. He may have paid over-large indemnities to the owners of property without having enough skill secretly to secure a proportionate rake-off for himself.

However this may be, Cicero had not in 54 sacrificed his political independence for nothing. He had scarcely signed his pact of allegiance with Caesar before he contrived to make it a profitable investment. We learn from his *Letters* that he supplemented the loan of Feb. 54 with contract profits or regular commissions or clandestine gratuities, which must have enabled him the following summer to arrange purchases of land at the order and for the account of his party leader.

All these transactions look somewhat shady, to put it mildly; and we should have known nothing about them but for the *Letters*. It is the *Letters* which hint at, when they do not reveal, the mean intrigues to which Cicero stooped, sacrificing his duties as pleader, his political liberty and even his personal dignity to his need for money. It is they also which undermine that reputation for incorruptibility which he had built up round his conduct of public affairs.

During the last century of the Roman Republic the expense of election to the magistracy had become ruinously costly. The amount of bribery required to secure election made heavy inroads into the candidate's private fortune, and successful candidates were accustomed periodically to make good the deficit, at the expense of the provincials. In virtue of the laws of Sulla, a man was called on the expiry of his curule office to take over the governorship of some province, and was invested with unlimited powers over the

---

[1] Pliny, *H.N.* XXXVI, 103: *Pyramidas regum miramur, cum solum tantum foro extruendo HS milies Caesar dictator emerit.*

[2] Suetonius, *Caes.* XXVI, 2: . . . *forum de manubiis inchoavit [Caesar] cuius area super sestertium milies constitit.* The agreement between the figures given by Suetonius and Pliny may well be due to their being based on the same official and contemporary document: perhaps one of the inscriptions carried in Caesar's triumph of 46 B.C., at which the Temple of Venus Genetrix was inaugurated in the centre of the *Forum Iulium.* See my *César* (3), p. 1009.

foreign subjects of Rome. This offered him incalculable possi-
bilities of enriching himself. To do justice to Cicero, he appears to
have abstained from these detestable practices, which imprisoned
the governing aristocracy in a vicious circle, in which extortion
was necessary to staunch the wounds caused by bribery and in its
turn accentuated the virulence of bribery.[1] On the conclusion of
his praetorship in 66 he was entitled to a province, and again after
his consulship of 63, but in each case he refused to claim it. Not
until after the passing the *Lex Pompeia de Provinciis* in 52 did he
avail himself of the constitutional practice and accept the proconsulship, to which he had for twelve years been entitled. He was
no doubt in part influenced by the hope of securing an easy
"triumph" to gratify his vanity and satisfy his ambition.

He was Proconsul of Cilicia from July 51 to July 50, and his
conduct there evoked the highest praise from Plutarch,[2] who fills
a whole chapter with the sonorous echoes of the *satisfecit*'s which
Cicero awarded to himself and which fill all his letters of this
period. Before paying homage, with grave respect, to the military
achievements—those pseudo-victories—of which the *Letters* speak
with excessive pride,[3] Plutarch exalts the beneficent kindliness on
which they love to dwell. This benevolent behaviour was supposed
to have nipped in the bud an insurrection brewing amongst the
natives of the province. Above all, Plutarch extols the frugal
simplicity of the Governor's life, the justice, solicitude and scrupulous integrity of his administration. He illustrates each of the
virtues he mentions by examples of his hero's conduct. His
humanity: never did Cicero order anyone to be beaten with rods or
to have his robe torn. Never, even when most roused to anger, did
he utter insulting words or add offending comment to the penalties
inflicted by his court. His frugality: he entertained at his own
expense people whose company he found pleasing, and he treated
them with liberality but without ostentation. No porter guarded
his door. No visitor ever found him still in bed. He rose early and
walked about outside his room, graciously greeting all who came to
pay their respects to him. His effective justice: he restored the
finances of impoverished cities by recovering for them what they
had lost. Without humiliating those who had betrayed their trust,
he compelled them to restore what they had taken. His integrity:

---

[1] Cf. my book, *Des Gracques à Sulla* (2), pp. 127–9, and my *César* (3), p. 1023.
[2] See the text of Plutarch, *Cic.* XXXVI, 1–2.   [3] Cf. below, p. 123.

he refused all gifts save those from kings; and he dispensed the province from paying the cost of his maintenance.

This time Plutarch was building his biography on firm rock; he had, it would seem, no need to fear that Cicero's Correspondence would belie him. It is certainly easy to find in the *Letters* the principal material for this idealisation, and it is no doubt on the *Letters* that Plutarch, or the author on whom he drew, based his findings.

Cicero calculated that no one else would be as well qualified as he to sing his praises, and he filled his letters from Cilicia with the tale of his popularity and of his dazzling virtues. To hearken to him, he has surpassed everyone "in disinterestedness, as in justice, accessibility and humanity".[1] Nor have ever "such incredible crowds, from fields, hamlets and houses and everywhere" poured forth to greet a Governor: "they come to life merely at my approach".[2] He leaves no detail unrecorded of the subtle diplomacy he employed in the public interest to establish harmony between the provincial towns and the farmers of taxes. He reduced the moneylenders' profits by subjecting their investments to the official rate of 1 per cent. per month.[3] At the same time he made it easier for them to recover their debts from the towns by re-floating the city treasuries in the manner sketched by Plutarch. Cicero himself proudly analyses his methods: "There had been amazing thefts from the towns committed by their own Greek magistrates. I myself made enquiries of all who had held office in the last ten years. They confessed openly. So without the disgrace [of exposure] they shouldered the burden of their defalcations and repaid the communities the money [taken from them]. Communities that had paid the tax-farmers nothing for the present quinquennium have now without a murmur paid up in addition the arrears of the previous quinquennium."[4]

We see him in the same way preening himself—if we may use

---

[1] *Ad Att.* V, 21, 5 (250 T.P.): *Vicimus omnes—hoc tu ita reperies—cum abstinentia, tum iustitia, facilitate, clementia.* From Laodicea, Feb. 13, 50 B.C.

[2] *Ad Att.* V, 16, 3 (208 T.P.): *Itaque incredibilem in modum concursus fiunt ex agris, ex vicis, ex domibus, ex omnibus. Mehercule etiam adventu nostro reviviscunt* . . . From Synnada in Phrygia, 51 B.C.

[3] *Ad Att.* V, 26, 11 (250 T.P.): . . . *cum ego in edicto translaticio centesimas me observaturum haberem* . . .

[4] *Ad Att.* VI, 2, 5 (256 T.P.): *Mira erant in civitatibus ipsorum furta Graecorum, quae magistratus sui fecerant. Quaesivi ipse de iis, qui annis decem proximis magistratum gesserant. Aperte fatebantur. Itaque sine ulla ignominia suis umeris pecunias populis rettulerunt. Populi autem nullo gemitu publicanis, quibus hoc ipso lustro nihil solverant, etiam superioris lustri [reliqua] reddiderunt.* From Laodicea, first half of May, 50 B.C.

the word—as he parades his modesty: "There are now no obstacles in my administration, I am mild and admirably courteous. The provincials have access to me with a minimum of difficulty: no question of an ante-room; before dawn I am walking up and down in the house, as I used to do when of old I was a candidate. These things are welcome and not burdensome to me, thanks to old times in military service."[1] Finally he raves above all about the marvellous, exceptional disinterestedness he has displayed. His behaviour as he travels rouses the wonder of the people "nor have I so far any charge to bring against any of my staff".[2] In Asia as in Greece he was welcomed with surprise: "for our coming does not cost anyone a farthing".[3] Once he had arrived in his own province he redoubled his scrupulous goodwill: "The burden on the towns is lightened, for no expense is incurred for me, nor for my Legates, nor for my Quaestor, nor for anyone. You must know that we do not even accept the hay, nor what is customarily given under the *Lex Iulia*,[4] not even firewood; nor when accepting a roof do we ever ask more than four beds; in many places we do not even ask a roof, but usually put up in a tent."[5]

What a contrast to the exactions and the greed, the violence and brutality of most of his compeers, and especially of his immediate predecessor in Cilicia, Appius Claudius Pulcher, whose conduct was "direful and savage, rather that of some wild beast than of a man!"[6] From what a lofty height Cicero looks down on them! How he outshines them in purity! Repudiating their cruelly oppressive lust for money, he refrained from demanding from the wealthy cities the large sums they used to pay in order to avoid having soldiers billeted on them during the winter. The

---

[1] *Ad Att.* VI, 2, 5 (256 T.P.): *Iam cetera iuris dictio nec impedita et clemens cum admirabili facilitate. Aditus autem ad me minime provinciales: nihil per cubicularium: ante lucem inambulabam domi, ut olim candidatus. Grata haec et magna mihique nondum laboriosa ex illa vetere militia.* With many editors I have emended the manuscript reading *imperita* to *impedita*.

[2] *Ad Att.* V, 11, 5 (200 T.P.): *Nos adhuc iter per Graeciam summa cum admiratione fecimus, nec mehercule habeo quod adhuc quem accusem meorum.*

[3] *Ad Att.* V, 14, 2 (204 T.P.): *Nos Asia accepit admirabiliter. Adventus noster nemini ne minimo quidem fuit sumptui.* From Tralles, July 51 B.C.

[4] On the *Lex Iulia de Repetundis* of 59 B.C. see my *César* (3), p. 720.

[5] *Ad Att.* V, 16, 3 (208 T.P.): *Levantur tamen miserae civitates, quod nullus fit sumptus in nos, neque in legatos, neque in quaestorem, neque in quemquam. Scito non modo nos foenum aut quod de lege Iulia dari solet non accipere, sed ne ligna quidem nec praeter quattuor lectos et tectum quemquam accipere quidquam, multis locis ne tectum quidem et in tabernaculo manere plerumque.* Aug. 51 B.C.

[6] *Ad Att.* V, 16, 2 (208 T.P.): . . . *non hominis sed ferae nescio cuius immanis.* Cf. ibid. VI, 1, 2 (252 T.P.): from Laodicea, Feb. 50 B.C.

island of Cyprus alone had paid under this head two hundred Attic talents to Appius Claudius; Cicero during his whole year as Proconsul had literally not asked and was not going to ask a penny.[1]

So mindful was he of the welfare of the Roman subjects under his care, that when the Aediles responsible for organising the games in the Roman amphitheatre requested him to arrange wild-beast hunts in the mountains of Cibyra to replenish their stocks, he first tried to evade the task and only with great regret eventually gave in. He first thanks Atticus for having spread in Rome the rumour that it simply could not be done.[2] Then he argues that he dislikes the idea of imposing this dangerous task on the people of Cibyra.[3] Finally, when further dunned by Caelius, he promises to do what he can to satisfy him, but he cannot guarantee success "because", he adds ironically, "there is an amazing scarcity of panthers, and what panthers there are, are said to be complaining that they are the only creatures for whom snares are laid in my province, and they are thinking of quitting it for Caria."[4]

Nor was this all. He was as generous towards the vassal kings as towards the subject cities. He was resolute in refusing all the tempting bribes offered him by the enemies of King Ariobarzanes, and he would not accept "even the value of a hair"[5] from his kingdom of Cappadocia. He scorned to bring pressure to bear even on rebels. When it came to dividing up the booty won by the capture of Pindenissus, the citadel of the revolt he had quelled, he claims to have given it all to the soldiers with the sole exception of the prisoners. On the third day of the Saturnalia of 51 he would seem to have auctioned them off as slaves and handed over to the Public Treasury the 12 million thereby realised.[6]

---

[1] *Ad Att.* V, 21, 7 (250 T.P.): . . . *civitates locupletes, ne in hiberna milites reciperentur, magnas pecunias dabant: Cyprii talenta Attica CC, qua ex insula . . . nummus nullus me obtinente erogabatur.*

[2] *Ad Att.* V, 21, 5 (250 T.P.): . . . *de Cibyratis pantheris, multum te amo quod respondisti M. Octavio te non putare . . .*

[3] *Ad Att.* VI, 1, 21 (252 T.P.).

[4] *Ad Fam.* II, 11, 2 (255 T.P.): *De pantheris per eos, qui venari solent, agitur mandatu meo diligenter, sed mira paucitas est, et eas, quae sunt, valde aiunt queri, quod nihil cuiquam insidiarum in mea provincia nisi sibi fiat, itaque constituisse dicuntur in Cariam ex nostra provincia decedere.* To Caelius, April 50 B.C.

[5] *Ad Att.* V, 20, 6 (228 T.P.).

[6] *Ad Att.* V, 20, 5 (228 T.P.): *Hilara sane Saturnalia militibus quoque, quibus* [*equis et mancipiis*] *exceptis aliquam praedam concessimus: mancipia venibant Saturnalibus tertiis, cum haec scribebam; in tribunali res erat ad HS $\overline{CXX}$.*

Greed and Unscrupulousness

If Cicero did in fact conduct himself as he says in his letters, we can well understand the gratitude said to be felt towards him even by the mountain peoples from beyond the Taurus.[1] We ourselves are carried away on the wave of enthusiasm which—so he says—led the Cilicians to wish to erect "statues and temples" to him, a tribute which he declined[2]; we are prepared to endorse the verdict he pronounced on himself that his government "had excelled the hopes of all"—*opiniones omnium superavit*.[3] At the same time, we cannot believe that the letters which echo to such a concert of praise could have been published with any hostile intent towards the writer. We have to read them through to the end to detect the false notes which sound in the dangerous turn of an imprudent phrase and which suddenly shatter this entrancing harmony.

As soon as our ear has once caught these false notes, we cease to take seriously the compliments which he so lavishly fires off on every possible occasion. We begin to question the perfect innocence of the intentions he proclaims; we suspect his ostentatious well-doing of being—bluff. We cannot suppose that he was really a skilful governor when we overhear him telling Atticus: "I frequently regret my decision, for not by any device can I extricate myself from this business. What job could be less suited to my temperament!"[4] And again: "A saddle has been placed on the ox: the burden is definitely not one for me."[5] Still worse, we lose faith in his sincerity when he admits that he is afraid his pose of disinterestedness will suffer if his governorship of Cilicia is prolonged: "the glory of my justice and self-restraint will I hope be all the brighter the sooner I depart."[6]

His boast of never having robbed the people of his province looks empty when, to reassure his creditors, he tells of a deposit he entrusted to the bankers of Ephesus before leaving his province.

[1] *Ad Att.* V, 21, 7 (250 T.P.): . . . *Postea vero quam Taurum transgressus sum, mirifica exspectatio . . . nostrarum dioecesium.*

[2] *Ad Att.* V, 21, 7 (250 T.P.): *Ob haec beneficia, quibus illi obstupescunt, nullos honores mihi nisi verborum decerni sino : statuas, fana . . . prohibeo.*

[3] *Ad Att.* V, 16, 3 (208 T.P.).

[4] *Ad Att.* V, 10, 3 (198 T.P.): *Reliqua sunt eius modi, ut meum consilium saepe reprehendam, quod non aliqua ratione ex hoc negotio emerserim. O rem minime aptam meis moribus!*

[5] *Ad Att.* V, 15, 3 (207 T.P.): *Clitellae bovi impositae sunt; plane non est nostrum onus.* Laodicea, beginning of Aug. 51 B.C.

[6] *Ad Att.* V, 17, 5 (209 T.P.): *Et simul hanc gloriam iustitiae et abstinentiae fore illustriorem spero si cito decesserimus.* Tarsus, summer, 51 B.C.

This amounts to a sum of 2,200,000 sesterces in good cistophori,[1] the silver coinage current in the provinces of Asia. The cistophorus weighed more than 12 grammes and was normally exchanged, at a loss, for three Roman denarii of 3.90 grammes each.[2]

Whether this sum was a modest one or a large one for a Proconsul of Cicero's day may be a subject for debate. It cannot, however, be disputed that since it was in local currency, it must have been the produce of his proconsulate. Poor André Lichtenberger, in his anxiety to save Cicero's good name, is gravely embarrassed by this silver harvest. He will not allow himself to explain this bank account as the proceeds of unseemly levies on the provincial people, and prefers to assume that it represents Cicero's due share of the booty taken after the capture of Pindenissus.[3] This is fighting a very feeble rearguard action; for Cicero, we remember, deliberately led us to believe that of all the Pindenissus loot he had kept nothing[4] for himself. If he intentionally misled us on this point, why should we suppose that he did not falsify the facts about other sources of more or less illegitimate gain?

So, as they lie before us, Cicero's letters about his administration of Cilicia are a blend of light and shade. They omit none of the panegyrics which the writer unweariedly lavished on himself, but they give little indications of self-contradiction which tend to discredit his own account of his stewardship. It is the more difficult to combat our suspicions when we detect in at least one instance a flagrant case of untruthfulness and dishonesty.

It will be remembered that on several occasions Cicero condescends to share his praises with his entire following and with his Quaestor in particular—while of course retaining for himself the major credit.[5] Now in regard to the Quaestor, one Lucius Mescinius Rufus, he has most certainly departed from the truth. Let us turn over a few pages of his Correspondence: Mescinius, this paragon of virtue, is no longer worthy of his esteem. In defiance of the regulations of the *Lex Iulia*, Cicero prevents his playing his

---

[1] *Ad Att.* XI, 1, 1 (406 T.P.): *Ego in cistophoro in Asia habeo ad HS bis et viciens.* Epirus, Jan. 48 B.C. *Ad Fam.* V, 20, 9 (302 T.P.): . . . *simul illud cogitare debes me omnem pecuniam quae ad me salvis legibus pervenisset, Ephesi apud publicanos deposuisse: id fuisse HS $\overline{XXII}$.* To Mescinius Rufus, from Rome, mid-Jan. 49 B.C. On this bank deposit, see above, p. 66.

[2] Cf. Mommsen, *Histoire de la monnaie romaine*, I, p. 63, quoted by A. Lichtenberger, op. cit., p. 39, note 7.

[3] A. Lichtenberger, op. cit., p. 40.

[4] See above, p. 122.　　　　　　　　　　　[5] See above, p. 121.

due part in drawing up the statements of accounts.[1] Nothing could be less trustworthy than the Quaestor Mescinius, whose successor is awaited.[2] He describes the man in lurid colours as "irresponsible, lustful and light-fingered".[3] Nor is this all. Reading further we find the robber robbed. Astute as he was, Mescinius lets himself be relieved in a trice of 100,000 sesterces by Cicero himself.

Truth is sometimes stranger than fiction. When requested to repay this sum, which he had weakly borrowed from his subordinate, Cicero had the face to put Mescinius off with a letter whose forced jocularity makes the reader blush: "It remains to mention the 100,000 sesterces about which I remember you wrote to me from Myrina . . . you should be able to bear the loss of the money cheerfully, and to consider that it was not so much your own property as the product of your maintenance allowance and of my generosity."[4] Turn these phrases as we will, they admit of one interpretation only: Cicero had turned a blind eye on the irregularities and exactions of his Quaestor; without committing such acts himself, he profited by those that others committed. He did not personally display such insatiable greed as many Proconsuls of the time, but it is proved that he was by no means the pure and stainless character whose legend the letters sought to create. A few such passages in the Correspondence suffice to disperse the cloud of incense; two or three of their pinpricks judiciously applied deflate the bubble of his superiority. Cicero proudly drapes himself in a robe of righteousness to which he could lay no valid claim. Like others, he was vulnerable; like them—though in lesser degree—he lacked fastidiousness and integrity. His Correspondence, while appearing to substantiate his claims, gives glimpses which turn his vanity to ridicule, unmask his bad faith and rob him of the reputation for incorruptibility that he assumed.

3. AN EVIL-DOER BY PROXY

The *Letters* betray the unworthy motives underlying every act of Cicero's public life, and show each tainted by breach of trust,

[1] *Ad Fam.* V, 20, 1f. (302 T.P.).

[2] *Ad Att.* VI, 4, 1 (268 T.P.): *Nihil minus probari poterat quam quaestor Mescinius.* Tarsus, June 50 B.C.

[3] *Ad Att.* VI, 3, 1 (264 T.P.): *Quaestorem nemo dignum putat. Etenim est levis, libidinosus, tagax.* June 50 B.C.

[4] *Ad Fam.* V, 20, 8 (302 T.P.): *Reliquum est de HS centum milibus de quibus memini mihi a te Myrina litteras esse adlatas . . .* (9) *Tu de HS centum aequo animo ferre debes et existimare eo minus ad te vel de tuis cibariis vel de mea liberalitate pervenisse.*

down to his renunciation of the province of Macedonia. Let us summarise this very simple episode.[1] In 64 Cicero was elected Consul for the following year, 63. His colleague was Caius Antonicus Hybrida, who during the election campaign had made common cause with Catiline in the canvass against Cicero. Catiline was the unsuccessful candidate. Concord between the two Consuls and unity of command was thus compromised at the very moment when the defeated candidate's revolutionary intrigues made such unity more necessary than ever. Cicero realised that this could only be secured if he could lure to his side the opponent whom he had freely insulted in his speeches of recent months,[2] but whom the caprice of the ballot box had foisted on him as colleague.

By great luck Cicero had a pull over Caius Antonius, uncle of the future Triumvir Marcus Antonius (Mark Antony), a degenerate aristocrat, glutton, drunkard and libertine. He was weighed down with debt, and if Cicero could help him to pay off his creditors he would have a good chance of securing at least a satisfactory neutrality from him, if not any devoted co-operation. According to the old *Lex Sempronia*[3] the new Consuls, before taking office, should draw lots to decide which of the two provinces assigned to them by the Senate each should take over on the termination of his Consulship. This gave Cicero the opportunity of wiping out all trace of their recent quarrels and of reconciling himself with Caius Antonius. Antonius felt he had been cruelly used by fate when he drew Cisalpine Gaul, a peaceful province where fighting had ceased, whose inhabitants were semi-citizens of Rome, enjoying the *Ius Latii*[4] secured for them in 86 by Pompey's father. Cisalpine Gaul was adjacent to Rome, easily and effectively controlled by the Senate, and hence it offered little scope for independent enterprise and money-making by its Proconsul. Fortune had perversely awarded to Cicero the province of Macedonia, whose distance and status, whose harmlessly restive population, whose varied agricultural and mineral resources opened up for its Governor a smiling prospect of cheaply won triumphs and of immense profits, some more and some less legitimate.

Cicero had observed Caius Antonius's disappointment and readily divined the cause. He proposed an exchange of provinces

---

[1] Cf. Drumann-Groebe, V, pp. 452–3.
[2] Cf. above, p. 23, the analysis of Cicero's speech *In Toga Candida*.
[3] See my *César* (3), p. 674.
[4] See my *Des Gracques à Sulla* (2), p. 396.

which suited his own tastes and needs, and to Antonius came, as it were, as an answer to prayer: with Cicero's glad concurrence his impecunious colleague set out in due course for Macedonia to recoup his fortunes. By this concession Plutarch concludes that "Cicero employed Antonius as it were a salaried actor to play second fiddle to him on the political stage in the service of his country".[1] Though the comparison is amusing, the compliment is somewhat lame. Plutarch in fact congratulates Cicero on his shrewd psychology and his skill in manoeuvre. Nothing more. At first sight the exchange to which Cicero agreed looks like disinterested generosity. Plutarch gives no such hint. This is strange. Stranger still: Cicero himself in speaking of it makes no such claim. When he made the announcement of it to the Assembly of the people in 63 he simply rejoiced that it foretold harmony between the two Consuls.[2] Thirteen years later, when he recalls it to Cato's memory, he mentions only his renunciation of a triumph.[3] Nowhere[4] does he expressly allude to other sacrifices which his decision might have entailed. Nowhere does he suggest that this exchange proves his magnificent indifference to money. Knowing Cicero's irresistible tendency to self-admiration, we suspect some glaring paradox. This is easily explained when we read the Correspondence. We find there that Cicero had made no sacrifice in renouncing Macedonia: he avoided facing the fatigue and boredom of a provincial exile while surreptitiously establishing a lien on a share of the profits to be extorted by the man taking his place.

A distant propraetorship or proconsulship had no attractions for him; he looked on it with fear and distaste. First because the price of it was usually a long sea-voyage, and we know that the highly pampered Cicero had a horror of seasickness.[5] When he resigned himself in 51 to travel to Cilicia he filled his letters to Atticus with wailings over the discomforts of the journey. When the sea was

---

[1] Plut. *Cic.* XII, 4.

[2] Cic. *De Leg. Agr.* II, 37, 103: *Concordia quam mihi constitui cum collega;* cf. *In Pis.* II, 5: *provinciam Galliam . . . cum Antonio commutavi.*

[3] *Ad Fam.* XV, 4, 13 (238 T.P.): *Itaque et provinciam ornatam et spem non dubiam triumphi neglexi.*

[4] Cf. Cic. *Phil.* XI, 10, 23 (Cicero is addressing Pansa): *Imitare me quem tu semper laudasti, qui instructam ornatamque a senatu provinciam deposui ut incendium patriae omissa omni cogitatione restinguerem.* The verb *deposui* applies rather to Cisalpine Gaul than to Macedonia. Cf. below, p. 128, note 5.

[5] Cf. above, pp. 76 and 81.

calm he was free of both the nausea and the terror which a storm provoked,[1] but he was irritated by the slowness of his craft. He began to grow acutely agitated as soon as the swell began; he thought sea-travel even in July a serious business: *negotium magnum est navigare atque id mense Quinctili*,[2] all the worse because the un-decked boats of Rhodes, in which he was sailing, were cruelly unsuited to withstand the waves.[3] As soon as the wind began to blow his sole thought was to take refuge in the nearest port. Once he had disembarked at Delos: "I don't mean to stir from Delos until I see all the peaks of Gyrae clear",[4] that is until the weather was clearing and calm was about to set in. It would, however, be a mistake to suppose that the only thing Cicero dreaded was the fatigue and danger of the voyage. What he most hated about a province was the uprooting from Rome. As a matter of fact, though Cisalpine Gaul was only a few days' march from the City, he avoided taking it over, just as much as he avoided Macedonia. When Caius Antonius handed it over to him in exchange, he hastened to get the permission of the Assembly to pass it on to Quintus Metellus Celer.[5] He was essentially a stay-at-home, too much in love with his comfort and his routine to feel anything but aversion for any change that threatened to upset the one and endanger the other. In his heart of hearts he hated having to put up with bad temper or bad manners or bad taste of any kind[6] from the people around him. It was only in the air of Rome that he could breathe and thrive: life elsewhere meant deterioration and decay.[7]

When eventually the possible glory of a triumph lured him into accepting the province of Cilicia, he had barely begun the journey before he was bitterly repenting his folly. All the way, from Actium to Athens, from Ephesus to Laodicea, he is haunted by the same grief: to have left Italy! and buoyed up by the same hope: to

[1] *Ad Att.* V, 13, 1 (203 T.P.): *Navigamus sine timore et nausea, sed tardius propter aphractorum imbecillitatem* . . .

[2] *Ad Att.* V, 12, 1 (202 T.P.).

[3] *Ad Att.* V, 12, 1 (202 T.P.): *Nihil quod minus fluctum ferre possit* . . .

[4] *Ad Att.* V, 12, 1 (202 T.P.): *Itaque erat in animo nihil festinare nec me Delo movere nisi omnia ἄκρα Γυρέων pura vidissem.*

[5] Cf. Drumann-Groebe, V, pp. 462–3. See in particular *Ad Fam.* V, 2, 3 (15 T.P.): *Nihil dico de sortitione vestra.* To Metellus Celer, beginning of 62 B.C.

[6] *Ad Att.* V, 10, 3 (198 T.P.): . . . *Sane scio et puto molestiora restare* . . . *sed angor intimis sensibus : ita multa vel iracunde vel insolenter vel in omni genere stulte insulse adroganter et dicuntur et tacentur cotidie.*

[7] *Ad Att.* V, 15, 1 (207 T.P.): *Est incredibile quam me negotii taedet,* etc.

return as soon as ever possible!¹ Feelings so strong and so often expressed inhibited him from pretending that his renunciation of Macedonia in favour of Caius Antonius was an act of virtuous unselfishness when in fact it was the indulgence of his own preferences. Never were his refusals of distant governorships prompted by self-abnegation. He certainly achieved the height of his ambition when, without leaving Italy or even the Forum, without breaking any one of the links which bound him to his beloved Rome, he was able to secure the advantages which would ill have compensated him for exile in barbarous Macedonia, by inducing the Proconsul whom he had despatched thither in his stead to hand over without undue delay a considerable share of the moneys which at his own risk and peril Caius Antonius would manage to squeeze out of the people of his province.

Promises of this kind have, of course, no legal value, since they are based on actual breach of the law and on disregard of the common decencies. They cannot therefore be made the subject of a formal agreement and can only be surreptitiously exchanged. So Cicero alludes to them only in cryptic phrases. But he cannot avoid writing about them, whether to ensure their being understood or to press for their fulfilment. Despite the obscurities in which he veils his meaning he was able to make it clear without giving himself away, and to make it more definite in one confidential communication after another. He entrusted to his letters secrets to which only his correspondents ought to have had the clue, but which were open to the public as soon as his Correspondence was published. No very careful study of the letters of this period about these matters is needed, to draw up a singularly compromising dossier from the opaque or transparent allusions they contain.

We may begin with the only letter addressed to Caius Antonius which the collection *Ad Familiares* has preserved for us. It dates from the beginning of 61 and strikes a harsh note very unusual

---

¹ *Ad Att.* V, 9, 2 (195 T.P.): *Memento curare per te et per omnes nostros, in primis per Hortensium, ut annus noster maneat suo statu, ne quid novi decernatur. Hoc tibi ita mando, ut dubitem an etiam te rogem, ut pugnes ne intercaletur.* Summer, 51 B.C.; ibid. V, 13, 3 (203 T.P.): *Per fortunas! quoniam Romae manes, primum illud praefulci atque praemuni, quaeso, ut simus annui, ne intercaletur quidem.* From Ephesus, July 51 B.C.; ibid. V, 15, 3 (207 T.P.): *Sed feremus [onus] modo, si me amas, sim annuus.* From Laodicea, Aug. 51 B.C.

From these repetitions in his letters it is clear that Cicero was most unwilling to see his governorship extended for a second year. He even goes so far as to hope that there will be no intercalary month inserted into the civil year 51 B.C., which would prolong his stay in the East by another month.

with Cicero. It begins with reproaches and ends with a threat. If Caius Antonius does not alter his behaviour towards Cicero, Cicero will not persevere in his devoted service. In the past Cicero has done everything in his power "to promote your convenience, your honour and your dignity".[1] Cicero's possible future exertions on his behalf "will demand much more zeal from me, more seriousness and more work".[2] If he sees that his efforts are not being squandered in vain and uselessly "I shall continue them with all my power".[3] If, on the other hand, he feels that he is getting no adequate return, why, so much the worse for Caius Antonius: "I will not take the risk of being thought a fool."[4] Writer and reader of this letter understood each other, but these wilfully contorted phrases require explanation.

There is no difficulty about the services which Cicero had already rendered to Caius Antonius. At the close of 64 we have seen Cicero surrendering the proconsulship of Macedonia,[5] where a bad governor was doing his worst. At the end of 62, as we shall presently see, Cicero helped to procure an extension or "prorogation" of his term of office which, while it would lengthen the list of his ill-doings, would equally prolong his opportunity of making profits.[6] As for possible future services, we can guess what they would be. The extortions of Caius Antonius had already been so scandalous that a strong feeling of disapproval had been aroused against him in Rome, and his return would certainly be greeted by a formal prosecution. In such circumstances, amid such embarrassments, faced by this alarming prospect, a threat of rupture of friendly relations smacks of blackmail. If anyone but Cicero were involved, historians would long since have given it this ugly name.

It is not so easy to be certain in what way Caius Antonius was at fault in his behaviour towards Cicero. Cicero expresses himself in veiled language and in roundabout phrases: "That you have never made any return for those services you are yourself the best witness. On the contrary, I hear from many that your conduct towards me

---

[1] *Ad Fam.* V, 5, 2 (18 T.P.): *Omnia enim a me in te profecta sunt quae ad tuum commodum, quae ad honorem, quae ad dignitatem pertinerent.* Jan. 61 B.C.

[2] *Ad Fam.* V, 5, 3 (18 T.P.): . ., . *reliqua, mihi crede, multo maius meum studium maioremque gravitatem et laborem desiderant.*

[3] *Ad Fam.* V, 5, 3 (18 T.P.): *Quae ego si non profundere ac perdere videbor omnibus meis viribus sustinebo* . . .

[4] *Ad Fam.* V, 5, 3 (18 T.P.): *Sin autem ingrata esse sentiam, non committam ut tibi ipsi insanire videar* . . .

[5] Cf. above, p. 126.   [6] Cf. below, pp. 131 and 135.

has had quite the opposite tendency. . . . But I should prefer you
to learn the things that have been reported to me, from Atticus—
to whom they have been no less distressing—rather than from my
letters."[1] Atticus was at the time living on his estates in Epirus and
was in a good position orally to discharge this unpleasant task, for
shortly before, in a letter dated Jan. 1, 61, Cicero, having no fear of
his friend's being indiscreet, had written freely, crossing the t's
and dotting the i's: "There is a freedman of mine, Hilarus by
name, a perfect blackguard, an accountant, and a client of yours.
Valerius the interpreter and Thyillus tell me that they are informed
that this fellow is living with Antonius, and that Antonius in
making his requisitions (from the people of his province) gives out
that a part of them goes to me, and that this freedman is commissioned by me to look after my share in the profits. I was not a
little annoyed, though I did not altogether believe it, but it has
caused some talk. I wish you would look into the matter and if
possible get the rascal out of the country altogether. . . ."[2]

From this it follows that Caius Antonius had let himself go and
was spreading damaging stories about his former colleague, with
whom he had exchanged places, and that he was trying to bolster
up these tales by pointing to the presence and the special
qualifications of Tullius Hilarus. Finally, Cicero wanted to scotch
these scandals and have the rascally freedman kicked out of Macedonia. Looking deeper, however, it is not easy to be sure which
actually carries more weight: the slanderous insinuations of Caius
Antonius or Cicero's angry denials.

Virtuous indignation is impressive, but proves nothing. It was
natural, it was necessary for Cicero to show extreme anger. If he
had quietly ignored the rumours coming from Macedonia he
would have shown them to be true. In the same way, unless he were
willing to acknowledge his complicity, he was forced to decry
Hilarus. To establish his own innocence it was essential fiercely

---

[1] *Ad Fam.* V, 5, 2 (18 T.P.): *Pro his rebus nullam mihi abs te relatam esse
gratiam tu es optimus testis: contra etiam esse aliquid abs te profectum ex multis
audivi . . . Sed ea quae ad me delata sunt malo te ex Pomponio, cui non minus
molesta fuerunt, quam ex meis litteris cognoscere . . .*

[2] *Ad Att.* I, 12, 2 (17 T.P.): *Libertum ego habeo, sane nequam hominem, Hilarum
dico, ratiocinatorem et clientem tuum. De eo mihi Valerius interpres nuntiat Thyillus-
que se audisse scribit haec: esse hominem cum Antonio; Antonium porro in cogendis
pecuniis dictitare partem mihi quaeri et a me custodem communis quaestus libertum
esse missum. Non sum mediocriter commotus neque tamen credidi, sed certe aliquid
sermonis fuit. Totum investiga, cognosce, perspice et nebulonem illum, si quo pacto
potes, ex istis locis amove.*

to denounce his confederate. His brutal abuse by no means carries conviction. What, we ask, should a freedman of Cicero's, who was a client of Atticus to boot and an accountant by profession—*ratiocinator*—be doing with Caius Antonius in Macedonia if he had not gone there to check the accounts? Again, if this Hilarus was the "blackguard" and the "rascal" that Cicero calls him in the letter of 61 and if, knowingly or unintentionally, he had had a share in slandering his patron, how did it come that in 45 he was still enjoying, or had recovered, Cicero's favour sufficiently to be chosen as the bearer of confidential messages[1] and then to be promoted to the delicate position of private secretary—*librarius*[2]—in his household? This promotion after an interval of fifteen years gives the lie to the wrathful exclamations of yore. The further course of the Correspondence gives an ugly look to Cicero's conduct in the Macedonian affair. The *Letters* convince us that in this case there was no smoke without fire; they prove that indirect bargainings were going on between Cicero and Caius Antonius and that a scandalous compact had been arrived at behind the scenes which justified Antonius in his assertions and reflected little credit on Cicero.

Three letters of Cicero's written at the same time and skirting round the same subject offer irrefutable evidence of this collusion. The first of these, addressed to Publius Sestius, was written round about Dec. 10, 62,[3] and is to be found in the collection *Ad Familiares*. The two others, written in Epirus and addressed to Atticus, are of Jan. 25[4] and Feb. 13,[5] 61. One single thread runs through them, and through the two letters to Atticus and to Caius Antonius (Jan. 1, 61,[6] and some time in the course of the same month[7]) which we have just been discussing. From this thread was woven the dark and mysterious intrigue carried on between Cicero and Caius Antonius at the expense of the Macedonians.

This intrigue is clearly to be detected in the elaborate prearranged complications of the message sent to P. Sestius. The

---

[1] *Ad Att.* XII, 37, 1 (579 T.P.): *A te heri duas epistolas alteram pridie datam Hilaro, alteram eodem die tabellario* . . . From Astura, May 4, 45 B.C.

[2] *Ad Att.* XIII, 19, 1 (631 T.P.): *Commodum discesserat Hilarus librarius IV Kal., cui dederam litteras ad te, cum venit tabellarius cum tuis litteris pridie datis* . . . From Arpinum, June 29, 45 B.C.

[3] L. A. Constans, I, p. 110, rightly proposes this date on account of the Tribune, Q. Fufius Calenus, being mentioned as having entered on his office. Cf. Cic. *Ad Fam.* V, 6, 1 (16 T.P.).

[4] *Ad Att.* I, 13, 6 (19 T.P.).

[5] *Ad Att.* I, 14, 7 (20 T.P.).

[6] Cf. above, p. 130.

[7] Cf. above, p. 129.

friendly relations between Cicero and this young politician start from this point and continue to grow steadily stronger from the publication in 60 of the first Catiline Oration. In this speech at the decisive point of his argument[1] Cicero with calculated flattery substituted the name of P. Sestius for the name of Catulus, which he had first used. Stronger the friendship grew till it culminated in 56 in Cicero's undertaking the defence of Sestius in the action *de vi* brought against him by Clodius.[2] In the summer of 62 Sestius had gone to Macedonia as Quaestor to the Proconsul Caius Antonius, and from thenceforth he acted as intermediary between his chief and Cicero. From the first lines of Cicero's letter to him— the only one that has been preserved—we gather that in the course of the preceding months (that is to say in the autumn of 62) he had written one or more letters to Cicero which have been lost or suppressed. In them he had begged Cicero to use his influence with the Senate in such a way that his own and his chief's interests would be safeguarded when the lots were drawn for the provincial posts of the succeeding year. Caius Antonius was anxious to have his governorship extended for another year, while Sestius on the other hand wanted to be relieved of his quaestorship. Then suddenly Sestius changed his mind and put as much urgency into asking to be continued another year in office as he had previously put into clamouring for a successor.

This sudden change of front disconcerted Cicero not a little, but he was nevertheless at pains to reassure Sestius. Having talked things over with the new Tribunes of the Plebs, he thinks he will be able to arrange matters.[3] The proconsular administration of Caius Antonius had already been severely criticised in the Curia, but Cicero had been successful[4] in defending him. As we see, harmony reigned between Cicero and the officials in Macedonia, and we are bound to recognise that relations had been established between them. This fact is vouched for not only by the *Letters*—of

---

[1] Cf. Th. Reinach, *R.E.G.*, 1904, pp. 5–11, and my *César* (3), p. 684. On the date of the publication by Atticus of the *Catiline Orations*, cf. *Ad Att.* II, 1, 3 (27 T.P.) and below, II, p. 475.

[2] Cf. Laurand, op. cit., pp. 44–5.

[3] *Ad Fam.* V, 6, 1 (16 T.P.): . . . *Omnino res tota in mensem Iaunuarium reiecta erat sed facile obtinebatur.* On Sestius's change of front, ibid.: . . . *ut operam darem ne tibi hoc tempore succederetur . . . tamen quod memoria tenebam cuius modi ad me litteras antea misisses . . .*

[4] *Ad Fam.* V, 6, 3 (16 T.P.): *Antonium, etsi eius in me officia omnes desiderant, tamen in senatu gravissime ac diligentissime defendi senatumque vehementer . . . commovi.*

which we have the one isolated sample—but also by the personal messengers whom Sestius sent to Rome and the personal conversations which he arranged for Cicero to have with his family. We have knowledge of the measures which Sestius arranged from Macedonia that his relations in Rome should take in order to make his wishes and his intentions clear. His brother-in-law, Quintus Cornelius, was to call on Cicero and his wife, Cornelia, on Terentia, Cicero's wife: *et Cornelia tua Terentiam convenit et ego cum Q. Cornelio locutus sum.*[1] After these conversations Cicero could not misunderstand the meaning of the letters he had received from Sestius which the visits were to expound, nor be in any doubt as to the direction his own activities were to take.

According to his own account, he acted in the matter with every hope of speedy and complete success: and he lays stress on the trouble he took to achieve success: *plurimumque in eo negotii habui.*[2] After this, and without appearing in any way to connect the two subjects, he makes an appeal for a substantial token of gratitude from the two men he has obliged: "Roused by your congratulations—for in a letter some time ago you wished me good luck on the completion of my purchase of a house from Crassus—I have bought that very house for $3\frac{1}{2}$ millions some time after your congratulations. So you may now picture me as being so deeply in debt as to be ready to join a conspiracy. . . ."[3]

Either these phrases are wholly irrelevant or they mean that in the earlier letters, all trace of which has been lost, and later in the *tête-à-tête* conversations which were not at the mercy of third-party indiscretions, particularly in the talk between Cornelia and Terentia, a connection had been quietly established between the obligations incurred by Cicero towards Crassus for the purchase of his house and the assistance given in the past, and possibly to be given in the future, by Cicero to the man who had taken his place in Macedonia. Naturally no figure will have been openly named; but if we remember that in the summer of 62 Cicero had got two millions from P. Sulla, it is hardly too rash to guess that he was counting on Caius Antonius to find him the one and a half million still needed. Let us pursue our researches. Our hypothesis begins

---

[1] *Ad Fam.* V, 6, 1 (16 T.P.).   [2] *Ad Fam.* V, 6, 1 (16 T.P.).

[3] *Ad Fam.* V, 6, 2 (16 T.P.): *Ego tua gratulatione commotus, quod ad me pridem scripseras velle te bene evenire, quod de Crasso domum emissem, emi eam ipsam domum $\overline{XXXV}$ aliquanto post tuam gratulationem. Itaque nunc me scito tantum habere aeris elieni ut cupiam coniurare . . .*

to take shape and assume the form of fact when we read in the *Letters* that after a certain amount of pressure Caius Antonius gave way and found the money.

On Jan. 1, 61, the Proconsul of Macedonia was still hesitating and Cicero, writing to Atticus, vigorously voices his annoyance: "This . . . business hangs fire—. . . *illa lentum sane negotium*—I never saw anything more shameless, artful and dilatory."[1] Cicero, however, was unwilling to give up hope. A line of Menander's came opportunely into his mind to comfort him: "Chance designs better than we ourselves."[2] Chance in this case meant that Pompey had returned to Italy and was nearing Rome. He was announcing far and wide that when he once got back to the City he would urge the immediate removal of Caius Antonius from the governorship of Macedonia.[3] In face of this intention of Pompey's and the support it found both among patricians and plebs, Cicero dared not venture to come to Caius Antonius's help. Moreover, after the Hilarus incident mentioned above[4] he did not want to.

But grumbling about Caius Antonius would not replenish his coffers, and Crassus was no doubt dunning him for his money, so a few days later Cicero thought again. His hand was strengthened by the general strong disapproval of his former colleague's administration, and he was able to put the slightly veiled pressure on the Proconsul of Macedonia which we saw in his half-reproachful, half-threatening letter of Jan. 61 on which we commented above.[5]

This letter was still on its way to Macedonia, and even if it had already arrived, he could not yet have received a reply to it. Nevertheless he was patting himself on the back for having balanced himself so neatly on the fence, and he was already anticipating the happy effect. On Jan. 25 he wrote to Atticus: "The . . . affair drags on, yet I still have hopes."[6] Eighteen days later, Caius Antonius was stirred to repentance by the fear of threatening disgrace, resigned himself to the inevitable and agreed. Cicero forthwith informed Atticus on Feb. 13, 61: " . . . has fulfilled her promises"—*promissa patravit*.[7] In other words—we are surely justified in assuming this—Caius Antonius has consented to

---

[1] *Ad Att.* I, 12, 1 (17 T.P.): *Nihil ego illa impudentius, astutius, lentius vidi.*
[2] *Ad Att.* I, 12, 1 (17 T.P.).
[3] *Ad Att.* I, 12, 1 (17 T.P.): *Nam mihi Pompeiani prodromi nuntiant aperte Pompeium acturum Antonio succedi oportere . . .*
[4] Cf. above, p. 131.   [6] *Ad Att.* I, 13, 6 (19 T.P.).
[5] Cf. above, pp. 129-30.   [7] *Ad Att.* I, 14, 7 (20 T.P.).

advance Cicero the balance due on the price of his Palatine mansion.

The texts would bear out this conclusion with absolute certainty if we could read the name of Caius Antonius in the places I have provisionally left blank in the above quotations. Three times, however, the space is filled by a feminine pseudonym: once in its original Greek form, $T\epsilon\hat{v}\kappa\rho\iota\varsigma$,[1] twice in its Latin transcription, *Teucris*, a translation of *Troia* or *Troiana*.[2] The Latin forms are probably due to the carelessness of the copyists rather than to the editor's intention. The context seems to point to a Roman ex-Consul, the text mentions a woman denoted by a Greek race-name: "the Trojan woman" or "our Trojan lady". What an odd use of terms! The most recent commentators, succumbing to the logic of the written word, imagine the existence of some woman in Caius Antonius's retinue whom he had chosen to be his representative in his dealings with Cicero.[3] But they fail entirely to identify her and equally to explain the exotic name with which she is encumbered. I believe that I am able to prove: first, that, the better to conceal what it was all about, Cicero changed the man into a woman; and secondly, that he improvised a name which in its oddity would suit the person spoken of and would enable Atticus to recognise at the first glance that he had Caius Antonius in the flesh before him.

Let us first look at this change of sex. Compare two phrases. In the letter to Atticus of Jan. 1, 61 we read: "This Trojan woman (Teucris) is a slow-coach and Cornelius has not called on Terentia since"—*Teucris illa lentum sane negotium, neque Cornelius ad Terentiam postea rediit*.[4] But in the letter to Sestius of the immediately preceding month (Dec. 62) we read: "Your wife Cornelia called on Terentia"—*Cornelia tua Terentiam convenit*.[5] The collation of the two passages makes it obvious that, as propriety would dictate, Terentia twice received a visit not from a man, Cornelius, but from Cornelia, a woman like herself. In the Atticus-letter "Cornelius" is a male disguise for Cornelia, the wife of Sestius, the first hint of whose activity is given in the Sestius letter. A similar metamorphosis, in the reverse direction, has transformed the Trojan into "the Trojan woman". These sex-interchanges were all the easier

---

[1] *Ad Att.* I, 14, 7 (20 T.P.).
[2] *Ad Att.* I, 12, 1 (17 T.P.) and 13, 6 (19 T.P.).
[3] Cf., for instance, L. A. Constans, I, p. 122.
[4] *Ad Att.* I, 12, 1 (17 T.P.).   [5] *Ad Fam.* V, 6, 1 (16 T.P.).

since Cicero contemptuously uses neuter adjectives in alluding to the man whom he considered little better than an animal: "I never met any*thing* more shameless, etc."[1]

Nor is it difficult to solve the riddle of why "the Trojan" and Caius Antonius were one and the same person. To the ancients, as to us, the pig and the swine represented the lowest and most repulsive type of animal[2]; and a Trojan swine was, so to speak, doubly a pig. We may remember too that the French word for sow, or she-pig (*truie*), is derived by direct descent from the Latin (*porca*) *troia* or (*porca*) *troiana*,[3] a term which was used in cooking when preparing a dish of pork, the most highly appreciated delicacy on the menu of a Roman gourmet from the first half of the second century before Christ onwards.[4] This favourite dish was prepared by stuffing the pig's carcase with chickens, thrushes, quails or partridges. When the server carved it in front of the guests, the birds poured out of its body as the armed Greek soldiers poured from the Trojan horse.[5] Hence its name, "Trojan pork".

Now we begin to see daylight. Cicero was fuming with impatience at the procrastinations and delays of Caius Antonius, and found it natural to think of him as a pig, the most despised of all domestic animals for its swinishness. When the Romans wanted to pillory an ignorant ass, they would gibe at him as "a pig trying to teach Minerva"—*sus Minervam docet*.[6] When they sought a metaphor to express their contempt for a glutton, a "slave to his belly", it was again the pig which sprang to mind:

Aut porcus Umber aut obesus Etruscus.[7]

And everyone remembers the line in which Horace makes merry over the pig-herd of Epicurus:

Cum ridere voles Epicuri de grege porcum.[8]

---

[1] *Ad Att.* I, 12, 1 (17 T.P.): *nihil ego illa impudentius, astutius, lentius vidi.*

[2] Cf. below.

[3] Cf. Dauzat, *Dictionnaire étymologique*, Paris, 1938, p. 731.

[4] This we learn from the passage of Macrobius quoted in the next note. He describes this dish in referring to the sumptuary laws which aimed at suppressing it. One of these was passed by C. Fannius Strabo in 161 B.C. Cf. my book, *Des Gracques à Sulla* (2), pp. 70–71.

[5] Macrobius, *Saturn.*, III, 13, 13: *Titius in suasione legis Fanniae obicit saeculo suo quod porcum troianum mensis inferant, quem illi ideo sic vocabant quasi aliis inclusis animalibus gravidum, ut ille Troianus equus gravidus armatis fuit.*

[6] Cf. Festus, p. 310 M.

[7] Catullus, XXXIX, 11.

[8] Horace, *Serm.* I, 4, 16.

137

The word is a common term of abuse[1], and we need not be surprised that in alluding to Caius Antonius Cicero added a further flavour to it by a supplementary allusion to the stuffed pig—*porc à la Troyenne*—which was the pride of his banquets.

For Caius Antonius enjoyed a well-founded reputation as a guzzler and a toper. Quintilian has handed down to us the ugly portrait which young Caelius drew of this sack of food and wine when he prosecuted the Proconsul of Macedonia in 59. This unworthy Roman had been guilty of allowing himself to be surprised by the enemy in the midst of one of his orgies: "Women, his usual attendants, filled the banqueting hall, lying about on all the couches or stretched out here and there on the floor. When they heard the enemy was at hand, half dead with fear, they tried to rouse Antonius; they called his name; they tried to lift him by the neck. Some of them murmured tendernesses in his ear, others treated him more roughly and even struck him. When he recognized voice or touch he stretched out his arms from force of habit, seized and tried to kiss the first he caught hold of. They shouted so loud to wake him that he could not sleep, but so drunk was he that he could not wake himself. Powerless to overcome this semi-slumber, he had to be carried out by his centurions and his mistresses."[2]

This passage is celebrated. We might almost think it had been specially written to justify the name of pig which Cicero had hit on for this gorged carcase, whose belly if it had been cut open would have spilt out food and wine, as the "Trojan pig" spilt out the quails and partridges with which the cook had stuffed it.

There is better to follow. The grotesque comparison which Cicero used was forcefully suggested by the abusive nickname of his former colleague, who as Pliny informs us was currently known as Hybrida,[3] the Half-breed. This may have been meant to imply that Caius Antonius was the offspring of an unequal mating of his father with a low-caste woman of more or less foreign origin,[4]

[1] The cheap pun to which the name of Verres lent itself should be borne in mind. Cf. Plut. *Cic.* VII, 3. and Cic. *Verr.* I, 46, 121: *Negabant mirandum esse ius tam nequam esse verrinum . . . Sacerdotem exsecrebantur qui verrem tam nequam reliquisset.* Here there is a double pun, playing on the name of Verres's predecessor as well as on the name of Verres himself.

[2] Quint. *Inst. Or.* IV, 2, quoted and translated into French by Gaston Boissier *Cicéron et ses amis*, p. 187.

[3] Cf. p. 139, note 2.

[4] Cf. Val. Max. VIII, 5, 4: *Q. Valerius propter obscurum ius civitatis Hybrida cognominatus.*

or more likely it was intended to stigmatise the blend of brutality and debauchery which his enemies thought characteristic of him.[1]

For us the typical half-breed is the mule, the result of mating a mare or a stallion with a donkey; for the Romans—as we learn from the Elder Pliny[2] and from the hint in an epigram of Martial's[3]—it was the result of cross-breeding between a boar and a sow, wild or domesticated, in any case a bastard pig. This being so, the *Teucris* of Cicero's letters is the equivalent of the nickname Hybrida: a masculine cognomen with a feminine ending, an ingenious and transparent substitution in which Atticus must at once have recognised Caius Antonius.

But we must be on our guard. This cryptography in which Cicero indulged, these not-quite-expressed meanings, these toyings with words, were usually designed to conceal the gravity of his matters behind the entertainment of his manner, and to protect himself against indiscreet revelations. He displayed his wit to cover his lapses, but he has, after all, given himself away. Once we know that Teucris is Caius Antonius, we know why Antonius replied to protests against his robberies and extortions that part of the swag was going to Cicero.[4] We cannot fail to see that Cicero, though himself unwilling to quit Rome, took sufficient toll of the takings of his locum tenens in Macedonia to pay Crassus the one and a half million still due, the payment of which would secure him possession of the princely house on the Palatine.[5] Finally, we are sure that Caius Antonius never demanded a penny back.

The *Letters* in fact contain no further reference to this ugly transaction. Not a word is said of demands by Caius Antonius for repayment, not a word of the financial embarrassment which Cicero would infallibly have felt when a large reimbursement of this sort fell due. Everything happens as if, while Cicero had begun by bleeding Antonius, the "stuffed pig" ended by having Cicero at his mercy. Cicero was henceforth pledged to the other's cause by the memory of their complicity and the absolute necessity of concealing it. Even at the risk of drawing down on himself the

---

[1] A more probable view. Cf. Drumann-Groebe, II, p. 390, note 3.
[2] Pliny, *N.H.* VIII, 213: *In nullo genere aeque facilis mixtura cum fero, qualiter natos antiqui hybridas vocabant ceu semiferos, ad homines quoque, ut in C. Antonium Ciceronis in consulatu collegam, appellatione tralata.*
[3] Martial, VIII, 22.
[4] Cf. above, p. 131.   [5] Cf. above, p. 134.

thunderbolts of Julius Caesar,[1] Cicero was compelled willy-nilly to defend the incompetent official whom Caelius prosecuted in 59 for extortion and malversation. Caius Antonius was condemned and went into exile in Cephallenia until 47.[2] To the very end Cicero had to back Caius Antonius, his old enemy of 64, and his unwanted colleague of 63. As late as 44 we still hear him hurling invectives at Mark Antony the Triumvir for his allegedly unjust treatment of this man's uncle, Antonius Hybrida.[3]

If we possessed no documents but Cicero's speeches, we could only admire his courage in 59 and his steadfast loyalty to an old friend in 44. It is fatally unfortunate for him that we have his Correspondence, which reveals the base motives for his conduct and robs him of this undeserved admiration. It was not from courage that Cicero in 59 risked the wrath of Caesar, who was hot on the track of the evil-living Proconsul of Macedonia, but from fear of revelations which would have wrecked his own political career. If his *Letters* bear witness to any steadfastness, it is his steadfast refusal to desist from the hypocritical practice of plundering the provinces by proxy. With Antonius Hybrida in Macedonia, and later with his Quaestor Mescinius Rufus[4] in Cilicia, he displayed a lamentable skill in profiting from other men's extortions. He never appeared as principal, but he always secured his profits. If we take into account the overwhelming evidence against him with which the publishers of his *Letters* have supplied us, we shall have no hesitation in applying to him the damning words of Dalberg about the Prince of Benevento: "He is a monkey who would not risk burning the tip of his paw, even though the chestnuts were for him alone."[5]

---

[1] The very day that Cicero defied the wishes of the Triumvirs by undertaking the defence of Caius Antonius, Caesar and Pompey arranged the adoption of Cicero's enemy, P. Clodius, into a plebeian family (*transitio ad plebem*). Cf. Drumann-Groebe, II, p. 395.
[2] Cf. Drumann-Groebe, II, p. 396, following Strabo, X, 2, 14.
[3] Cic. *Phil.* II, 38, 99.
[4] Cf. above, pp. 124–5.
[5] Louis Madelin, *Talleyrand*, Paris, 1944, p. 273.

Chapter III

UNSTABLE FAMILY LIFE

JUDGING from his Correspondence, the passion for money was so deeply rooted in Cicero's heart that it dominated his married life, infected his most intimate feelings and perverted his dearest family affections.

His married life was distinguished neither by good management nor by logic. About 79[1] he married Terentia, who bore him two children, Tullia and Marcus Cicero.[2] After thirty-three years of life together, he divorced Terentia, at latest at the beginning of 46.[3]

In Dec. 46 he married a second time, a young girl, Publilia, from whom he separated almost at once, in the July following.[4] It was not love but love of money which seems to have accounted for the abrupt variations of temperature in his sentimental relationships.

Apart from the *Letters* we have very little information about Terentia. History has kept no record of her parentage, and gives her no relations except a half-sister, Fabia, who became one of the Vestal Virgins. In 73 Fabia was accused of incest, but after a defence by M. Pupius Piso the judges found her innocent and sent her back to her duties in the temple.[5] We know nothing about Terentia's looks, but we can judge of her jealous affection for Cicero by her anger at Clodia's attempted flirtation with him and the zeal with which she egged him on against Clodius.[6] There is no doubt that she had many qualities: a most unusual constitution which, in spite of the rheumatic pains of her young days,[7] allowed

---

[1] Cf. Drumann-Groebe, VI, p. 610. Cicero was twenty-seven at the time and Terentia ten years or so younger.
[2] See below, p. 146f. and p. 155f.   [3] See below, p. 145f.
[4] Drumann-Groebe, VI, p. 612; and below, p. 148f.
[5] On these facts see the texts collected by Weinstock, *P.W.*, Va, c. 710.
[6] Plut. *Cic.* XXIX, 4.
[7] *Ad Att.* I, 5, 8 (1 T.P.): *Terentia magnos articulorum dolores habet.* 68 B.C.

her to outlast all her contemporaries and to live till over a hundred[1]; an intelligence and force of character of which she gave ample proofs as Cicero's wife,[2] and which in her maturity induced the historian Sallust to marry her after his own divorce, and later after Sallust's death attracted the orator Messalla Corvinus,[3] who became her third husband; lastly, a handsome fortune, the importance of which is not to be overlooked nor its value denied.

Plutarch, who estimated Cicero's patrimony at 900,000 sesterces, calculated Terentia's dowry[4] at 1,200,000 sesterces, and the *Letters* show that this estimate was markedly too modest. Amongst Terentia's properties were at least two blocks of tenement flats, the one at Argiletum, the other on the Aventine, the total income from which varied from year to year between 80,000 and 100,000 sesterces.[5] In the suburbs of Rome, near Tusculum, she also owned some woods, which Cicero visited and thoroughly explored. His jesting reference to them betrays a pleasure not unmixed with pride.[6] She also owned a farm—*vicus*—the position of which we do not know, but the price of which if she had sold it in 58 would have alleviated the distress of her exiled husband.[7] Finally, like many other large land-owners, she had rounded off this property, or perhaps some other we do not know of, by occupying without scruple some State lands which she was making use of just as she chose, without paying the trifling rents rightly claimed by the tax-collectors of the *ager publicus*.[8]

[1] Val. Max. VIII, 13, 6: *Terentia Ciceronis tertium et centesimum explevit annum.*
[2] Cf. below, p. 143f.
[3] St. Jerome, *Adv. Iovin.* I, 48: *Illa interim coniunx egregia et quae de fontibus Tullianis hauserat sapientiam nupsit Sallustio inimico eius et tertio Messallae Corvino.* It is only right to recognise that the Moderns cast doubt on this last marriage with a man the same age as her son: cf. Drumann-Groebe, VI, p. 611; Hammer, *Prolegomena to an Edition of the Panegyricus Messalae,* New York, 1925, p. 91, both of whom treat St. Jerome's information as pure invention.
[4] Plut. *Cic.* VIII, 3.
[5] *Ad Att.* XII, 32, 2 (568 T.P.) of March 28, 45 B.C.; XV, 17, 1 (749 T.P.) of June 14, 44 B.C.; XVI, 1, 5 (769 T.P.) of July 8, 44 B.C. This income alone presupposes a capital of over one and a half million sesterces. Cf. above, pp. 45 and 53.
[6] *Ad Att.* II, 4, 5 (31 T.P.): *Terentiae saltum perspeximus. Quid quaeris? Praeter quercum Dodonaeam nihil desideramus quo minus Epirum ipsam possidere videamur.* From Tusculum, 59 B.C.
[7] *Ad Fam.* XIV, 1, 5 (82 T.P.): *Quod ad me, mea Terentia, scribis te vicum vendituram,* etc. To Terentia, 58 B.C. On the meaning of *vicus* cf. *Ad Att.* I, 4, 3 (9 T.P.): *Quod si adsequor supero Crassum divitiis atque omnium vicos et prata contemno.*
[8] *Ad Att.* II, 15, 4 (42 T.P.): *Terentia pergrata est adsiduitas tua et diligentia in controversia Mulviana. Nescit omnino te communem causam defendere eorum qui agros publicos possideant. Sed tamen tu aliquid publicanis pendis. Haec etiam id recusat.* End of April, 59 B.C.

Not a doubt, this rich woman thoroughly understood how to handle her wealth. Strong in the independence which a marriage *sine manu*[1] conferred on Roman matrons of her rank, she entrusted the management of her affairs to no one, but ran them advantageously herself with the assistance of her steward Philotimus.[2] Though she did not willingly allow her husband to interfere in her business, she lent a skilful hand to Cicero in political matters and in the struggle with Catiline gave moral support with omens taken piously at home.[3] If we are to believe malicious gossip, she was capable of urging him on to take part in transactions which were more remunerative than commendable, especially in helping himself to the confiscated property of convicted men.[4] In any case, as we know, she did not hesitate to play a useful part in her husband's most—or perhaps least—delicate pecuniary negotiations, as we have seen in the case of P. Sestius.[5]

She most assuredly was not the modest housewife who confines herself to domestic duties, but was Cicero's full partner in good or evil fortune, who co-operated in her husband's schemes and at need shared his anxieties and his ambitions.[6] In Cicero's *Letters* we are witnesses of the moral courage with which Terentia sustained him in the days of his worst distress. In the letters of 58, written at the beginning of his exile, she figures not only as a gentle angel of consolation but as the noble instrument of his salvation.

After two thousand years these letters still have power to move us by their passionate sincerity. In one, he seeks to forget his own pain in thinking only of the trials that have overtaken his beloved partner. "Unhappy man that I am! To think that a woman of your virtue, fidelity, uprightness and kindness should have fallen into such troubles on my account!"[7] At the same time he draws comfort and arguments against despair from the courageous example

---

[1] On this form of marriage and its implications see my *Daily Life in Ancient Rome*, Eng. trans. 1941, p. 82f.

[2] Cf. above, p. 102, and below, p. 146.

[3] Plut. *Cic*. XX, 3; Dio Cass. XXXVII, 35, 4. On Terentia's piety cf. *Ad Fam*. XIV, 4, 1 (62 T.P.): . . . *neque di, quos castissime coluisti* . . . and *passim*.

[4] Ps.-Sall. *In Cic*. 3.   [5] Cf. above, p. 132f.

[6] See the portrait of Terentia which Plutarch has drawn, *Cic*. XX, 2. It is no doubt based on Tiro: "neither weak nor timid, but on the contrary ambitious, and, as her husband tells us, taking a larger share in Cicero's political activities than she allowed him to take in her affairs."

[7] *Ad Fam*. XIV, 1, 1 (82 T.P.): *Me miserum, te ista virtute, fide, probitate, humanitate in tantas aerumnas propter me incidisse*. From Dyrrachium, Nov. 25, 58 B.C.

set by his wife: "I learn both from the letters of many and from
the conversation of all whom I meet that you are showing a forti-
tude and courage surpassing belief; and that you give no sign of
fatigue in mind or body from your labours."[1] In another letter he
takes pains to point out that there is no one to whom he writes at
greater length than to her,[2] and in another place that he receives the
letters she sends with so much emotion that "I almost blotted them
out with my tears."[3] He begs her not to rob herself and their boy in
order to supply his needs: "In the name of our unhappy fortunes
beware how we put the finishing stroke to the boy's ruin."[4] He
begs her to take care of herself: "Do not, as you love me, overtax
your delicate constitution," for in the last resort "I see that everything depends on you."[5] Again, he urges her not to attempt to
come out to him: "knowing that a large part of this burden is
borne by you, I should like you to remain where you are."[6] He
calls her, now "my life", now "my beloved".[7] He has the vision
of her "day and night before my eyes".[8] When he thinks of the
future, it is for her sake that he hopes some day to be reinstated
and to recover some of his property: "If fortune has reserved for
me any hope of recovering at any time any position again, I was
not utterly wrong (i.e. in not committing suicide). If these miseries
are to be permanent, I only wish, my darling, to see you as soon
as possible and to die in your arms."[9]

How much happier it would have been for Cicero if nothing had
come down to us but these loving and passionate expressions! For

[1] *Ad Fam.* XIV, 1, 1 (82 T.P.): *Et litteris multorum et sermone omnium per-
fertur ad me, incredibilem tuam virtutem et fortitudinem esse, teque nec animi neque
corporis laboribus defatigari.*
[2] *Ad Fam.* XIV, 2, 1 (79 T.P.): *Noli putare me ad quemquam longiores epistolas
scribere.* From Thessalonica, Oct. 5, 58 B.C.
[3] *Ad Fam.* XIV, 3, 1 (84 T.P.): *Accepi ab Aristocrito tris epistolas, quas ego
lacrimis prope delevi.* Nov. 29, 58 B.C.
[4] *Ad Fam.* XIV, 1, 5 (82 T.P.): *Per fortunas miseras nostras, vide ne puerum
perditum perdamus.*
[5] *Ad Fam.* XIV, 2, 3 (79 T.P.): . . . *valetudinem istam infirmam, si me amas,
noli vexare* . . . ; *video in te esse omnia.*
[6] *Ad Fam.* XIV, 3, 5 (84 T.P.): *Cum sciam magnam partem istius oneris abs
te sustineri, te istic esse volo.*
[7] *Ad Fam.* XIV, 2, 3 (79 T.P.): *Obsecro te, mea vita* . . . ; 4, . . . *valete, mea
desideria, valete.* Cf. below, note 9.
[8] *Ad Fam.* XIV, 2, 3 (79 T.P.): *Mihi ante oculos dies noctesque versaris;*
3, 2 (84 T.P.): . . . *mi ante oculos dies noctesque versatur squalor vester et maeror;*
5: . . . *vale, mea Terentia, quam ego videre videor.*
[9] *Ad Fam.* XIV, 4, 1 (62 T.P.): *Quod si nos ad aliquam alicuius commodi aliquando reciperandi spem fortuna reservavit, minus est erratum a nobis; si haec mala
fixa sunt, ego vero te, quam primum, mea vita, cupio videre et in tuo complexu emori.*
From Brundisium, April 29, 58 B.C.

they form a painful contrast with the dry curtness of the notes[1] written in the quiet and prosperous years that followed. It seems as if Cicero was appreciative of Terentia's virtues only when he was in the midst of perils from which they might rescue him. A dozen years later he would seem to have blue-pencilled these passionate pages and repudiated the sacred debt of which they speak so fervently, as he made up his mind to part from Terentia. His divorce, after more than thirty years of a fertile marriage, rich in noble devotion, was severely judged by his contemporaries. It supplied a favourite subject of abuse to his enemies,[2] and it has reduced his admirers to desperate efforts to find excuses for him—excuses which the inexorable *Letters* render vain.

Plutarch, for instance, admits that Terentia had meantime begun to feel a certain coolness towards her husband; that she showed complete indifference to the disastrous position in which he found himself in 48 in consequence of his having belatedly espoused the tottering cause of Pompey, so soon to be entirely lost; that she even refused to accompany their daughter to Brundisium to comfort him on his melancholy return after Pompey's fatal defeat at Pharsalia.[3] These plausible explanations do not hold water in face of the *Ad Familiares*. These letters prove that the reason why Terentia did not hasten to join him at Brundisium was a letter Cicero wrote to her from there dissuading her from doing so. It is dated Nov. 4, 48. Briefly and coldly he writes: "I trust you may continue to feel your joy at my safe arrival in Italy. . . . But I am afraid that I have taken a course which it is not easy to find a way out of. . . . Therefore give me all the help you can. But I cannot imagine what you can do. It is no good your setting out at this time of the year. The journey is long and dangerous and I do not see that you could be of any use to me, if you were to come."[4] What a change of tone from the eager cries of 58! Evidently the bonds of affection between the two had snapped, and the *Letters* suggest what miserable questions of finance had been the cause of their breaking.

[1] Cf. G. Boissier, *Cicéron et ses amis*, p. 100.
[2] Dio Cass. XLVI, 18, 3.   [3] Plut. *Cic*. XLI, 2.
[4] *Ad Fam.* XIV, 12 (415 T.P.): *Quod nos in Italiam salvos venisse perpetuo gaudeas velim; sed . . . metuo ne id consilii ceperimus, quod non facile explicare possimus. Quare quantum potes, adiuva. Quid autem possis mihi in mentem non venit. In viam quod te des hoc tempore, nihil est; et longum est iter et non tutum; et non video quid prodesse possis, si veneris. Vale. D. pridie Nonas Novembr. Brundisio.*

As we know, Terentia had always been jealous of her financial independence[1]; but we have also seen—if only from Cicero's strong protests against her doing anything of the kind—that she was prepared to sell her property to come to her husband's aid when he was being persecuted by their common enemy Clodius.[2] She continued, after that, to administer her own fortune herself with the aid of her freedman Philotimus. But there is no indication in the letters of the next period that she ever renewed her first generous gesture. Quite the opposite. She may have felt uneasy at Cicero's extravagant expenditure; perhaps she was displeased at seeing him reject Caesar's overtures[3]; in any case, everything seems to indicate that she turned a deaf ear to her husband's requests, and refused to spend a penny to finance outlays of which she disapproved or to make good mistakes which she in his place would not have made. Never again has Cicero opportunity for expressing thanks to her in his letters; worse than that, he has begun to distrust her, and he constantly reiterates instructions to Atticus to keep all his business transactions safe from the curiosity or interference of Philotimus, that is to say of Terentia, whose accountant the freedman was.[4]

When he was away from Italy, he could not avoid letting Terentia take a hand in his affairs, but he distrusted her loyalty and suspected her of contemptible misappropriations at his expense. It is stupefying to read in his own hand a letter to Atticus dated from Brundisium, Aug. 6, 47, which runs: "But as regards Terentia—I pass over innumerable other things—can you beat this? You had written asking her to remit to me here by bill of exchange 12,000 sesterces, that being the balance of the money. She sent me 10,000, saying that was the whole balance. When she makes such a petty theft from so small a sum, you can imagine what she has done in larger matters."[5]

Two months later he addressed to her direct the last of the letters which figure under her name in the *Ad Familiares*. The tone

---

[1] Cf. above, p. 143. [2] Cf. above, pp. 141 and 143.
[3] This is a plausible conjecture. Cf. Neubauer, *Terentia*, in *Wiener Studien*, XXXI, 1909, p. 228.
[4] Cf. above, pp. 102–3.
[5] *Ad Att.* XI, 24, 3 (441 T.P.): *De Terentia autem—mitto cetera quae sunt innumerabilia—quid ad hoc addi potest? Scripseras ut HS $\overline{XII}$ permutaret, tantum esse reliquum de argento. Misit illa HS $\overline{X}$ mihi et ascripsit tantum esse reliquum. Cum hoc tam parvum de parvo detraxerit, perspicis quid in maxima re fecerit? . . . VIII Idus Sextil.*

of it is not only laconic and extremely casual, but actually insulting! "I expect to arrive in Tusculum on Oct. 7 or 8. Let everything be ready there. For there will probably be several people with me, and I think we shall be staying there for some time. If there is not a tub (*labrum*) in the bathing room, let one be put there: similarly, with all other things necessary for life and health. Goodbye."[1]

The comparison of these two documents is instructive. The exact date of Cicero's divorcing Terentia is uncertain; it cannot have been later than the beginning of 46, but it is clear that as early as Oct. 47[2] the idea was present to his mind. This is indicated by his venturing to issue curt orders to his wife as if she were a serving woman, an insult which Terentia's pride could not tolerate. It is no less certain that Cicero was led to this course by the way in which Terentia was tightening the purse-strings and reducing him to living on his own resources. It might look as if he wanted to divorce her because of a derisory discrepancy of 2000 sesterces which she was supposed to have pocketed. But in fact he did not come to this decision on this pretext, a trifling one bordering on the absurd, but for the deeper reason underlying it. A careful calculation of the debits and assets of his wife had convinced him that Terentia had not the slightest intention of using her £ s. d. to caulk the leaks in his budget—a process of which she had grown weary; he realised that henceforward she was determined to carry on her person the keys of her private cash-box. The partner who for thirty-three years had shared his life was now refusing to subsidise him further. He could make up the loss of wifely contributions by levying them from another. His plan of divorce was the first step towards finding a new wife, a rich and compliant one, whose income he could enjoy and whose dowry he could consume at will.

Some months later, when people noticed this elderly man, who would never see his sixtieth birthday again,[3] fluttering round with

---

[1] *Ad Fam.* XIV, 20 (449 T.P.): *In Tusculanum nos venturos putamus aut Nonis aut postridie. Ibi ut sint omnia parata. Plures enim fortasse nobiscum erunt et, ut arbitror, diutius ibi commorabimur. Labrum si in balineo non est, ut sit: item cetera quae sunt ad victum et ad valetudinem necessaria. Vale. Kal. Octobr. de Venusino.*

[2] On June 3, 47 B.C., at Brundisium Cicero had already been contemplating a divorce. This was why he was anxious that Atticus should persuade Terentia to make a will in favour of Tullia and young Marcus Cicero. *Ad Att.* XI, 16, 5 (431 T.P.): *. . . ut Terentiam moneatis de testamento. Tempora monent, ut videat ut satisfaciat quibus debet . . .*

[3] Cf. the text quoted on p. 148, note 2, and the date fixed, p. 149.

an adolescent girl, they thought he was merely suffering from one
of those amorous attacks to which men entering on the last lap are
notoriously liable, and more than one of his circle with lewd or
contemptuous wit made merry over this belated outburst of
romance. For a moment Cicero joined in the laughter, and when
they teased a man of his age and with his infirmities[1] for flirting
with a mere girl, he retorted with gallant gaiety, "but she'll be a
woman tomorrow!"[2] Plutarch reports the rumour that Cicero was
carried away by the fresh beauty of Publilia and could not resist
the desire it roused in him.[3] But at the same time he explodes this
theory by referring to Tiro's biography of his master. In this Tiro
denies any basis for this interpretation. The truth, according to
Cicero's freedman—who cannot be suspected of ill-will—is quite
different: Cicero married for the second time—to pay his debts.
Publilia's father had died leaving a large fortune. The Voconian
Law of 169 deprived the daughter of a rich man of the right of
inheriting from her father. Since he could not make his daughter
his heir, the father had recourse to the usual device of the day, and
entrusted a large share of his property to Cicero as trustee and
guardian of Publilia, on the understanding that it should be handed
over to her on her marriage. To avoid having to make restitution,
Cicero could think of nothing better than to marry his ward himself. Bartolo was at least in love with Rosine, while Cicero—on
Tiro's evidence—was in love only with Publilia's fortune.[4] The
Letters certainly give us no direct clue to the motives which suddenly plunged Cicero into so ill-assorted a match. This omission
leaves us a choice between the two explanations current in Rome—
it is hard to say which is the less flattering; it is easily explained if
the hostile publishers of Cicero's Correspondence had the idea
that it would be no harm to leave this ugly uncertainty to damage
his memory.

---

[1] Cf. Fufius Calenus *ap.* Dio Cass. XLVI, 18, 3.

[2] Quint. *Inst. Or.* VI, 3, 75: *Cicero obiurgantibus quod sexagenarius Publiliam virginem duxisset, cras mulier erit, inquit.*

[3] This rumour is said to have been corroborated by Terentia, cf. Plut. *Cic.*
XLI, 4: ". . . married a young maiden for the love of her beauty, as Terentia
upbraided him."

[4] Plut. *Cic.* XLI, 5: ". . . married a young maiden . . . for her riches, to
discharge his debts. For the young woman was very rich, and Cicero had the
custody of her estate, being left guardian in trust; and being indebted many
myriads of money, he was persuaded to marry her and use her money to satisfy
his creditors."

On the *Lex Voconia* see my book *Des Gracques à Sulla* (2), p. 70.

Unstable Family Life

On the other hand the *Letters* add a touch of comedy to this marriage, by mile-stoning the ridiculously short time it lasted. A letter written to Atticus in Oct. or Nov. 46 shows Cicero already anxious to remarry, but hesitating between various possible choices, amongst whom Publilia is not one.[1] Now, as early as March 28, 45, he was already so much out of love with his young wife that he fiercely opposed the wish she had expressed to come and rejoin him in the loneliness of Astura, where he had gone for peace and quiet, and to hide his grief over the death of his daughter Tullia.[2] Rather than meet Publilia he would prefer, he said, to fly somewhere else, and he begged Atticus to let him know the latest date to which he could safely prolong his stay without running the risk of a meeting which he wanted to avoid at any cost.[3] On July 26, 45, he instructed Atticus to come to an arrangement as soon as possible with Publilia's brother—to whose guardianship she would be transferred after a divorce—about the conditions of a separation which was already being gossiped about in Rome and which he was impatient to push through.[4] So, three months after his second marriage, Cicero was already regretting it, and the divorce which dissolved it followed seven months[5] after the wedding. This speedy disillusionment hardly favours the theory of an invincible passion, any more than his previous hesitation over the choice of a desirable bride.

Plutarch, still, it would seem, following Tiro, explains Cicero's haste to break the matrimonial knot so recently tied, by the cruel way Publilia had wounded him in making no secret of her pleasure at the death of Tullia[6] (about mid-Feb. 45), of whom she was jealous. Here again the *Letters* provide no precise evidence either to weaken or to strengthen a story which Cicero's friends have

[1] *Ad Att.* XII, 11 (502 T.P.): Tyrrell and Purser date this brief letter, in which Cicero is hesitating between various *partis* (one of them Pompey's daughter), in the second intercalary month of 46 B.C., which fell between October and November of the Julian Calendar. Cf. my *César* (3), pp. 736 and 1030 and my memoir on *César et Cléopatre*, Ghent, 1937, p. 49.

[2] Cf. above, p. 51.

[3] *Ad Att.* XII, 32, 1 (568 T.P.): *Illud autem quod fore video, ipsum volo vitare, ne illi* (i.e. Publilia, her brother and her mother) *ad me veniant. Et una est vitatio, ut ego (avolem). Nolim, sed necesse est. Te hoc nunc rogo ut explores ad quam diem hic ita possim esse, ut ne opprimar.*

[4] *Ad Att.* XIII, 34 (647 T.P.): *Tu velim . . . illud in primis cum Publilio me absente conficias, de quo quae fama sit, scribes . . . Non mehercule arbitror. Etenim haec decantata erat fabula.*

[5] Cf. Drumann-Groebe, VI, p. 622.

[6] Plut. *Cic.* XLI, 7: "His grief was so excessive that he put away his new-married wife, because she seemed to be pleased at the death of Tullia."

been pleased to seize on as a proof of his paternal affection, and which his worst enemies have no doubt exploited in support of the disgraceful rumours they were spreading about his relations with his daughter.[1] At the same time, the *Letters* give colour to another most unpleasant suggestion that would reduce both the divorce and the marriage to the proportions of an "affair".

None of the later letters about Publilia or her family mention anything but the practical arrangements for liquidating the marriage. On July 30, 45, Cicero was already wishing that the whole matter might be cleared up before his return from Astura, which was expected on Aug. 5,[2] and that Atticus would be able in his absence to finish the necessary transactions with the Publilii: *me enim absente omnia cum illis transigi malo.*[3] But he had to come off his horse. The divorced girl's brother seems to have indulged in a lot of bargaining in his discussions with Atticus: *Publilius tecum tricatus est.*[4] This was quite natural, for it was Publilius who stood to gain by an arrangement which automatically released Publilia from the authority of the husband she had lost, only to place her under her brother's. If it was tempting for Cicero to get some reward for the transfer of the property which reverted of right to the brother as his sister's guardian, it was natural that Publilius for his part should devote some ingenuity to losing as few feathers as possible in the cock-fight. It seems not improbable that he was at one moment so disgusted that he thought of renouncing the privileges which Cicero was trying to whittle away, and actually tried to enlist Caerellia's influence to bring about an impossible reconciliation between husband and wife.[5] At last an agreement was reached. About July 11, 44, Publilius was able to put 200,000 sesterces in the bank, out of the 400,000 which Cicero recognised as due.[6] From the imperfect record, we get the impression that Cicero, after having replenished his treasury by an improvised marriage with his ward, for whom he was trustee, managed to get something for his pains from the formalities which attended the divorce that ended it.

[1] Cf. above, p. 82.
[2] *Ad Att.* XIII, 34 (647 T.P.): . . . *ne ante Nonas mihi illuc veniendum sit.*
[3] *Ad Att.* XIII, 47B, 2 (654 T.P.).
[4] *Ad Att.* XIV, 19, 4 (725 T.P.). From Pompeii, May 8, 44 B.C.
[5] Cf. above, p. 61. *Ad Att.* XIV, 19, 4 (725 T.P.): *Huc enim Caerellia missa ab istis est legata ad me* . . . May 8, 44 B.C.; ibid. XV, 1A, 4 (730 T.P.): *Caerellia vero facile satisfeci, nec valde laborare mihi visa est* . . . May 17, 44 B.C.
[6] *Ad Att.* XVI, 2, 1 (772 T.P.): . . . *(nos) qui de residuis $\overline{CCCC}$ HS $\overline{CC}$ praesentia solverimus* . . .

This is not all. From the chronological data they give us we may gather from the Cicero letters a clue as to his change of mind and an idea why he suddenly allowed the quarry he had marked down for himself to escape, and threw Publilia over with her accompanying subsidies. Cicero's letter to Atticus in which he set in motion the procedure for his divorce, consigning his love to the scrap-heap, was written, as we have seen, on July 26, 45.[1] Now another letter to Atticus, near neighbour to this in the collection, was written on Aug. 2, 45. From it we learn that Cicero had just had a conversation with Balbus about the conditions under which an auction of the properties left by Cluvius would take place, for the benefit of the co-heirs, who could not otherwise equitably divide up the assets: *de auctione proscribenda equidem locutus sum cum Balbo*.[2] This means that we can reckon that the death of the rich banker who had placed Cicero's name in his will must have taken place at least a fortnight before. This important legacy,[3] bequeathed without restriction or reserve, was much better value than a trustee-guardianship saddled with matrimonial slavery. Whatever our opinion may be about an actual connection of cause-and-effect between the inheritance of Cluvius and the repudiation of Publilia, it cannot be gainsaid that the former immediately preceded the first hint we get of the second. There is a disturbing coincidence between the two. At least in Cicero's Correspondence, the second divorce follows the second marriage just as the expedients of a debtor, logical in their inconsistency, vary as receipts happen to grant or to deny him respite.

2. TOO CASUAL A FATHER

It is even worse to find, as we read the Correspondence, that even Cicero's paternal feelings seem to have been blunted by his personal ambition.

First with regard to his son. Reading his other works, we easily find traces of affectionate solicitude for him. It was for Marcus and with him as interlocutor that the father composed in 46 the dialogue *Partitiones Oratoriae*, and it was to him that he dedicated his Essay on Duty, the *De Officiis*,[4] in which he inserted a proud

---

[1] Cf. above, p. 149.

[2] *Ad Att.* XIII, 37, 4 (657 T.P.).   [3] Cf. above, pp. 107-8.

[4] *Ad Att.* XV, 13A, 6 (795 T.P.): Nos hic φιλοσοφοῦμεν—quid enim aliud?—et τὰ περὶ τοῦ καθήκοντος magnifica explicamus προσφωνοῦμενque Ciceroni. Qua de re enim potius pater filio? Deinde alia. Quid quaeris?

account of the young man's gallantry in Pompey's army at Pharsalia.[1] Other writers give us the same impression. Plutarch calls to witness the series of letters which Cicero addressed in Greek to the Athenian rhetorician Gorgias, to whom he had entrusted the boy's education. He was alarmed by the lax morals of this bad master and the alarming tolerance he showed towards the escapades of his pupils, and with a harshness of tone unusual with him bade the man be ashamed of such deplorable lack of control.[2] Quintilian praises Cicero as a purist who, he says, never failed when writing to his son to impress sternly on him the need for correct speech.[3] Now, we have none of the letters to Gorgias, none of the letters Cicero wrote to his son, and none which Marcus wrote to his father. Though these were overflowing with affectionate kindness[4]—as we know—the publishers of the collections which have come down to us have left them out. The most they have condescended to do is to preserve the commonplace effusion in which Marcus confesses his past errors to Tiro, promises to avoid repeating them, and renews his demand—a thing on which he had set his heart—for a slave, preferably a Greek, competent to act as his secretary and to copy out his lecture notes, "which waste a lot of my time."[5]

From the *Letters*, as we have them, we get the impression that Cicero's relations with his son were never anything but intermittent, spasmodic and indirect.[6] In the Atticus letters, where his name frequently recurs, it is not so often a question of eloquence or morals as of economy and the balancing of his budget.

No doubt Cicero loved this boy, whose entry into the world he

---

[1] Cic. *De Off.* II, 13, 45: *Cum te Pompeius alae alteri praefecisset, magnam laudem et a summo viro et ab exercitu consequebare, equitando, iaculando, omni militari labore tolerando.*

[2] Plut. *Cic.* XXIV, 4.

[3] Quint. *Inst. Or.* I, 7, 34: *In filio, ut epistolis apparet, recte loquendi asper quoque exactor.*

[4] *Ad Fam.* XVI, 21, 1 (786 T.P.): *Cum maximam cepissem laetitiam ex humanissimi et carissimi patris epistola.* Marcus Cicero to Tiro, Sept. 44 B.C.

[5] *Ad Fam.* XVI, 21, 8 (786 T.P.): *Peto a te ut quam celerrime mihi librarius mittatur, maxime quidem Graecus; multum mihi enim eripietur operae in exscribendis hypomnematis.* This haste to get hold of a good secretary throws doubt on the sincerity of Marcus's good resolutions. This letter was shortly after followed by a note where Marcus complains with some asperity how rarely Tiro writes to him and says how much he enjoys informal news from home (*Ad Fam.* XVI, 25 = 793 T.P.).

[6] Contemporaries, especially young Quintus, reproach Cicero for his harsh conduct towards his son. Cf. *Ad Att.* XIII, 37, 2 (657 T.P.): *Ciceronem meum vexari.* From Tusculum, Aug. 2, 45 B.C.

had greeted with more pride than enthusiasm[1]; he took an interest in his studies; he was worried about his amusements; he applauded his progress: but only when he had nothing else to do, and then without overmuch eagerness or curiosity. The older the boy grew, the more the father seems to have delegated his parental responsibility to the tutors he chose for him: Paeonius,[2] then Dionysius,[3] and finally those who were to complete the young orator's apprenticeship in Athens.[4] After that, Cicero's main concern was to secure an income for his offspring that would reflect credit on himself.[5] In this matter he displayed what would seem an extravagant generosity if it had not aimed solely at increasing his own importance.[6] Marcus would have been content with 72,000 sesterces a year.[7] Cicero started him off straight away with an allowance of 80,000, for which he assigned the rents of the tenements at the Argiletum and on the Aventine. These, by the way, were the property of his wife, which means that it was from Terentia's purse that the father's liberality was financed.[8] With these large sums at his disposal, and released from scruples by the counsel of the frivolous Gorgias, we can well imagine that Marcus kept more than secretaries and copyists in his train, and the

---

[1] *Ad Att.* I, 2, 1 (11 T.P.): *Filiolo me auctum scito, salva Terentia.* After July 17, 65 B.C. There is more tenderness in two letters alluding to Marcus's babyhood, one of Jan. 20, 60 B.C. *Ad Att.* I, 18, 1 (24 T.P.) in which he says he has no other happiness than in the time spent at home with his wife, little Tullia and sweet little Marcus: *ut tantum requietis habeam quantum cum . . . mellito Cicerone consumitur :* the other of Nov. 25, 58 B.C. *Ad Fam.* XIV, 1, 1 (82 T.P.) in which he sympathises with Terentia on the small boy's being so early aware of sorrow and misery: *Quid ego de Cicerone dicam? Qui cum primum sapere coepit, acerbissimos dolores miseriasque percepit.* The father's pen never again strikes so affectionate a note.

[2] *Ad Q. Fr.* III, 3, 4 (151 T.P.). 54 B.C.

[3] *Ad Att.* VIII, 4, 1 (335 T.P.). Feb. 22, 49 B.C.; and VI, 1, 12 (252 T.P.). 50 B.C.

[4] On Gorgias cf. above, p. 152; on Herodes and Leonidas cf. *Ad Att.* XIV, 16, 3 (721 T.P.). May 44 B.C. On Bruttius, Cassius, Cratippus and Epicrates cf. Marcus's letter to Tiro, Sept. 44 B.C. *Ad Fam.* XVI, 21, 4 and 5 (786 T.P.).

[5] *Ad Att.* XIII, 47A, 2 (664 T.P.): *Turpe enim nobis illum, qualiscumque est, hoc primo anno egere.*

[6] *Ad Att.* XIV, 16, 4 (721 T.P.): *Nihil enim deesse Ciceroni cum ad officium tum ad existimationem meam pertinet*; XV, 15, 4 (748 T.P.): *id etiam ad dignitatem meam pertinere.* 44 B.C.

[7] *Ad Att.* XVI, 1, 5 (769 T.P.). July 8, 44: *HS LXXII satis esse, adfatim prorsus.*

[8] *Ad Att.* XII, 32, 2 (568 T.P.): . . . *accommodet ad mercedes Argileti et Aventini, et cum ei proposueris, ipse velim reliqua moderere, quemadmodum ex iis mercedibus suppeditemus ei, quod opus sit.* March 28, 45 B.C.; cf. ibid. XV, 20, 4 (752 T.P.): . . . *de mercedibus dotalium praediorum; quae si fideliter Ciceroni curabuntur, quamquam volo laxius, tamen ei propemodum nihil deerit.* June, 44 B.C.

rumour of his escapades from time to time reached even Rome. Cicero of course regretted them, but he put off the necessary remonstrances and refrained from cutting down supplies to check his son's goings on. Though these were becoming almost a scandal, they were not unflattering to his pride.[1]

In the spring of 44 he talked, it is true, of a trip to Athens to bring the wayward student back into the narrow way, but this was only a pretext to cover his own wish to disappear opportunely and escape the difficulties with which the political situation in Italy was bristling.[2] He was in reality flying from the explanations which he ought to have demanded, and from the responsibilities which lay heavy on him. Whether it was a question of planning the stages of his son's journey,[3] or of the falling due of the allowance promised him, or of discreetly keeping an eye on the young man's mode of life in Athens, he shirked all these tiresome jobs and shuffled off on to third parties the duties which were his alone. Trebonius, travelling in Attica, was to look Marcus up and politely deliver messages from his father[4]; Tiro was to see about the supplementary subsidies which were being asked for[5]; Atticus, banker,[6] mentor[7] and confidant, heard all about Marcus's plans for his future before Cicero senior was consulted.[8]

Possibly Cicero was a good father to Marcus.[9] But from his Correspondence he emerges with the appearance of a casual and

[1] *Ad Att.* XIII, 47A, 2 (664 T.P.): . . . *Post moderabimur diligentius.* Aug. 13, 45 B.C., cf. ibid, XIII, 1, 1 (601 T.P.).

[2] *Ad Att.* XIV, 16, 3 (721 T.P.): *Cupio . . . excurrere in Graeciam. Magni interest Ciceronis, vel mea potius, vel mehercule utriusque, me intervenire discenti.* May 44 B.C. Other texts are quoted by Drumann-Groebe, VI, p. 634, note 5.

[3] *Ad Att.* XII, 32, 2 (568 T.P.): *Itaque velim videas . . . quid viatici, quid instrumenti satis sit.* March 28, 45 B.C.

[4] *Ad Fam.* XII, 16, 1 (736 T.P.): . . . *Vidi filium tuum deditum optimis studiis summaque modestiae fama.* From Trebonius, May 25, 44 B.C.

[5] *Ad Att.* XV, 15, 4 (748 T.P.): *Scripsit hoc autem ad Tironem sibi post Kal. Apriles . . . nihil datum esse.* If we read aright the passage of the letter which Marcus wrote to Tiro at the end of August or the beginning of Sept. 44 B.C. the young man had been driven to helping himself from Tiro's purse. Cf. *Ad Fam.* XVI, 21, 7 (786 T.P.): . . . *cum sciam communem nobis emptum esse istum fundum* . . .

[6] Cf. above, p. 152.

[7] *Ad Att.* XIII, 1, 1 (601 T.P.): *Ad Ciceronem ita scripsisti ut neque severius neque temperatius scribi potuerit.* May 23, 45 B.C.

[8] *Ad Att.* XII, 7, 1 (500 T.P.): Marcus having fought for Pompey at Pharsalia, now wanted to join Caesar in Spain and fight against Pompey's sons.

[9] In the very middle of the Civil War, Cicero intrigued to get his son a place in the College of Pontiffs. Cf. *Ad Br.* I, 5, 3 (852 T.P.); 12, 3 (609 T.P.); 14, 1 (913 T.P.), letters ranging between May and July 43 B.C. This was, however, a question involving Cicero's pride, rather than proving any special thought or affection for his son.

absent-minded parent, all too ready to hand on to others the trouble, and even the joy, of superintending his boy's upbringing —a task which it was his to fulfil.

It was much the same in the case of Tullia. That Cicero felt a passionate affection for his elder child, his daughter,[1] is a fact in which all testimony[2] is at one, and which is corroborated even by the unworthy calumnies to which I have already alluded.[3] Her affection, her modesty and her quick intelligence were all a delight to him. He was enchanted to recognise the likeness to his own of her features, of her voice, of her mind, as if she were a new edition of himself.[4] Now this feeling is only fleetingly revealed in the Correspondence, which has preserved for us not a single letter of Tullia's to her father, nor any letter of his addressed exclusively to her.[5] The *Letters*, on the contrary, abound in signs of a detachment unusual in a father, in all the critical episodes of the girl's short life.

For, though Tullia died at the age of thirty or thirty-five,[6] she had been three times married, and on each occasion we are struck by the scant attention paid in her father's letters to events so crucial. We scarcely catch a glimpse of the first of her husbands as he makes his entrance through the modest door of the betrothal. At the beginning of 66, or it may be the close of 67,[7] Cicero casually adds a word or two to the last line of a letter to Atticus: "We have betrothed our little Tulliola to Caius Piso Frugi, the son of Lucius."[8] He makes no comment on the news; and this silence borders on indifference. Not a word about this young man who belonged to the family of the Calpurnii, one of the noblest houses of the senatorial aristocracy. Not a word in the later letters about the wedding itself. It was certainly solemnised before the end of 63, since in his fourth Catiline oration, which was delivered to the

---

[1] *Ad Att.* I, 5, 8 (1 T.P.): *Tulliola deliciae nostrae*; XI, 6, 4 (418 T.P.) and *Ad Fam.* XIV, 19 (417 T.P.): *excruciat me valetudo Tulliae nostrae . . .* Letters written during an illness of the child's in 48 B.C.

[2] Cf. Plut. *Cic.* XLI, 7 and 8. Cicero himself liked to call up a picture of his daughter in his speeches: *Verr.* II, I, 44, 112: *mihi qui mea filia maxime cordi est*; cf. *Pro Sestio*, LXIII, 131.

[3] Cf. above, pp. 84 and 89.

[4] *Ad Q. Fr.* I, 3, 3 (66 T.P.): *Quid quod . . . desidero filiam? qua pietate, qua modestia, quo ingenio, effigiem oris, sermonis, animi mei.* June 13, 58 B.C.

[5] Except the letters *Ad Fam.* XIV addressed jointly to "Terentiae et Tulliis suis". On the existence of these letters, cf. *Ad Att.* VI, 1, 10 (252 T.P.).

[6] If she was born about 79 B.C. Cf. Drumann-Groebe, VI, pp. 614 and 622.

[7] On the date cf. Drumann-Groebe, II, p. 88.

[8] *Ad Att.* I, 3, 3 (8 T.P.): *Tulliolam C. Pisoni L. f. Frugi despondimus.*

Senate on Dec. 5 of that year,[1] Cicero salutes his son-in-law's presence among the Fathers.[2] But we cannot look to the *Letters* to fix the date for us: the ceremony is not alluded to, and there is nowhere the slightest mention of the first marriage of the dearly loved Tulliola.

Five years later, in his letters written in exile to his wife and children, he pays increasingly warm tribute to Piso's political loyalty and devotion.[3] But he remains as silent as ever about the young couple's domestic affairs. We deduce that their marriage was happy from an allusion Cicero slips into his plea for Sestius; speaking of his return from exile, he tells how he landed at Brundisium on Aug. 5, 57, and met his daughter for the first time since her heavy grief and bereavement: *filiae quam ex gravissimo tum primum desiderio luctuque conspexi.*[4] So Piso had just recently died, and we might expect that his daughter's sorrow, to which he pays such eloquent tribute in his speech, would find some echo in his letters of the period. Not a bit of it. To read the account in the *Ad Atticum* collection of Cicero's arrival at Brundisium no one would dream that so cruel a bereavement had cast a shadow over it: "I arrived at Brundisium on Aug. 5. There my dear Tulliola met me on what was her own birthday, which happened to be also the Commemoration Day of the founding of the colony of Brundisium, and the Foundation Day of the temple of your neighbour the Goddess Health. This coincidence was noted by the multitude and celebrated with warm congratulations by the citizens of Brundisium."[5] We may seek in vain for any cloud dimming this radiant scene. Cicero kept the display of his family sorrows to adorn his resounding orations in the Forum, and quietly passed over in his letters all painful memories which might have

---

[1] On the Notes of Dec. 63 B.C. cf. Cic. *Ad Att.* I, 19, 6 (25 T.P.): *Ego autem, ut semel Nonarum illarum Decembrium . . . eximiam quamdam atque immortalem gloriam consecutus sum . . .*

[2] Cic. *Cat.* IV, 1, 3: *Stat in conspectu meo gener.*

[3] Cf. *Ad Fam.* XIV, 4, 4 (62 T.P.): *Pisonem ut scribis, spero fore semper nostrum.* April 17, 58 B.C.; 2, 2 (79 T.P.): *Pisonem nostrum merito eius amo plurimum.* Oct. 5, 58 B.C.; 1, 4 (82 T.P.): *Pisonis humanitas, virtus, amor in nos tantus est ut nihil supra possit . . .* Nov. 25, 58 B.C.; 3, 3 (84 T.P.): *Pisonem nostrum mirifico esse studio in nos et officio, et ego perspicio et omnes praedicant.* Nov. 29, 58 B.C.

[4] Cic. *Pro Sestio,* LXIII, 131.

[5] *Ad Att.* IV, 1, 4 (90 T.P.): *Brundisium veni Nonis Sex(tilibus). Ibi mihi Tulliola mea fuit praesto natali suo ipso die, qui casu idem natalis erat et Brundisinae coloniae et tuae vicinae Salutis. Quae res animadversa a multitudine summa Brundisinorum gratulatione celebrata est.* On the position of the temple of *Salus,* the Goddess of Health, cf. Platner-Ashby, *Top. Dict.* s.v. *Aedes Salutis.*

cast a gloom on his egocentric joy at return from exile to the arms of his darling daughter amid the acclamations of the populace.

"The dead are soon forgotten": so it was in Ancient Rome. A year after the loss of Piso, his widow was engaged anew to one Furius Crassipes. We know almost nothing about this second match except that the patrician husband was well provided with a large fortune, which Cicero will certainly have considered a good recommendation. He warmly encouraged a plan which would make his daughter one of the wealthiest ladies in Rome, and would allow him to enjoy a little of the luxury which would surround her. By the end of March 56 he was hoping to see the matter concluded, and he speaks of it without the slightest sentimentality as a business transaction: "As to our Tullia, who by Hercules is very warmly attached to you," he writes to his brother Quintus, "I hope we have arranged the affair with Crassipes."[1] A few days later the deed was done. He confirms that "our dear Tullia was betrothed to Crassipes on April 4."[2] Next day he adds: "on April 6 I gave the betrothal dinner in honour of Crassipes."[3] In a letter to Atticus he remarked, not without regret, that this was eating into his savings: "Crassipes is swallowing up my travelling-money"—*viaticum Crassipes praeripit.*[4] Not for a moment did he rise above the question of material considerations. He never enquired into the qualities of head or heart which a father worthy of the name would hope to find in a future son-in-law. Shortly after, when he had to thank the Proconsul, Lentulus Spinther, for his congratulations on the betrothal, he confined himself to an evasive and commonplace phrase: "In your congratulations to my daughter and Crassipes I am obliged to you for your kindness, and do indeed expect and pray that this connection may be a source of pleasure to us."[5] These lines, hastily added to a long letter about literary and political developments, are either entirely meaningless or they show that Cicero in re-marrying his daughter was primarily concerned with himself, his own pleasure and his own advantage.

[1] *Ad Q. Fr.* II, 4, 2 (105 T.P.): *De nostra Tullia, tui mehercule amantissima, spero cum Crassipede nos confecisse.*
[2] *Ad Q. Fr.* II, 5, 1 (106 T.P.): ... *erat scriptum Tulliam nostram Crassipedi pridie [Non(as)] Apri(les) esse desponsatam.*
[3] *Ad Q. Fr.* II, 6, 1 (106 T.P.): *a.d. VIII Id(us) Apr(iles) sponsalia Crassipedi praebui.* On Furius Crassipes cf. *P.W.* VII, c. 351–2.
[4] *Ad Att.* IV, 5, 3 (108 T.P.).
[5] *Ad Fam.* I, 7, 11 (114 T.P.) *Quod mihi de filia et de Crassipede gratularis, agnosco humanitatem tuam, speroque et opto nobis hanc coniunctionem voluptati fore.*

One of these advantages which delighted him was the pleasure of reclining at a luxuriously laid table set up in the gardens of Crassipes, which rivalled those of Julius Caesar,[1] on the bank of the Tiber. In a letter from Antium, written in the last days of May 55, he informed Atticus that he intended to return to Rome on June 1, and invited him and his wife Pilia to dine with him the next day. He had another—and better—engagement for the evening of the 1st when he got back: "I think of dining in the gardens of Crassipes as at a kind of country-inn." For fear of ruffling Atticus, he added as an explanation that he was making as it were a final halt in a country house outside the City before coming in.[2] The food was certain to be exquisite and elegantly served, and in any case the setting of the dinner magnificent. When he wanted to set the seal on his reconciliation with Crassus in the autumn of 54, before the new Proconsul of Syria set out for the Parthian War, Cicero could imagine no more princely entertainment to offer him. "It might almost be said that Crassus started for his province from my hearth," he wrote to Lentulus, "for on his own invitation he dined with me in the gardens of my son-in-law Crassipes."[3] Cicero considered himself entirely as if he were at home in the sumptuous surroundings in which his son-in-law held receptions in honour of his guests.

The following winter he felt himself personally as hard hit as if the disaster had directly affected himself by the damage caused when a rise in the Tiber wrecked the property of Tullia's husband. "There has been a remarkable flood at Rome. . . . The promenade of Crassipes with his gardens and pavilions has been swept away."[4] Cicero had obviously fallen under the spell of these trees and shrubberies, and was so delighted to have so magnificent a host as

---

[1] On the gardens of Caesar see the latest thesis by Grimal.

[2] *Ad Att.* IV, 12 (125 T.P.): *Sed, si me diligis, postridie Kalend. cena apud me cum Pilia. Prorsus id facies. Kalend. cogito in hortis Crassipedis, quasi in deversorio, cenare.*

[3] *Ad Fam.* I, 9, 20 (153 T.P.): *Crassusque . . . paene a meis laribus in provinciam est profectus. Nam cum mihi condixisset cenavit apud me in mei generi Crassipedis hortis.*

[4] *Ad Q. Fr.* III, 7, 1 (156 T.P.): *Romae . . . mira alluvies Crassipedis ambulatio ablata, horti tabernae plurimae . . .* Dec. 54 B.C. I take *horti* and *tabernae* to refer to Crassipes's property. But it is equally possible to interpret them in a more general sense, "people's gardens, etc." This catastrophe occurred within a few months of an illness of Tullia's which induced Cicero, for fear of causing her anxiety, to remain silent against Clodius during the trial of Procilius; cf. *Ad Att.* IV, 15, 4 (143 T.P.): *verita est enim pusilla quae nunc laborat, ne animum Publii [Clodii] offenderet.* July 54 B.C.

son-in-law that it never crossed his mind that Tullia could fail to
be happy with so rich a husband or might be growing tired of him.
But he had to recognise the fact when the marriage went to pieces
somewhere between 53 and 51.[1] This divorce must have been a
painful business for Tullia, but Cicero pays no attention to it in
his *Letters*. They let us infer that the separation was completed
before 51 only from the fact that at that date he was looking out for
a third husband for Tullia. At the same time they show how easily
Cicero forgave the rupture of the marriage to the man who was no
longer his son-in-law.

He did not himself break off friendly relations, nor renounce the
pleasures and advantages which they secured him. He continued to
see Crassipes, to write to him[2] and to entertain him, especially in
49 in his *villa* at Formiae.[3] Even in 51, when Tullia's divorce was
quite recent, he did not hesitate to beg the goodwill of Crassipes,
then Quaestor of the province of Bithynia,[4] in favour of a company
of bankers who were no doubt clients of his. His own interests
and those of his financier clients took precedence over his family
disappointments. Deep as his fatherly affection for Tullia may have
been, he did not in his *Letters* carry it to the point of quarrelling
with a man whose good offices he valued, merely because the fellow
had more or less wrecked his daughter's happiness.

We must, however, do him the justice of admitting that for some
time he did his best to repair the damage; and that at least in 51
his confidences to Atticus show that he was anxious to find a husband for Tullia who would compensate her for her earlier disappointments. He had to leave Rome for Cilicia at the beginning
of May without having succeeded. On his journey he was still
thinking over the thorny problem, different solutions of which
appealed to him though he had come to no fixed decision. From one
of his first stages, Beneventum, he thanks his friend for promising
to take over, during his absence, a job which lay so very near his
heart. Knowing that Atticus would be leaving Rome in his turn,

---

[1] As we shall see below, p. 161, it was in 51 B.C. that Cicero began to make
enquiries in his letters about a third husband for Tullia.
[2] *Ad Att.* VII, 1, 8 (284 T.P.): Autumn, 50 B.C.
[3] *Ad Att.* IX, 11, 3 (367 T.P.): *Pridie autem apud me Crassipes fuerat.* March
20, 49 B.C.
[4] *Ad Fam.* XIII, 9, 1 (237 T.P.): *Non dubitavi haec ad te scribere . . .*
3: *Id cum mihi gratissimum feceris . . . tibi . . . promitto et spondeo, te socios
Bithyniae, si iis commodaris, memores esse et gratos cogniturum . . .* End of 51 B.C.
or beginning of 50 B.C.

Cicero felt anxious about what might happen. One unnamed suitor had applied for Tullia's hand whom he had not rejected, not that he thought much of him, but "we must be content with him for want of a better". There was a second one, Servius Sulpicius, who seemed about to propose, but Cicero feared that "Tullia could not be persuaded" to accept him. It was difficult to know just how things stood. Atticus might please try to get Servilia to use her influence with Servius Sulpicius if he was undecided. For the rest, "the result is uncertain and I don't see how I can *do* anything."[1] Two months later, Cicero arrived at Tralles. He was impatient to hear whether Atticus had been able to accomplish all the tasks entrusted to him, "especially that at my own hearth, than which, as you know, I have nothing more at heart".[2]

A few days later he wrote from Tarsus about a third candidate for Tullia's hand and wanted Atticus's views on the matter.[3] But no decision had been arrived at by Feb. 50: "Now for family matters. As to our 'home secret', I am of your opinion—Postumia's son, since Pontidia is playing fast and loose."[4] Weary of war and in face of the increasing difficulties of "settling" Tullia, which Atticus has from time to time told him about, he is inclined to abate his original pretensions: he would now be content to substitute a mere Roman *eques* for a member of the senatorial aristocracy, on one of whom he had at first set his heart.[5] The weeks pass, one possibility follows another without any coming to fruition, and without any capturing Cicero's attention, except in a fleeting way. His most serious effort at solving his problem always consisted in giving it up and leaving decisions to the friends representing him in Rome.

It is true that he turned to several different ones at the same time,

---

[1] *Ad Att.* V, 4, 1 (187 T.P.): *Ac de illo . . . inopia cogimur eo contenti esse. De illo altero, quem scribis tibi visum esse non alienum, vereor adduci ut nostra possit, et tu ais δυσδιάγνωστον esse. Equidem sum facilis sed tu aberis, et me absente res habebit mei rationem? Nam posset aliquid, si utervis nostrum adesset, agente Servilia, Servius fieri probabilis. Nunc, si iam res placeat, agendi tamen viam non video.*

[2] *Ad Att.* V, 14, 3 (204 T.P.): *Nihil mihi gratius facere potes, nisi tamen id erit mihi gratissimum, si, quae tibi mandavi, confeceris, in primisque illud ἐνδόμυχον, quo mihi scies nihil esse carius.*

[3] *Ad Att.* V, 17, 4 (209 T.P.). *Sestius ad me scripsit quae tecum esset de mea domestica et maxima cura locutus et quid tibi esset visum.*

[4] *Ad Att.* V, 21, 14 (250 T.P.): *Reliqua sunt domestica. De ἐνδομύχῳ probo idem quod tu, Postumiae filio, quoniam Pontidia nugatur.*

[5] *Ad Att.* VI, 1, 10 (252 T.P.): *De Tullia mea tibi adsentior, scripsique ad eam et ad Terentiam mihi placere. Tu enim ad me iam ante scripseras "ac vellem te in tuum veterem gregem rettulisses . . ."* From Laodicea, Feb. 24, 50 B.C.

without, it would seem, informing the one about the other. While
Atticus was hesitating between the various suitors we have mentioned, Caelius, also on the lookout, sprang a surprise on them all
by producing on the quiet a rival claimant, and one who soon
carried the day: Publius Cornelius Dolabella. In this very month
of Feb. 50, when Cicero was doing his best to rekindle Atticus's
zeal, he got a letter from Caelius in which this disquieting figure
made his appearance, with innuendoes still more disquieting: "I
remember the commission you gave me as you were leaving, and
I think you won't have forgotten what I wrote to you. It is not yet
the time for going into further details. I can only give you this hint;
if you like the suggestion do not, all the same, betray your feelings
at the present moment, but wait and see how he comes out of this
case. Take care that the matter does not bring discredit on you if
it leaks out."[1] We do not know what sort of a welcome Cicero gave
to these suggestions. It was a pity from his point of view that
Caelius wrapped them so prudently up in circumlocutions. It is as
if in his calculations he were thinking only of the political situation
of the moment, and particularly of the prosecution which Dolabella had just initiated of Appius Claudius Pulcher, Cicero's predecessor in Cilicia, with whom it was most important to avoid
becoming embroiled. Caelius obviously took it for granted that
this curious father was a man who would subordinate the question
of his daughter's marriage to the momentary exigencies of his own
convenience and career, rather than consider Tullia's preferences
and her chances of future happiness.

On reflection her chances of happiness with Dolabella were
pretty slim. He was a gay spark, already notorious in Rome for
disorders and violence, and considerably younger than his future
wife.[2] Cicero's eloquence alone had—with some difficulty—twice
saved him when he was prosecuted for capital offences.[3] A

---

[1] Caelius, ap. Cic. *Ad Fam.* VIII, 6, 2 (242 T.P.): *Quid mihi discedens mandaris
memini : quid ego tibi scripserim te non arbitror oblitum. Non est iam tempus plura
narrandi. Unum illud monere te possum : si res tibi non displicebit, tamen hoc
tempore nihil de tua voluntate ostendas et expectes quem ad modum exeat ex hac
causa : vide ne qua invidiosum tibi sit, si emanarit . . .*
We learn from Quintilian, *Inst. Or.* VI, 3, 78, that the name of Dolabella's
wife was Fabia and that she divorced him.
[2] Assuming that, as Appian, *B.C.* II, 129, tells us, this "adolescent", as
Cicero calls him (see the letter following, of 50 B.C.) was born in 69 B.C.
[3] *Ad Fam.* III, 10, 5 (261 T.P.): *. . . tantam temeritatem in eo adolescente,
cuius ego salutem in duobus capitis iudiciis summa contentione defendi . . .* To
Appius Pulcher, from Laodicea, May 50 B.C.

clear-sighted and disinterested father was bound to reject so disreputable a suitor for his daughter. Cicero could all the more easily have opposed the match with Dolabella since a distinguished man, Tiberius Claudius Nero—who afterwards married Livia—had come as a candidate into the field.[1] But to believe his letters Cicero did not venture either to give or to refuse his consent to an alliance the disastrous consequences of which in the nearer or more distant future he could plainly foresee. In the immediate present, however, this alliance would contribute to his party intrigues the support of an energy unhampered by scruples. So he let things take their course. If they went wrong, he could always throw the responsibility for such a risky choice on to his wife or daughter. In writing to Appius Claudius Pulcher he contended that the betrothal had taken place without his knowledge.[2]

In writing to Atticus, he feigned astonishment, confessed his fears and expressed his regrets. "While employed in my province in doing everything for the honour of Appius, I suddenly became father-in-law to his accuser (Dolabella). 'Heaven prosper it!' you say. So say I, and I am sure you wish it. But believe me, it was the last thing I expected: in fact, I had even sent confidential messengers to my wife and daughter about Tiberius Nero, who had made proposals to me, but they arrived in Rome after the betrothal had taken place."[3]

A little later, it was open to Cicero, according to his mood, to moderate his fears or augment his anxiety, by pondering over the curious congratulations which Caelius sent: "I congratulate you on a son-in-law who is, so help me God, the best of men, for that is what I think of him. Some other things, by which he has up to now done himself no good, have fallen from him with the years, and if any faults remain I feel sure that they will be quickly overcome under the influence of your companionship and authority and the pure example of Tullia. For he is not obstinately set on vice, nor so dull as not to appreciate the better way. Lastly, and

---

[1] Cf. below, note 3.

[2] *Ad Fam.* III, 12, 2 (275 T.P.): *Ego vero velim mihi Tulliaeque meae, sicut tu . . . optas, prospere evenire ea quae me insciente facta sunt.*

[3] *Ad Att.* VI, 6, 1 (276 T.P.): *Ego dum in provincia omnibus rebus Appium orno, subito sum factus accusatoris eius socer. Id quidem, inquis, Di approbent! Ita velim teque ita cupere certo scio. Sed crede mihi nihil minus putaram ego: quin de Ti. Nerone, qui mecum egerat, certos homines ad mulieres miseram, qui Romam venerunt factis sponsalibus . . .*

this is the most important point, I love him well."[1] Cicero's only desire was to cradle himself in illusions. Finally, he seemed to resign himself: "My son-in-law makes himself very agreeable to me, to Tullia and to Terentia; he has any amount of natural ability, or should I say culture; so I am satisfied. His other qualities, which you wot of, must be put up with."[2]

Let us admit it. From the evidence of his letters Cicero accepted with far too good a grace and for far too long this gloomy necessity of "putting up" with Dolabella. The young man made life intolerable to his wife, forced her to leave his house and to take refuge with her father though she was expecting a child. After her confinement, he let her pine away from bitterness and fatigue in her father's country seat at Tusculum. Yet after the divorce and even after his daughter's death, Cicero continued to remain on good terms with Dolabella, as long as this incredible tolerance served to further his intrigues and to save his pocket.

Open to criticism as such conduct was, it offered every advantage from the moment when Dolabella, as a faithful adherent of Caesar's, offered Cicero a guarantee against any hostile measures by his chief. It is hardly an accident that Tullia's third marriage was celebrated in Aug. 50, when the double acquittal of Appius Claudius Pulcher had smoothed away the main obstacle which might have deterred Cicero from consenting to it.[3] And at a time too when signs heralding an approaching crisis showed him that he must try, by the favour of the new son-in-law, to gain a footing in Caesar's camp.[4] When war broke out, his letters ingenuously reveal the worldly-wise reflections which had actuated him six months before.

When the news arrived that Caesar, the Proconsul of the Two

---

[1] Caelius *ap.* Cic. *Ad Fam.* VIII, 13, 1 (271 T.P.): *Gratulor tibi adfinitatem viri me dius fidius optimi. Nam hoc ego de illo existimo. Cetera porro, quibus adhuc ille sibi parum utilis fuit, et aetate iam sunt decussa et consuetudine atque auctoritate tua, pudore Tulliae, si qua restabunt, confido celeriter sublatum iri. Non est enim pugnax in vitiis, neque hebes ad id, quod melius est, intellegendum. Deinde, quod maximum est, ego illum valde amo.* June 50 B.C.

[2] *Ad Att.* VII, 3, 12 (294 T.P.): *Quid superest? Etiam: gener est suavis mihi, Tulliae, Terentiae: quantumvis vel ingenii vel humanitatis, satis est. Reliqua, quae nosti, ferenda.* Dec. 9, 50 B.C.

[3] On this double acquittal and the election of Appius Claudius Pulcher to the censorship which followed immediately on his acquittal in the summer of 50 B.C., see *P.W.* III, c. 2852, with references to *Ad Fam.* III, 11 and 12.

[4] It was in the summer of 50 B.C. that the first of the senatorial manoeuvres took place, which was completely successful and compelled Caesar to send the 15th Legion back to Pompey. Cf. my *César* (3), p. 849.

Gauls, had crossed the Rubicon and was marching on Rome as a conqueror, the sole feeble hope that he and his would escape the usurper's violence lay in the influence of Dolabella. On Jan. 23, 49, Cicero wrote from Minturnae to his wife and daughter in Rome: "If Caesar is coming quietly to Rome you can stay at home in safety for the present; but if in madness he is going to plunder the city, I fear Dolabella himself will not be able to be of sufficient use to us."[1] By the end of March he breathed again. Caesar showed no sign of the expected and dreaded violence and, better still, he sent a most friendly and flattering letter hoping that Dolabella could arrange for Cicero to meet him in Rome, and adding, "No one, you must know, is more agreeable to me than your Dolabella."[2] To counterbalance this, in May 49, a few days after Tullia had been prematurely brought to bed of a seven-months boy who no doubt did not survive,[3] Cicero grew alarmed, not indeed for Tullia but for himself. His dear Dolabella had got himself into trouble by his rashness and extravagance, and Cicero was afraid that this might undermine his son-in-law in Caesar's favour, and thereby upset the balance of his own position.[4] Fortunately the "favourite" did not fall into disgrace, but was summoned by Caesar to various commands in his fleet and his army.[5] During the whole period of his absence, which lasted till the end of 48, he gave his wife no cause of complaint and he rendered many services to his father-in-law. These were the more valuable because Cicero's initial vacillations and his final rally to the lost cause of Pompey had most dangerously exposed him to the vengeance of the victor. Dolabella had tried in vain, in May 48, to induce Cicero patiently to maintain a wise neutrality.[6] And it was to Dolabella that Cicero owed Caesar's letter of pardon permitting him in Dec. 48 if not to

[1] *Ad Fam.* XIV, 14, 1 (309 T.P.): *Si ille [Caesar] Romam modeste venturus est, recte in praesentia domi esse potestis : sin homo amens diripiendam Urbem daturus est, vereor ut Dolabella ipse satis nobis prodesse possit.*

[2] *Ad Att.* IX, 16, 3 (374 T.P.) transmits to Atticus on March 26, 49 B.C. the letter just received from Caesar in which the phrase occurs: *Dolabella tuo nihil scito mihi esse iucundius.*

[3] *Ad Att.* X, 18, 1 (404 T.P.): *Tullia mea peperit XIIII K. Iun(ias)* [May 19] *puerum* ἑπταμηνιαῖον; *quod* ηὐτόκησεν *gaudeo; quod quidem est natum perimbecillum est.*

[4] To Caelius, *Ad Fam.* II, 16, 5 (394 T.P.): *Dolabellam meum, vel potius nostrum, fore ab iis molestiis, quas libertate contraxerat, liberum. Velim quaeras, quos ille dies sustinuerit, in Urbe dum fuit, quam acerbos sibi quam mihimet ipsi socero non honestos.* Beginning of May, 49 B.C.

[5] Cf. *P.W.* IV, c. 1301.

[6] Dolabella to Cicero, *ap.* Cic. *Ad Fam.* IX, 9 (409 T.P.). From Epirus, May 48 B.C.

return to Rome at least to land in Italy without fear of reprisals.[1] What is sad is that his selfish hope of a complete amnesty made him hesitate to dissolve his daughter's marriage, which had saved him from immediate danger, though it was evident that it spelt nothing but unhappiness for Tullia.

Dolabella returned to Rome in Dec. 48 to assume the office of Tribune of the Plebs, a post which he had secured by means of an *adrogatio* on the same lines as that which had formerly allowed Clodius to be adopted into a plebeian *gens*.[2] No longer restrained by the presence of his chief, for Caesar was first immobilised in Egypt and then mobilised in Asia against Pharnaces, Dolabella gave the rein to his excesses. Hunted by his creditors, he hastily adopted the revolutionary proposals of his predecessor Caelius. These included the cancellation of the half of all debts and a moratorium for the remaining half, and he called the people to arms to carry them into effect. Mark Antony, who was at the time in command of the Dictator's cavalry and represented Caesar in the city, led out his troops to meet the revolutionaries, massacred 800 of them and scattered the rest.

Dolabella was lucky enough to escape the brutal suppression of the insurrection he had provoked.[3] Proud of his immunity as Tribune, the sedition-monger plunged into a frenzy of shameless debauchery. Full of drink and lust, he kept the Romans awake with the din of his nocturnal riotings, and burst into their houses with his dissolute companions. He was a close friend of a notorious libertine, the son of Aesopus the actor, and the two were rivals for the cheap favours of ex-Consul Lentulus Spinther's wife. To everyone's knowledge Dolabella won in the competition for the lady's favour.[4] This was enough to rouse the wrath of any father with the slightest care for the happiness and dignity of his daughter. Cicero, however, was compulsorily detained in Brundisium. If he was fully aware of the notorious scandals that were reported, and which were causing acute torment to his Tullia, he did not venture to remonstrate or interfere with his son-in-law. The year before,

---

[1] *Ad Att.* XI, 7, 2 (420 T.P.): *Tum ad eum [Antonium] misi L. Lamiam, qui demonstraret illum [Caesarem] Dolabellae dixisse, ut ad me scriberet, ut in Italiam quam primum venirem, eius me litteris venisse.* From Brundisium, Dec. 17, 48 B.C.

[2] Cf. *P.W.* IV, c. 1301–1302. In a letter to Terentia written from Brundisium in Dec. 48 B.C. Cicero complains of having received bad news from Rome about the health of both Dolabella and Tullia. *Ad Fam.* XIV, 9 (419 T.P.): *Ad ceteras meas miserias accessit dolor et de Dolabellae valetudine et de Tulliae.*

[3] See my *César* (3), pp. 990–91. [4] Cf. below, p. 167.

when Dolabella impatiently clamoured at each pay-day[1] for the next instalment of Tullia's dowry, which he was gradually squandering,[2] Cicero took fright to the point of calmly contemplating a divorce, a step which Atticus was then already recommending.[3] Now that it seemed the necessary course to take, he had not the courage to face it. In his fear of the trouble-maker and his uncertainty about Caesar's final intentions, he either said nothing at all or waited to speak till Dolabella should seem to want to open the subject.

There is no doubt that towards the end of 48 and in the early months of 47 he was gravely disturbed by the physical and moral distress which poor Tullia was suffering. He grieved over the weakness she complained of—*imbecillitas corporis me exanimat*[4]—and racked with grief by her illness—*excruciat me valetudo Tulliae nostrae*[5]; he did not know what to think, or what to wish for her—*quid scribam? aut quid velim?*[6] He was in despair over the ruin which her husband's extravagance had brought on the unfortunate woman—*istam miseram patrimonio, fortuna omni spoliatam.*[7]

The present misbehaviour of his son-in-law and the rumour of his misdeeds—*accessisse ad superiores aegritudines praeclaras generi actiones*[8]—were added to his previous worries. The tales which were current in May 47 about the adventures of Dolabella and the son of Aesopus completed his discouragement.[9] Ere long the shame he felt about his son-in-law's carryings-on in Rome made him dread showing his face in Brundisium.[10] But no manly decision resulted from these vain groanings.[11] The only measure he took to comfort

---

[1] *Ad Att.* XI, 2, 2 (407 T.P.): *De dote, quod scribis, per omnes deos te obtestor ut totam rem suscipias . . . Iam illa HS $\overline{LX}$ quae scribis, nemo mihi unquam dixit ex dote esse detracta; nunquam enim essem passus.* Feb. 5, 48 B.C.

[2] *Ad Att.* XI, 3, 1 (411 T.P.): *. . . periculum tantae pecuniae . . .* June 13, 48 B.C.

[3] *Ad Att.* XI, 3, 1 (411 T.P.): *Quod ad Kal. Quinct(iles) pertinet* [the payment of the third instalment of the dowry] *quid vellem? Utrumque grave est, et tam gravi tempore periculum tantae pecuniae, et dubio rerum exitu, ista, quam scribis, abruptio.* June 13, 48 B.C.

[4] *Ad Att.* XI, 6, 4 (418 T.P.). Nov. 27, 48 B.C.

[5] *Ad Fam.* XIV, 19 (417 T.P.). Nov. 48 B.C.

[6] *Ad Att.* XI, 7, 6 (420 T.P.). Dec. 17, 48 B.C.

[7] *Ad Att.* XI, 9, 3 (423 T.P.). Jan. 3, 47 B.C.

[8] *Ad Att.* XI, 12, 4 (427 T.P.). March 8, 47 B.C.

[9] *Ad Att.* XI, 15, 3 (430 T.P.): *Quin enim Aesopi filius me excruciat.* May 14, 47 B.C. On the son of Aesopus and Metella, cf. Hor. *Sat.* II, 3, 39.

[10] *Ad Att.* XI, 14, 2 (429 T.P.): *Etsi omnium conspectu horreo, praesertim hoc genero.* April or May 47 B.C.

[11] *Ad Att.* XI, 14, 2 (429 T.P.): *Tamen in tantis malis quid aliud velim non reperio.*

his daughter was to get her away from her painful surroundings and to invite her to share his temporary retirement. Tullia joined him in Brundisium on June 12, 47, and stayed with him till August.[1] Prostrated by seeing her again in so exhausted and worn-out a state,[2] he felt acute remorse to think that all the unhappiness and misery which had overtaken his daughter were his fault,[3] the fault he committed in consenting to a marriage which he should have done everything to prevent—a fault which he then aggravated by not making up his mind promptly to dissolve the marriage. In July 47 he laid bare his dilemma in a letter to Atticus. Why did he not cut the painter? It was high time to do so; Atticus was pressing him to it and Dolabella had given him just cause a hundred times over: by his drunkenness and his seditious riots, by his night-burglaries and by his parade of his liaison with Metella.[4] In such painful circumstances no solution would have been better than a divorce: and Cicero himself agreed in principle.[5] He agreed, but did nothing. His intentions and his regrets were all expressed in the past tense. He regretted having paid over in July 48 the second instalment of Tullia's dowry,[6] yet in July 47 he had not the courage to refuse the third. If Dolabella did not accept it—that would mean divorce. If he claimed it, why, then . . . it was up to Atticus to decide whether it should be paid only when the request came from him, or whether he should be forestalled by its being paid before.[7] Atticus, however, did not take the responsibility off Cicero's shoulders. The bad husband pocketed the third instalment like the two first; the wretched marriage was patched up again.

---

[1] On this stay, cf. *Ad Fam.* XIV, 15 (435 T.P.): *Ad Att.* XI, 17, 1 (432 T.P.), June 14, 47 B.C., in which Cicero wonders whether he should not send Tullia back to her mother; XI, 23, 3 (437 T.P.); XI, 25, 3 (436 T.P.), etc.

[2] *Ad Att.* XI, 17, 1 (432 T.P.): . . . *non modo eam voluptatem non cepi, quam capere ex singulari filia debui, sed etiam incredibili sum dolore adfectus, tale ingenium in tam misera fortuna versari.* Brundisium, June 14, 47 B.C.; XI, 25, 3 (436 T.P.): *Ego huius (Tulliae) miserrima facultate confectas conflictor.* July 5, 47 B.C. I retain the reading of the *Mediceus.*

[3] *Ad Att.* XI, 17, 1 (432 T.P.): . . . *idque accidere nullo ipsius Tulliae delicto summa culpa mea*; 23, 2 (437 T.P.): . . . *equidem in meo tanto peccato* . . .

[4] *Ad Att.* XI, 23, 3 (437 T.P.): *Aliquid fecissemus ut viri vel tabularum novarum nomine vel nocturnarum expugnationum vel Metellae* . . . *Memini omnino tuas litteras* . . . Brundisium, July 9, 47 B.C.

[5] *Ad Att.* XI, 23, 3 (437 T.P.): *Melius quidem in pessimis nihil fuit discidio* . . . *Placet mihi igitur et idem tibi nuntium remitti.*

[6] *Ad Att.* XI, 25, 3 (436 T.P.): . . . *in pensione secunda caeci fuimus* . . . Brundisium, July 5, 47 B.C. On the days payment fell due cf. ibid., 3, 1 (411 T.P.): *quod ad Kal(endas) Quinct(iles) pertinet* . . . June 13, 48 B.C.

[7] *Ad Att.* XI, 23, 3 (437 T.P.): *Petet fortasse tertiam pensionem. Considera igitur tumne, cum ab ipso nascetur, an prius* . . .

So much the worse for Tullia! So much the better for Tullia's father, whose interests were thus preserved! While Dolabella got ready to rejoin Caesar in Africa, Cicero received in Sept. 47 a final pardon, and permission to leave Brundisium and return to Rome.[1]

In May 46 Dolabella returned to Rome from Africa[2] and resumed life with his wife. In Jan. 45—that is to say exactly nine months later, remembering the intercalary months which the reformed Julian Calendar inserted between September and December, thus prolonging the end of 46—Tullia brought a little son into the world.[3] This is the boy whom his grandfather called Lentulus. Cicero asked Atticus kindly to go and see the child in his stead.[4] A first glance at this chronology might lead us to think that Dolabella had learnt wisdom in the war, and had at last made it possible for Tullia peaceably to enjoy the affection of her third husband. Alas! The reality was very different. Cicero's Correspondence furnishes proof that after a few months—perhaps after only a few weeks—discord had once more arisen between the couple. Both sides soon came to the conclusion that a separation was inevitable, and this was arranged by mutual consent at latest by Oct. 46. In the course of November[5] Cicero was busy trying to recover from Dolabella, before he should set out for the Spanish campaign and on a date agreed on, a first fraction of his daughter's dowry.[6] It was three months later, probably in Cicero's house in Rome, where Tullia had been obliged to take refuge, that little Lentulus was born.[7]

[1] Cf. Drumann-Groebe, VI, p. 621.

[2] *Ad Fam.* IX, 7, 2 (462 T.P.): *Adventat enim Dolabella.* To Varro, May 46 B.C.

[3] *Ad Fam.* VI, 18, 5 (534 T.P.): . . . *me Romae tenuit omnino Tulliae meae partus.* To Lepta, Jan. 45 B.C.

[4] *Ad Att.* XII, 28, 3 (564 T.P.): . . . *velim Lentulum puerum visas.* From Astura, March 24, 45 B.C.; 30, 1 (567 T.P.): *Quod Lentulum invisis, valde gratum.* From Astura, March 27, 45 B.C.

[5] Since the letter quoted in my note next following belongs to the second of the intercalary months of 46 B.C. On the Julian reform of the Calendar, cf. my *César* (3), p. 1030f., and my essay on Caesar and Cleopatra in the *Études d'Archéologie romaine,* published by the Ghent Institut des Hautes Études, 1937, pp. 48–9. The rupture was not yet foreseen when at Tusculum in July 46 B.C. Cicero was exchanging with Dolabella lessons in good talking for lessons in good eating. Cf. above, p. 80.

[6] *Ad Att.* XII, 8 (501 T.P.): *De prima pensione ante videamus. Adest enim dies et ille (Dolabella) currit.* Second intercalary month of 46 B.C. Dolabella's haste defeated Cicero's impatience, for in Jan. 45 B.C. Cicero was still trying to extract the first instalment of the dowry from Dolabella's agents. Cf. *Ad Fam.* VI, 18, 5 (534 T.P.): . . . *teneor tamen dum a Dolabella procuratoribus exigam primam pensionem.* To Lepta.

[7] As appears from the letter to Lepta quoted above, note 3. Cf. the reservations formulated in note 2 to p. 169.

To crown her misfortune, Tullia was destined not to recover from a pregnancy so overladen with anxieties and vexations. After her confinement she went to Tusculum, hoping no doubt that the quiet of the country and the air of the Alban Hills would restore her health.[1] But it had been undermined by too many shocks and disappointments, and a few days after her arrival at her father's *villa* she succumbed to consumption and to sorrow. For many a day her death robbed Cicero of his pleasure in the most dearly loved of all his country seats.[2]

In his *Letters* and in his philosophical treatises he returned again and again to the great sorrow that this premature loss had caused him. In his philosophical works he expresses it simply and soberly with an emotion all the more touching for its restraint[3]; whereas in his *Letters* he lets himself go with a sort of boastfulness that shocks our feelings and makes us doubt the sincerity of his. Of all the condolences which we know he received on his loss,[4] the

---

[1] The letters quoted below seem to contradict the contrary information given by Plutarch, *Cic.* XLI, 7, and by Asconius, *In Pis.*, p. 502: *Cicero filiam P. Lentulo collocavit, apud quem illa ex partu decessit.* Cf. Drumann-Groebe, VI, p. 623.

[2] He had striven against and overcome this feeling by May 15, 45: *Ad Att.* XII, 44, 3 (590 T.P.): *Ego hinc* [from Astura] . . . *postridie Idus* [*Maias*] *Lanuvii, deinde postridie in Tusculano. Contudi enim animum et fortasse vici, si modo permansero.*

Cf. *Ad Att.* XIII, 26, 1 (591 T.P.): *Revolvor identidem in Tusculanum.* May 14, 45 B.C.; and XII, 46, 1 (592 T.P.): *Vincam, opinor, animum et Lanuvio pergam in Tusculanum. Aut enim mihi in perpetuum fundo illo carendum est—nam dolor idem manebit . . .—aut nescio quid intersit utrum illuc nunc veniam an ad decem annos.* May 15, 45 B.C.

I recognise of course that there is another interpretation, more damning to Cicero's memory, which would allow us to reconcile the phrases of the *Letters* with the statements of Plutarch and Asconius. According to them Tullia would have borne her child and died in the house of the husband from whom she was separated: and Cicero, who did not want to leave Rome till Dolabella's agents had paid up the first instalment of her dowry, would not have stayed to watch over the health of his daughter and his baby grandson. He would have gone off —as if there were nothing amiss—to Tusculum and there have been overtaken by the news of his bereavement. His Tusculan *villa* would in that case have become hateful to him, not because his Tullia had died there, but because he was there when the news reached him. This explanation fits in with the dates, very close together, of Tullia's confinement and death (Jan. and Feb. 45 B.C. respectively). I do not like to accept this explanation for fear I should be accused of prejudice against Cicero in my use of his Correspondence.

[3] See, for example, Cic. *De Natura Deor.* I, 4, 9: . . . *animi aegritudo fortunae magna et gravi commota iniuria*; and *Acad. Post.* I, 3, 11: *fortunae gravissimo percussus vulnere.*

[4] Notably from Caesar and from Dolabella then in Spain. Cf. *Ad Att.* XIII, 20, 1 (634 T.P.): *A Caesare litteras accepi consolatorias datas pridie Kal(endas) Maias Hispali*; and *Ad Fam.* IX, 11, 1 (576 T.P.), in which Cicero replying to Dolabella writes:—*Quod scribis*—and adds: *hilaritas illa nostra et suavitas quae te praeter ceteros delectabat, erepta mihi omnis est: firmitatem et constantiam . . . eandem cognosces quam reliquisti.* On Brutus's condolences, *Ad Att.* XII, 13, 1 (549 T.P.). Cf. below, p. 174, note 2.

publishers of his *Letters* have, somewhat basely, preserved only the rather studied and scholastic effusion of Servius Sulpicius.[1] On the other hand, they have maliciously selected all those in which Cicero dwells on his mourning in terms which do less to recall the dear image of the dead daughter than to glorify for the edification of the public the noble thoughts of the father.

Scarcely had he reached the solitude of Astura, where he professed to have gone to brood over his grief,[2] than he conceived the vainglorious idea of erecting an imperishable monument[3] to his daughter's memory. Not a mere tomb, not a vulgar cenotaph, but a veritable sanctuary whose composite beauty should unite all the perfections which the artistic genius of Greece and Rome had in the past produced.[4] He told Atticus his wishes on March 11, 45, and asked him to put his whole heart into the grandiose scheme. He had already decided on the plan itself and the form the monument should take, and had approved the plans of his architect, Cluatius. But he had not yet definitely made up his mind about the site. This is the question he invited Atticus to think about,[5] for he felt that he had made a vow and would like to fulfil it as quickly as possible.[6] A little later he wrote to his friend that everything must be complete before the end of the summer.[7] He did not know what

[1] This is the famous letter reproduced by Cicero, *Ad Fam.* IV, 5 (555 T.P.), whose commonplaces were repeated by St. Ambrose and for which Boissier expresses an admiration which I cannot succeed in sharing, *Cicéron et ses amis*, p. 107.

[2] *Ad Att.* XII, 18, 1 (549 T.P.): . . . *quasi fovebam dolores meos*. On Cicero's retreat in Astura, cf. above, p. 51. The first letter from Astura is dated March 7, 45 B.C., *Ad Att.* XII, 13 (545 T.P.): that which I shall be quoting in notes 4 to 6 below is of March 11, 45 B.C.

[3] These lines were already written before I read the excellent article of Pierre Boyancé, *L'apothéose de Tullia*, in the *R.E.A.*, 1944, pp. 179–84, in which the writer has shown that Cicero had borrowed from Crantor the mystic idea that certain souls were predestined to divinisation and achieved it by migration to the stars. He believes that Cicero had set himself the task of acclimatising this faith in Rome by this apotheosis of his daughter. But in his heart Cicero was really exploiting his grief in order by his scheme to launch his metaphysical innovations and to increase his own fame as a philosopher. In this plan he betrayed his personal preoccupations. As we shall see later (below, p. 174), it was not incompatible with other designs either, with which spiritualism at any rate had nothing to do.

[4] *Ad Att.* XII, 18, 1 (549 T.P.): *De fano illo dico, de quo tantum, quantum me amas, velim cogites* . . . *Profecto illam consecrabo onmi genere monimentorum ab omnium ingeniis sumptorum et Graecorum et Latinorum.* Amongst these "monuments" we must reckon the writings mentioned below, p. 175.

[5] *Ad Att.* XII, 18, 1 (549 T.P.): *Equidem neque de genere dubito—placet enim mihi Cluatii—neque de re—statutum est enim—de loco non numquam.*

[6] *Ad Att.* XII, 18, 1 (549 T.P.): *Quasi voto quodam . . . me teneri puto.*

[7] *Ad Att.* XII, 19, 1 (552 T.P.): *Cogito . . . ita tamen, ut haec aestate fanum absolutum sit.* From Astura, March 14, 45 B.C.

site to choose: Tullia's island birthplace at Arpinum?[1] or the park
at Tusculum which Atticus suggested and which for a moment
appealed to him?[2] or the sea-coast at Ostia?[3] or, better still,
some place in Rome itself, in some splendid garden on the banks of
the Tiber?[4] He begged Atticus to look out for one for him. Pending
the purchase of some such garden and as if this business were
already disposed of, he begs Atticus to "settle the contract with
Apella of Chios for the (marble) columns"[5] and to stir up and urge
on the architect Cluatius.[6]

The *Letters* now introduce us to an endless procession of sellers
unwilling to sell, a perpetual criss-crossing of arrangements which
were concluded only to be again abandoned from one letter to the
next. Arpinum is definitely too far off[7]; there is not enough room
at Ostia, that idea must be given up.[8] The ground which the lovely
Clodia possessed, where today the Farnese palace stands, would
have suited Cicero admirably, but Clodia has not the slightest wish
to sell.[9] Drusus and Silius are too grasping. There remain Scapula's
gardens, which Cicero prefers, but they are coveted by the millionaire Roscius Otho.[10] Completely unruffled, Atticus collected all
these contradictory instructions and did exactly nothing. He had
noted the bottomless pit which this megalomania was digging, and
he did not intend to fall into it or to let it swallow up Cicero's

---

[1] *Ad Att.* XII, 12, 1 (556 T.P.): *Insula Arpinas . . .* From Astura, March 16,
45 B.C.
[2] Cf. especially *Ad Att.* XII, 37, 2 (579 T.P.): *. . . valde probo rationem tuam
de Tusculano.* Astura, May 4, 45 B.C.
[3] *Ad Att.* XII, 23, 3 (559 T.P.), Astura, March 19, 45 B.C.
[4] *Ad Att.* XII, 19, 1 (552 T.P.); 22, 3 (558 T.P.); 23, 3 (559 T.P.); 25, 1
(561 T.P.), etc.
[5] *Ad Att.* XII, 19, 1 (552 T.P.): *Tu tamen cum Apella Chio confice de columnis.*
Astura, March 14, 45 B.C.
[6] *Ad Att.* XII, 36, 3 (578 T.P.): *. . . velim cohortere et exacuas Cluatium.*
Astura, May 4, 45 B.C.
[7] *Ad Att.* XII, 12, 1 (556 T.P.): *Insula Arpinas habere potest . . .* ἀποθέωσιν
sed vereor ne minorem τιμὴν *habere videatur* ἐκτοπισμός.
[8] *Ad Att.* XII, 29, 2 (565 T.P.): *De illo Ostiensi nihil est cogitandum.* Astura,
March 25, 45 B.C.
[9] *Ad Att.* XII, 38, 4 (582 T.P.): *Clodiae sane placent, sed non puto esse venales.*
Astura, May 7, 45 B.C.; 42, 1 (586 T.P.): *Scripsti nescio quid de Clodia . . .*
May 10. On the question of site, see the remarkable study of Giuseppe Lugli,
Mélanges de l'École de Rome, 1939, p. 1f.
[10] On Silius cf. especially *Ad Att.* XII, 30, 1 (567 T.P.) and 31, 3 (568 T.P.):
Cum Silio non video confici posse. March 28, 45 B.C.; 41, 3 (588 T.P.): *Drusus aget
iniuste.* On Scapula's gardens and Otho's competition see especially *Ad Att.* XII,
37, 2 (579 T.P.): *. . . maxima est in Scapulae celebritas*; and 41, 3 (588 T.P.):
Si quaeris quid optem, primum Scapulae. May 11, 45 B.C.; XIII, 29, 2 (605 T.P.):
Othonem vincas volo; 33, 12 (616 T.P.): *Othonem quod speras posse vinci, sane
bene narras.* Tusculum, May 27 and June 3, 45 B.C. respectively.

resources. He groused.[1] He temporised. And ultimately his patience won the day. June 23, 45, Cicero was still sighing for Scapula's gardens: *de Scapulanis hortis toto pectore cogitemus*.[2] His letters of June 25, 26 and 27 are silent.[3] On the 28th he condescended to contemplate the more modest suggestion put forward by Atticus to plant the future building in a wood bought for the express purpose. Before accepting this advice, however, he would like more information "about the neighbourhood", and, once more, he would prefer the gardens on the banks of the Tiber.[4] Having obtained the details he wanted, he was disinclined, on July 4, to accept the idea of the small wood: "In the case of a shrine for human beings I don't think well of a grove, because it is too deserted; yet there is something to be said for it. However, this shall be settled as you think best—as everything is"[5]—and we hear no more talk of Scapula's gardens. He decided to give up all idea of them too on July 9, for he had just heard that they were to be engulfed in the vast town-planning scheme by which Caesar hoped to double the area of the Campus Martius and change the face of Rome. It was Capito who told him of the Dictator's extension plans and warned him against indulging in any ambition of his own which might appear to stand in their way: "for the law will be carried. Caesar wishes it."[6] The gardens were thus consigned to the same oblivion as the grove, and we should search the rest of the Correspondence in vain for even an allusion to the plan of which Cicero had for four months been passionately day-dreaming. His enthusiasm died down as quickly as it had flared up, and the reasons that quenched it were no more cogent than those that kindled it.

Cicero had never reared Tullia's temple in imagination save as a tribute to himself. The shrine had to be princely, to bear brilliant witness to the profundity of his grief and the nobility of his feel-

---

[1] On the attitude of Atticus to this whole business see Drumann-Groebe, V, p. 42, and especially *Ad Att.* XII, 25, 2 (561 T.P.): . . . *obsequere, ut facis, huic errori meo*; 41, 3 (588 T.P.): *me . . . iam etiam gravius quam patitur tua consuetudo*; 43, 1 (589 T.P.): *ferendus tibi meus error*. Letters dated respectively March 21 and May 11 and 12, 45 B.C.

[2] *Ad Att.* XIII, 12, 4 (626 T.P.).

[3] *Ad Att.* XIII, 13, 14, 15 and 16 (627, 628, 629 T.P.).

[4] *Ad Att.* XIII, 18 (630 T.P.): *Vides propinquitas quid habeat. Nos vero conficiamus hortos.*

[5] *Ad Att.* XIII, 22, 4 (635 T.P.): *Lucum hominibus non sane probo quod est desertior : sed habet* εὐλογίαν. *Verum hoc quoque ut censueris, quippe qui omnia.*

[6] *Ad Att.* XIII, 33, 4 (636 T.P.): *Cave facias, inquit Capito, nam ista lex perferetur. Vult enim Caesar.*

ings, for the edification of posterity on whom his eyes were fixed.[1]
It had to be called a "shrine"—*fanum*—so that generations to
come might there celebrate the "apotheosis" of his daughter,[2] and
in order that posterity might "regard it as hallowed" it had to be
of the largest size and built for permanence,[3] and it had to be built
on land independent of a *villa* which would be subject to changes
of ownership,[4] yet not too far removed from the crowds who were
to learn the way to it.[5] All these conditions once laid down, a solution of the problem was bound to be difficult and costly. Though
Cicero began by proclaiming that he was indifferent to cost and
that no price is too high for a thing you want,[6] he ended by shrink-
ing from the enormous expense. He realised that to meet it he
would be driven to borrowing[7] or to start again making loans on a
profitable system—a delicate and risky business—as he had done
to Faberius.[8] Faberius turned a deaf ear; lenders refused to oblige.
It was this lack of funds, which Atticus had no doubt foreseen,
rather than Caesar's town-planning which explains Cicero's final
abandonment of his scheme.

Even in the height of his mourning Cicero was never blind to his
own interests. At least one of his letters proves that in dedicating a
temple, a shrine, to the memory of Tullia, rather than a tomb or a

---

[1] *Ad Att.* XII, 18, 1 (549 T.P.): *Longumque tempus cum non ero, magis me movet
quam hoc exiguum, quod mihi tamen nimium longum videtur.* Astura, March 11,
45 B.C. Cf. ibid., 35, 2 (577 T.P.): . . . *nollem illud ullo nomine nisi fani appellari.*

[2] *Ad Att.* XII, 18, 1 (549 T.P.): . . . *de fano illo dico* . . . Nine times out
of ten Cicero uses the word *fanum* as a technical term. The idea of "apotheosis"
recurs again and again expressed by the Greek ἀποθέωσις. Cf. ibid, XII, 12, 1
(556 T.P.); 36, 1 (578 T.P.); 37, 4 (580 T.P.). It is worth remarking that, apart
from these passages, Cicero never uses the word "apotheosis" except when
glorifying his own consulship. Cf. ibid. I, 16, 13 (22 T.P.). July 61 B.C.

[3] *Ad Att.* XII, 36, 1 (578 T.P.): *Mihi videor adsequi posse ut posteritas habeat
religionem.* Astura, May 3, 45 B.C.

[4] *Ad Att.* XII, 36, 1 (578 T.P.): *Quod poteram, si in ipsa villa facerem, sed,
ut saepe locuti sumus, commutationes dominorum reformido.*

[5] Hence his motto: *Sequor celebritatem: Ad Att.* XII, 27, 1 (563 T.P.); cf.
ibid., 19, 1 (552 T.P.); *Nihil enim video quod tam celebre esse possit*; 37, 2 (579
T.P.): *Maxima est in Scapulae celebritas.*

[6] *Ad Att.* XII, 23, 3 (559 T.P.): *Nec tamen ista pretia hortorum pertimueris*;
and a few lines higher up: *bene emitur quod necesse est.* March 19, 45 B.C.

[7] *Ad Att.* XII, 22, 3 (558 T.P.): *Omnibus meis eorumque quos scio mihi non
defuturos, facultatibus—sed potero meis—enitendum mihi est.* March 18, 45 B.C.
Two days later he admits that his own available funds will not suffice and he
looks round for lenders. Ibid., XII, 23, 3 (559 T.P.): . . . *video etiam a quibus
adiuvari possim.*

[8] He had first thought of Hermogenes, *Ad Att.* XII, 25, 1 (561 T.P.); 31, 2
(569 T.P.). But in the end he would have to revert to Faberius (see above, p. 56),
as he often said at the time. See especially ibid. XII, 21, 2 (557 T.P.); 25, 1
(561 T.P.); 31, 2 (569 T.P.); and finally XIII, 33, 2 (616 T.P.).

cenotaph, he oddly blended the sacred and the profane, the spiritual and the temporal, the outpourings of a fatherly devotion and the precautions of a capitalist who looks after his wealth and protects it with all-embracing care. This is the letter in which he frankly owned that the building of a sacred shrine would not only serve to raise his daughter to the heavens, but would absolve him from pouring into the public treasury sums equal to the excess of his expenditure above the limit which the sumptuary laws had set to the cost of luxury monuments to the dead.[1] So much is this so, that if we confine ourselves to the *Letters* we are justified in maintaining that while his pride played as large a part as his grief in his plans for a sanctuary to the divinity of Tullia, he sacrificed both his grief and his pride to an avarice more potent than the two together. We can understand why, in order to immortalise his sorrow without squandering his £ s. d., he abandoned the idea of buildings which would have impoverished him and wrote a book instead, which cost him nothing but his knowledge and his talent.

We gather in fact from his letters that Tullia's ashes were not yet cold before he had set to work. His daughter died about the middle of Feb. 45.[2] On March 8 he was in a position to hand over to his copyists, in order to send to Atticus, the book of comfort he had written[3] to relieve his sorrow: *librum de luctu minuendo . . . scripsimus*.[4] Cicero said in his *Tusculan Disputations* that he had conceived and composed the *De Consolatione* in the midst of mourning and sorrow.[5] Nevertheless, though we possess only some miserable fragments of this work preserved for us by the Elder

[1] *Ad Att.* XII, 35, 2 (577 T.P.): *Nunquam mihi venit in mentem, quo plus insumptum in monumentum esset quam nescio quid, quod lege conceditur, tantumdem populo dandum esse.* May 1, 45 B.C.; and 36, 1 (578 T.P.): *Fanum fieri volo neque hoc mihi erui potest. Sepulchri similitudinem effugere non tam propter poenam legis studeo quam ut quam maxime adsequor ἀποθέωσιν.* May 3, 45 B.C.

[2] As O. E. Schmidt has observed in his *Briefwechsel des M. Tullius Cicero*, Leipzig, 1893, p. 271, this date is fixed by the date on which he received Brutus's condolences from Cisalpine Gaul. These reached him in Astura before March 7, 45 B.C. *Ad Att.* XII, 13, 1 (545 T.P.): *Bruti litterae scriptae et prudenter et amice mihi tamen lacrimas attulerunt.* Allowing for the delays in transmission, this means that Brutus could have been informed only towards the end of February of a death which had taken place from six to ten days previously.

[3] *Ad Att.* XII, 14, 3 (546 T.P.): *Quem librum ad te mittam si descripserint librarii.*

[4] *Ad Att.* XII, 20, 2 (553 T.P.). March 15, 45 B.C.

[5] *Tusc.* IV, 29, 63: *. . . in Consolationis libro, quem in medio (non enim sapientes eramus) maerore et dolore conscripsimus.*

Pliny, Lactantius and St. Jerome,[1] the tone of the *Letters* forbids us to imagine we hear the heart-rending cry of a soul in despair.[2]

Nothing raises a man to greater spiritual heights than a great sorrow. Cicero would have been ennobled by his grief if he had listened only to his heart, and, like Victor Hugo at Villequier, he had immortalised the lamentations wrung from him by the torturing thoughts of his dead child. But on the pretext of solacing his pain Cicero degraded it to the level of a schoolboy's essay and profaned it by his literary vanity.

There was in fact amongst classical writers a fashion, which the Greeks introduced into Rome, for composing essays of consolation, in which they vied with each other in trying to bring soothing words of comfort to help their friends or benefactors to overcome the trial of bereavement,[3] Cicero had never tried his hand in this line before. With feverish haste he seized this melancholy occasion to show that he could excel in this style as in every other. He set out to display his mastery of it by surpassing the models which he studied unremittingly, and by giving a touch of personal originality to his work by applying to his own case the arguments which his predecessors with natural modesty had used to comfort others.[4] The neo-academician Crantor of Soli had written his Περὶ πένθους to ease the grief of Hierocles, whom Fate had bereft of his children,[5] and Cicero had no hesitation in adapting for his own use the arguments of Crantor, whom he acknowledged as his chief inspirer. One phrase of Crantor's, literally transcribed, occurs at the beginning of *De Consolatione*.[6]

Cicero has by no means exaggerated his morbid appetite for reading. Despite his haste after Tullia's funeral to quit the City

[1] See quotations from these authors in the notes which follow. The text printed at Venice in 1583 is apocryphal. It was written by the humanist Sigonius. Cf. Schanz-Hosius, *Röm. Literaturgeschichte* I, 2, p. 376.

[2] Mérimée, who made a thorough study of the Correspondence, fails equally to hear it, see Chap. XI of *Colomba*: "Cicero, in despair over the death of his daughter Tullia, forgot his grief in mentally rehearsing all the beautiful thoughts that could be expressed on the subject."

[3] On the *Consolatio* as a literary fashion cf. Buresch, *Consolationum Historia Critica* in the *Leipziger Studien*, IX, 1887.

[4] *Ad Att.* XII, 14, 3 (546 T.P.): *Quin etiam feci, quod profecto ante me nemo, ut ipse me per litteras consolarer.* March 8, 45 B.C.

[5] Plut. *Consol. ad Apoll.* VI, P. 104 C. On Crantor in general see Arnim's article, *P.W.* XI, c. 1587.

[6] Pliny, *H.N.*, Praef. 22: *Crantorem, inquit Cicero, sequor.* Cf. St. Jerome, *Ep.* 60, 5: . . . *legimus Crantorem, cuius volumen ad confovendum dolorem suum secutus est Cicero.*

and the world for a bitter solitude,[1] he made a point of staying on in Rome long enough to consult in Atticus's library the books which dealt with this subject.[2] He methodically devoted himself to a survey of all the misfortunes akin to his own which before his time had overtaken the most distinguished men of Rome,[3] to an analysis of the platitudes in which his predecessors had displayed their ingenuity, in short to the delicate and laborious patchwork of which his own treatise consisted. "Yet after all," he wrote to Atticus, "I go no further than the greatest philosophers allow; all whose writings of whatever kind bearing on this subject I have not only read—which was itself the deed of a strong man . . . but have carried over into my own essay. This surely was not the effort of a crushed and broken mind."[4]

He was trying, he says again, to conquer his feelings.[5] Many will think that he succeeded only too quickly and too well, and will endorse the view so admirably expressed by Lactantius: "Someone may perhaps contend that after Tullia's death Cicero was out of his mind from excess of grief. Yet . . . his thought shows no indication of pain, and I for my part do not think that he could have written with so much variety, richness and elegance if his suffering had not been softened by the promptings of his reason, by the sympathy of his friends and by the passage of time."[6] Only,

[1] *Ad Att.* XII, 13, 1 (545 T.P.): *Me haec solitudo . . . stimulat.* March 7, 45 B.C.; 15 (547 T.P.): *. . . in hac solitudine careo omnium colloquio.* March 9, 45 B.C.; 23, 1 (559 T.P.): *itaque solitudinem sequor.* March 19, 45 B.C.

[2] *Ad Att.* XII, 14, 3 (546 T.P.): *Quod me ab hoc maerore recreari vis, facis ut omnia, sed me mihi non defuisse tu testis es. Nihil enim de maerore minuendo scriptum ab ullo est quod ego non domi tuae legerim.* March 8, 45 B.C.

[3] Cic. *De Div.* II, 4, 22: *Clarissimorum hominum nostrae civitatis gravissimos exitus in consolatione collegimus.* The *Letters* corroborate this assertion. See in particular the letter in which Cicero requests the learned Atticus to tell him "whether Cn. Caepio, father of Claudius's wife Servilia, perished by shipwreck before or after his father's death: *Ad Att.* XII, 20, 2 (553 T.P.): *. . . velim me facias certiorem proximis litteris, Cn. Caepio Serviliae Claudii pater, vivone patre suo naufragio perierit an mortuo . . . Pertinent ad eum librum quem de luctu minuendo scripsimus.* Other questions of trifling importance: ibid. 22, 2 (558 T.P.). March 18, 45; 23, 2 (559 T.P.). March 19, 45 B.C., and 24, 2 (560 T.P.), March 20, 45 B.C.

[4] *Ad Att.* XII, 21, 5 (557 T.P.): *Neque tamen progredior longius quam mihi doctissimi homines concedunt, quorum scripta omnia, quaecumque sunt in eam sententiam, non legi solum, quod ipsum erat fortis . . . sed in mea etiam scripta transtuli, quod certe adflicti et fracti animi non fuit.* March 17, 45 B.C.

[5] *Ad Att.* XII, 46, 1 (592 T.P.): *Vincam, opinor, animum.* May 15, 45 B.C.

[6] Lactantius, *Inst. Div.* I, 15, 21: *. . . fortasse dicat aliquis prae nimio luctu delirasse Ciceronem.—Atqui . . . haec ipsa sententia nullum praefert indicium doloris; neque enim puto illum tam varie, tam copiose, tam ornate scribere potuisse, nisi luctum eius et ratio ipsa et consolatio amicorum et temporis longitudo mitigasset.*

time had nothing to say in the matter, for we know from his letters that Cicero immediately began to use his sorrow as a subject of philosophical reflection. Just as Montesquieu's worst misfortunes could not withstand an hour's reading, Cicero's acutest sorrow transmuted itself at once into literature.[1] He had sought this sublimation as an infallible cure for his grief,[2] but at moments he regretted it: "I write all day long . . . and sometimes I feel myself to be doing wrong and sometimes that I shall be doing wrong if I don't."[3]

If we remember that the *De Consolatione* was immediately followed at Astura by the *Academica*,[4] then by the *De Finibus Bonorum et Malorum*[5] and the beginning of the *Tusculan Disputations*,[6] no one will dare to blame him for having so splendidly enriched Latin letters with the researches and reflections which the loss of his daughter inspired; but neither can anyone avoid suspecting that his thought would have been less active and his pen less productive if the grief that afflicted him had been as profound as he said. His attitude to Dolabella prevents our believing that it was.

3. TOO EASY-GOING A FATHER-IN-LAW

After the irreparable had occurred, we might have expected that the man whose infidelities had assuredly, and whose brutalities had probably, forced Tullia to look on divorce and perhaps even death itself as a deliverance, would have been for ever barred from his ex-father-in-law's friendship. To our surprise, the Correspondence abounds in proofs to the contrary. Dolabella, who could do no less than follow Caesar's example, had sent at the same time as his chief a letter of condolence to Cicero on Tullia's death. He was writing from Spain, where the last battles of the civil war were

---

[1] Since the manuscript was finished on March 14, 45 B.C., cf. above, p. 174.

[2] *Ad Att.* XII, 21, 5 (557 T.P.): *Ab his me remediis noli . . . vocare, ne recidam.* March 17, 45 B.C.

[3] *Ad Att.* XII, 14, 3 (546 T.P.): *Totos dies scribo . . .; idque faciens interdum mihi peccare videor, interdum peccaturus esse nisi faciam.*

[4] *Ad Att.* XII, 45, 1 (590 T.P.): *Ego hic duo magna συντάγματα absolvi.* This applies to the two books of the *Academica*. The letter is of May 13, 45 B.C. Cf. Schanz, op. cit. I, 2, p. 351.

[5] *Ad Att.* XIII, 12, 3 (626 T.P.): *Nunc illam περὶ τελῶν σύνταξιν sane mihi probatam Bruto, ut tibi placuit, despondimus.* June 28, 45 B.C.

[6] In the first book of the *Tusculan Disputations* (10, 21 and 24) Cicero quotes Dicaearchus. Now in a letter of May 29, 45 B.C., Cicero asks Atticus *Dicaearchi περὶ ψυχῆς utrosque mittas et καταβάσεως,* cf. XIII, 32, 2 (610 T.P.); so he was about to start the *Tusculan Disputations,* which were not finished till the following year. Cf. Schanz, op. cit., loc cit., p. 356.

being fought out. Like all the letters of condolence—except one[1]—
those of Caesar and Dolabella are missing from our collections;
but the reply which Cicero did not disdain to make to Dolabella
has come down to us. At the risk of ascribing to his daughter the
blame for the divorce which had so dismally preceded her death,
the inconsolable father wrote with shocking amiability: "I had
rather that my own death had been the cause of your being without
a letter from me than the event which has fallen so heavily upon
me; I should certainly have borne it more easily if I had had you,
for your wise conversation and the remarkable love you bear me
would have lightened it, but since—as I think—I am to see you
before long you shall find me in a state of mind to receive much
assistance from you."[2]

So much tolerance and forgiveness would be incredible if we
were to forget the date of these courtesies. The letter in question
was written at the end of April 45. Now, the battle of Munda had
been fought and won by Caesar on the preceding March 17.[3] It
took a month for Rome to learn of this victory, which paved the
victor's way to universal power.[4] Cicero was therefore writing to
Caesar's right-hand man under the direct impact of this epoch-
making news. His tone was certainly inspired by his overwhelming
desire to curry favour with the master-powers of the day. Just as,
when writing at the end of March to commend Praecilius, he had
paid court to Caesar in a half-chaffing note quite out of tune with
his recent mourning,[5] he now set out to flatter Dolabella so as to
get the continued benefit of his influence with the Dictator. Knowing that his ex-son-in-law was shrewd enough to see through the
game, he added to his letter—which should have been devoted
wholly to Tullia's memory—before sealing it, a few business lines
about his hopes and wishes:[6] "You tell me", he writes, without

---

[1] See above, p. 170.
[2] *Ad Fam.* IX, 11, 1 (576 T.P.): *Vel meo ipsius interitu mallem litteras meas
desiderares quam eo casu, quo sum gravissime adflictus; quem ferrem certe moderatius, si te haberem; nam et oratio tua prudens et amor erga me singularis multum
levaret; sed quoniam brevi tempore, ut opinio nostra est, te sum visurus, ita me
adfectum offendes, ut multum a te possim iuvari.* Ficulea, end of April, 45 B.C.
I have to thank my former teacher, M. René Durand, for having helped me to
interpret the obscure opening of this passage.   [3] *C.I.L.* I (2), p. 312.
[4] With extraordinary speed Caesar had covered the distance between Rome
and Obulco in twenty-seven days. Cf. my *César* (3), p. 949, note 284.
[5] *Ad Fam.* XIII, 15, 1–2 (571 T.P.). From Astura, end of March, 45 B.C.
[6] *Ad Fam.* IX, 11, 2 (576 T.P.): *Quod scribis proelia te mea causa sustinere,
non tam id laboro, ut, si qui mihi obtrectent, a te refutentur, quam intellegi cupio,
quod certe intellegitur, me a te amari.*

transition, "that you have to fight my battles; I don't so much care about your refuting those who slander me, as I wish it to be known —as is plainly the case—that I retain your affection." When he penned these lines, all thought of Tullia had obviously had to give way to the necessities of the situation.

Nor did the dead woman's shade rise to separate Cicero and his ex-son-in-law when Dolabella returned with the advance-guard[1] from Spain and came one morning,[2] June 17, 45, to stay with Cicero in the *villa* of Tusculum, where Tullia had breathed her last[3] and on the walls of which—if we are to believe the letters I have already quoted—her tragic image had stamped an ineffaceable mark.[4] Her hearth and home had been wrecked by the amorous liaisons of her husband, and Cicero had for years been well aware— as was the whole Roman public—of Dolabella's relations with the wife of Lentulus Spinther, and now Dolabella's return coincided with Lentulus Spinther's divorce of Dolabella's mistress Metella.[5] Nevertheless, far from forbidding Dolabella to cross the threshold sanctified by Tullia's death, Cicero welcomed his guest with open arms and felt no shame at the pleasure he took in their conversation: "We had much talk to a late hour in the day. I cannot exaggerate its cordial and affectionate tone." Cicero lost no time in profiting by this indecent visit: "While I had Dolabella with me Torquatus most opportunely arrived. In the kindest manner Dolabella repeated to him what I had been saying. . . . My earnestness seemed to gratify Torquatus."[6, 7] Tullia was dead, but the influence of Dolabella was very much alive and active, and merrily

---

[1] Caesar was not to set out till after mid-July. Cf. my *César* (3), p. 955. Dolabella had been wounded and was obliged to convalesce. Cic. *Phil.* II, 30, 75.

[2] *Ad Att.* XIII, 9, 1 (623 T.P.): *Hodie mane Dolabella.* It would seem that this visit was paid on Cicero's invitation. He sent Tiro to meet the guest.

[3] Cf. above, pp. 168-9. Cf. *Ad Att.* XII, 5, 4 (621 T.P.): *Ego misi Tironem Dolabellae obviam.* Mid-June 45 B.C. [4] See above, p. 169, note 2.

[5] *Ad Att.* XII, 52, 2 (599 T.P.): *Sed quid est, quod audio Spintherem fecisse divortium?* May 21, 45 B.C.; XIII, 7, 1 (619 T.P.). *Lentulum cum Metella certe fecisse divortium.*

[6] *Ad Att.* XIII, 9, 1 (623 T.P.): *Multus sermo ad multum diem. Nihil possum dicere ἐκτενέστερον, nihil φιλοστοργότερον.* June 17, 45 B.C.

[7] *Ad Att.* XIII, 9, 1 (623 T.P.): *Εὐκαίρως ad me venit, cum haberem Dolabellam, Torquatus humanissimeque Dolabella quibus verbis secum egissem exposui . . . Quae diligentia grata est visa Torquato.*

A. Manlius Torquatus had been Quaestor in 52 B.C. He had embraced the cause of Pompey and had been obliged to live in exile in Athens until the end of 46 B.C. He was anxious to regain Caesar's favour. Cf. Tyrrell and Purser, IV, pp. lxxix and lxxx, and the article of *P.W.* XIV, c. 1196-9. We may note that about the same time Cicero, through the mediacy of Dolabella, had obtained an amnesty for Trebianus. Cf. *Ad Fam.* VI, 11, 1 (622 T.P.).

Cicero manipulated and exploited it, thrusting his grief and resentment into the background.

In his excess of zeal he was within an ace of dedicating one of the essays he had written to stifle his sorrow, to this libertine, who was assuredly hungrier for large fortunes than for serious literature. He drew the line, however, at this tactlessness, which would have been also a breach of good taste. He admits that a less difficult and more political thesis[1] would be better adapted to Dolabella. So in the summer of 45 he dedicated the *Academica* to Varro[2] and the *De Finibus* to Brutus[3] and put off the complimentary dedication to Dolabella to a later date. The question put his ingenuity to a severe test: "I don't know which way to turn," he confessed to Atticus on June 25, 45; "I want to satisfy Dolabella's urgent desire to have a book dedicated to him. I don't see my way to a suitable subject and at the same time 'I fear the Trojans'. Now even if I do hit on a subject, I shall not be able to escape criticism."[4] So Cicero was reckoning Dolabella—with Caesar—as a "Trojan" in a hostile camp. But he would have been angered if anyone noticed this, and he did not abandon his flattering attentions towards Caesar's powerful and dangerous partisan. At the close of Dec. 45 he took advantage of being at Puteoli to send to Dolabella, who was at that time staying at Baiae,[5] if not a book written expressly for him, at least a copy of his "little speech" for Deiotarus, and in a gracious letter accompanying the gift he apologised for the modest nature of the present, which is "slight and weak" and "not very worthy of being committed to writing".[6]

Caesar's death changed nothing in these good relations. We shall

---

[1] *Ad Att.* XIII, 10, 2 (624 T.P.): *Ad Dolabellam, ut scribis, ita puto faciendum,* κοινότερα *quaedam et* πολιτικώτερα. June 18–20, 45 B.C. The words "as you write" indicate that Atticus had warned Cicero against the blunder he was about to commit.

[2] *Ad Att.* XIII, 12, 3 (626 T.P.). June 23, 45 B.C.: cf. letters 14, 15 and 16 (627–9 T.P.) and 19 (631 T.P.).

[3] As the title of the dialogue proves and the Correspondence confirms: cf. *Ad Att.* XIII, 23, 2 (637 T.P.): . . . *item libros quos Bruto mittimus in manibus habent librarii.*

[4] *Ad Att.* XIII, 13, 2 (627 T.P.): *Nunc* ἀπορῶ *quo me vertam. Volo Dolabellae valde desideranti: non reperio quid, et simul* αἰδέομαι Τρῶας *neque, si aliquid, potero* μέμψιν *effugere.* June 25, 45 B.C. Cicero adds: "I must either give it up or think out something else"—*Aut cessandum aut aliud aliquid excogitandum.*

[5] *Ad Fam.* IX, 12, 1 (680 T.P.): *Gratulor Baiis nostris si quidem, ut scribis, salubres repente factae sunt.* Puteoli, after Dec. 17, 45 B.C.

[6] *Ad Fam.* IX, 12, 2 (680 T.P.): *Oratiunculam pro Deiotaro, quam requirebas, habebam mecum . . . itaque eam tibi misi, quam velim sic legas ut causam tenuem et inopem nec scriptione magno opere dignam.*

be the less surprised at this when we recall that Dolabella replaced the murdered Dictator in the consulship, and that Cicero wanted to support him in opposition to the other Consul, the future Triumvir, Mark Antony. Until April 44 these two "Presidents of the Roman Republic" governed in harmony. Towards the end of the month, however, Mark Antony committed the imprudence of leaving Rome for Campania to get on with the apportionment of land to his veterans. Dolabella, who would not have been sorry to supplant Antony, got into touch with the "tyrannicides", forbade the worship of the murdered "god", the celebration of which was held in the Forum on the spot where Caesar's body had been cremated, knocked down the commemorative column which had been put up there, and stamped out with death and torture the revolt provoked by these reactionary measures. Cicero, on the other hand, was naturally delighted and on May 1, 44, he burst out into cries of rejoicing: "O, my admirable Dolabella! For now I call him mine. Before this, believe me, I had my secret doubts. . . . It is indeed a marvellous achievement: execution from the rock, on the cross, removal of the column, the contract given out for repaving the place. In short, positively heroic!"[1] Two days later, fresh ecstasies in a letter to Cassius; and for Dolabella himself warmest congratulations. In these Cicero claims a share; for, he says, public opinion associates him with the young Consul's exploits, and Dolabella must not feel it any detraction from his glory or dignity, "as it was none to that of Agamemnon himself, the 'king of kings', to have Nestor to assist him in his deliberations".[2]

The truth is that, whether he would have wished it or not, Dolabella by his impulsive action had made himself dependent on the anti-Caesar "conspirators" and could now make no headway against Mark Antony, of whom he had made an enemy, without forming an alliance with them, nor without Cicero's support in the Senate. Hence Cicero's rejoicing. He was only too happy to acknowledge Dolabella as his "leader" while at the same time

[1] *Ad Att.* XIV, 15, 2 (720 T.P.): *O mirificum Dolabellam meum. Iam enim dico meum, antea, crede mihi, subdubitabam.* Cf. ibid. 16, 2 (721 T.P.). May 2, 44 B.C. It would seem that Atticus reproved Cicero for such warmth. Ibid. 18, 1 (726 T.P.): *. . . saepius me iam agitas quod rem gestam Dolabellae nimis in caelum videar efferre.*
[2] *Ad Att.* XIV, 17A=*Ad Fam.* IX, 14, 1 (722 T.P.): *Non possum non confiteri cumulari me maximo gaudio, quod vulgo hominum opinio socium me adscribat tuis laudibus . . . (2) et tamen non alienum est dignitate tua, quod ipsi Agamemnoni regum regi fuit honestum, aliquem in consiliis capiendis Nestorem habere.*

having this leader under his thumb.[1] Hence too the presence of mind with which he immediately cashed in on the advantages of a situation in which Dolabella had breached his own consular authority and hampered his own freedom of action.

He exploited his influence in favour of Atticus, who was busy trying to get a sentence of confiscation revoked which Caesar had passed on the people of Buthrotum in Epirus, of whom Atticus was a creditor. They had refused to obey a requisition of Caesar's and he had punished them by this confiscation order. If this were upheld, the debtors would be expropriated and in consequence rendered insolvent and unable to pay their creditors. From Tusculum he propounded this subject to Dolabella, and on June 26, 44, he received satisfactory promises from him. Dolabella had done and was ready to do anything Atticus wanted.[2]

First and foremost, however, he exerted pressure on Dolabella in his own interests. For the first time since Tullia's death[3] he let himself remember that Dolabella had married his daughter, and that after their divorce it was up to the ex-husband to repay her dowry. The payment was five months overdue and Cicero took courage to demand it. On May 8, 44, he pilloried the rapacity of Dolabella, whose procrastinations exasperated him,[4] and he decided to show his teeth. Dolabella should have paid up on the preceding Jan. 1. He had paid nothing, though he had only to plunder the treasury of the Goddess of Assistance (*Ops*) for the assistance (*opem*) that he needed.[5] Driven to extremes, he wrote

---

[1] *Ad Att.* XIV, 20, 4 (727 T.P.): *Nunc autem videmur habituri ducem : quod unum municipia bonique desiderant.* May 11, 44 B.C. Cicero outlines the plan he was later to try to put into practice against Octavian. What an illusion!

[2] *Ad Att.* XV, 14, 1 (758 T.P.): . . . *vi Kal. Iulias accepi a Dolabella litteras, quarum exemplum tibi misi in quibus erat omnia se feciosse quae tu velles.* Then follows the text of Cicero's letter of thanks to Dolabella.

[3] Just after Tullia's divorce, when her time was nearly complete, in Jan. 45 B.C., Cicero had thought he might be driven to force Dolabella's agents to pay up the first instalment. Cf. *Ad Fam.* VI, 18, 5 (534 T.P.): . . . *dum a Dolabellae procuratoribus exigam primam pensionem* (letter to Lepta) and he had explained that the possible need for these steps was the reason of his staying on in Rome. Cf. above, pp. 169–70. After that, nothing till May 44 B.C.

[4] There are various readings of the text: *aritia* probably stands for *avaritia*, "rapacity", *Ad Att.* XIV, 19, 1 (745 T.P.): *Cum Dolabellae aritia magna desperatione adfectus essem.*

[5] *Ad Att.* XIV, 18, 1 (726 T.P.): *O hominem pudentem [Dolabellam]! Kal. Jan. debuit : adhuc non solvit praesertim cum opem ab Ope petierit.* May 9, 44 B.C. The pun, restored by a correction of Cobet's, is all the more pleasing since the war-funds collected by Caesar for a Parthian campaign had been deposited in the temple of Ops, next door to his residence as Pontifex Maximus. Perhaps Cicero is speaking in this passage of the second instalment. Cf. above, p. 169, and below, pp. 183–4.

Dolabella so stinging a letter that "even if it does no good, I think he will be unable to face me when we meet".[1]

It is surely a thousand pities that this letter has not been preserved. But we can divine the acid tone of it from the irony of Cicero's phrases to Atticus: "You say that I make a good deal of Dolabella's achievement; so I do, but it would be a still greater achievement if he would pay me what he owes me."[2] Next day, writing from Puteoli, where he had been hearing praises of a harangue Dolabella had delivered to the Assembly of the people to set them against Lucius Antonius's agrarian schemes for the Pontine Marshes, Cicero kept to his point. He was willing to compromise if he received immediate satisfaction that the principle was recognised: "By all means let him keep the money (the capital), provided he pays (the interest) on the Ides."[3] On May 24 Cicero despatched Tiro to his recalcitrant debtor with another letter and with verbal instructions.[4]

This time, without yet making any money payment to Cicero, Dolabella paid him with a favour of infinitely greater value. Having been appointed to the governorship of Syria for the year 43 he entered his father-in-law's name on the list of his *legati* on June 5, 44. At the moment Italy could not offer personal security to anyone. The rival political factions were eyeing each other and only waiting to fly at each other's throats, and Cicero was, most naturally, longing for a change of air. The *legatio* which his ex-son-in-law suddenly put at his disposal came most opportunely. It gave him a guarantee of safety all the more valuable that he could avail himself of it without seeming to take flight. He could quit Rome under the pretext of serving the State in undertaking a distant mission entrusted to him by one of the Consuls and

---

[1] *Ad Att.* XIV, 18, 1 (726 T.P.): *Satis aculeatas ad Dolabellam litteras dedi, quae, si nihil profecerint, puto fore ut me praesentem non sustineat.*

[2] *Ad Att.* XIV, 19, 5 (725 T.P.): *Tibi vero adsentior maiorem* πρᾶξιν *eius fore, si mihi quod debuit dissolverit.* May 8, 44 B.C.

[3] *Ad Att.* XIV, 20, 2 (727 T.P.): *L. Antonii horribilis contio, Dolabella praeclara. Iam vel sibi habeat nummos, modo numeret Idibus.* The Ides were, of course, the recognised "pay-days" when debts fell due. See my article in the *Mélanges Radet*, Bordeaux-Paris, 1940.

[4] *Ad Att.* XV, 4B, 5 (735 T.P.): *Ad Dolabellam Tironem misi cum mandatis et litteris.* From Arpinum, May 24, 44 B.C. Tiro was also to plead for Atticus in the Buthrotum business which is the subject of this letter; cf. 12, 1 (745 T.P.): *Bene de Buthroto. At ego Tironem ad Dolabellam cum litteris, quia iusseras, miseram.* Astura, June 10, 44 B.C.

endorsed by the other.[1] It is true that the post was a sinecure whose duties he could not have defined and the uselessness of which was a favourite subject of mirth between him and his intimate friends.[2]

In the course of the summer the relative positions of Cicero and Dolabella were abruptly reversed. In June, Cicero, with an eye to his *legatio*, was making enquiries about means of transport[3] and a route which would reduce sea-crossings to a minimum.[4] By July 17 he had set out.[5] But however he might seek to mislead people about his real wishes, it was obvious enough that he had no great enthusiasm about the journey, and that he was scanning the horizon for some signal bidding him retrace his steps. If this had not been so, he would not have sailed for Greece by way of the Tyrrhenian Sea,[6] nor would he have put so often into Italian ports.[7] As soon as he learned that Brutus and Cassius had, on Aug. 4, flung down the gauntlet to Mark Antony,[8] he realised that he would have allies in the war he was burning to wage against Antony. Relieved of his fears, he decided to turn back, and he landed at Pompeii on Aug. 19, completing the circular tour he had begun from that place thirty-two days before. Dolabella, on the other hand, whose place at the head of the opposition to Antony was being taken by Octavian, was now interested in getting into closer touch with Antony. As for Cicero and Dolabella, their relationship was thereby finally and fatally ruined.

[1] Dolabella, Consul and Proconsul Designate, nominated Cicero as one of his *legati* on June 2 and Cicero learned of his appointment on the 7th, the evening before his letter to Atticus, *Ad Att.* XV, 11, 4 (744 T.P.) . . . *sed heus, tu ne forte sis nescius, Dolabella me sibi legavit a. d. IIII Nonas Iunias. Id mihi heri vesperi nuntiatum est.* Antony's acquiescence had been sought in anticipation as early as May 31; cf. ibid. 8, 1 (741 T.P.): . . . *scripsi ad Antonium de legatione, ne, si ad Dolabellam solum scripsissem, iracundus homo commoveretur.* Oppius also gave his approval at the beginning of July. Cf. *Ad Fam.* IX, 29, 1 (762 T.P.).

[2] *Ad Att.* XV, 19, 1 (751 T.P.): *A Dolabella mandata habebo, quae mihi videbuntur, id est nihil.* June 16–19, 44 B.C.

[3] He applied to Dolabella for mules: *Ad Att.* XV, 18, 1 (750 T.P.): *Scripsi ad Dolabellam me, si ei videretur, velle proficisci petiique ab eo de mulis vecturae itineris.*

[4] He consulted Atticus about the route: *Ad Att.* XV, 25 (759 T.P.): *De meo itinere variae sententiae . . . ; sed tu incumbe, quaeso, in eam curam*, etc. June 44 B.C.

[5] See following note.

[6] *Ad Att.* XVI, 3, 6 (773 T.P.): *Haec ego conscendens e Pompeiano tribus actuariolis decemscalmis.* July 17, 44 B.C.

[7] He ought to have embarked at Brindisi or Otranto (Brundisium or Hydrus). *Ad Att.* XV, 21, 3 (753 T.P.). Now, leaving Pompeii on July 17th, he was at Velia on the 20th: *Ad Fam.* VII, 20, 1 (774 T.P.); at Vibo on the 25th, *Ad Att.* XVI, 6, 1 (775 T.P.); at Rhegium on the 28th: *Ad Fam.* VII, 19 (786 T.P.); his last port of call was Leucopetra on Aug. 6: *Ad Att.* XVI, 7, 1 (783 T.P.).

[8] Cf. *Ad Fam.* XI, 3 (782 T.P.) the letter of the two Praetors, Brutus and Cassius, to the Consul Marcus Antonius from Naples, Aug. 4, 44 B.C.

Cicero could not immediately resign himself to the breach. Anticipating the reconciliation which he feared between Dolabella and Antony, he first tried to prevent it. In the first open attack which he launched against Antony on Sept. 2, 44, when Dolabella was presiding over the meeting of the Senate, he took the precaution of scrupulously dissociating Dolabella's cause from Antony's. While vigorously accusing Antony in the first of his *Philippics*, he pointedly showered compliments on Dolabella, referring in the most flattering terms to his past conduct and in fulsome words to him as "one most dear to me": *Dolabella qui est mihi carissimus*.[1] On Sept. 19, the day on which he was to have pronounced that masterpiece of invective the second of the *Philippics*, he was definitely less prodigal of compliments to Antony's colleague. And when it came to circulating the text of this oration in copies made for him by Atticus's scribes, he touched it up in such a way as to pluck yet more blossoms from the meagre garland of praise with which he had adorned the brow of his sometime son-in-law.[2] But he was still careful not to burn his boats, fearing on the one hand that he might merely drive Dolabella into Antony's arms, and on the other that he might ruin all chance of ever recovering Tullia's dowry. So he abode by his determination to nurse Dolabella at any cost.[3]

His methods, however, were not over-subtle, and Dolabella was not the kind of man to be taken in by blarney that was so obviously interested. He was himself a past-master in the arts of dissimulation and deceit. He set himself first to allay suspicion and then to do his ex-father-in-law in the eye. One deceiver was up against a deceiver and a half. Somewhere about Oct. 26, 44, Cicero, completely reassured, wrote from Puteoli telling Atticus of a message he had just received from "that fine fellow Dolabella": "He wrote to me from Formiae—a letter which reached me just as I had left the bath—saying that he had done his best about assigning debts to me. He lays the blame on Vettienus, who of course has his

---

[1] Cic. *Phil.* I, 12, 29. It is significant that these words are recorded only in some secondary MSS., as if they had disappeared from a revised version of the authorised text transmitted by the Medicean codex (M).

[2] *Ad Att.* XVI, 11, 2 (799 T.P.): *De laudibus Dolabellae deruam cumulum.* As a matter of fact, the only praise of Dolabella that is to be found in the *Second Philippic* relates to his military exploits. Cic. *Phil.* II, 30, 75: *Ter depugnavit Caesar cum civibus, in Thessalia, Africa, Hispania. Omnibus adfuit his pugnis Dolabella; in Hispaniensi etiam vulnus accepit.*

[3] Just as he nursed Octavian. Cf. *Ad Att.* XV, 12, 2 (745 T.P.): *Sed tamen alendus est et, ut nihil aliud, ab Antonio seiungendus.* June 10, 44 B.C.

dodges (for delaying payment) like a true business man. But he says that Sestius has taken over the whole affair. He is indeed an excellent man and very much attached to us."[1] What a nice letter! While he was thus encouraging Cicero's illusions, Dolabella was secretly preparing to play him a mean trick, and on the sly took ship for Macedonia and Syria. A fortnight later this debtor who had seemed so honest and accommodating was sailing off to his province and his doom, sailing probably as an accomplice of Mark Antony's and most certainly without having paid a penny to Cicero.[2]

Robbed, hoaxed and laughed at, the victim wrathfully explodes: "To come to business. If Dolabella had not treated me in the most dishonourable way I should perhaps have hesitated whether to be somewhat easy with him or fight to the limit of the law. As it is, however, I rejoice that an opportunity is given me of showing him and everybody else that I have become estranged from him. I will make that very plain, as also that I detest him, not only for my own sake for also for the sake of the Republic."[3]

Do these last words imply a painful memory of Tullia, the young wife whom Dolabella drove to despair, the beloved daughter whose loss Cicero vowed he would never cease to mourn? We cannot be sure. But if they do, Cicero had taken a long time to feel the influence of the tragic past. Worn out by over-strain and trial, Tullia had died in Feb. 45 and the above letter is dated mid-Nov. 44. Three months later Cicero delivered the eleventh *Philippic* demanding from the Senate Dolabella's head, the head of the man convicted of the cowardly murder of Trebonius, the head of a scoundrel and a parricide.[4]

Chronology therefore offers us the choice between two interpretations only. At best, Cicero repressed his well-justified wrath for twenty months and gave it vent only after having been cheated

[1] *Ad Att.* XV, 13A, 5 (795 T.P.): *Dolabella vir optimus est . . . Ad me ex Formiano scripsit, quas litteras, cum e balineo exissem, accepi, sese de attributione omnia summa fecisse; Vettienum accusat, tricatur scilicet ut monetalis; sed ait totum negotium Sestium nostrum accepisse, optimumque quidem illum virum nostrique amantissimum . . .* Puteoli, Oct. 26–29, 44 B.C.

[2] See *Ad Att.* XVI, 3, 5 (773 T.P.). It looks as if Dolabella had left on Cicero's hands nothing but an unpromising law-suit. *Ad Att.* XVI, 15, 2 (807 T.P.).

[3] *Ad Att.* XVI, 15, 1 (807 T.P.): *Ego si me non improbissime Dolabella tractasset, dubitassem fortasse, utrum remissior essem an summo iure contenderem. Nunc vero etiam gaudeo mihi causam oblatam, in qua et ipse sentiat et reliqui omnes me ab illo abalienatum, idque prae me feram, et quidem me mea causa facere et reipublicae, ut illum oderim.* After Nov. 11, 44 B.C.

[4] See in particular Cic. *Phil.* XI, 12, 29.

as creditor and betrayed as statesman. At worst, he had been
conscious of no wrath until stung to anger by his personal morti-
fication. It required loss of money and political disappointment to
rouse that hatred for Dolabella with which neither the bitterness
of his grief, nor his fatherly love, nor concern for his personal
honour had inspired him. Whichever way we look at it, this lack
of humanity—in the fullest sense of the word—surprises and
horrifies the modern mind.

This unnatural indifference has worried and disconcerted the
most fervent admirers of Cicero. In order to reconcile it with their
worship of the great man, they go so far as to generalise it. They
throw the responsibility for it on to the difficulty of the terrible
times in which he lived, on to the manners of a period one of whose
most repellent features is illustrated by his example.[1] But is it not
unjust and over-daring to attribute to a whole generation that
hardness of heart which they cannot deny, and yet are loth to
blame, in Cicero? People of noble and delicate feeling breathed the
air in that iron age. Virgil was born in it, and there died about the
same time as Cicero that Roman matron—identified on insufficient
grounds with Turia—whose *laudatio*, or funeral oration, engraved
on her tomb, exhales a breath of Christian graciousness before
Christianity had come.[2] Cicero's Correspondence, moreover, rich
though it is in psychological material, offers no basis for comparisons which would entitle us to extend to the whole of Roman
society those ugly features which disfigure Cicero's face.

The unwelcome but obvious truth is that the publication of his
Letters debases him even in his role of loving father. His love for
Tullia was the strongest, the purest feeling he possessed. Nevertheless so superficial was it that it gave way either before his love
of lucre or before his personal ambition. Legend tells us that in
obedience to the oracles and for the salvation of the Greeks,
Agamemnon sacrificed his daughter Iphigenia—but he sacrificed
only her life. The *Letters* show us that Cicero sacrificed the very
memory of Tullia to the shifting intrigues of his politics. They
damn their writer all the more thoroughly when they relentlessly

[1] See, in particular, Tyrrell and Purser, IV, p. lxxxiii: "The extraordinary
unconcern with which marriage connections were broken off, as well as the
absence of any ill-feeling between the families of the separated parties, is a
remarkable feature in the social life of Rome."

[2] *C.I.L.* VI, 1527 and 31670=Dessau *I.L.S.* 8393. On this *laudatio* see
Marcel Durry's edition, translation and commentary, which M. Durry was kind
enough to let me read.

expose those political intrigues, the incoherence and pettiness of his motives, the hesitations of his conduct and the futility of its results.[1]

[1] Before embarking on a discussion of Cicero's "politics" as revealed in his *Letters* we should need a whole chapter on his bad relations with his brother Quintus and the other members of this disunited family. To minimise in Caesar's eyes his responsibility for having suddenly and belatedly thrown in his lot with Pompey, Cicero brazenfacedly represented Quintus as the instigator of this impulsive action. Cf. *Ad Att.* XI, 9, 2 (423 T.P.). Jan. 3, 47 B.C. And without a blush he represented his brother as having denounced him to the conqueror. Ibid. 8, 2 (422 T.P.). We are spared nothing of the squabbles of Quintus with Pomponia—sister of Atticus—in the course of a marriage which was already in 48 B.C. threatening to end in divorce, for if we are to believe *Ad Att.* XIV, 13, 5 (718 T.P.) Quintus was in April 44 B.C. thinking of marrying Aquilia.

The life of Quintus and Pomponia had been a perpetually stormy one; as long as the two lived under one roof, it was filled with mean and petty naggings recorded for us in the *Letters*: cf. *Ad Att.* V, 1, 3-4 (184 T.P.). Nor are we spared the quarrels of the estranged couple with their son—the younger Quintus —who would insolently espouse the cause now of the one parent and now of the other, according to circumstances; cf. *Ad Att.* XIV, 10, 4 (713 T.P.). We hear too all about the lapses in speech and conduct of this spoilt boy, of which both uncles, Cicero and Atticus, in turn complain; cf. *Ad Att.* XIII, 42, 1 (681 T.P.).

But I must limit this revelation of family misery and dissension, and here simply note that it provides one further proof of the hostile intention of the persons who published Cicero's Correspondence. It was not for the pleasure of wreaking posthumous vengeance on allies or relatives who had given him trouble that Atticus transgressed Cicero's formal instructions (*Ad Att.* X, 12, 3; 397 T.P.) and washed the family's dirty linen in the Forum. The important thing was, by defamation of the Ciceros, to cover the stain with which Octavian's Triumvirate was besmirched by having put to death Marcus Tullius Cicero, his brother Quintus, and his nephew, the three persons proscribed in Dec. 43 B.C.

PART II

CICERO'S POLITICS AS SEEN IN HIS LETTERS

WHATEVER political reputation other authorities ascribe —or leave—to Cicero, his Correspondence most effectually destroys. The *Letters* reduce to nothingness his most deserving attempts at intervention, prick the bubble of his most eloquent and resounding speeches and give the lie to the noblest declarations of his philosophical treatises. They illuminate fully— or re-illuminate—the events in which he played an inglorious part. In order not to prejudice Cicero, Plutarch passes over these in silence or prudently tones them down, or by ingenious little touches—of which but for the *Letters* we should be unaware— distorts or travesties them in a greater or less degree.

Worse still: Cicero's Correspondence, revealing the real motives which underlay certain of his actions, motives known only to himself and his intimates, reduces the majority of them to pettiness and convicts the writer of an incompetence which was veiled by his gift of speech. The *Letters* reveal the greatest orator of the Roman Republic as a politician with no convictions, no loyalty and no courage. His inordinate vanity led him to entertain extravagant illusions. Under the weight of his blunders and his faults, he inevitably sank into inexcusable mistakes and irreparable failure. Apart from his *Letters*, Cicero would retain in the eyes of History at least some features of the statesman he claimed to be. In his *Letters* we find only the hateful, pitiable, or ludicrous caricature of a statesman.

Chapter I

THE BLUNDERS OF A CAREER THAT FAILED

LET us look at the major episodes in the long public life of Cicero: his conduct of the highest offices of the City-State, the praetorship and the consulship; his exile; his eclipse at the time of the First Triumvirate; his timid participation in the Civil War; and his attempt to seize power after Caesar's death as leader of the incongruous coalition which included Brutus and Octavian amongst its members. Everywhere we are struck by the same contrast as we have noted in the case of his proconsulship of Cilicia[1]: between, on the one hand, the frank apologia contained in his writings and the veiled apologia of Plutarch's biography—based no doubt on Tiro's[2]—and, on the other, the stealthy or openly savage attacks which the confidences of his *Letters* were bound to provoke.

I. PRAETOR AND CONSUL

The series of letters relating to his two senior magistracies begins in 68, when he had just completed his year of office as Aedile[3] and was on the eve of assuming the praetorship, to which he had been elected in 67 and in which he officiated in 66.[4] The *Letters* at once put us on our guard against the over-indulgent statement of Plutarch that Cicero's praetorian decrees won him a great reputation for integrity.[5] His own words disclose the truth that belies the two examples of his virtue quoted by his biographer.[6] The first

---

[1] Cf. above, p. 119. [2] Cf. above, p. 42.
[3] Drumann-Groebe, V, p. 349f. [4] Cf. Drumann-Groebe, V, p. 377f.
[5] Plut. *Cicero*, IX, 1: "This verdict was considered very creditable to Cicero, as showing his careful management of the Courts of Justice"; and a few lines earlier: "He managed the decision of causes with justice and integrity."
[6] This is quite natural if the two examples were included in Tiro's earlier biography.

refers to the trial of Caius Licinius Macer, who was accused of extortion. The defendant, trusting in the weight of his own and his relatives' influence, felt so certain of his impunity that when the Praetor closed the debate to allow the jury to proceed with their voting, he hastened home to tidy up and put on a fresh toga, so as to reappear triumphantly in the Forum. He had a bitter disillusionment. As he was leaving his house Crassus informed him that the jury had unanimously found him guilty. Licinius Macer was shattered by the blow, took to his bed and died shortly afterwards. Plutarch ends his account of the affair not by expressing sympathy for the fatal consequences of this severe condemnation, but by praising Cicero for the zeal with which as president of the court he had conducted the trial and made the sentence possible.[1]

Untimely zeal, immoral zeal it was, if we are to believe the letter which Cicero wrote to Atticus after the conclusion of the sitting. The self-satisfaction with which he writes disarms criticism: "I have conducted the case of Caius Macer with such marked popular approval as you would scarcely have believed possible. Though I might have taken a lenient view of the case, I gave judgment against him and I reaped much greater advantage from the people's approval of his condemnation than I could have gained from his good offices had he been acquitted."[2] What is there to be said? Only one thing: Cicero was inclined to believe in the innocence of the accused, nevertheless, preferring popularity to justice, he lightheartedly influenced the jury to bring in a verdict of guilty—the consequences of which proved tragic. This letter implicitly belies the undeserved praise which Plutarch accorded Cicero in the matter.

Similarly, the *Letters* rob Cicero of the credit his biographer gives him in the second example he quotes, the trial of Manilius for extortion. Cicero cited Manilius shortly before his judicial office expired. The accused requested an adjournment. Contrary to custom, which permitted a respite of ten days, the Praetor for sole answer fixed the trial for the following day. This apparent harshness displeased the crowd at first and stirred up the Tribunes of the Plebs. The harshness was only feigned. Cicero had in fact granted Manilius the last opportunity that he as Praetor would

---

[1] Plut. *Cicero*; cf. a variant in Val. Max. IX, 12, 7.
[2] *Ad Att.* I, 4, 2 (9 T.P.): *Nos . . . incredibili ac singulari populi voluntate de C. Macro transegimus. Cui cum aequi fuissemus, tamen multo maiorem fructum ex populi existimatione illo damnato cepimus quam ex ipsius, si absolutus esset, gratia cepissemus.*

have of procuring a favourable verdict for him. He had hurried on the trial only in order to be sure of securing an acquittal.[1] Cicero was therefore convinced that the defendant's case was good. It certainly was; but the case was good in his eyes not because Manilius was innocent but because Manilius was a friend of Pompey and a favourite of the people. Quintus reminded his brother of this fact one day—making no bones about it—when totting up the chances Cicero had in 64 of being elected to the consulship. He is careful not to forget amongst others "that you have won the city populace . . . by undertaking the cause of Manilius."[2] In this as in the former case Cicero's Correspondence strips him of undeserved credit. The letters make it clear that he was by no means the pure and incorruptible Praetor that Plutarch, following Tiro, wished to depict for us, but an intriguing rhetorician more easily swayed by public opinion than by truth and prepared to sacrifice justice to his own electoral prospects. To reverse a famous saying to his disadvantage, we see him in his Praetorian court not rendering judgments but services. In other words, his decisions, whether indulgent or severe, were dictated, as his *Letters* admit, solely by consideration of his own personal advantage.

Passing on from his praetorship to his consulship. Like all his other works—speeches, dialogues or poetry—his *Letters* are full of dithyrambic passages devoted to the glory of his magistracy.[3] It is easy to imagine that his perpetual harping on this theme and inviting everyone else to join in the chorus[4] ended by wearying and boring everybody.[5] But his *Letters* are absolutely silent about the actual facts which they incessantly and extravagantly extol.[6] We have no single letter of 63, the *annus mirabilis*[7] in which Consul Cicero defeated the agrarian law of Rullus; quieted, by an improvised speech, the murmurings of the theatre against the privileges of the Equites and their champion Roscius Otho; by his defence of the aged Senator Rabirius upheld the legality of the quasi-dictatorship which in cases of disturbance the *Fathers* used to

[1] Plut. *Cic.* IX, 3–5.
[2] *Comm. Pet.* XIII, 51 (12 T.P.): *Iam urbanam illam multitudinem . . . adeptus es . . . Manilii causa recipienda.*
[3] Praises in the Correspondence of 62 and 61 B.C. Cf. below, p. 250f. For what follows see Drumann-Groebe, V, p. 512f.
[4] Cf. the letter to Lucceius, *Ad Fam.* V, 12 (109 T.P.) of 56 B.C.
[5] Cf. Plut. *Cic.* XXIV, 1.
[6] Cf. Sen. *De Brev. Vit.* V, 1: *Non sine causa sed sine fine laudatus . . .*
[7] The chapter on Cicero's consulship in Rice Holmes's *Roman Republic* is entitled *Annus Mirabilis*.

confer on the supreme magistrates; and finally saved Rome from the horrors of civil war by unmasking and suppressing the conspiracy of Catiline.[1]

Our collections contain no letters between 65 and the beginning of 62,[2] as if during this lapse of time the indefatigable letter-writer had written to no one. In 62 his letters re-echo to the self-admiration which fills him as he remembers his recent and most famous victory, and we soon weary of this sonorous insistence.[3] In 65 they recall facts which would otherwise be buried in merciful oblivion and which retrospectively tarnish the glory of which he is so proud. They show us the future prosecutor of Catiline not only disposed to forgive his crimes but fully prepared to conclude an abominable alliance with him. At the beginning of July 65, Cicero with cynical calm foresaw that by dint of collusion—a possibility which he records without raising an eyebrow—between the accused and his judges, Catiline, indicted for undeniable exploitation, but now and henceforth certain of securing an iniquitous acquittal, intended to stand for the Consulship at the same time as he himself. "Catiline will be a certain competitor if the jury bring in a verdict that the sun does not shine at noonday."[4] Towards the end of the same month Cicero went further and confessed to Atticus an idea that had occurred to him—though he ultimately gave it up[5]—that he was thinking "at the moment" of himself undertaking the defence of this blackguard.

Picturing himself in the role that he would in that case be playing, he unblushingly adds: "We have a jury to our mind with the full consent of the prosecutor. I hope that if he is acquitted he will be more closely united with me in the conduct of our canvass; but if things turn out otherwise, I shall bear it with resignation."[6]

So Cicero, to increase his chances of securing the consulship (in 64 for 63), was calmly contemplating in 65 concluding an electoral

---

[1] *Ad Att.* II, 1, 3 (27 T.P.) gives a list of his consular speeches. This letter dates from 60 B.C.

[2] Letter No. 12 in Tyrrell and Purser's edition (*Comm. Petitionis*) dates from the beginning of 64 B.C.; letter No. 13 (*Ad Fam.* V, 2) is of Jan. or Feb. 62 B.C.

[3] Cf. *Ad Fam.* V, 2 (13 T.P.), 1 and 2; *Ad Att.* I, 16, 5 (22 T.P.).

[4] *Ad Att.* I, 1, 1 (10 T.P.): *Catilina, si iudicatum erit meridie non lucere, certus erit competitor.*

[5] Cf. above, pp. 24–5, where this passage and that following are quoted and commented on from the point of view of Asconius's use of them.

[6] *Ad Att.* I, 2, 1 (11 T.P.): *Hoc tempore Catilinam, competitorem nostrum, defendere cogitamus. Iudices habemus quos voluimus summa accusatoris voluntate. Spero, si absolutus erit, coniunctiorem illum nobis fore in ratione petitionis; sin aliter acciderit, humaniter feremus.*

pact with this man "sunk in debt and crime" whom two years later he blasted with all the thunders and lightnings of his eloquence. It makes no difference whether he did or did not in fact undertake Catiline's defence.[1] It is sufficient shame that even for a moment he toyed with the thought of doing so, and that meantime he lent himself to the infamous judicial farce which was to whitewash the robber whose victims had caught him with his hand in their pocket. It was certainly a feat to have made the Curia and the Forum quiver under the "useful"[2] reverberation of the Catiline orations. It was, above all, a feat to have reduced to naught the revolutionary plot woven by Catiline, though the success was bought, it is true, at the cost of murderous executions in the dungeon of the Tullianum and a pitched battle on the plain of Pistoria.

But how much better it would have been for Cicero to have forestalled all these attempts at bloody revolution by making common cause—while there was yet time, and common honesty demanded it—with his fellow-citizens who were clamouring for a death-sentence on this bandit, an execution which would once and for all have wiped Catiline off the political map! In very truth the glory which he claims for having cleansed the Roman State of Catiline's criminal enterprises is ruined by the dishonour which besmirches him for having contributed to making such enterprises possible by the semi-complicity which his Correspondence betrays.

2. EXILE

Moreover, this very glory became dangerous when his enemy Clodius, now an elected Tribune of the Plebs, sought a means of turning it against the self-glorifier. Clodius promulgated the draft of a law which, without expressly naming Cicero, condemned to perpetual banishment the Consul guilty of slaying the Catiline conspirators without having appealed to the people to ratify the capital sentence. Immemorial custom guaranteed this right of appeal to the humblest of Roman citizens. Cicero had silently ignored it, and he now abandoned himself most pitiably to despair.

Two courses were open to him, as he later wrote to his wife: he could either give up his resistance to the Triumvirs and accept the *legatio* offered him by Caesar in his province of Gaul, or he could

---

[1] Cf. above, p. 25.
[2] The word is Sallust's, *Cat.* XXXI, 6: *M. Tullius consul orationem habuit luculentam atque utilem reipublicae.*

The Blunders of a Career that Failed

resist his enemies, who in the circumstances were also the enemies of free senatorial government, and try to overcome them in the *Comitiae* by the magic of his words. If, despite his eloquence and the evidence of the facts, he were to fall under their blows, he would bequeath to them the odium of his death rather than be false to himself by a cowardly submission to their iniquitous persecution.[1]

He followed neither course. He was too full of himself to believe in the reality of his danger; too full of himself to evade it by an arrangement which would place him in a subordinate position. When the danger actually overtook him, he had not the force of character to face it. After some days of humiliating and theatrical supplications,[2] panic seized him and at nightfall on March 20, 58, on the eve of the Assembly which would reject or pass the plebiscite proposed by Clodius, he fled, without waiting for the result of the voting, like a criminal who has the courage neither to fight nor to uphold his rights. After this, having without a battle left the field to his opponents, he spent eleven months[3] filling the letters which strewed the route of his exile—from Brundisium, from Thessalonica, from Dyrrhachium—with recrimination and remorse, with groans and fears, which betray the chaos in his mind, the weakness of his character and his utter lack of dignity: "I am so heart-broken and dejected"[4] . . . "I am the most miserable man alive and am being worn out with the most poignant sorrow"[5] . . . "I am very wretched and can scarcely bear my life"[6] . . . "Tears do not allow me to write"[7] . . . "I cannot write the rest, so copious are my tears"[8] . . . "How much weeping do you

[1] *Ad Fam.* XIV, 3, 1 (84 T.P.): *Meum fuit officium vel legatione vitare periculum vel diligentia et copiis resistere vel cadere fortiter.* Nov. 29, 58 B.C. On the *legatio* cf. *Ad Att.* II, 18, 3 (45 T.P.): *A Caesare valde liberaliter invitor in legationem illam sibi ut sim legatus, atque etiam libera legatio voti causa datur.* June or July, 59 B.C.

[2] He made approaches to Piso and to Pompey; he left his beard untrimmed, his hair uncut; he put on mourning: cf. Plut. *Cic.* XXX, 4, and XXXI, 1-3; Ciaceri, *Cicerone e i suoi tempi,* Milan, 1930, II, p. 49.

[3] From the end of March 58—*Ad Att.* III, 1 (59 T.P.)—to the beginning of 57 B.C.—ibid. III, 27 (88 T.P.).

[4] *Ad Att.* III, 2 (57 T.P.): . . . *ita sum animo perculso et abiecto.* April 8, 58 B.C.

[5] *Ad Att.* III, 5 (60 T.P.): *Ego vivo miserrimus et maximo dolore conficior.* April 10, 58 B.C.

[6] *Ad Att.* III, 6 (61 T.P.): *Me vix misereque sustento.* April 17, 58 B.C.

[7] *Ad Q. Fr.* I, 3, 10 (66 T.P.): . . . *me lacrimae non sinunt scribere.* June 13, 58 B.C.

[8] *Ad Fam.* XIV, 1, 5 (82 T.P.): *Non queo reliqua scribere, tanta vis lacrimarum est.* Nov. 25, 58 B.C.

think it has cost me to write these things?"[1] . . . "When I write to you or read your letters I am so weakened with tears that I cannot endure it."[2] He sobs as he thinks of all he has lost: his rights as a citizen, his worldly wealth, the people whom he loves, in short: "I miss . . . myself."[3] When he compares his present misery with his past glory, his sobs redouble: "Can I forget what I was and not feel what I am?"[4]

So great is his sorrow, so profound his despair, that those who saw him in Macedonia were struck by his emaciated condition and so anxious about his dazed and agitated state and his lack of will-power—which he confesses to Atticus[5]—that they spread in Rome the rumour that he was gradually going mad.[6] When he now and again masters his despondency, it is only to call down curses on the men who had hunted him down or those who had betrayed him.[7] When he interrupts his wailings it is only to cheer himself by a childish boastfulness, magnifying the height from which he fell and the depth of his fall, which he contends has had no parallel in history. It is as if he were so much accustomed to think of himself as occupying the first place that he derives a bitter satisfaction from yielding to none the first place even in misfortune.[8] Only one manly note seems to make itself heard in this monotonous series of lamentations, when Cicero beats his breast for having preferred life to honour, vowing in one place that he wishes he had committed suicide, and in another that he means to have done with a

---

[1] *Ad Q. Fr.* I, 3, 3 (66 T.P.): *Haec ipsa me quo fletu putas scripsisse?* June 13, 58 B.C.
[2] *Ad Fam.* XIV, 4, 1 (62 T.P.): *Conficior lacrimis sic ut ferre non possim.* April 29, 58 B.C.
[3] *Ad Att.* III, 15, 2 (73 T.P.): *Desidero enim . . . me ipsum.* Aug. 17, 58 B.C.
[4] See in particular *Ad Att.* III, 10, 2 (67 T.P.): *. . . vitavi ne viderem fratrem, ne . . . me, quem ille florentissimum reliquerat, perditum illi afflictumque offerrem.* June 17, 58 B.C. Cf. *Ad Q. Fr.* I, 3, 6 (66 T.P.).
[5] Cf. *Ad Att.* III, 10, 3 (67 T.P.): *Ad te minus multa scribo quod . . . maerore impedior,* etc. . . . *Ad Att.* III, 8, 4 (64 T.P.): *Ex epistolarum . . . inconstantia puto te mentis meae motum videre.* On Cicero's physical deterioration, cf. *Ad Att.* III, 15, 1 (73 T.P.): *Crassi libertum ais tibi de mea sollicitudine macieque narrasse.* Aug. 17, 58 B.C.
[6] *Ad Att.* III, 13, 2 (71 T.P.): *Quod scribis te audire me etiam mentis errore et dolore adici, mihi vero mens integra est;* 15, 2 (73 T.P.): *a mente non deserar.*
[7] Especially Hortensius. Cf. *Ad Att.* III, 9, 2 (65 T.P.) and *Ad Q. Fr.* I, 3, 8 (66 T.P.), and Cato, cf. *Ad Att.* III, 15, 2 (73 T.P.).
[8] *Ad Att.* III, 7, 2 (63 T.P.): *Hoc adfirmo, neminem umquam tanta calamitate esse adfectum;* 13, 2 (71 T.P.): *. . . debes ignoscere, cum ita me adflictum videas ut neminem umquam nec videris nec audieris,* etc.

The Blunders of a Career that Failed

life which has become intolerable[1] from the humiliations that it has heaped upon him.

Since however—if we are to believe him—nothing but the tears and entreaties of his friends and relatives restrained his hand,[2] we must express some doubt as to the sincerity of these melancholy vapourings. A man fiercely bent on suicide shows more discretion. In this particular case Cicero's best chance of being a second time dissuaded from carrying out his fatal intention was to confide it in good time to those who had made his first attempt a failure. His letters really sound too like a paraphrase of the famous line in the comedy: "Hold me back or I'll do something desperate!" The false heroism with which they deck him out puts us off even more than the mawkish tears with which they drip.

Some of the historians are exasperated, others saddened by these ugly pages of the Correspondence. "Pitilessly, inhumanly",[3] Drumann criticises Cicero's flabbiness.[4] Ciaceri assumes that Cicero was plunged into these extremes of despair by his passionate love of his country. Love of Rome was so deeply rooted in his soul that he lost all self-command when he found himself cut off from the City. It would be unjust to condemn him for having been driven into distraction and hysteria by his banishment, when the mere threat of exile had sufficed a few years before to break the nerve of a soldier of the mettle of Lucullus.[5] Unfortunately this is

---

[1] See especially *Ad Att.* III, 3, 1 (56 T.P.): *Illam diem videam cum tibi gratias agam quod me vivere coegisti.* Beginning of April, 58 B.C.; 7, 2 (63 T.P.): *Quod me ad vitam vocas, unum efficis ut a me manus abstineam, alterum non potes ut me non nostri consilii vitaeque paeniteat,* etc. April 29, 58 B.C. Note that in paragraph 1 of the same letter Cicero puts a distance of four days' march between himself and Autronius, a conspirator whom he suspects of murderous intentions. *Ad Fam.* XIV, 4, 1 (62 T.P.): *Quod utinam minus vitae cupidi fuissemus!* Note that in this letter to Terentia he lays on himself and his desire for life the blame for having *not* committed suicide, which blame he tries to share with Atticus in the preceding letter written on the same day. *Ad Q. Fr.* I, 4, 4 (72 T.P.): *Lacrimae meorum me ad mortem ire prohibuerunt.* Beginning of Aug. 58 B.C.; and ibid. 3, 6 (66 T.P.): *Illud quidem nec faciendum est nec fieri potest, me diutius . . . in tam misera tamque turpi vita commorari*; and 2: *Sed testor omnes deos me hac una voce a morte esse revocatum, quod omnes in mea vita partem aliquam tuae vitae repositam esse dicebant.* June 13, 58 B.C.

[2] See the passages quoted in the preceding note: He was deterred from suicide by Atticus, by his family, by the thought of his brother, whose future was in some sort linked with his own, but above all by his own lust for life—*cupiditas vitae*. Oblivious of facts, he goes so far as to make a grievance of the advice given him in the matter by Atticus and others: *Ad Att.* III, 9, 1 (65 T.P.): *In hunc me casum vos vivendi auctores impulistis.* June 13, 58 B.C.

[3] The phrase is Ciaceri's, op. cit. II, p. 62: *critica spietata e disumana.*

[4] Drumann-Groebe, V, p. 636f.

[5] Ciaceri, *Ciceroni e i suoi tempi*, II, pp. 62–3. On Lucullus beseeching Caesar cf. Suet. *Caes.* XX, 4; Plut. *Luc.* XLII, 6; and Dio. Cass. XXXIII, 75.

only a hypothesis, for which Plutarch goes bail, but which is belied by the Correspondence. The biographer indeed represents the exile as "an unhappy lover" who in his bewilderment "ceaselessly turns his eyes to Italy".[1] The *Letters* show not a trace of this patriotic passion: in them Cicero mourns not Rome herself but the honours, the riches, the dignity, the happiness which he enjoyed in Rome.[2] Equally indulgent and equally unconvincing, L. A. Constans maintains that "Cicero lived in an age when even the most gallant warrior was not ashamed to shed tears"[3] and he suggests that there is "a certain modesty of moral suffering which the Latins do not seem to have felt to the same degree as we do." He skilfully adduces the example of "pious Aeneas" and recalls his over-facile outbursts of tenderness; but this is not enough to justify an opinion which is unsupported by either Plutarch or the *Letters* themselves. The biographer, who had read the *Letters*, considers that Cicero overstepped the limits allowed to pusillanimous hearts when he allowed adversity to make him "so poor-spirited, so humiliated and dejected by his misfortunes, as none could have expected in a man who had devoted so much of his life to study and learning."[4] We see from the *Letters* themselves that Atticus again and again reproached him for his low spirits,[5] bidding him be ashamed of his weakness and speaking so vigorously that Cicero began sadly to complain[6] and ended by repudiating his friend's reproof with sulky wrath.[7]

The only valid excuse for Cicero has been supplied by L. Laurand. The admiration which this first-class humanist professed for Cicero is well known. Nevertheless his hero's lack of steadfastness in this case damps his enthusiasm. He does not go so far

---

[1] Plut. *Cic.* XXXII, 3: "He yet continued disheartened and disconsolate, like an unfortunate lover often casting his looks back upon Italy."

[2] There is one exception in a phrase of *Ad Att.* III, 26 (87 T.P.): . . . *potius vita quam patria carebo.* Beginning of 57 B.C. But the point at which he would "prefer to be deprived of life rather than of my country" is the very eve of his return. Previously, he wept only over the ruin of his fortunes: *Ad Q. Fr.* I, 3, 6 (66 T.P.): . . . *nunc in hac tam afflicta perditaque fortuna neque me neque meos lugere diutius possim.* June 13, 58 B.C.; *Ad Att.* III, 15, 6 (73 T.P.): *Quid de bonis? quid de domo?* Aug. 17, 58 B.C., etc.

[3] L. A. Constans, *Lettres*, II, p. 27.   [4] Plut. *Cic.* XXXII, 3.

[5] Cf. especially *Ad Att.* III, 10, 2 and 3 (67 T.P.). June 17, 56 B.C.; and 13, 2 (71 T.P.). Aug. 5, 58 B.C., etc.

[6] *Ad Att.* III, 10, 2 (67 T.P.): *Nam quod me tam saepe et tam vehementer obiurgas et animo infirmo esse dicis* . . . 3: *Haec ego scripsi ut potius relevares me, quod facis, quam ut castigatione aut obiurgatione dignum putares.*

[7] *Ad Att.* III, 11, 2 (68 T.P.): *Consolari iam desine, obiurgare vero noli.* June 27, 58 B.C.

as to formulate expressly the blame which he feels due, only because he thinks it unfair to hold up against Cicero confidential outpourings which were never intended for our ears: "Never," he writes, "was any man so cast down. He sighs, he weeps. He writes pitiable letters, which unfortunately for his reputation his correspondents carefully preserved. They have been delivered to posterity, for whom they were by no means intended."[1] That is evident enough. And the excuse becomes plausible the moment we recognise a truth which neither Laurand nor any of his predecessors ever suspected, but which stares us in the face when we re-read the letters written during his exile: Cicero's Correspondence was published to gratify the hate of an enemy rabidly hostile to his memory.[2]

3. RETURN FROM EXILE

Cicero re-entered Rome on Sept. 4, 57, greeted by a popular ovation which he describes to Atticus without sparing his friend a single detail.[3] It was a triumphant return, but one destined to have few fellows. Intoxicated by the public enthusiasm with which he was received and at the same time deceived by the seeds of discord which he thought he detected sprouting between the "three men", he imagined for a while that he was in a strong enough position to speak and act as he liked, to hack any opponent to pieces at his own good pleasure, and to resume, if necessary against general opposition, his ascendancy over the Senate.

The very day after his return, on the pretext of thanking the Fathers for his restoration, he launched into panegyrics on the one hand, and on the other soundly berated the outgoing Consuls, Gabinius and Piso, who by their inertia, if not by their connivance, had tolerated the intrigues of Clodius.[4] A few days later he repeated this performance before an Assembly of the people,[5] and again on Sept. 29 before the College of Pontiffs.[6] On March 11, 56 he stepped to the bar to defend P. Sestius, one of the Tribunes of the

---

[1] L. Laurand, *Cicéron, Vie et Œuvres*, Paris, 1933, p. 41.
[2] Those who published the *Letters* wanted Cicero to be condemned out of his own mouth: cf. *Ad Fam.* XIV, 3, 1 (84 T.P.): *Hoc miserius, turpius, indignius nobis nihil fuit.* Nov. 29, 58 B.C.
[3] *Ad Att.* IV, 1, 4 and 5 (90 T.P.).
[4] On the date, see *Ad Att.* IV, 1, 5 (90 T.P.): . . . *postridie in senatu qui fuit dies Nonarum Septembr(ium) senatui gratias egimus* . . .
[5] *Ad Att.* IV, 1, 6 (90 T.P.): *Eo biduo . . . habui contionem.* This would be Sept. 7, 57 B.C.
[6] *Ad Att.* IV, 2, 2 (91 T.P.): *Diximus apud pontifices pridie Kal. Octobres.*

year before, who had shown conspicuous zeal in trying to get the laws of Clodius annulled. In the course of an extempore cross-examination he thundered against one of the witnesses for the prosecution, P. Vatinius, who despite his spirited insolence withdrew trembling and badly mauled from the unequal duel.[1] Finally, on April 4, he appeared for the defence of young M. Caelius, whom Clodia accused of an attempt to poison her. He amused and terrified his hearers by his account of the basenesses of this prostitute in the circles of high society.[2] Any chance was good enough for him to wreak vengeance on his persecutor Clodius or on his enemy's relatives or friends.

Up to this point the masters of the hour noted his blows without displeasure.[3] Cicero felt he was sailing before a favourable wind.[4] He thought the moment had come to assert his independence. The day after Caelius's acquittal, the application of Caesar's agrarian law relating to the *Ager Campanus* was on the agenda of the Senate. Hoping for a revision of the law, Cicero had, in a session of the preceding December, urged a vote of adjournment,[5] making a pretext of Pompey's absence at the time. He had the joy of taking part in a debate so stormy that no decision could be arrived at.[6] He was so chicken-hearted, however, that this first gesture of opposition to Caesar was also his last.

Towards the middle of April 56 the Proconsul of the Two Gauls, having just received a visit from Crassus at his headquarters in Ravenna, had a meeting with Pompey at Luca. It had been thought that Caesar and his son-in-law were on the point of falling out, but

---

[1] *Ad Q. Fr.* II, 4, 1 (105 T.P.): *Sestius noster absolutus est a. d. Idus Martias . . . Quid quaeris? Homo petulans et audax, Vatinius, valde perturbatus debilitatusque discessit.*

[2] The acquittal of Caelius is implicit in *Ad Q. Fr.* II, 11, 2 (135 T.P.). On this trial cf. Schanz, I, 2, p. 264.

[3] Before taking a lead Cicero was, as usual, anxious to be sure that he would find followers. Cf. *Ad Q. Fr.* II, 3, 5 (102 T.P.): *. . . ut humanissimi gratissimique et ipsi* (i.e. Sestius, whose defence he is about to undertake) *et omnibus videremur.* Feb. 15, 56 B.C.

[4] *Ad Q. Fr.* II, 4, 6 (105 T.P.): *In iudiciis ii sumus qui fuimus; domus celebratur ita ut cum maxime.* Shortly after March 11, 56 B.C.

[5] *Ad Q. Fr.* II, 1, 1 (93 T.P.): *Idcirco taceo, quod non existimo, cum Pompeius absit, causam agri Campani agi convenire.* Dec. 10, 57 B.C.

[6] *Ad Q. Fr.* II, 5, 1 (106 T.P.): *Non(is) April(ibus) vehementer actum de agro Campano clamore Senatus prope contionali.* Moreover, in another context Cicero lets it be understood that it was on his motion that the Senate decided to refer the question of the Campanian land to a full meeting of the Senate on May 15, 56 B.C.: *Marcellino et Philippo consulibus, Nonis Aprilibus mihi est senatus adsensus, ut de agro Campano frequenti senatu Idibus Maiis referretur.* To P. Lentulus Spinther, Dec. 54 B.C., *Ad Fam.* I, 9, 8 (153 T.P.).

at this meeting they strengthened their alliance. Cicero was warned of this reconciliation both by his brother Quintus and by a special messenger, Vibullius, sent to him by Pompey. Any formally expressed resistance[1] to the wishes of the Triumvirate could result only in provoking against him the united anger of all three. In his own mind Cicero hastened to make amends, and refrained from engaging in a struggle whose consequences for him might well be tragic. The final debate on the *Ager Campanus* was due to open on May 15. To avoid having either to repeat or to withdraw his objections to the allotment of lands ordered by Caesar, Cicero left Rome for an opportune visit to the country. Shortly after, May 16 he wrote to Quintus how pleased he was over this transparent device: "I was at Antium because the debate on the *Ager Campanus* was said to be coming on, on the 15th or 16th, which in fact it did. In this matter I am in a fix—*in hic causa mihi aqua haeret.* But I have said more than I meant to say. Till we meet then— *coram enim.*"[2] But the Triumvirs were not satisfied by his mere abstention. They wanted pledges. Cicero provided them. When the opponents of the Triumvirate introduced, towards the end of the month, a plan under which the Two Gauls would be included amongst the provinces to be allotted to the outgoing Consuls of 55, it was Cicero who opposed it and got a measure passed under which the Consuls of 55 would draw lots for Syria and Macedonia. These two Proconsulships were at the time still held by Gabinius and Piso, the ex-Consuls of 58. In moving this measure Cicero appeared to be slaking his ancient malice against the allies of his old enemy Clodius, who would be compelled to surrender their governorships. But in reality, by excluding the Two Gauls from the *sortitio provinciarum*, his aim was to maintain Caesar in the extraordinary command on which his power was based.[3]

No one was taken in by this manœuvre, not even Cicero. While extolling Caesar's worth, dwelling on the necessities of war, the overriding interests of Rome and her Empire, he did not hesitate to wind up by saying: "Even if Gabinius and Piso were the most

---

[1] See the same letter, *Ad Fam.* I, 9 (153 T.P.): paragraph 9, where Pompey conveys reproof to Cicero through Quintus, and paragraph 10, where he sends Vibullius to him armed with the same gently threatening message.

[2] *Ad Q. Fr.* II, 6, 2 (117 T.P.): *Eram Antii, quod Idibus et postridie fuerat dictum de agro Campano actum iri, ut est actum. In hac causa mihi aqua haeret. Sed plura quam constitueram: coram enim.* Soon after May 16.

[3] Chapters 7, 8, 14, 17–19 and the peroration of the *De Provinciis Consularibus* should be specially noted.

The Blunders of a Career that Failed

excellent of men, yet in my opinion Julius Caesar ought not yet to be superseded."[1] He thus gave its full significance to his speech *De Provinciis Consularibus*. He was aiming at giving a guarantee of the genuineness of his unexpected conversion. Fear has been called the beginning of wisdom. It had taken only a month for Cicero's wisdom to advance from opposition to silence and from silence to open and publicised submission.

The Correspondence is, moreover, the only source from which we learn how far Cicero had advanced along this new path; only the *Letters* enable us to appreciate the meaning and the range of this change of mind.

We can certainly find indications in the speeches he delivered between 56 and his departure for Cilicia in 51. Of some of these we possess the text, of others fragments or analyses.[2] From them we can feel that Cicero was now less keen to threaten reprisals against those responsible for his banishment than to curry favour with the powerful men who had instigated them. There is no doubt that the bitter memory of his trials in 58 was with him when he gave rein to a fierce attack in the Senate in 55 against the Consul Piso, who with his colleague Gabinius had been the author of his misfortunes; with him too when the next year he stood by an Aedile, Cnaeus Plancius, who was threatened with the cancellation of his election. Plancius was one of the friends who had given the fugitive the most affectionate welcome in Macedonia.[3] But his other speeches were inspired directly or indirectly by nothing more than a sudden desire to please Caesar and Pompey. It was to oblige Pompey that Cicero undertook in 54 the defence of M. Aemilius Scaurus, Pompey's brother-in-law,[4] whom Triarius was prosecuting for extortion. For the same reason he appeared at the bar for C. Rabirius Postumus,[5] the financier whom Gabinius—one of Pompey's faithful adherents—when Governor of Syria had in-

---

[1] Cic. *De Prov. Cons.* VIII, 18: *Quodsi essent illi [Gabinius et Piso] optimi viri, tamen ego mea sententia C. Caesari succedendum nondum putarem.*

[2] A list of these in chronological order will be found in Laurand's *Cicéron est intéressant*, pp. 55 and 56.

[3] *Ad Att.* III, 14, 2 (70 T.P.): *Sed iam extrudimur, non a Plancio, nam is quidem retinet.* Thessalonica, July 21, 58 B.C.; 22, 1 (81 T.P.): *Me adhuc Plancius sua liberalitate retinet.* Nov. 25, 58 B.C.; *Ad Fam.* XIV, 1, 3 (82 T.P.): *Plancius homo officiosissimus, me cupit esse secum et adhuc retinet.* To Terentia, same date.

[4] On Pompey's marriage to Aemilia cf. Plut. *Pomp.* IX, 3 and my *Sylla*, p. 188.

[5] On this person see the studies of Paul Guiraud in the *Revue de Paris*, 1903, pp. 355–78, and of Dessau in *Hermes*, XLVI, 1911, pp. 603–20.

stalled as minister of finance to the King of Egypt, Ptolemy Auletes. Rabirius was to help the Egyptian king conveniently to put more pressure on the *fellahin*, and in return for his services was to have a share of the exactions.

Nothing but his eagerness to obey the slightest sign from Julius Caesar accounts for the warmth with which he defended the Roman citizenship of Balbus. Balbus was a native of Gades (Cadiz) to whom Pompey had granted Roman citizenship, and he became in 61 an intimate friend of Julius Caesar, then Propraetor of Spain, who in 58 was appointed Proconsul for the Two Gauls.[1] In the same way it was fear of Caesar and Pompey together that robbed Cicero of speech when in 52 he was defending Milo for the murder of Clodius. We admire today the *Pro Milone*, but the title and the recorded version of the speech convey nothing of the feeble and halting delivery which proved fatal to the cause of the accused.[2]

To judge by the content only, Cicero's speeches might be interpreted as precautionary efforts called forth by the occasion, as isolated opportunist manœuvres, binding him to nothing when the moment of their delivery was past and leaving him otherwise complete liberty of action. If, on the other hand, we read them in the light thrown by the *Letters* on what lies behind them, and compare them with others which Cicero made at the same time but did not trouble to publish, but of which traces are to be found in his Correspondence, they stand out in striking relief. To Cicero's shame they testify not to a pardonable skill in changing his mind, but to the base and perpetual betrayal of loyalty and principle.

4. GREAT RECANTATIONS

It was thus that he retracted his attacks on Piso. When he heard at Arpinum that Gabinius, who had returned from Syria on Sept. 27, 54, had immediately been confronted by an accusation for the crime of *maiestas* against the State, he would have liked to see the same fate overtake Piso; for he considered that "there is nothing viler than Gabinius, though Piso runs him close".[3] Yet he did nothing. Then when Piso published his reply to the attacks

---

[1] *Ad Att.* II, 3, 3 (29 T.P.): . . . *nam fuit apud me Cornelius: hunc dico Balbum, Caesaris familiarem.* Dec. 60 B.C.
[2] Dio. Cass. XL, 54, 2.   Cf. above, p. 111.
[3] *Ad Q. Fr.* III, 1, 24 (148 T.P.): *Nihil illo [Gabinio] turpius. Proximus est tamen Piso.*

made on him the preceding year and Quintus urged his brother to issue a retort, Cicero evaded the question with a neat pirouette: "The next thing is about Piso's speech. I am surprised at your thinking that I ought to answer it, particularly as no one is likely to read that speech unless I write an answer to it, while every schoolboy learns off, like a lesson, the one I did write against Piso."[1] The Triumvirs had in fact made him decide to let his quarry go free: Pompey because Piso had drawn closer to him by sharing in the defence of Aemilius Scaurus, his brother-in-law[2]; and Caesar, who by his marriage with Calpurnia had in 59 become Piso's son-in-law. When his daughter Julia died, Caesar was rebuffed by Pompey's refusal to marry his other daughter Octavia and so cement a new matrimonial alliance between them. In Sept. 54 Caesar had to abandon the hope of achieving a change of father-in-law by repudiating Calpurnia (Piso's daughter).[3] Out of consideration for both Caesar and Pompey, Cicero resigned himself to silence in Piso's case.[4] God alone knew how Cicero detested Vatinius. But on instructions from Caesar and Pompey he was forced to change over from his prosecutor to counsel for his defence. We have proof of the hatred and contempt he felt for the man both in his *In Vatinium* and in his *Letters*. In April 59 he was lampooning this counterfeit of an *epulo*-priest who was so ignorant of the most elementary rules of social etiquette as to

---

[1] *Ad Q. Fr.* III, 1, 11 (148 T.P.): *Alterum est de Calventii Marii* (a mocking nickname for Calpurnius Piso) *oratione. Quod scribis miror, tibi placere me ad eam rescribere, praesertim cum illum nemo lecturus sit, si ego nihil rescripsero, meam in illum pueri omnes tamquam dictata perdiscant.*

[2] Scaurus was acquitted on Sept. 2, 54 B.C. Cf. Asconius, p. 18, Or.: *L. Domitio Ahenobarbo et Appio Claudio Pulchro consulibus . . . a. d. iiii Nonas Septembr(es).* He had had Piso and Pompey as witnesses for the defence. Cf. Asconius, p. 28 Or.

[3] Cf. Suet. *Caes.* XXVII, 1. On these facts see my *César* (3), pp. 835–6.

[4] In the same way and for the same reasons he avoided plunging into the electoral campaigns of 53 B.C. for the consulship. Valerius Messalla and Domitius Calvinus were both candidates, but the two elected Consuls were Memmius and Scaurus. Caesar favoured Memmius, who combined his canvassing with that of Domitius Calvinus, both of them supported by the Consuls of the day. Pompey leaned towards Scaurus; cf. *Ad Att.* IV, 15, 7 and 9 (143 T.P.). July 27, 54 B.C. Cicero's sympathies were with Messalla, and he boasts to Quintus that Messalla was greatly pleased with him, but he adds: "So I think is Memmius." He contrived to win the attachment of Scaurus by defending him, but at the same time to satisfy Domitius; cf. *Ad Q. Fr.* III, 1, 16 (148 T.P.): *Cui* [*Messallae*] *vehementer satisfacio rebus omnibus, ut arbitror, etiam Memmio. Domitio ipsi multa iam feci, quae voluit quaeque a me petivit. Scaurum beneficio defensionis valde obligavi.* It is comic to see Cicero being "all things to all men" because he is not sure which way the cat will ultimately jump. Ibid.: *adhuc erat valde incertum . . . qui consules futuri essent.* He no longer dared risk offending anyone.

attend a funeral banquet dressed in a dark toga.[1] He grew indignant over the excesses of the "three unbridled men" who could even contemplate "investing the wen of Vatinius with the double-dyed toga of the augur."[2] About the same time he was rejoicing in the air of his *villa* at Antium, "a town so near to Rome where many have never seen Vatinius."[3] When in 56 as prosecutor he charged full tilt at him in the Sestius case and hewed him into small pieces, he felt overjoyed at remembering the blows he had dealt his victim.[4] Two years later he slyly made fun of a letter in which Vatinius sought to vilify him, and professed the most complete contempt for any dirty tricks the loathsome fellow might try to play on him: "I laughed about the letter of Vatinius . . . I can swallow his hatred and digest it too."[5] We may well think so. In the interval, towards the end of Aug. 54 to be exact, a few days before the Scaurus trial, Cicero undertook—no doubt to the general amazement—the defence of Vatinius, whom at the expiration of his praetorship Licinius Calvus was accusing of corrupt practices. It is no use for Cicero to strike a note of light-hearted detachment in breaking this astounding news to his brother: "I am turning up in the afternoon on the same day to defend Vatinius. It's going to be an easy job."[6] We may be allowed to doubt this. The Triumvirate's support of the accused would have made it easy for anyone else, but it was a peculiarly ticklish business for Cicero. First, from the legal point of view, because the prosecutor in drawing his indictment had cited the terms of the law relating to bribery and corruption to which Cicero during his consulship had given his name.[7] Lastly, and above all, in fact, because at the time of the contested election he had confided to Quintus his disgust at the way the Triumvirs had favoured Vatinius at the

[1] *Ad Att.* II, 7, 3 (34 T.P.): *Illa opima (legatio)* . . . *ut opinor* . . . *epuloni Vatinio reservatur.* On this allusion cf. *In Vat.* XII, 30.

[2] *Ad Att.* II, 9, 2 (36 T.P.): *Cum ea [senatus potentia] non ad populum sed ad tres homines immoderatos redacta sit, quid iam censes fore? Proinde isti licet farciant quos volent cons(ules), tr(ibunos) pl(ebis), denique etiam Vatinii strumam sacerdoti* διβάφῳ *vestiant* . . . April 17 or 18, 59 B.C.

[3] *Ad Att.* II, 6, 2 (33 T.P.): *Esse locum tam prope Romam ubi multi sint qui Vatinium nunquam viderint.* First half of April, 59 B.C.

[4] *Ad Q. Fr.* II, 4, 1 (105 T.P.): *Vatinium* . . . *arbitratu nostro concidimus dis hominibusque plaudentibus.* After March 11, 56 B.C.

[5] *Ad Q. Fr.* III, 9, 5 (160 T.P.): *De epistula Vatinii risi. Sed me ab eo ita observari scio, ut eius ista odia non sorbeam solum, sed concoquam.* Dec. 54 B.C. Vatinius was spying on Cicero on Caesar's behalf.

[6] *Ad Q. Fr.* II, 15, 3 (147 T.P.): *Ego eodem die post meridiem Vatinium eram defensurus. Ea res facilis est.* Aug. 54 B.C.

[7] See my *César* (3), pp. 675–6.

expense of Cato.[1] But nothing now weighed in Cicero's false scales: neither justice nor fact nor even his own private loathing of the accused. The Triumvirs had given him a signal: it was his business to obey, and he airily sacrificed himself.

In the same way he complied without a murmur when his masters bade him fly to the assistance of another of his pet aversions, the ex-Proconsul of Syria, Gabinius. Gabinius had no easy task if he was to justify his crimes. This grasping Governor had deliberately infringed all the orders and instructions given him by the Fathers before he set out. Just before leaving his province he had despatched troops to restore Ptolemy Auletes to the Egyptian throne, and then had accepted a commission of ten thousand talents[2] as the price of his services. This shocking case of corruption had exasperated the majority of the Senate. But it had not ruffled any of the Triumvirs except Crassus, who had been appointed to succeed Gabinius and who had been looking forward to fishing in Egyptian waters on his own account. His two partners calmed his indignation by dangling before his eyes the glory and profit he could reap from an expedition against the Parthians.[3] Caesar and Pompey, for their part, had secretly encouraged Gabinius in the course he took:[4] Caesar perhaps because he had been the lover of Lollia, Gabinius's wife,[5] and Pompey because Gabinius was his unscrupulous tool; and both of them because this Egyptian adventure served their schemes for getting a grip on the resources of that fabulous country and fitted into their plans of imperial aggrandisement. Feeling sure of their connivance, Gabinius took an audacious line and requested the Senate to grant him a public thanksgiving (*supplicatio*) to thank the gods for his initial successes—a ceremony which would by implication have ratified all his doings. Cicero of course, who during the Sestius trial had just severely manhandled Gabinius in public[6] and was to attack him again in 55 and 54 in the course of his defence of Plancius[7] and his prosecution of Piso,[8] treating him as Catiline's "lantern-

---

[1] *Ad Q. Fr.* II, 7, 3 (120 T.P.). After Feb. 11, 55 B.C.
[2] This figure is quoted by the Bobbio Scholiast, p. 271 Or. It corresponds to 27 million Poincaré francs.
[3] Cf. my *César* (3), p. 786f.
[4] Amongst other authorities, see Plut. *Pomp.* XXV, 2.
[5] Suet. *Caesar*, L, i; cf. *P.W.* XIII, c. 1393.
[6] Cic. *Pro Sestio*, XXV, 55, and XLIII, 93.
[7] Cic. *Pro Plancio*, XXXV, 86.
[8] Cic. *In Pis.* XXI, 48 and 49; XXII, 51.

bearer",[1] passionately hoped that the *supplicatio* would be refused. But knowing the contrary wishes of the Triumvirs he had not the courage to defy them. When the day came for the debate, he took refuge in abstention, and we hear him congratulating himself in one of his letters to Quintus on an overwhelming refusal which came like an answer to prayer without his being in any way responsible for it: "On May 15 the Senate, which was well attended, acted splendidly in refusing the *supplicatio* asked for by Gabinius. Procilius swears that never was anyone so snubbed. Out of doors there is wild applause. Pleasing as this is to me in itself, it is even more pleasing because it happened in my absence, for it was an unbiassed judgment of the Senate without any attack or support on my part. I was away in Antium."[2]

Cicero could not in truth cover a more complete retreat with a more sanctimonious piece of hypocrisy. This feeble lapse of his on May 15, 56, was destined to bring in its train other, much more serious, lapses two years later. Towards the end of the summer of 54 Gabinius was advancing by short marches towards the City, where he would have to give an account of his governorship of Syria. He had moderated his ambitions and realised how much hostility he would have to meet. So he halted in front of Rome on Sept. 19 and for several days hesitated to come in and face the music. Cicero, who was still up in arms, was delighted by his discomfiture: "Gabinius", he writes to Quintus, "arrived outside Rome on Sept. 19. Nothing was more humiliating, nothing more ignored (than his arrival)."[3] Gabinius had scarcely set foot in the City, by night on the 27th, before he encountered a perfect hail of accusations.[4] He had first to answer to the crime of *maiestas*, of which a cloud of enemies united in accusing him. To believe the Correspondence, three groups of them had been formed to convict him of having impaired and degraded the majesty of the State "by

---

[1] Cic. *In Pis.* IX, 20: *Catilinae lanternarius*. In the *Pro Plancio* Cicero renewed his metaphors without changing their object; he there called Gabinius Catiline's "dancing boy": *saltator Catilinae*, XXXV, 87.

[2] *Ad Q. Fr.* II, 6, 1 (117 T.P.): *Idibus Maiis senatus frequens divinus fuit in supplicatione Gabinio deneganda. Adiurat Procilius hoc nemini accidisse. Foris valde plauditur. Mihi cum sua sponte iucundum, tum iucundius, quod me absente; est enim* εἰλικρινὲς *iudicium, sine oppugnatione, sine gratia nostra. Eram Antii.* From Antium, April 16, 54 B.C.

[3] *Ad Q. Fr.* III, 1, 15 (148 T.P.): *Ad Urbem accessit a. d. XII, Kal. Octobr. Nihil turpius nec desertius.* Written on different days during Sept. 54 B.C.

[4] *Ad Q. Fr.* III, 1, 24 (148 T.P.): *Gabinius a. d. iiii Kal. Octobr. noctu in Urbem introierat.*

violating its edicts". The speakers for these three groups were: "L. Lentulus, son of the *Flamen*; Tiberius Nero, with sturdy backers; and C. Memmius, Tribune of the Plebs, with L. Capito."[1] Pompey had made great efforts during the preceding days to reconcile Cicero with Gabinius, and induce him to take up the cause of the accused man. But Cicero turned a deaf ear: "Pompey has been trying hard", he writes to his brother, "to persuade me to be reconciled to him, but as yet he has not succeeded at all, nor if I retain a shred of liberty will he succeed."[2] The days passed, Cicero's attitude stiffened. He was encouraged by public opinion and the hope that "he will be crushed", which was to be expected "unless our friend Pompey, to the disgust of gods and men, upsets the whole business".[3] After Oct. 11 especially Cicero was buoyed up by furious hatred. There had been a session of the Senate on that day, and an altercation arose between him and Gabinius in the course of which Gabinius hurled at Cicero the taunt of "Exile!" which the majority of the Senate drowned in shouts.[4] About the same time "Memmius gave Gabinius such a splendid warming" that no one could find a word in answer to the Tribune of the Plebs.[5] Excited by all this effervescence round him, Cicero would have dearly liked to join the accusers' hue-and-cry. He was thinking of it, as he confessed to Quintus: "I refrain from prosecuting—with difficulty, by Hercules—but refrain I do."[6] Above all things he had no wish to become involved in a quarrel with Pompey.[7] So he would choose a middle course. He would neither plead in favour of Gabinius—as Pompey wished him to do—nor

[1] *Ad Q. Fr.* III, 1, 15 (148 T.P.): *Gabinium tres adhuc factiones postulant. L. Lentulus, flaminis filius, qui iam de maiestate postulavit, Ti. Nero cum bonis subscriptoribus, C. Memmius tribunus pleb. cum L. Capitone.*

[2] *Ad Q. Fr.* III, 1, 15 (148 T.P.): *Pompeius a me valde contendit de reditu in gratiam, sed adhuc nihil profecit nec, si ullam partem libertatis tenebo, proficiet.*

[3] *Ad Q. Fr.* III, 2, 1 (150 T.P.): *Quid quaeris? Probe premitur Gabinius, nisi noster Pompeius dis hominibusque invitis negotium everterit.* Oct. 11, 54 B.C.

[4] *Ad Q. Fr.* III, 2, 2 (150 T.P.): *Cum a me maxime vulneraretur [Gabinius], non tulit et me trementi voce exulem appellavit. Hic (o di! nihil umquam honorificentius nobis accidit) consurrexit senatus cum clamore ad unum sic ut ad corpus eius accederet.*

[5] *Ad Q. Fr.* III, 2, 1 (150 T.P.): *Eodem die a. d. vi Idus Octobr.* (Oct. 10, 54 B.C.) *Gabinium ad populum luculente calefecerat Memmius sic ut Calidio verbum facere pro eo non licuerit.*

[6] *Ad Q. Fr.* III, 2, 2 (150 T.P.): *Ego tamen teneo ab accusando, vix me hercule, sed tamen teneo.*

[7] *Ad Q. Fr.* III, 2, 2 (150 T.P.): *Vel quod nolo cum Pompeio pugnare, vel quod iudices nullos habemus.* Ἀπότευγμα *formido.*

against him, as he himself longed to do. He would act as a witness in court. Nothing more; nothing less.[1]

The enemies of Gabinius, delighted by Cicero's diatribes against him in his speeches *In Pisonem*, counted more on his evidence than on anyone's. When the trial came on, however, they were disappointed. Cicero had had time to reflect and the result of his reflections was: "No, I shan't risk a battle with the Triumvirs." He havered and hedged, he balanced his evidence so skilfully, he seemed equally to avoid saying anything to exonerate Gabinius or anything to accuse him. In fact, he seemed to be speaking for the express purpose of saying nothing.[2] The jury acquitted Gabinius by 38 votes to 32.[3] And Gabinius, anticipating the effect which Cicero's dubious intervention might have had on them, hastened before the court rose to thank Cicero for his prudent, his noble words.[4]

Cicero had, in fact, executed a skilful retreat which presently became a rout and ended in the most complete surrender. For Gabinius, who had just barely been acquitted on the charge of *maiestas*, was involved in a prosecution for extortion, and Pompey —who had justly assessed Cicero's powers of resistance—demanded that in this second trial he should appear for the defence of the accused, his enemy. For the interests of Pompey's client the banker Rabirius Postumus and of his friends the *publicani* were more or less identical with those of Gabinius. This time Pompey's command admitted of no evasion or withdrawal[5], and in the course of Nov. 54 Cicero gave in. His defence of Gabinius does not figure amongst his speeches. But it is certain that, making the best of a

---

[1] This middle course offered complete security. He hoped to help to bring about the condemnation without seeming to do so, without risking a failure, without risking a success more dangerous than a failure: *timeo ne illi me accusante aliquid accidat, nec despero rem et sine me et non nihil per me confici posse (Ad Q. Fr. III, 2, 2).* Cicero seems to have been a hardened habitual hypocrite.

[2] In a letter to Atticus, Cicero tries to brazen it out: *Ad Att.* IV, 18, 1 (154 T.P.): *Quaeris ego me ut gesserim? Constanter et libere.* End of Oct. 54 B.C. Shortly after he gave Quintus a glimpse of what his constancy and his liberty were worth; cf. *Ad Q. Fr.* III, 9, 1 (160 T.P.): *Feci summa cum gravitate, ut omnes sentiunt et summa cum lenitate quae feci. Illum Gabinium neque ursi neque levavi; testis vehemens fui, praeterea quievi.* Dec. 54 B.C.

[3] Cf. *Ad Q. Fr.* III, 4, 1 (152 T.P.): . . . *sententiis condemnatus XXXII cum LXX tulissent;* and *Ad Att.* IV, 18, 1 (154 T.P.): *ac tamen XXXII condemnarunt, XXXVIII absolverunt.*

[4] *Ad Q. Fr.* III, 4, 3 (152 T.P.): *Mihi illud iucundum est, quod, cum testimonium secundum fidem et religionem gravissime dixissem, reus se dixit, si in civitate licuisset sibi esse, mihi se satisfacturum, neque me quicquam interrogavit.*

[5] Although Cicero, fearing a condemnation, would still have preferred to shirk the task. Cf. *Ad Q. Fr.* III, 4, 1 (152 T.P.): . . . *ut videatur reliquis iudiciis periturus et maxime de pecuniis repetundis.* Oct. 24, 54 B.C.

bad job, he delivered it with all the warmth and vigour he could command and, as he said himself a few days afterwards, put his zeal and his talent at the service of this unexpected client: *summo studio [Gabinium] defenderim*.[1] It was all of no avail. For the court was presided over by the puritanical Cato, and Gabinius was condemned.[2] Cicero realised that day the depths of shame to which he had sunk. He was doubly disgraced: first, by having taken on the case, secondly by having lost it. He was nakedly revealed as the contemptible character he had been reduced to: a cowardly puppet whose strings the relentless Triumvirs could manipulate at will.

He still put a bold face on it in public, no doubt. And in his *Pro Rabirio Postumo* he has tried to bluff us by boasting of the innate generosity which led him to sacrifice "ephemeral enmities to preserve undying friendships".[3] It was no good. I can trace no tradition of anyone except Valerius Maximus, who has even soft-pedalled this impossible *leit-motif*: "Cicero passionately defended Gabinius whom he had as Consul expelled from the City. And twice in public courts he appeared for Vatinius, who had always been hostile to him. He must not be blamed for levity, but rather praised; for it is a finer thing when injuries are overcome by benefits than when they are requited by the obstinacy of mutual hatred."[4] This hesitant voice has been silenced by the evidence and has awakened no echo. Despairing of being able to justify such unpardonable acrobatics, Plutarch has preferred to bury in oblivion the years in which they were performed. Rather than seek to explain to his readers how Cicero was induced to speak and act against his conscience in favour of men whom he detested and whose evil deeds he had previously never ceased to condemn, he

---

[1] Cic. *Pro Rab. Post.* VIII, 19: *Quem [Gabinium] ex tantis inimicitiis receptum in gratiam summo studio defenderim* . . .

[2] Cf. Drumann-Groebe, III, p. 55. Gabinius in his turn took the road to Thessalonica, to return only in 49 B.C., cf. Dio Cass. XXXIX, 63, 5. His condemnation entailed the dropping of the prosecutions for *ambitus* (bribery and corruption in canvassing) which were pending against him. On this point see *Ad Q. Fr.* III, 3, 2 (151 T.P.): *Gabinium de ambitu reum fecit P. Sulla* . . . October 21, 54 B.C.

[3] Cic. *Pro Rab. Post.* XII, 32: *Neque me vero paenitet mortales inimicitias, sempiternas amicitias habere.*

[4] Val. Max. IV, 2, 4: *Aulum . . . Gabinium repetundarum reum summo studio defendit, qui eum in consulatu suo Urbe expulerat idemque P. Vatinium dignitati suae semper infestum duobus publicis iudiciis tutatus est, ut sine ullo crimine levitatis, ita cum aliqua laude; quia speciosius aliquanto iniuriae beneficiis vincuntur quam mutui odii pertinacia pensantur.*

leaps in his chronological narrative without transition from 57 to
52, from his hero's return from exile to the murder of Clodius and
the *Pro Milone*.[1]

Moreover in a period and on a subject where apology is vain
nothing but silence could save Cicero's reputation. But we possess
the Correspondence, which breaks the silence, and whose unim-
peachable evidence undoes all the good of Plutarch's omissions and
the eloquent excuses of Valerius Maximus. Having mercilessly
enumerated the contradictions in which Cicero bogged himself
down, the *Letters* leave us ignorant of nothing: neither the
reckless selfishness of the motives which actuated him, nor
the reward he was not too proud to pocket as the price of his
apostasies.

The *Letters* prove that he was perfectly conscious of the nature
of the acts he was committing and the baseness with which they
stamped him, without doing anything to avoid the former or
cleanse himself from the latter. When he writes of these things, he
does so without the embarrassment or the blushes which would
provide a certain extenuation. On the morrow of his speech about
the Consular Provinces, the words of which had been put into
his mouth by the Triumvirs, and which contributed more than
anything to thrust the laws of the Republic into abeyance, he was
making no confession of guilt as he jested with Atticus: "For a
long time now I have been nibbling at what after all I've got to
swallow—my recantation did seem a trifle discreditable. But good-
bye to upright, honest and straightforward policy! . . .[2] I wanted
to make my escape from this new alliance impossible lest I should
drift back to those who when they should pity me never cease to
be jealous of me. . . . Since those who are powerless will not
love me, let me take pains to make myself well liked by those

---

[1] Cf. Plut. *Cic.* XXXIV (Cicero's revenge on Clodius) and XXXV, 1: "After
this, Milo killed Clodius and being arraigned for the murder, he procured
Cicero as his advocate."

[2] *Ad Att.* IV, 5, 1 (108 T.P.): *Quid? etiam (dudum enim circumrodo quod
devorandum est) subturpicula mihi videbatur esse παλινῳδία. Sed valeant recta,
vera, honesta consilia.* June 56 B.C.
L. A. Constans is so much dismayed by this indecent farewell that he comments on it in a note which the text does not seem to bear out: "Cicero is
not bidding farewell to virtue, loyalty and honour, but to the politics to which the
optimates have enslaved him on the pretext of faithfulness to these lofty principles." *Correspondance*, II, p. 154, note 2. The truth is that Cicero is saying
good-bye to the principles he has hitherto proclaimed as his own, because it
now looks as though it would be more dangerous than profitable to live up
to them.

who have power.[1] You will say: 'That is what I should long ago have wished.' Yes, I know you did wish it, and I have been a perfect ass. But now the time has come for me to show some affection for myself."[2]

When he shocked and horrified all decent people by that other recantation implied in his legal assistance to P. Vatinius, he showed the same lack of regret. He addressed a letter on the subject to the Proconsul of Cilicia, P. Lentulus. From its carefully studied form and its metrically balanced phrases it was obviously intended for circulation in numerous copies amongst the governing circles in the City. In it he openly admits his compliance with the wishes of the Triumvirs and the favours this compliance brings him. He proclaims the amazing, the divine, generosity of Caesar to his brother and to himself—*divina Caesaris in me fratremque meum liberalitas*.[3] Then he goes on: "About Caesar, that you 'have no fault to find'; I am glad that you approve my policy. But as to Vatinius, first Pompey had brought about a reconciliation immediately after he was made Praetor. Though it is true that I had opposed his candidature in very strong language in the Senate, yet I did so not so much for the purpose of attacking him as of defending and doing honour to Cato. Then, later on, there followed a remarkably pressing request from Caesar that I should defend him."[4] Now that the name of Caesar had been introduced into the discussion P. Lentulus was bound to be convinced. If, however, he showed so much bad taste as to insist on his point of view, Cicero would have no difficulty in reducing him to silence by quoting examples of similar political veerings and tackings which he could easily dig up from the history of Lentulus's own past: "But I beg that you will not ask why I praised either this defendant or the others, lest

[1] *Ad Att.* IV, 5, 2 (108 T.P.): *Ego mehercule mihi necessitatem volui imponere huius novae coniunctionis, ne qua mihi liceret labi ad illos, qui etiam tum, cum misereri mei debent, non desinunt invidere . . . Quoniam, qui nihil possunt, ii nolunt amare, demus operam ut ab iis qui possunt, diligamur.*

[2] *Ad Att.* IV, 5, 3 (108 T.P.): *Dices: vellem iam pridem. Scio te voluisse, et me asinum germanum fuisse. Sed iam tempus est me ipsum a me amari.*

[3] *Ad Fam.* I, 9, 18 (153 T.P.): Dec. 54 B.C. Cf. L. A. Constans, *Correspondance*, III, p. 126, No. CLIX.

[4] *Ad Fam.* I, 9, 19 (153 T.P.): *De Vatinio autem, primum reditus intercesserat in gratiam per Pompeium, statim ut ille praetor est factus, cum quidem ego eius petitionem gravissimis in senatu sententiis oppugnassem, neque tam illius laedendi causa quam defendendi atque ornandi Catonis: post autem Caesaris, ut illum defenderem, mira contentio est consecuta.* Dec. 54 B.C. This statement is simply indecent. In order to excuse his defence of Vatinius, Cicero stoops so low as to maintain that he had previously attacked the fellow merely to gratify Cato. In every way he proclaims his complete absence of sincerity.

The Blunders of a Career that Failed

I retaliate by asking you the same question when you come back. Although indeed I can ask you even in your absence, for remember for whom you sent favourable testimony even from the ends of the earth."[1] Instead of evading criticisms which, in his own heart, he knew to be unanswerable, Cicero nimbly turned them against the critic. Without showing the slightest trace of remorse, his letter closes on a note of ill-concealed insolence beneath which gleams a mild suggestion of blackmail. Finally, when hints reached him about the attitude he would be wise to take up towards Gabinius, he was neither indignant at their being offered nor ashamed of having heeded them. He never looked the business fearlessly in the face. He never asked himself on which side truth and justice lay; he thought of nothing but his own immediate advantage and convenience. He was certainly furious over the initial acquittal of his future client; but he betrays his wrath only in writing to his brother: "The trial is generally considered so disgraceful that it looks as if he would be convicted in the other cases, especially in the prosecution for extortion. But as you see, the Republic, the Senate and the Courts all count for naught, and for naught the position of any of us therein."[2] But once this first outburst of temper was over, he assumed, even with Quintus, an air of serene indifference to it all. In alluding to a disastrous flooding of the Tiber, for instance, he noted that it coincided with the acquittal of Gabinius, and that it had evidently been let loose to punish men,

> Who wrench the law to suit their crooked ends
> And drive out justice, recking naught of Gods.[3]

Having relieved his feelings by this quotation from Homer, he immediately pulled himself up: "But I have made up my mind not to worry about such things"—*sed haec non curare decrevi.*[4]

The fact is that, when he had to choose between his feelings—all

---

[1] *Ad Fam.* I, 9, 19 (153 T.P.): *Cur autem laudarim, peto a te, ut id a me neve in hoc reo neve in aliis requiras, ne tibi ego idem reponam cum veneris. Tametsi possum vel absenti: recordare enim quibus laudationem ex ultimis terris miseris.* For this and the preceding quotations I have made use of the excellent translation of L. A. Constans.

[2] *Ad Q. Fr.* III, 4, 1 (152 T.P.): *Est omnino tam gravi fama hoc iudicium, ut videatur reliquis iudiciis periturus et maxime de pecuniis repetundis. Sed vides nullam esse remp(ublicam), nullum senatum, nulla iudicia, nullam in ullo nostrum dignitatem.* Oct. 24, 54 B.C.

[3] *Ad Q. Fr.* III, 7, 1 (156 T.P.): *Cadit enim in absolutionem Gabinii:*

οἳ βίῃ εἰν ἀγορῇ σκολιὰς κρίνωσι θέμιστας,
ἐκ δὲ δίκην ἐλάσωσι, θεῶν ὄπιν οὐκ ἀλέγοντες.

Autumn 54 B.C. Homer, *Iliad*, XVI, 387–8.

[4] *Ad Q. Fr.* III, 7, 1 (156 T.P.).

the stronger because they were feelings of resentment—and his political and material interests, he did not hesitate, but at once took the line that seemed to promise personal advantage. What he would have liked to do, if he had felt free, would have been to prosecute Gabinius, as Sallust advised him. But he was no longer at liberty to give the rein to either his loves or hates.[1] He had Pompey to reckon with; he must avoid Pompey's displeasure, he must avert Pompey's vengeance: "Pompey would have looked on the clash with me not as a question of the safety of the accused but one of his own dignity. He would have entered the City [in arms]; it would have been a regular battle. I should have been like Pacideianus matched against Aeserninus the Samnite. He would, as like as not, have bitten off my ear . . ."[2] In other words, Cicero was afraid of getting hurt, and so he filed away his speech for the prosecution of Gabinius and presently substituted a speech for the man's defence.

Yet the idea of having to defend Gabinius made his gorge rise. It is true that he pushed the bitter draught aside when Pansa, acting as the messenger, or perhaps only the interpreter, of the Triumvirs' wishes, came semi-officially to offer it to him. But he rejected it only half-heartedly and solely because he would expose himself to some danger by quaffing it, "for if I had defended Gabinius, as Pansa thinks I ought to have done, I should have been ruined: those who hate him would have begun to hate me equally".[3] But when the detestable task was ultimately forced on him, he made no attempt to escape it, for he hoped it would guarantee him "ease and peace", which above all else he longed for.[4] So dearly did he love these things that to attain them he was ready to throw himself into the arms of his enemies and publicly espouse a cause which he had previously in public torn to ribbons.

He was discredited beyond hope. And he knew it. He had made

[1] *Ad Q. Fr.* III, 5, 4 (155 T.P.): *Angor, mi suavissime frater . . . inimicos a me partim non oppugnatos, partim etiam esse defensos, meum non modo animum, sed ne quidem odium esse liberum.* Autumn 54 B.C.

[2] *Ad Q. Fr.* III, 4, 2 (152 T.P.): *Aiunt non nulli, ut Sallustius, me oportuisse accusare . . . sed me alia moverunt. Non putasset Pompeius de illius salute, sed de sua dignitate mecum esse certamen: in Urbem introisset, ad inimicitias res venisset, cum Aeserino Samnite Pacideianus comparatus viderer, auriculam fortasse mordicus abstulisset.*

[3] *Ad Q. Fr.* III, 5, 5 (155 T.P.): *Gabinium, si, ut Pansa putat oportuisse, defendissem, concidissem: qui illum oderunt . . . me ipsum odisse coepissent.*

[4] *Ad Q. Fr.* III, 5, 5 (155 T.P.): *Et in omni summa, ut manes, valde me ad otium pacemque converto.*

The Blunders of a Career that Failed

his choice. He preferred the gold-lined belt to his good name. He had a horror of any form of suffering. He recalled with a shudder the hardships of his exile.[1] He clung passionately, as a man in dire danger of losing them, to the good things of this world: his "beloved studies", the "joys of eloquence", and at the same time his leisure, his wealth, his well-being, his mansion on the Palatine, his *villae* in the country. He could not bear to recall the height from which he had already fallen once; he dared not slip again into the abyss out of which he had succeeded in climbing.[2] That is why, taking the line of least resistance, he made himself the eloquent but despised tool of the Triumvirs, who not only confirmed him in the enjoyment of his delights but raised his price to a level at which he could satisfy not only his needs but his desires.

We have only to turn to his *Letters*—many of which we have discussed in earlier chapters—to see the accumulation round him of the gratifications and profits with which his masters, Caesar at their head, padded the fetters of their slave[3]: a *legatio* for his brother in Gaul[4]; a post for his friend Trebatius on the Proconsul's staff[5]; and for himself not only sovereign protection against any hostile happenings[6] but an immediate loan of 800,000 sesterces[7] and a rake-off, probably still more substantial, on the expropriations of the *Forum Iulium*.[8]

The documents written in the shelter of his own fireside show Cicero, the politician of this period, as a man cowardly, versatile and venal. From the time of his return from Thessalonica to his departure for Cilicia and the preliminary signs of civil war, Cicero, as painted by himself and his intimates, was never so lavishly

---

[1] *Ad Q. Fr.* III, 4, 2 (152 T.P.): *Cum Clodio quidem certe redisset in gratiam* [*Pompeius*].

[2] *Ad Att.* IV, 18, 2 (154 T.P.): *Multa mihi dant solacia . . . ad litteras et studia nostra. Dicendi laborem, delectatione oratoria consolor, domus me et rura nostra delectant: non recordor unde ceciderim sed unde surrexerim.* Oct. 54 B.C.; *Ad Q. Fr.* III, 9, 2 (160 T.P.): *Litterae me et studia nostra et otium villaeque delectant, maximeque pueri nostri.* Dec. 54 B.C.

[3] The word is not too strong: cf. T.P. V, p. liii: "Cicero at this time, after the complete breakdown of his opposition to the Triumvirs . . . was their obedient slave . . ."

[4] See, in particular, *Ad Q. Fr.* II, 12 (139 T.P.); 13 (141 T.P.); 15 (147 T.P.); III, 1 (148 T.P.); *Ad Fam.* I, 9, 21 (153 T.P.): *Quintus frater meus legatus est Caesaris.* It seems that at the same time Cicero obtained from Pompey a *legatio* for himself: *Ad Att.* IV, 19, 2 (158 T.P.): *. . . sed heus tu, scripseramne tibi me esse legatum Pompeio*; cf. *Ad Q. Fr.* III, 1, 18 (148 T.P.). Not to risk irritating Caesar, he treated this *legatio* as a sinecure.

[5] *Ad Fam.* VII, 6–22.　　　　　　　　[6] Cf. above, p. 213–14.
[7] Cf. above, p. 63.　　　　　　　　　　[8] Cf. above, p. 116f.

provided for as in those years when he had sold his liberty, bidden
farewell to scruples, and lost the last shred of his moral authority
by unpardonable lapses from principle. His enemies have naturally
cast his treacheries and betrayals of this period in his teeth, and
the Pseudo-Sallust does not hesitate to call him "the most adroit
of all turn-coats".[1] But the Correspondence itself hits him harder
than the most damaging of his enemies' pamphlets, for it shows us
Cicero the deserter comfortably provided for and taking his ease
in his infamy.

5. THE STRESSES OF THE CIVIL WAR

By this infamy he had at least achieved the goal for which his
self-love had striven. Later, the same sordid practices caused him
the loss of it. From the confidential disclosures of his later letters,
we know that he continued to disgrace himself by variations of
allegiance dictated apparently by caprice; but these were unsuccessful in securing peace for him during the Civil War or in
saving his life when once Mark Antony had become reconciled
with Octavian.

If we were to rely on Plutarch's narrative nothing could have
been happier or more consistent than Cicero's behaviour during
the bloody struggle between Caesar and Pompey for the domina-
tion of Rome. Discouraged by the obstacles he encountered in his
efforts to preserve peace, and then by the difficulty he found in
making his choice between the two warring parties, he ended by
acrimoniously rejecting Caesar's overtures to him. Immediately
after Caesar had set out for Spain, Cicero took ship to join Pompey
in Epirus.[2] Such is the version of events—a very flattering version
—which Cicero later sketched in his *Philippics*,[3] supplementing it
with corroboratory evidence. This is the version which Plutarch
tries to make more credible by claiming that he has taken his data
"from the very words of the Correspondence".[4]

Now, when we examine the *Letters* more closely they are very
far from showing this version to be well founded; in fact they
expressly give the lie to the essentials of it. Cicero's letters fix to
within a day or two—April 6 or 7, according to the Roman,

[1] Ps.-Sall., *In Cic.* 7.
[2] Plut. *Cic.* XXXVIII, 1: "As soon as Caesar had marched into Spain, he
immediately sailed away to join Pompey."
[3] Cic. *Phil.* II, 23, 57. Quoted by Drumann-Groebe, VI, p. 197, note 15.
[4] Cf. below, p. 221, note 6.

The Blunders of a Career that Failed

March 8 or 9 according to the Julian Calendar—the date in 49 when Caesar left Rome for Spain.[1] It was not until June 7 (Roman) or May 7 (Julian) of the same year that Cicero embarked for Epirus.[2] Instead of the two events being coincident, as Cicero and Plutarch contend, a long interval of two entire months separated them. Those two months were filled with urgent questionings, agonising hesitations, irrational caprices, and with advances and retreats on Cicero's part. These are measured by the march of events and accompanied by a vast amount of reticence and dissimulation.

Before he even entered Rome on his return from Cilicia, Cicero had proclaimed his adherence to Pompey's cause: *Cn(aeo) Pompeio adsentior*,[3] and on Dec. 10, 50, he had a *tête-à-tête* conversation with him, lasting about two hours.[4] Soon, however, he began to fear that he had committed himself too deeply. Towards the end of the year, after quiet reflection at Formiae, he began to have doubts: "We should have resisted Caesar when he was weak." With a sort of impassioned dismay he started totting up the forces now at Caesar's disposal: "Eleven legions, as much cavalry as he wants, the peoples from beyond the Po (the *Transpadani*) the city rabble . . . a leader of such influence and such audacity."[5] As he was on the point of returning to Rome for his birthday on Jan. 3, 49 Cicero clung to the hope that war would not break out after all[6]: "Peace is what is needed. From victory, many evils will arise: a tyrant most certainly."[7] Primarily the tyranny of Pompey.

[1] The date is inferred to within twenty-four hours from comparison of the following letters: (1) *Ad Att.* IX, 15, 1 (373 T.P.) notifies Caesar's arrival at Capua from Brundisium on the 7th of the Kalends of April; (2) *Ad Att.* IX, 17, 1 (375 T.P.) admits that Caesar will preside at the meeting of the Senate on April 1; (3) *Ad Att.* X, 3 (380 T.P.) and 3A (381 T.P.), from Arcanum, wonder whether on April 7—*a. d. vii Id(us)*—Caesar had not already left Rome.

On the question of the necessary corrections to the Roman Calendar of the period, according to which the following dates are quoted, see my *César* (3), pp. 736 and 858. Henceforward I shall quote the first of these dates only and refer the reader once for all to the equations given in my *César*.

[2] *Ad Fam.* XIV, 7, 2 (405 T.P.): . . . *in eam [navem] simul atque conscendi haec scripsi* . . . 3 : . . . *D. vii Id(us) Iun(ias)*. To Terentia from Formiae.

[3] *Ad Att.* VII, 3, 5 (294 T.P.).

[4] *Ad Att.* VII, 4, 2 (295 T.P.): *Pompeium vidi iiii Id(us) Decembres ; fuimus una horas duas fortasse.*

[5] *Ad Att.* VII, 7, 6 (298 T.P.): *Imbecillo resistendum fuit, et id erat facile. Nunc legiones XI, equitatus tantus quantum volet, Transpadani, plebs urbana . . . tanta auctoritate dux, tanta audacia . . .*

[6] *Ad Fam.* XVI, 11, 2 (301 T.P.). To Tiro Jan. 12, 49 B.C.; and *Ad Att.* VII, 5, 3 (296 T.P.).

[7] *Ad Att.* VII, 5, 4 (296 T.P.): *Pace opus est : ex victoria cum multa mala tum certe tyrannus exsistet.* End Dec. 50 B.C.

The Blunders of a Career that Failed

Atticus had approved Cicero's professions of allegiance to Pompey and now urged him to go out and fight, rather than to become a slave. Cicero in reply quoted the dread consequences of a war which could have only one of two results for him: proscription if his side were defeated; enslavement, if it were victorious.[1] He found another reason for doing nothing: had Atticus forgotten that if he kept his word and rallied to the side of Pompey, Caesar would demand repayment of the money he had lent him?[2] He was in truth dancing on hot bricks,[3] and he compared the preparedness of Caesar with Pompey's lack of foresight—"who has begun too late to fear Caesar"[4]—with apprehension all the more lively since he had accepted from Pompey the duty of seeing to the defence of the Campanian coast.[5]

Instead of feverishly executing these orders, he was biting his nails with annoyance at having let himself be induced to undertake the job, and he kept changing his mind and trying to gain time.[6] In his bewilderment he did not know what advice to give to his wife and daughter, who had stayed on in Rome subject to the threat of an invasion of the city by Caesar. So vague and changeable were his instructions that when he thought he had convinced them that it was better for them to remain where they were, he had the surprise of seeing them suddenly turn up in Formiae[7] on Feb. 2, 49. He eagerly kept his ears open to catch any rumours of peace-talks between the belligerents.[8] When these faded, he relapsed despondently into perplexity. Should he join Pompey or not? No; if he considered—and we cannot but be aghast at the considerations which weighed with him—the severities of winter, the inconvenient presence of the lictors whom he had brought back

[1] *Ad Att.* VII, 7, 7 (298 T.P.): *Depugna, inquis, potius quam servias. Ut quid? Si victus eris, proscribare; si viceris tamen servias.* End of Dec. 50 B.C.

[2] *Ad Att.* VII, 8, 5 (299 T.P.): *Mihi autem illud molestissimum est, quod solvendi sunt nummi Caesari* . . . End of Dec. 50 B.C.

[3] *Ad Fam.* XVI, 11, 2 (301 T.P.): *Incidi in ipsam flammam civilis discordiae.*

[4] *Ad Fam.* XVI, 11, 3 (301 T.P.): *Pompei nostri qui Caesarem sero coepit timere.*

[5] *Ad Att.* VII, 11, 5 (304 T.P.): *Vult enim me Pompeius esse, quem tota haec Campana et maritima ora habeat ἐπίσκοπον ad quem dilectus et summa negotii deferatur.* Jan. 19, 49 B.C.

[6] *Ad Att.* VII, 12, 3 (305 T.P.): . . . *an cuncter et tergiverser?* Jan. 22, 49 B.C.

[7] *Ad Fam.* XIV, 18, 1 (306 T.P.): *Considerandum vobis etiam atque etiam, animae meae, diligenter puto quid faciatis.* Jan. 22, 49 B.C.; *Ad Att.* VII, 14, 3 (310 T.P.): *Scire velim quid cogites de exeundo.* Jan. 25, 49 B.C.; 17, 5 (315 T.P.): *In Formiano, quo Capua redieram, mulieres exspectabam quibus quidem scripseram* . . . *ut Romae manerent.* Feb. 2, 49 B.C.; 18, 1 (316 T.P.): . . . *iiii Non(as) Febr(uarias) mulieres nostrae Formias venerunt.* Feb. 3, 49 B.C.

[8] *Ad Att.* VII, 14, 1 (310 T.P.): *Spero in praesentia pacem nos habere.*

with him from his proconsulate and whom he could not yet make up his mind to dismiss, the incompetence and shortsightedness of the leaders of the Senate. Yes; if he gave ear to the friendship which bound him to Pompey, the soundness of a cause which honourable people upheld, the dishonour of aiding a tyrant when you didn't know whether he would turn out to be a Phalaris or a Pisistratus.[1] Furthermore, not one item of news came in which did not chill him: the exit of the magistrates from Rome, followed by the fall of Corfinium on Feb. 21, Pompey's flight from Brundisium and from Italy on March 9.[2] He was racked by embarrassment and indecision: *mira me ἀπορία torquet*.[3] If he was quite clear whom to fly from, he was not clear whom to follow,[4] and as Pompey suffered one reverse after another Cicero overwhelmed him with criticisms,[5] as if to exonerate himself in advance if he were ultimately to fail to keep his promises.

We know that in the end he kept them; but at the last moment, as it were, in despair of the cause and in curious circumstances. On this point also the *Letters* correct Plutarch's statements and contradict the benevolent conclusions the biographer strove to deduce from them. According to Plutarch, Cicero made up his mind under the pressure of righteous wrath and noble feeling. In the name of his chief (Caesar), Trebatius implored his friend and protector (Cicero) to rally the ranks and raise the hopes of Caesar; or at least, if Cicero's age no longer allowed him to take an active part in hostilities, at least to withdraw to Greece and live there outside the fighting zone without committing himself to either party. Offended because Caesar had not addressed him directly, Cicero angrily replied to Trebatius that he would never do anything "unworthy of himself and of his policy".[6] That at least,

---

[1] *Ad Att.* VII, 20, 2 (318 T.P.): *Ad manendum hiems, lictores, improvidi et neglegentes duces, ad fugam hortatur amicitia Gnaei, causa bonorum, turpido coniugendi cum tyranno qui quidem incertum est Phalarimne an Pisistratum sit imitaturus.* Feb. 5, 49 B.C.
[2] On these facts and their dates, see my *César* (3), pp. 871-2.
[3] *Ad Att.* VII, 21, 3 (319 T.P.). Cicero adds: *Iuva me consilio, si potes;* cf. ibid. 9, 5 (300 T.P.): *Ad ea quae dixi adfer si quid habes : equidem dies noctesque torqueor.* This letter is of the end of Dec. 50 B.C.: the other is of Feb. 8, 49 B.C. One day follows another, all alike.
[4] *Ad Att.* VIII, 7, 2 (338 T.P.): *Ego vero, quem fugiam habeo, quem sequor non habeo.* Feb. 24, 49 B.C.
[5] Cf. *Ad Att.* VIII, 7, 2 (338 T.P.); cf. *Ad Att.* VII, 21, 3 (319 T.P.). Feb. 8, 49 B.C., etc.
[6] Plut. *Cic.* XXXVII, 3: "Wondering that Caesar had not written himself, Cicero gave an angry reply, that he should not do anything unbecoming his past life."

The Blunders of a Career that Failed

Plutarch triumphantly announces, is a sentiment which emerges from every letter of Cicero's Correspondence.[1]

But that is just what we do *not* find; or, rather, we find exactly the opposite!

(1) From the *Letters* we know that it is untrue to say that Caesar failed to try personally and directly to influence Cicero; Atticus preserved a copy of three letters from Caesar in which the same pressing request appears couched in most flattering terms. About March 7, 49, when he was approaching Brundisium by forced marches, Caesar dictated a first message direct to Cicero: "Above all, I beg of you, as I feel sure I shall speedily be coming to the City, that I may see you there so that I may be able to avail myself of your counsels, influence, position and support of every kind. I shall recur to this subject: pray forgive my haste and the shortness of this letter."[2] He returned to the charge on March 26 with substantially the same words.[3] On April 16, as he was travelling to Spain, he sent a request, which was also a warning, putting Cicero on his guard against any attempt to declare himself for Pompey's cause: "Finally, what can be more becoming to a good man, and a peaceable citizen, than to hold aloof from civil strife?"[4]

(2) The Correspondence, which has preserved sixteen letters from Cicero to Trebatius,[5] contains none from Trebatius to Cicero. It does contain one written jointly by Matius and Trebatius, announcing to Cicero that Pompey had left Brundisium on March 17, 49, but not conveying any message from Caesar for him.[6]

(3) It includes, on the other hand, a letter of Feb. 2, 49 in which Cicero incidentally gives Atticus a résumé of a letter he had just received from Trebatius and the answer which he had sent by return of courier.[7] It is perfectly true that Trebatius had informed him that Caesar—and this was as early as Feb. 2—was inviting

---

[1] Plut. *Cic.* XXXVII, 3: "Such is the account to be collected from his letters."

[2] Letter from Caesar *ap. Ad Att.* IX, 6A (357 T.P.): *In primis a te peto, quoniam confido me celeriter ad Urbem venturum ut te ibi videam, ut tuo consilio, gratia, dignitate, ope omnium rerum uti possim. Ad propositum revertar: festinationi meae brevitatique litterarum ignosces.* About March 7, 49 B.C.

[3] Caesar *ap. Ad Att.* IX, 16, 3 (374 T.P.): *Tu velim mihi ad Urbem praesto sis, ut tuis consiliis atque opibus, ut consuevi, in omnibus rebus utar.* Dated *a. d. vii Kal. Apr.,* viz. March 26, 49 B.C.

[4] Caesar *ap. Ad Att.* X, 8B, 2 (385 T.P.): *Postremo, quid viro bono et quieto et bono civi magis convenit quam abesse a civilibus controversiis.* Letter dated by Caesar *XV Kal(endas) Maias ex itinere,* viz. April 16.

[5] *Ad Fam.* VII, 6–22.

[6] Matius and Trebatius *ap. Ad Att.* IX, 15, 6 (373 T.P.).

[7] See the following two notes.

him to come to Rome and was conveying in flattering terms how much his presence there would be valued.[1] It is no less true that Cicero had replied—to Trebatius rather than to Caesar, who had not written with his own hand—by dismissing the case.[2] But, according to his own account, he betrayed not the slightest quiver of pride or anger. He confined himself to arguing politely that it was practically impossible to leave his country estate at the moment. To strengthen this excuse, which was so transparent that it could deceive no one, he added assurances designed to deceive at least Caesar—on a point about which no one had questioned him. He brazen-facedly asserted in fact that he was refraining from all activity on Pompey's behalf.[3] A little further on in the same letter to Atticus he confirmed his return to Formiae from Capua, where he had had to go to inspect the military preparations of which Pompey had put him in charge.[4]

(4) Most important of all: the texts of the Correspondence in the form in which the original publishers have transmitted them to us[5] cut clean across the connection which Plutarch made between the Trebatius letter and the sudden decision of Cicero's, taken when summer was near, to rejoin Pompey's armies.[6] The chronology is unanswerable. The aforementioned letter conveys instructions issued by Caesar on Jan. 22, 49.[7] It must have reached Cicero either at the end of January or at latest on Feb. 1. And Cicero did not weigh anchor at Pompeii till—the 7th of the following June.[8] Between these two dates Cicero went on racking his brains trying

---

[1] *Ad Att.* VII, 17, 3 (315 T.P.): *Trebatius quidem scribit se ab illo Caesare ix Kal. Febr(uarias) rogatum esse, ut scriberet ad me ut essem ad urbem : nihil ei me gratius facere posse. Haec verbis plurimis.*

[2] *Ad Att.* VII, 17, 3 (315 T.P.): *Illud admiror non ipsum ad me scripsisse, non per Caelium egisse, quamquam non aspernor Trebatii litteras a quo me unice diligi scio.* 4: *Rescripsi ad Trebatium—nam ad ipsum Caesarem qui mihi nihil scripsisset nolui, quam illud hoc tempore esset difficile, me tamen in praediis esse . . .* Cicero shows surprise (*admiror*), but no sign of anger.

[3] *Ad Att.* VII, 17, 4 (315 T.P.): *Rescripsi . . . me . . . neque dilectum ullum neque negotium suscepisse.*

[4] *Ad Att.* VII, 17, 5 (351 T.P.): *Ego iiii Non(as) Febr(uarias) in Formiano quo Capua redieram . . .* On Cicero's business in Capua, cf. above, p. 221.

[5] From *Ad Att.* X, 11, 4 (396 T.P.) and 12A, 1 (397 T.P.). Drumann-Groebe has inferred—wrongly as I think—that some further approach was made by Trebatius apart from the one here analysed. But even if so, the fact that Trebatius was with Cicero, a fact confirmed by both these letters, excludes his having written a letter during May 49 B.C.

[6] Cf. above, p. 221.

[7] *Ad Att.* VII, 17, 3 (315 T.P.): *Trebatius quidem scribit se ab illo ix Kal. Febr. rogatum esse . . .* viz. Jan. 22.

[8] Cf. above, p. 219.

to find some new solution, to which each day raised a fresh objection, and his mind veered this way and that like a weather-cock at the mercy of every breeze, hesitating between contradictory schemes. He appeared courteously receptive to all the suggestions with which Caelius,[1] Dolabella[2] and Mark Antony[3] bombarded him in Caesar's name—in the absence of Caesar—while all the time he never ceased to follow the fluctuations of the battle-line, subordinating the dictates of his conscience to the fortunes of war. It would be tedious to follow the details of the tergiversations of which all his letters of these days are full.[4] It is enough to note that they came to an end, and he hearkened to the voice of duty bidding him choose adherence to Pompey only when the good weather was at hand and sea-sickness was less acutely to be feared,[5] and above all when the news from the west exaggerated the temporary check which Caesar had suffered in front of Massilia (Marseilles), and convinced him that Pompey's forces were on the eve of victory in Spain.[6] He then forgot the persuasions to which he had seemed to be listening with sympathy,[7] and without waiting any longer—

[1] *Ap. Ad Fam.* VIII, 16, 1–3 (383 T.P.) and Cicero's reply *Ad Fam.* II, 16, 1 (394 T.P.).

[2] *Ad Att.* VII, 17, 3 (315 T.P.): *Illud admiror non ipsum Caesarem ad me scripsisse, non per Dolabellam, non per Caelium egisse.* Cf. Dolabella's letter *ap. Ad Fam.* IX, 9 (409 T.P.). May 48 B.C.

[3] See the letter from Mark Antony enclosed in *Ad Att.* X, 8A, 2 (391 T.P.) and the final threatening request—*ne profugias*; also the allusions to Caesar's command that no one at all should be allowed to leave Italy, see especially *Ad Att.* X, 10, 2 (395 T.P.): *Partes mihi Caesar has imposuit ne quem omnino discedere ex Italia paterer.*

[4] See passim *Ad Att.* X, 12B, 4 (398 T.P.): *Quid provideam?* May 6, 49 B.C.; 14, 1 (400 T.P.): *O vitam miseram! maiusque malum tam diu timere quam est illud ipsum, quod timetur.* May 8, 49 B.C.

[5] Cf. above, p. 221, note 1, and *Ad Att.* X, 11, 4 (396 T.P.): . . . *navigans quam fuerim sollicitus.* May 4, 49 B.C.; and 16, 2 (402 T.P.): . . . *navigatio modo sit, qualem opto!* May 14, 49 B.C.

[6] *Ad Att.* X, 10, 4 (395 T.P.): *De Massiliensibus gratae tuae mihi litterae.* May 3, 49 B.C.; X, 12A, 2 (397 T.P.): *Sit modo recte in Hispaniis . . . Ab Hispaniis autem iam audietur.* May 5, 49 B.C.; 12B, 6 (398 T.P.): *Hispanias spero firmas esse. Massiliensium factum cum ipsum per se luculentum est, tum mihi argumento est recte esse in Hispaniis.* May 6, 49 B.C.; 14, 2 (400 T.P.): *Conquire de Hispaniis, de Massilia; quae quidem satis bella Servius adfert.* May 8, 49 B.C. It is odd: even if Caesar were going to win, the Spanish War seems to Cicero to justify his rallying to Pompey: *Ad Att.* X, 8, 2 (392 T.P.): *Si pelletur Caesar Hispaniis quam gratus aut quam honestus erit ad Pompeium noster adventus? . . . Relinquitur ut, si vincimur in Hispania, quiescamus. Id ego contra puto : istum enim victorem magis re inquendum quam victum . . . Nam caedem video.* May 2, 49 B.C.

[7] Pure humbug according to his own confession. Cf. his strange confession about Mark Antony's impending visit, *ap. Ad Att.* X, 10 (395 T.P.): *Omnino excipiam hominem . . . Temptabo, audiam : nihil properare, missurum ad Caesarem me clamabo, Cum paucissimis alicubi occultabor, certe hinc istis invitissimis evolabo.* And so indeed the bird the Caesarians thought they had tamed did in fact take wing.

as would have been prudent and as his family were urging him to do[1]—for further news from the Spanish front, news for which he had been anxiously clamouring only the day before,[2] he staked his future on a throw of the dice and embarked for the campaign that was doomed to end at Pharsalia.

So Plutarch was guilty of a grave misreckoning. Perhaps he was misled by some apologist in whom he placed his faith, and I incline to identify the source of his material with Tiro's biography[3] of his master. The Correspondence on which he thought he could rely brings back into their true light the facts he has wrested, and pitilessly reveals the real features of the unchanged face which he has sought to beautify. In 49 Cicero was still "the most adroit of turncoats" whom the Pseudo-Sallust had jeered at in 54.[4] But this time his adroitness was punished, for in full view of both parties he had betrayed them both. His precipitate and yet belated rally to Pompey's cause succeeded only in arousing the contempt and suspicion of those to whom in desperation he brought his support, from motives of mere personal opportunism,[5] and the well-deserved wrath of the man whom he deserted after having welcomed his advances.

What insults and what dangers was he not exposed to by his presence in Pompey's camp? In default of his Correspondence, which was completely interrupted during the second half of 49 and reduced to a few notes of a strictly private character during the first ten months of 48,[6] we have Plutarch's evidence. Plutarch is compelled to admit that after a somewhat chilly reception from his companions in arms, Cicero played practically no part at all among them.[7] Plutarch makes up for this by amusing his reader with the jokes that Cicero, incurable jester that he was, cracked about them all, but we should be wrong to imagine that they, with Cato at their head, failed to pay him back with interest in his

---

[1] *Ad Att.* X, 8, 1 (392 T.P.): . . . *cum ad me saepe mea Tullia scribat orans, ut quid Hispania geratur exspectem*; 9, 2 (393 T.P.): *lacrimae meorum me interdum molliunt precantium, ut de Hispaniis exspectemus.*

[2] Again, on May 19, *Ad Att.* X, 18, 2 (404 T.P.): *Si quid de Hispaniis perge, quaeso, quaerere.*

[3] Cf. above, pp. 42 and 192.   [4] Cf. above, p. 218.

[5] Just as Cicero himself had foreseen. Cf. *Ad Att.* X, 8, 2 (392 T.P.), quoted above, p. 224, note 6.

[6] There is no letter of 49 B.C. after that of June 7 to Terentia: *Ad Fam.* XIV, 7 (405 T.P.): seven letters to Atticus and to Terentia between the beginning of Jan. 48 and his arrival at Brundisium early at Nov.: *Ad Att.* XI, 1 (406 T.P.); 2 (407 T.P.), 3 (411 T.P.), 4 (413 T.P.): *Ad Fam.* XIV, 8 (410 T.P.), 21 (412 T.P.), and 6 (414 T.P.).   [7] Plut. *Cic.* XXXVIII–XXXIX.

own coin. There was clearly nothing but enmity and distrust between him and them. While military operations hung fire he exerted himself in recriminations and slanging-matches, and when things began to warm up he took care to go sick. He did not put in an appearance on the battlefield of Pharsalia, and when, in the council of war after the defeat, the survivors suggested that as the senior ex-Consul present he should take over the command, he refused in terms which foreshadowed his desertion. He was within a hair's-breadth of being murdered out of hand, but he stuck to his intention, and set sail for Italy with all the haste of a fugitive who spends his last energy in fleeing from the scene of the fight and pins all his hopes to the conqueror's clemency—having in his inmost heart already surrendered to the victor.

According to Plutarch this clemency was accorded as a matter of course, and the biographer puts it on record in three brilliant sentences. He represents Cicero as having waited at Brundisium for the conqueror to return from his campaign in the East. No sooner had he happened to meet Caesar on the Tarentum road than the great soldier dismounted and conversed in a friendly way and forthwith forgave him without Cicero's having to do or say anything derogatory to his dignity.[1] In the interval, however, the thread of the Correspondence has been resumed, and according to the *Letters* things were far from passing off with such ease and elegance.

Firstly, it was in fear and trembling that Cicero disembarked at Brundisium in the early days of Nov. 48. He was a fugitive, haunted by the memory of the lies and the shams of which he was guilty towards Caesar. Terentia had sent an express messenger with a letter congratulating her husband on his safe return to Italy; in trembling tones he replied: "How I wish that your joy over my having got back safe and sound to Italy might prove everlasting! But distraught by mental anguish and the great injustices I had suffered, I fear I took a decision from the consequences of which I cannot easily disentangle myself."[2] Assuredly many in Rome,

---

[1] Plut. *Cic.* XXXIX, 2: "There was no necessity for him either to speak or to do anything unworthy of himself; for Caesar, as soon as he saw him coming . . . came down to meet him, saluted him, and leading the way, conversed with him alone for some furlongs. And from that time forward he continued to treat him with honour and respect."

[2] *Ad Fam.* XIV, 12 (415 T.P.): *Quod nos in Italiam salvos venisse gaudes, perpetuo gaudeas velim. Sed perturbati dolore animi magnisque iniuriis metuo ne id consilii ceperimus, quod non facile explicare possimus.* To Terentia dated: *prid. Nonas Novemb(res) Brundisio*, i.e. Nov. 4, 48 B.C.

foremost among them Vatinius, would have asked nothing better than to come to his aid, but in view of Caesar's estrangement he considered that these good friends could be of no use to him.[1] From day to day his worry and anxiety increased; he felt stifled in the confined atmosphere of gossip-ridden Brundisium, and he earnestly longed for some secluded retreat in an unknown spot where he could take refuge until the moment came when he would be given the chance to justify himself.[2] In vain Balbus and Oppius sought to console him with reassuring messages. He did not dare to trust these assurances and would not venture to come nearer Rome until, thanks to their intercession combined with similar good offices from Trebonius, Pansa and others, Caesar should deign to grant him express permission.[3]

At this point he received, instead of the anticipated permission, a copy of a letter of Caesar's, communicated to him by Mark Antony, which strictly interpreted would compel him to leave Italy.[4] At Lamia's request, he and Laelius had both been expressly excepted from the expulsion order.[5] But it was a near thing, and his terror redoubled. If the unfortunate man had even enjoyed a quiet conscience and could have foreseen the future clearly! But the future looked blacker and blacker and his conscience was racked with remorse. While he was exercising all his ingenuity to forestall by words and actions the blows which Caesar might deal him, he took refuge behind the most irritating casuistries against the attacks of Caesar's enemies. With incredible effrontery he maintained at one point that since Pompey was now assassinated no one could blame him for having deserted his standards[6]; and at another he justified himself for not having gone over to Africa, where the Senate was concentrating the remnant of its forces, by asserting

[1] *Ad Att.* XI, 5, 4 (416 T.P.): *Quod de Vatinio quaeris, neque illius neque cuiusquam mihi praeterea officium deesset, si reperire possent qua in re me iuvarent.* Nov. 48 B.C.

[2] *Ad Att.* XI, 6, 1 (418 T.P.): . . . *qui quidem [dolor] non modo non minuitur . . . sed etiam augetur . . .* 2: *Brundisii iacere in omnes partes est molestum . . . In oppido aliquo mallem resedisse quoad arcesserer; minus sermonis subissem, minus accepissem doloris.* Nov. 27, 48 B.C.

[3] *Ad Att.* XI, 6, 3 (418 T.P.): *Mitte nunc ad Oppium et Balbum quonam his placeret modo proprius accedere, ut hac de re considerarent . . . Explora cum istis . . . quo magis factum nostrum Caesar probet quasi de suorum sententia factum adhibeantur Trebonius, Pansa, si qui alii . . .* Nov. 27, 48 B.C.

[4] *Ad Att.* XI, 7, 2 (420 T.P.): Brundisium, Dec. 17, 48 B.C.

[5] *Ad Att.* XI, 7, 2 (420 T.P.): *Tum ille edixit ita ut me exciperet et Laelium nominatim.*

[6] *Ad Att.* XI, 7, 3 (420 T.P.): *Dicebar debuisse cum Pompeio proficisci; exitus illius minuit eius officii praetermissi reprehensionem.*

his unconquerable aversion from an alliance concluded with the Barbarians of the Numidian tribes "against a frequently victorious army".[1] His whole position was so utterly false that it was a torture to him.

Since no one knew exactly where Caesar was or what point matters had reached in Alexandria[2]; since Fortune's wheel might yet take another turn; since Spain was on the point of rising in rebellion like Africa,[3] Cicero, a prisoner in Italy and yet shut out from Rome,[4] felt himself spied upon, attacked from every side at once, and was hideously a prey to distress, regrets and fears. As in the days of his exile, he could find nothing better to do than to dissolve in tears.[5]

Towards the close of the spring of 47 a letter from Caesar reached him, the ambiguity of which would have alarmed him if he had not suspected it of being apocryphal[6] and if he had not just then heard talk of Caesar's expected return. On hearing this news, his first impulse was to rush to meet the conqueror. Atticus thought this eagerness excessive, and in face of his cautious counsels Cicero seemed to give up the idea.[7] Then without altogether giving it up, he modified and cut it down. He would send his son to the port to plead his cause.[8] At the beginning of August, Caesar's ship had not yet been sighted, but Cicero had received a letter from the Dictator, a genuine one this time, whose generosity reawakened his original plan. He thereupon decided neither to sit still in

---

[1] *Ad Att.* XI, 6, 2 (418 T.P.): *Me discessisse ab armis numquam paenituit . . . tanta cum barbaris gentibus coniunctio.* Nov. 27, 48 B.C.; 7, 3 (420 T.P.): *Sed ex omnibus nihil magis tamen desideratur quam quod in Africam non ierim. Iudicio hoc sum usus, non esse barbaris auxiliis fallacissimae gentis rempublicam defendendam praesertim contra exercitum saepe victorem.* Dec. 17, 48 B.C.

[2] *Ad Att.* XI, 15, 1 (430 T.P.): *Ille [Caesar] enim ita videtur Alexandream tenere.* May 14, 47 B.C.

[3] *Ad Att.* XI, 10, 2 (425 T.P.): *Accedit Hispania . . .* Jan. 19, 47 B.C.

[4] *Ad Att.* XI, 9, 1 (423 T.P.): *. . . nec in ulla sum spe, quippe qui exceptionibus edictorum retinear.* Jan. 3, 47 B.C.

[5] *Ad Att.* XI, 7, 6 (420 T.P.): *Lacrimae enim se subito profuderunt.* Dec. 17, 48 B.C.; 8, 1 (422 T.P.): *Quantis curis conficiar.* Dec. 25, 48 B.C. He gets to the point of cursing the day he was born: ibid. 3, 9 (423 T.P.): *Haec ad te die natali meo suscripsi: quo utinam susceptus non essem . . . Plura fletu prohibeor.* Jan. 3, 47 B.C.

[6] *Ad Att.* XI, 16, 1 (431 T.P.): *Nam et exigue scripta est epistola et suspiciones magnas habet non esse ab illo [Caesare].*

[7] *Ad Att.* XI, 16, 1 (431 T.P.): *De obviam itione ita faciam, ut suades. Neque enim ulla de adventu eius opinio est.*

[8] *Ad Fam.* XIV, 15 (435 T.P.): *Constitueramus, ut ad te antea scripseram, obviam Ciceronem Caesari mittere, sed mutavimus consilium, quia de illius adventu nihil audiebamus.* To Terentia June 19, 47 B.C.

Brundisium, as Atticus had probably suggested, nor yet to send young Marcus as a substitute, which was his later idea, but he began again to think of taking the initiative himself and going in person to meet Caesar.[1]

Plutarch, reporting the Correspondence, has told us how he did in fact carry out this plan and the comfort he got from his interview with Caesar towards the end of Sept. 47 on the road between Tarentum and Brundisium. Having been granted an amnesty by the master, Cicero rejoined his wife in Tusculum on Oct. 7,[2] and towards the end of the year installed himself once again in the Roman house which he had not lived in since he left for Cilicia in May 51.[3] A short time afterwards he confided to Varro his joy at being once more reconciled to his oldest and dearest friends, his books. "I had not abandoned their society because I had fallen out with them, but because I felt somewhat ashamed. For methought that in flinging myself into the raging vortex of politics with most untrustworthy companions I had not shown due respect for their teachings."[4]

The truth is that his apparent lightheartedness here rings the melancholy note of a farewell. To enjoy the benefits of Caesar's forgiveness he had to bid goodbye to politics, for no policy of his could be compatible with Caesar's absolutism. From 47 to the Ides of March 44 when the Dictator was slain Cicero was, *nolens volens*, a slave to that almighty will. He resigned himself to being "softer than the lobe of the ear"[5] and he emerged from his self-effacement only to give added proofs of the degree to which he was domesticated. When he put in an appearance in the Senate

---

[1] *Ad Fam.* XIV, 23 (443 T.P.): *Redditae mihi tandem sunt a Caesare litterae satis liberales, et ipse opinione celerius venturus esse dicitur. Cui utrum ob viam procedam an hic eum exspectem, cum constituero, faciam te certiorem.* To Terentia, Aug. 12, 47 B.C.

[2] *Ad Fam.* XIV, 20 (449 T.P.): *In Tusculanum nos venturos putamus aut Nonis aut postridie.* To Terentia, from Venusia, Oct. 1, 47 B.C.

[3] Deduced not so much from the allusion of Macrobius (*Sat.* II, 3, 5) to the suffete consulship of Vatinius as from the letter quoted in the following note.

[4] *Ad Fam.* IX, 1, 2 (456 T.P.): *Scito enim me, posteaquam in urbem venerim, redisse cum veteribus amicis, id est cum libris nostris in gratiam: etsi non idcirco eorum usum dimiseram, quod iis suscenseram, sed quod eorum suppudebat. Videbar enim mihi, cum me in res turbulentissimas infidelissimis sociis demisissem, praeceptis illorum non satis paruisse.* To Varro, beginning of 46 B.C.

[5] This is the expression which Cicero used as early as 54 B.C. in a letter to Quintus: *Ad Q. Fr.* II, 13, 4 (141 T.P.): *Tu quem ad modum me censes oportere esse et in republica et in nostris inimicitiis, ita et esse et fore oricula infima scito molliorem.* I borrow the translation "lobe of the ear" from Alfred Ernout, *C. R. Ac. Inscr.* 1938, p. 483.

The Blunders of a Career that Failed

it was only to endorse Caesar's proposals[1] with closed eyes and without even noticing what they were about. When he spoke in public, it was only to extol the greatness and the magnanimity of Caesar.[2] When he took the risk of publishing his speeches, he first procured Caesar's approval.[3] When he renewed his former correspondence with old friends of the senatorial party, he did so as Caesar's courtier and henchman, to induce them to give their allegiance to the personal régime which in his secret soul he abhorred. But for his own peace of mind he set himself to get others round him to follow his lead.[4] It is true that we owe the most glorious of Cicero's literary achievements to Caesar, who sent the author and philosopher back to his beloved studies. From the *Letters*, however, we see what a terribly heavy price he had to pay for the privilege: with the tears, the anxieties and the humiliations of Brundisium, above all with the apparently final downfall of the Roman statesman.

A little later we shall see—time and again—how, after having nearly pulled himself together in the months that followed Caesar's murder, he completed his own destruction by a repetition of the same weaknesses and monstrous miscalculations. We see why he fell a victim to the swords of Octavian and Mark Antony, whom he flattered himself he could everlastingly play off the one against the other. The warrant for his death set the seal on an alliance which was fore-written in the nature of things.[5]

[1] His signature was appended to *Senatus consulta*, of which he had never read a word, going out to places as far afield as Armenia. Cf. *Ad Fam.* IX, 15, 4 (481 T.P.): *Romae cum sum et urgeo forum, senatus consulta scribantur apud amatorem tuum, familiarem meum. Et quidem, cum in mentem venit, ponor ad scribendum et ante audio senatus consultum in Armeniam et Syriam esse perlatum, quod in meam sententiam factum esse dicatur, quam omnino mentionem ullam de ea re esse factam.* To Paetus, Sept. 46 B.C.

[2] Cf. the famous examples furnished by the *Pro Ligario* and *Pro Marcello* speeches; the letters to Ligarius *ap.* Cic. *Ad Fam.* VI, 13 (489 T.P.) and to Marcellus, *ap.* Cic. *Ad Fam.* IV, 7 (486 T.P.); 8 (485 T.P.); and 9 (487 T.P.) all dating from Sept. 46 B.C.

[3] *Ad Att.* XIII, 19, 2 (631 T.P.): *Scripsit enim ad me Balbus et Oppius mirifice se probare Ligarianam: ob eamque causam ad Caesarem eam se oratiunculam misisse.* June 45 B.C. If we cannot, strictly speaking, say that Cicero had to apply for official approval, the precaution he here took speaks volumes for his "liberty".

[4] Ciaceri, op. cit., II, pp. 272–7, has drawn up a list, as far as the Correspondence makes it possible, of these tentatives of Cicero's to enlist adherents for Caesar: Ligarius and Marcellus, cf. note 2 above; Cn. Plancius, *Ad Fam.* IV, 15 (484 T.P.); P. Nigidius Figulus, *Ad Fam.* IV, 13 (483 T.P.); A. Caecina, *Ad Fam.* VI, 5 (533 T.P.); 6 (488 T.P.); 7 (532 T.P.); Domitius Ahenobarbus, junior, *Ad Fam.* VI, 22 (465 T.P.); Trebianus, *Ad Fam.* VI, 10 (491–2 T.P.); T. Ampius Balbus, *Ad Fam.* VI, 12 (490 T.P.). The first and the last two of these were the only efforts that were completely successful.

[5] Cf. above, p. 218, and below, II, p. 383.

The Blunders of a Career that Failed

Thus on Dec. 7, 43, the blood of the proscribed man sealed the long series of misreckonings, reverses and misfortunes which from the time of his consulship to his assassination, during the course of well-nigh twenty consecutive years, marred his public life. His *Letters*, every page of which reveals the eccentricities of his mind and the vices of his heart, the faults and defects of his personality, explain the perpetual bankruptcy which were their consequence and their penalty. In reading them we see why, in spite of his extraordinary culture, his dazzling gifts and his immense talent, Cicero met with nothing but failure and frustration in politics. He possessed none of the qualities which make and he had all the faults which destroy a statesman.

Chaper II

THE DEFECTS OF A STATESMAN

WHAT do we ask for in a statesman worthy of the name? We want, above all, burning convictions, to sustain him in the struggle for power and maintain him when he reaches power. Then, he must have a clear and cool intellect to distinguish the vital from the inessential, day-dreams from realities. Next, he must possess enough firmness of character to look opponents and difficulties in the face; courage to shoulder responsibility and tackle danger, and in critical moments to make prompt and calm decisions. Lastly, in his human relations he must have enough self-respect to impress everyone, and enough modesty not uselessly to wound anyone, and an adaptability consistent with integrity, and a good faith towards loyal followers which creates confidence and confirms allegiance. Far from reflecting even some features of this brilliant and ideal personage, the *Letters* of Cicero, like a faithful yet distorting mirror, show us nothing but a looking-glass caricature.

I. A DOCTRINAIRE WITHOUT A DOCTRINE

Cicero prided himself on possessing and preaching a true doctrine. He never tired of repeating to his friends: "Do not call me an orator, call me a philosopher. I cling to philosophy as the yardstick of all my acts. For me eloquence is only the instrument of my political ideas".[1] And we all know that between 54 and 51 he composed the six books of his treatise on the best form of government, his *De Republica*.[2] He was, however, only an armchair

---

[1] Plut. *Cic.* XXXII, 4: "He often desired his friends not to call him orator, but philosopher, because he had made philosophy his business, and had only used rhetoric as an instrument for attaining his objects in public life."

[2] On the date of its composition, begun in May 54 B.C., cf. *Ad Q. Fr.* II, 12, 1 (139 T.P.); on the date of its publication *Ad Att.* V, 12, 2 (202 T.P.) and *Ad Fam.* VIII, 1, 5 (192 T.P.) from Caelius. These letters are dated, respectively, July and June 51 B.C.

theorist, and he kept a water-tight bulkhead between thought and act, between the writing of his books and the conduct of his life. People have lately been busy trying to prove the opposite; the Germans especially. Some have wanted to interpret the *Republic* as the sanctification of Pompey's powers and some as a prophetic anticipation of the Principate of Augustus.[1] In my opinion they are wrong. For Pierre Grenade has justly emphasised what he calls the "ideality" of these pages, the inspiration of which Cicero owed less to the observation of contemporary facts than to the Greek philosophers, whose aloof speculations he had filtered into Latin for the benefit of the Roman public. Grenade adds that it is this idealistic quality which lends them "at once their Utopian character, their grandeur and their nobility".[2] He would be entirely correct but for the *Letters*, which rob them of everything except their Utopian character. Just as in the days when, in the *Tusculan Disputations*, he was furbishing up the Platonic and Pythagorean proofs of the immortality of the soul, he erased them at one stroke when he confided to Toranius that "death is the end of all things",[3] so the variations of his Correspondence wilfully obliterate the last trace of the principles which he laid down in the *Republic*. The fact is that in his Treatises the artist in him harmonised all the memories he retained from his reading, whereas into his *Letters* he put himself—with his elusive and ever-changing nature, with the scepticism which he owed both to his temperament and to the teachings of the New Academy,[4] with those changes of mind like so many changes of mood which beat time to his erratic progress amid the complication of events and the scene-shiftings in the State. The utter lack of idealism in the *Letters* contrasts with the formal "ideality" of the *Republic*.

[1] I refer the reader to my *César* (3), p. 855, note 330.
[2] Pierre Grenade, "Remarques sur la théorie cicéronienne dite du Principat" in the *Mélanges de l'École française de Rome*, pp. 32–63. The passage quoted occurs at the end of this excellent article.
[3] Cicero pleads in favour of the immortality of the soul in the names of Plato and Pythagoras (following Posidonius?) in Chapters 17–21, Book I, of the *Tusc. Disp.*, which were begin at the end of May 45 B.C., *Ad Att.* XIII, 32, 2 (610 T.P.). And he brutally denies it in his letter to Toranius of the preceding month. Cf. *Ad Fam.* VI, 21, 1 (573 T.P.): . . . *una ratio videtur, quicquid evenerit ferre moderate, praesertim cum omnium rerum mors sit extremum.* Cf. below, p. 256, note 6, Cicero's phrase *Ad Fam.* V, 21, 4 (458 T.P.). 46 B.C.
On the subjects which seem to have been nearest his heart (cf. below, p. 247) he has to read the Greeks. See, for instance, how insistently he urges Atticus to get him a copy of Demetrius of Magnesia, *De Concordia: Ad Att.* VIII, 11, 7 (342 T.P.) and IX, 9, 2 (364 T.P.).
[4] Cf. the earliest in date of his treatises, the *Academica*, and below, p. 237.

The Defects of a Statesman

Of late years—again in Germany—an attempt has been made to extract from the *Letters* a theory about class-harmony which Cicero professed to consider as the foundation and the goal of Roman policy.[1] The formulators of this theory have, I fear, mistaken for a dogma what was only an effective slogan, whose alluring sound was designed temporarily to cover electoral tactics and an opportunist fusion of interests.

The expression *concordia ordinum*—the harmony of the Orders—frequently flowed from Cicero's pen during the years following his consulship. Sending Atticus the news of Rome on Dec. 5, 61, he congratulated himself on having made a great speech four days before, which lasted for two sessions of the Senate. The subject of it was "the honour and harmony of the classes",[2] a harmony "which I evoked and which our efforts must preserve".[3] In the following letter of Jan. 20, 60, he sadly noted that he had not been listened to: the two buttresses of the State which he had built up singlehanded had been overthrown and the "harmony of classes" broken up.[4]

If by that we were to understand a sort of general entente, a universal fusion, this extension of their meaning would rob the words of all significance, and they would imply nothing more than that union of all good citizens which every politician in every country and in every age solicits for support and co-operation.[5] If, on the other hand, we confine them—as we should [6]—to the two upper classes, who had achieved the dignity of being known as "Orders", the Senators namely and the Equites, or as we should say today the nobility and the bourgeoisie, they aimed only at achieving solidarity by a practical cartel, in which their rivalry

[1] Strasburger, *Concordia Ordinum, Eine Untersuchung zur Politik Ciceros*, Leipzig, 1931. See the arrangement of texts, pp. 71–4.

[2] *Ad Att.* I, 17, 9 (23 T.P.): . . . *multa a me de ordinum dignitate et concordia dicta sunt K(alendis) Decembr(ibus) et postridie.*

[3] *Ad Att.* I, 17, 10 (23 T.P.): *Tueor, ut possum, illam a me conglutinatam concordiam.* And it is his system: . . . *sic ego conservans rationem institutionemque nostram* (ibid.).

[4] *Ad Att.* I, 18, 3 (24 T.P.): *Sic ille annus duo firmamenta reipublicae per me unum constituta evertit: nam et senatus auctoritatem abiecit et ordinum concordia diiunxit.*

[5] On the *boni cives* or simply the *boni*, see the texts cited by Strasburger, op. cit., pp. 59–61. On the *bonorum consensio* cf. *Ad Att.* I, 16, 9 (22 T.P.). July 61 B.C.

[6] Cf. for instance *Ad Att.* I, 14, 4 (20 T.P.): *Etenim haec erat ὑπόθεσις de gravitate ordinis, de equestri concordia.* Feb. 13, 61 B.C.; L. A. Constans, I, p. 135, has well expressed it: the theme of the speech was: the dignity of the Senatorial order and the harmony between it and the Equestrian order.

would be reduced and their power and profits increased, combining landlord and financier, territorial magnate and owner of mobile capital: merchants, manufacturers, bankers and tax-farmers. This was a big programme, we must admit. But it lacks breadth and perspective. It was not calculated to regenerate the State; at most it might have reduced for the moment its most glaring imperfections. It lacked any plan of reform, any view of the future[1]; it was limited to stabilising the present, by drawing the possessing classes together to safeguard their wealth and fortune. This was no profession of faith, but simply a reflex action of self-preservation.

As a pleader at the bar, working for wealthy clients, Cicero pursued, or sought to pursue, in the Forum the policy that suited the men to whom he was attached by every fibre of his heart and all the ties of business in which he was involved with them. It was the rich whom he thought of as the "good people", whose affection and whose applause intoxicated him[2]; it was for their sake that he upheld the sanctity of credit,[3] opposed the allotment of public lands,[4] and defeated the revolutionary plans of Catiline and his followers. Neither in the Rome of his day nor elsewhere at any time did the wealthy venture openly to proclaim the profound affinity which linked them together despite superficial antagonisms, nor did they dare to form a distinct "party of the rich". Yet it was certainly to this party, unnamed and unrecognised, but numerous and as strong as an army, that Cicero tacitly vowed his fervent allegiance: *is enim est noster exercitus hominum, ut tute scis, locupletium . . .*[5] We might have expected some heartfelt conviction, strengthened by serious reflection; we find nothing but the instinctive clinging of a privileged person to his privileges.

Why should Cicero, whose faith and sense of certainty[6] had been shattered by the teachings of the School that wisdom consists in suspending judgment, why should he have obstinately sought to

---

[1] Cicero asks nothing more. Cf. *Ad Att.* I, 18, 2 (24 T.P.): *adductus . . . spe non corrigendae sed sanandae civitatis.*

[2] *Ad Q. Fr.* I, 2, 16 (53 T.P.): *nostra antica manus bonorum ardet studio nostri et amore.*

[3] *Ad Att.* II, 1, 10 (27 T.P.): *. . . vindicem aeris alieni . . .*

[4] Cf. above, p. 203 and below, note 5.   [5] *Ad Att.* I, 19, 4 (25 T.P.).

[6] We must not forget that in the *Academica* Cicero defended against Lucullus the opinion of Carneades, as expounded by Clitomachus, according to which, since certainty is unattainable, it is the part of wisdom to suspend judgment: *Acad. Pr.* II, 24, 78 . . . *sequitur omnium adsentionum retentio . . .*; 32, 104 . . . *adiungit [Clitomachus] adsensus sustinere sapientem.* Clitomachus had written four books *de sustinendis adsentionibus* (31, 98), etc.

find it amid the shifting sands of politics? To hear him, it is inevitable that ideas should change with changing circumstances, and it was nothing but necessity which accounted for the perpetual changeableness of which this unstable philosopher never cured himself. Towards the end of his life he confessed that he was unable to foresee, even a few days ahead, what Brutus and Cassius might do, "because", he said, "decisions depend on circumstances and you can see these changing from hour to hour."[1] Ten years earlier he had told Lucullus the rules which guided his conduct: "Never to fight against overwhelming power, not obstinately to cling to the same view when things had changed and the best public opinion had altered, but rather to bow to circumstances."[2]

His system—if we can call it a system—was whole-hearted opportunism. He adjusted himself to circumstances not in order to control them, but to submit to them with the perfect freedom of indifference, without any marked preference or preconceived desire—except the desire to succeed.[3] While a true statesman consents to swerve only in order to direct events the more surely to his chosen goal, Cicero veers and tacks, as it were on principle, and takes his direction solely from the wind.[4] Thiers is credited with having coined the phrase: "It is only imbeciles who never change." Cicero had anticipated him and gone even further, for according to him: "Persistence in the same view has never been regarded as a merit in men eminent for their guidance of the State."[5]

[1] *Ad Att.* XIV, 20, 4 (727 T.P.): *Consilia temporum sunt, quae in horas commutari vides.*

[2] *Ad Fam.* I, 9, 21 (153 T.P.): *De quo sic velim statuas, me haec eadem sensurum fuisse, si mihi integra omnia ac libera fuissent; nam neque pugnandum arbitrarer contra tantas opes . . . neque permanendum in una sententia conversis rebus ac bonorum voluntatibus mutatis, sed temporibus adsentiendum.* Dec. 54 B.C.; cf. below, p. 238, note 2, the formula on the decree of March 17, 44 B.C.

[3] His aim is to keep his place by means of his popularity—*dignitatem tueri gratia,* cf. *Ad Att.* I, 17, 6 (23 T.P.); and to preserve his resources; see next note.

[4] The *concordia ordinum* is only a means to an end and even while making use of it he is thinking of throwing it over: cf. *Ad Att.* I, 17, 10 (23 T.P.): *Sed tamen quoniam ista sunt tam infirma* [it is here a question of his *ratio*, of his *institutio*, of his *concordia* [*ordinum a se*] *conglutinata*] *munitur quaedam nobis ad retinendas opes nostras, tuta, ut spero, via*: and the context following shows that it is the alliance with Pompey. So Cicero is able to execute an "about turn" as easily as he can tack; and he tacks even at the cost of not making port. *Ad Fam.* I, 9, 21 (153 T.P.): *. . . in navigando tempestati obsequi artis est, etiam si portum tenere non queas . . .*

[5] *Ad Fam.* I, 9, 21 (153 T.P.): *Numquam enim in praestantibus in republica gubernanda viris laudata est in una sententia perpetua permansio.* He had got so far as triumphantly to hail in advance his coming recantations: *Ad Att.* II, 9, 1 (36 T.P.): *Quarum* [*orationum*] *exspecta divinam* παλινῳδίαν.

In the same letter he contrives to shelter this strange eulogy of inconsistency under the great name of Plato, and quotes that passage of the *Crito*[1] in which we are advised no more to do violence to our country than to our father.[2] In other words, he limits the art of leaders to letting themselves be led,[3] and their wisdom to giving way under stress of need.[4]

This negative conclusion reduces his ambition to a craving for material advantage and the satisfaction of his pride: things to which he clung with puerile tenacity even in the most tragic days of the terrible drama. It led him, for instance, into the most preposterous intrigues, whether to procure for a friend that a legal exception should be made in his favour when he had just refused to grant the same to an opponent,[5] or to get his son a place in the College of Pontiffs[6] (July and May 43). What is still more important, it implies his own repudiation of all moral sense. In thus making light of all political good faith, henceforth confusing it with the acquisition or preservation of influence and power— influence which he no longer knew how to employ, power which he could no longer use—his muddled mind was prepared to justify every compromise, to tolerate every paltering with principle, and to reduce every opinion to the level of the immediate success that it might be expected to bring. Having got so far, it was only one step to speak without believing a word of what he said, and Cicero, having by his curious philosophy freed himself of all scruples, all too often took that final step.

He was not the dupe of his own eloquence. He was himself unmoved by the oratorical efforts which shook his fellow-citizens and swept them off their feet. From his *Letters* we know that eloquence was for him nothing but the exercise of a musician—

---

[1] Plato, *Crito*, 51 C.

[2] *Ad Fam.* I, 9, 18 (153 T.P.): *Id enim iubet eidem ille Plato, quo ego vehementer auctore moveor : tantum contendere in republica quantum probare tuis civibus possis ; vim neque parenti nec patriae adferre oportere.*

[3] *Ad Fam.* I, 9, 18 (153 T.P.): *Itaque tota iam sapientium civium . . . et sententia et voluntas mutata esse debet.*

[4] *Ad Fam.* IV, 9, 2 (487 T.P.): *Necessitati parere, semper sapientis est habitum.* To Marcellus. Sept. 46 B.C.

[5] While he reproached Brutus for seeking to get his nephews excepted from the confiscation of Lepidus's, their father's, property, he asked Decimus Brutus to consent to a similar exception in favour of his friend Appius Claudius. Cf. *Ad Br.* I, 12 and 13 (909 and 908 T.P.) and *Ad Fam.* X, 29 (911 T.P.) and XI, 22 (912 T.P.).

[6] On this misplaced application, see *Ad Br.* I, 6, 1 (867 T.P.) and I, 7, 1 (868 T.P.).

whatever Plutarch avers to the contrary—playing for his public the airs it loved. These are, for instance, the terms in which he described to Atticus the joust in the Senate in Feb. 61, from which he emerged as victor. "As for my own speech, ye Gods, how I did show off before my new auditor Pompey! If I ever brought every art into play, I did then—period, transition, antithesis, deduction —everything. In short: cheers. For the subject of my speech was the dignity of the Senate; its harmony with the Equites; the unanimity of Italy; the dying embers of the conspiracy; cheap prices; peace. You know my thunder when these are my themes. So loud was it, indeed, that I may write the more briefly, since I think you must have heard it even over there [in Epirus]."[1] Hence, by his own admission, we know that the "harmony of the classes" was itself only one tune with more or less brilliant variations. When his audience tired of it, all Cicero had to do was to choose another, and at need to tear his own decrees to ribbons.[2]

He found no pleasure in indulging superfluous regrets over upheavals which, once they had taken place, he preferred to think had been inevitable. In a fit of low spirits he confessed: "I have so completely lost my nerve that I prefer to live under a tyranny in the peace in which we now languish, rather than to fight with the best possible hope."[3] This being so, we need not be surprised at the sort of insensibility with which he anticipated the disappearance of a form of government under which he had been happy, but which events seemed to have doomed. The fall of the Republic wrung from him not a tear: "We have lost, my dear Pomponius, not only the sap and blood but the very colour and former appearance of our State. . . . 'And can you lightly bear that?' you will ask. Even so." If someone asks how he stands

---

[1] *Ad Att.* I, 14, 4 (20 T.P.): *Ego autem ipse, dei boni! quo modo ἐνεπερπερευσάμην novo auditori Pompeio! Si umquam mihi περίοδοι, si καμπαί, si ἐνθυμήματα, si κατασκευαί, suppeditaverunt illo tempore. Quid multa? Clamores. Etenim haec erat ὑπόθεσις, de gravitate ordinis, de equestri concordia . . . Nosti iam in hac materia sonitus nostros: tanti fuerunt, ut ego eo brevior sim, quod eos usque istinc exauditos putem.* Feb. 13, 61 B.C.

[2] As, for instance, his decree of March 17, 44 B.C., which amnestied Caesar's murderers and ratified their deeds. *Ad Fam.* XII, 1, 2 (723 T.P.): *At enim ita decrevimus. Fecimus id quidem temporibus cedentes, quae valent in republica plurimum.* To Cassius, May 3, 44 B.C.

[3] *Ad Att.* II, 14, 1 (41 T.P.): *Ego autem usque eo sum enervatus, ut hoc otio, quo nunc tabescimus, malim ἐντυραννεῖσθαι quam cum optima spe dimicare.* End April 59 B.C.

it, he replies "Admirably. And by Hercules, I congratulate myself."[1]

Nor is this all. Since truth was for him dependent on men's acceptance of it, it seemed to him the natural thing to abandon what he yesterday thought to be the truth, but what has today ceased to be true because public opinion has turned away from it. Just as he made speeches without conviction, he admitted that he spoke against his conviction, and—amongst his friends at least—he explained this without the least embarrassment.

When Atticus was pressing him in 59 to publish a speech as he had promised, he evaded the request quite naturally "because I did not want to praise the man I didn't like".[2] Two years before, he had written to the same correspondent: "Here's another piece of cool insolence on the part of the Equites: hardly to be borne! Which I have not only put up with but embellished."[3] "The tax-farmers who had contracted with the censors for (collecting the taxes of) Asia complained in the Senate that, misled by their eagerness, they had contracted at too high a price, and they demanded that the contract should be cancelled. I led in their support. . . . The case is scandalous, the demand disgraceful and a confession of insolence. Yet there was grave danger that if they got nothing they would be completely alienated from the Senate. Here again I supported the case to the maximum. . . ."[4] Talleyrand used to maintain that speech was given to man to conceal his thought. Cicero was before him, in going so far as to distort his thought and deliberately to exploit the resources of his talent for the purpose.[5]

[1] *Ad Att.* IV, 18, 2 (154 T.P.): *Dices: Tu ergo haec quo modo fers? Belle, me hercule et in eo me valde amo. Amisimus, mi Pomponi, omnem non modo sucum ac sanguinem, sed etiam colorem et speciem pristinam civitatis . . . Idne igitur inquies facile fers? Id ipsum*, etc. Oct. 54 B.C.

[2] *Ad Att.* II, 7, 1 (34 T.P.): *. . . alteram* [*orationem*] *non libebat mihi scribere . . . ne laudarem eum quem non amabam.* April 59 B.C.

[3] *Ad Att.* I, 17, 9 (23 T.P.): *Ecce aliae deliciae equitum vix ferendae! Quas ego non solum tuli sed etiam ornavi.* Dec. 5, 61 B.C.

[4] *Ad Att.* I , 17, 9 (23 T.P.): *Asiam qui de censoribus conduxerunt questi sunt in senatu se cupiditate prolapsos nimium magno conduxisse: ut induceretur locatio postulaverunt. Ego princeps in adiutoribus . . . Invidiosa res, turpis postulatio et confessio temeritatis. Summum erat periculum ne, si nihil impetrassent, plane alienarentur a senatu. Huic quoque rei subventum est maxime a nobis. . . .*
Another subject, the same tactics: Cicero spoke with force and fluency in a cause he felt to be shameful. Ibid. 8: *in causa non verecunda admodum gravis et copiosus fui.*

[5] According to the theory he expounds to Marcellus, *Ad Fam.* IV, 9, 2 (487 T.P.): *. . . tibi ipsi dicendum erit aliquid quod non sentias aut faciendum quod non probes.* Sept. 46 B.C.

The Defects of a Statesman

2. CHRONIC BLINDNESS

There was a distressing lack of conscience about Cicero which impaired his splendid intelligence and destroyed what little strength of will he possessed.

Cicero was fond of comparing the statesman with the pilot of a ship rocked by the waves.[1] He should have reflected that without the stars whose course directs him, the pilot would never, except by a miracle, reach port. He, on the contrary, seized the helm without even knowing where he was going, and attempted to govern without any guiding principles. We need not be surprised, therefore, that since he never raised his eyes to scan the stars, he was throughout his stormy life the helpless plaything of cloud and billow. His gaze was riveted on the contingencies of each fleeting hour; no wonder that he understood nothing of the needs of his time, and that in his narrow calculations a myopia akin to blindness led him invariably to back the wrong horse.

Even more perhaps than his speeches, his *Letters* were interlarded with historical reminiscences drawn from ancient Rome or distant Greece, which saved him the trouble of reflecting on the present, and in general buried its distinctive features under a mass of miscellaneous and irrelevant precedents.[2] They are full of delightful pictures, of entertaining anecdotes, of silhouettes sketched from the life. They lack, on the other hand, those impressive résumés which reduce a century to a flash of lightning, those revelations which illuminate a remark of Bonaparte's, a paragraph of Lamartine's, a page of the *Mémoires d'Outre-Tombe*, and which, of a sudden, throw a searchlight into the future. When everything was going from bad to worse, Cicero, on his own showing, could only cower in his tent and groan over the decadence which he was doomed to witness.[3] If he had had the power to rebuild the crumbling edifice, he would have done it with the materials and in the forms of the past.[4] Hypnotised and dazed by the slightest disturbances of the Curia or the Forum, he perceived below their heaving surface neither the permanent currents which

---

[1] Cf. above, p. 236, note 5, and Cic. *De Off.* I, 25, 8; *De Rep.* I, 6, 11 and 40, 62.

[2] Precedents: Socrates remaining in Athens under the tyranny: *Ad Att.* VIII, 2, 4 (332 T.P.); Themistocles anticipating Pompey's strategy: *Ad Att.* VII, 11, 3 (304 T.P.) and X, 8, 4 (392 T.P.), etc.

[3] Cf. above, p. 238.

[4] Cf. J. Vogt, *Ciceros Glaube an Rom*, Stuttgart, 1935, pp. 56 and 66f.

were flowing there nor the great evils which had provoked those attacks of fever and which were wearing and tearing at the society, the state and the empire of Rome.

The panacea he preached was the restoration of senatorial authority,[1] ignoring the crisis which racked the aristocracy wielding this authority.[2] He barely alluded, and that only incidentally, to the formidable problem that for more than a century had been created by the fall in Italy's birth-rate.[3] He overlooked the revolutionary factors introduced into the old City institutions by the conquest of innumerable subject peoples. Even when transplanted to the eastern extremity of the Mediterranean, his interest still centred in the daily incidents of municipal life in Rome. From the depths of Cilicia he still felt the frontiers of his country to be bounded by the City walls.[4] This orator, so acutely conscious of the power of his own words, was barely aware of the irresistible power of military might, and it required a second civil war, following thirty-five years later on the war of Marius and Sulla, to wring the recognition from him.[5]

He was as far from piercing into the secrets of the human soul as he was from following the trend of events, perhaps because the overflowing of his own ego swamped for him the egos of his fellow men. In his relations with Caesar he was susceptible to the man's charm, but imperceptive of his greatness, and he had no inkling either of Caesar's genius or of his gigantic schemes. He equated Caesar's stature with his own and attributed to him in all seriousness and sympathy the vacuity of his own conceptions, the vacillations of his own invertebrate character. "Even if", he writes to Paetus, "he should desire the continued existence of the Republic, as perchance he does, and as we ought all to pray for, he yet does not know how to achieve it, so much is he entangled with so many things and people. But I am going too far: for (I must remember that) I am writing to you. Be sure of this, however, not I alone—who am not in his counsels—but even the leader himself does not know what is going to happen. For while we are all his slaves, he is the slave of circumstance. Hence neither can he know

[1] Cf. above, p. 234f. [2] Cf. J. Vogt, op. cit., p. 66.
[3] *Ad Att.* I, 19, 4 (25 T.P.): . . . *et Italiae solitudinem frequentari posse arbitrabor*. March 15, 60 B.C.
[4] Cf. J. Vogt, op. cit., p. 67.
[5] *Ad Fam.* IX, 17, 1 (480 T.P.): . . . *valebunt autem semper arma.* To L. Papirius Paetus, Aug. 46 B.C. How much more of a realist Caelius was: *Ad Fam.* VIII, 14, 3(280 T.P.), and Dolabella: ibid. IX, 9, 1–3 (409 T.P.).

what circumstances will demand, nor can we know what he is thinking of."[1] After the Ides of March he thought that the mantle of Caesar might fall to Dolabella and he attributed to this nitwit ne'erdowell the qualities of "the leader whom the municipalities and all 'good men' demand".[2] To make up for this, he had hailed a month before the arrival of Octavian in Italy as a casual incident, about which as a matter of course he asked for details, but which he obviously considered of no importance whatever.[3]

Cicero had no more luck with his prophesyings than with his opinions. It is staggering to find in his *Letters* so many gross mistakes, ridiculous misunderstandings, and predictions which a few days sufficed to falsify. In 60 Pompey, Crassus, and Caesar had secretly come to an agreement six months before to exercise jointly a power which as long as their concord lasted no one could dispute. But Cicero was still doubting the alliance between them, though their messengers had been humane enough to give him warning of it.[4] In 59 he took seriously the futile opposition of Bibulus to the Triumvirate, and intermittently put faith in the effectiveness of his Platonic edicts and his consultations with the heavens.[5] From society conversations in which people's discontented grumblings were given free rein, he concluded that a crash was near, even more complete than he would have wished.[6] Not only did no crash occur, but on Jan. 1, 58. Bibulus gave up

[1] *Ad Fam.* IX, 17, 2 and 3 (480 T.P.): *Qui si cupiat esse rem publicam, qualem fortasse et ille vult et omnes optare debemus, quo id faciat tamen non habet: ita se cum multis colligavit. Sed longius progredior: scribo enim ad te. Hoc tamen scito, non modo me, qui consiliis non intersum, sed ne ipsum quidem principem scire quid futurum sit. Nos enim illi servimus, ipse temporibus: ita nec ille quid tempora postulatura sint nec nos quid ille cogitet scire possumus.* To L. Papirius Paetus. Aug. 46 B.C.

[2] *Ad Att.* XIV, 20, 4 (727 T.P.): *Nunc autem videmur habituri ducem, quod unum municipia bonique desiderant.* May 11, 44 B.C. Dolabella was both physically and morally a dwarf. Cf. Macrobius, *Sat.* II, 3, 3.

[3] *Ad Att.* XIV, 5, 3 (707 T.P.): *Sed velim scire quid adventus Octavii, num qui concursus ad eum, num quae νεωτερισμοῦ [coup d'état?] suspicio. Non puto equidem sed tamen quidquid est scire cupio.* Cf. below, II, p. 361.

[4] *Ad Att.* II, 3, 3 (29 T.P.): *Is adfirmabat [Balbus] illum Caesarem omnibus in rebus meo et Pompeii consilio usurum daturumque operam ut cum Pompeio Crassum coniungeret.* The hesitations of this letter show that in spite of the warning he had received, Cicero was still doubtful of its accuracy. Now this letter was written in Dec. 60 B.C. and the Triumvirate had been formed for, and by, Caesar's election to the consulship in the preceding July. This we know from Livy, *Per.* CIII: *Eoque Caesare consulatus candidato rempublicam invadere coniuratio facta est.*

[5] *Ad Att.* II, 15, 2 (42 T.P.); 20, 6 (47 T.P.), etc.

[6] *Ad Att.* II, 19, 2 (46 T.P.): *Scito nihil umquam fuisse tam infame, tam turpe, tam peraeque omnibus generibus, aetatibus offensum quam hunc statum qui nunc est; magis mehercule quam vellem, non modo quam putaram.* Mid-July 59 B.C.

his office without having been able to deliver the ritual speech of a
Consul retiring again into private life,[1] and on March 20 in the
same year Cicero was compelled to fly into exile by night.[2] To
reduce Bibulus to silence and drive Cicero into banishment,
Caesar employed as his tool the Tribune P. Clodius. Cicero ought
to have been put on his guard by the rancour of this old enemy,
but up to the last moment he denied any danger, lulled by the
absolutely lying assurances concocted by young Curio, who
whispered them into his all-too-willing ear. Hear how Cicero
jested to Atticus on April 19, 59: "But observe the coincidence. On
my way from Antium I had just emerged on to the Appian Way
at Three Taverns, on the very day of the Cerealia (April 18),
when my friend Curio ran into me coming from Rome. At the
same place and at the very same moment a slave of yours turned
up with letters. Curio asked me whether I had heard the news.
I said 'No.' 'Publius Clodius,' said he, 'is a candidate for the
Tribuneship of the Plebs.'—'What?'—'And extremely hostile to
Caesar. He is going to rescind every act of his.'—'And what does
Caesar say?' I asked.—'He denies having proposed any law for the
adoption of Clodius (as a plebeian).' Then he poured out his own
hate and the hate felt by Memmius and Metellus Nepos for Caesar.
Having embraced the young man, I bade him farewell, being in
haste to get to your letters."[3] The simpleton had not suspected
the manœuvre, and in spite of his silences or the brevity of his
speech, he had given himself away. For if—as turned out to be the
case—Clodius was secretly working hand in glove with Caesar,
Curio was acting as one of their *agents provocateurs*. At the Three

---

[1] Dio Cass. XXXVIII, 12, 3. [2] Cf. above, p. 197.

[3] *Ad Att.* II, 12, 2 (37 T.P.): *Sed vide* συγκύρημα. *Emerseram commodum ex
Antiati in Appiam ad Tres Tabernas, ipsis Cerialibus, cum in me incurrit Roma
veniens Curio meus. Ibidem ilico puer abs te cum epistulis. Ille ex me nihilne audissem
novi: ego negare.* "Publius," *inquit*, "tribunatum pl(ebis) petit." "Quid ais?" "Et
inimicissimus quidem Caesaris, et ut omnia," *inquit*, "ista rescindat." "Quid
Caesar?" *inquam.* "Negat se quidquam de illius adoptione tulisse." *Deinde suum,
Memmii, Metelli Nepotis exprompsit odium. Complexus iuvenem dimisi, properans
ad epistulas.* April 19, 59 B.C.

Cicero ought to have distrusted the business, for in fact it was Caesar who
had manipulated the whole affair of Clodius's adoption by a plebeian (Suetonius,
Caes. XX, 4, etc.) and he ought to have known what to believe about Memmius
and Metellus Nepos. Cf. below, p. 263. But Cicero, completely duped by young
Curio, swallowed everything he said. *Ad Att.* II, 7, 3 (34 T.P.); 8, 1 (35 T.P.)
and 18, 1 (45 T.P.). This did not, however, prevent his writing to Caelius in
May 50 B.C. that he had always thought Curio was one of Caesar's creatures.
Ad Fam. II, 13, 3 (257 T.P.): *Caesarem nunc defendit Curio? Quis hoc putaret?
praeter me, nam, ita vivam putavi.*

Taverns he had killed two birds with one stone: while he had talked in such a way as to encourage Cicero's illusions, the cordiality of their conversation enabled him to destroy any doubt which Caesar still entertained about Cicero's feelings. No one could have fallen more clumsily into a more childish trap.

His trials of 58 made Cicero more timorous, but not more clearsighted. The Triumvirate had prostrated him. Compromising with the three he proclaimed them invincible, just at the moment when it was obvious that their alliance was about to break up. In Jan. 55 he announced to Lentulus: "You will learn the whole state of public affairs from Plaetorius. It is not easy to write what it is like. It is certainly, however, well under our friends' [i.e. the Triumvirs'] control, and in such a way that any change in it would seem unlikely to occur during the lifetime of the present generation."[1] Would seem unlikely! What a short-sighted view! Two years later Julia, Caesar's daughter and Pompey's wife, died, in Sept. 54. Crassus perished in the disaster of Carrhae the following summer. These two events first weakened and then disrupted the coalition of the Three.

It would be tedious to record the weary list of Cicero's successive blunderings during the Civil War which brought about the rupture of this monopoly government. Cicero announced in May 49 that Caesar's reign could not last six months,[2] and prophesied Caesar's defeat in Spain just three months before brilliant victories delivered the two provinces of the Iberian peninsula into the hands of the "usurper's" legions. Hither Spain was won from Afranius and Further Spain from Varro in Sept. 49.[3] It was perhaps at the end of his life that Cicero's forecasts reached the peak of their absurdity. In the spring of 43 one of the victors of Mutina, Decimus Brutus, feeling very doubtful of the good faith of the other, Octavian, feared a renewed attack by the defeated Mark Antony which might bring relief to Lepidus. Instead of attacking Antony he sent

---

[1] *Ad Fam.* I, 8, 1 (119 T.P.): *Ex eodem [Plaetorio] de toto statu rerum communium cognosces, quae quales sint non facile est scribere. Sunt quidem certe in amicorum nostrorum potestate, atque ita, ut nullam mutationem umquam hac hominum aetate habitura res esse videatur.* Jan. or Feb. 55 B.C., to Lentulus.

[2] *Ad Att.* X, 8, 7 (392 T.P.): . . . *iam intelleges id regnum vix semestre esse posse.* May 2, 49 B.C.

[3] *Ad Att.* X, 12, 6 (398 T.P.): *Hispanias spero firmas esse. Massiliensium factum cum ipsum per se luculentum est, tum mihi argumento est recte esse in Hispaniis. Minus auderent, si aliter esset: et scirent, nam vicini et diligentes sunt.* May 6, 49 B.C. On the Spanish campaigns, see my *César* (3), pp. 882–8.

appeals to Rome expressing his fears.[1] Cicero turned a deaf ear to his well-justified apprehensions and persistently assured him that all was for the best,[2] and that one supreme effort would consolidate for ever a victory which as he believed—for some days at least—would secure the liberty of the Republic for centuries.[3] This, on the very day when Plancus had told him of Lepidus's defection,[4] and three months only before Octavian's *coup d'état* in Rome and only six months before the proscriptions in which Cicero himself was to perish. It is true to say that nowhere has history recorded such appalling blunders, so soon and so cruelly expiated.

3. AN IMPENITENT TRIMMER

Nor has history perhaps any record of a so-called man of action who displayed such faltering will. There is no counting the letters in which Cicero anxiously implored his correspondents to advise him what to do, and sighing with weariness at the difficulties surrounding him, sought their advice like a favour from heaven: "I could wish I had Homer's Minerva here in the guise of Mentor and could say:

How shall I go then, O Mentor, and how shall I bear me before him?"[5]

What was troubling him just then in 49 was how to choose between Caesar and Pompey, and he could not arrive at a decision as to which side to take.[6] In 44, when conflict between Mark Antony and the "tyrannicides" was imminent, his perplexity was worse than ever. His first impulse was to seek in Greece a refuge from

---

[1] On June 3, 43 B.C., Decimus Brutus, writing from his camp at Cularo (Grenoble), consoled himself by sadly recalling his prophetic warnings: *Ad Fam.* XI, 26, 1 (892 T.P.): *Maximo meo hoc solacio utor quod intellegunt homines non sine causa me timuisse ista, quae acciderunt.* And of these we find a trace in Cicero, *Ad Fam.* XI, 14 (886 T.P.): cf. below, note 4.

[2] *Ad Fam.* XI, 24, 1 (894 T.P.): *Quam multa quam paucis! Te recte valere operam dare ut cotidie melius . . . nos oportere confidere.* June 6, 43 B.C.

[3] *Ad Fam.* XI, 14, 3 (886 T.P.): *Die tuo natali.* (April 26, 43 B.C.) *victoria nuntiata in multa saecula videbamus rempublican liberatam.* End May, 43 B.C.

[4] Decimus Brutus had told Cicero of his forebodings. Cicero was quite unmoved, *Ad Fam.* ibid.: *Id si ita est* (viz. if Lepidus does not join Antony) *omnia faciliora, sin aliter magnum negotium cuius exitum non extimesco : tuae partes sunt.* Now, Plancus on June 6, 43 B.C., on the eve of committing his own treachery, wrote from Cularo (Grenoble) to Cicero—who did not get the news till ten days later—*Lepidus . . . se cum Antonio coniunxit a. d. IV Kal(endas) Iunias* (i.e. May 29, 43 B.C.). Cf. *Ad Fam.* X, 23, 2 (895 T.P.).

[5] *Ad Att.* IX, 8, 2 (363 T.P.): *Hic ego vellem Homeri illam Minervam simulatam Mentori, cui dicerem :* Μέντορ, πῶς τ' ἄρ ἴω, πῶς τ' ἄρ προσπτύξομαι αὐτόν Homer, *Odyssey,* III, 22. The letter is of March 14, 49 B.C.

[6] Cf. above, p. 224f.

The Defects of a Statesman

the impending war, and to this end to accept the *legatio* which Dolabella was offering him.[1] That he resisted. He then regretted his refusal, but without going back on it. On April 12, 44, he was reproaching himself for his folly, but did not stir an inch.[2] On the 15th, in a panic of fear, he was thinking of going.[3] On the 26th he was again uncertain.[4] On May 1 he gave the idea up.[5] On the 9th he was again talking of setting out.[6] On the 11th he was quivering with impatience: "Let us think of flight. Anything rather than fighting."[7] By May 14 his eagerness was quenched; all things considered, he had come to the conclusion that if he went away his departure might expose him to the vengeance of Cassius and Brutus without protecting him against Mark Antony's hate, and he decided to give himself a pause for reflection up to June 1.[8] On June 2 his appointment as *legatus* was signed.[9] By the 15th his nerves were all on edge because Dolabella had not yet provided the necessary mules and means of transport.[10]

On July 2 he was resting at Arpinum before starting for the coast, and for his sea journey chose the very opposite port from what might reasonably have been expected. He proposed to sail via the Tyrrhenian Sea.[11] He reached Puteoli on the 7th.[12] On the 9th he suddenly thought he would strike overland to Venusia and on to Hydruntum (Otranto) on the Adriatic, but with the idea at the back of his mind that if neither port were safe he would return to Puteoli.[13] He did none of these things, however, and when

[1] Cf. above, p. 183.
[2] *Ad Att.* XIV, 5, 2 (707 T.P.): *En meam stultam verecundiam qui legari noluerim* . . .
[3] *Ad Att.* XIV, 7, 2 (709 T.P.): *Omnino, si ego, ut volo, mense Quinctili in Graeciam* . . .
[4] *Ad Att.* XIV, 13, 2 and 4 (718 T.P.).
[5] *Ad Att.* XIV, 15, 3 (720 T.P.): *Incipit res melius ire quam putaram, nec vero discedam, nisi cum tu me id honeste putabis facere posse.*
[6] *Ad Att.* XIV, 18, 4 (726 T.P.): *De Graecia cotidie magis et magis cogito.*
[7] *Ad Att.* XIV, 21, 4 (728 T.P.): *Quare talaria videamus. Quidvis enim potius quam castra.*
[8] *Ad Att.* XIV, 22, 2 (729 T.P.): *Habent in ore nos ingratos. Nullo modo licebit quod tum et tibi licuit et multis.*
[9] *Ad Att.* XV, 11, 4 (744 T.P.): *Dolabella me sibi legavit a. d. iiii Nonas.*
[10] *Ad Att.* XV, 18, 1 (750 T.P.): *Petiique ab eo [Dolabella] de mulis vecturae itineris.*
[11] *Ad Att.* XV, 26, 3 (763 T.P.): *Ego itinera sic composueram ut Nonis Quinctilibus Puteolis essem.*
[12] See last note.
[13] *Ad Att.* XVI, 5, 3 (770 T.P.): *Itaque dubito an Venusiam tendam et ibi exspectem de legionibus: si aberunt . . . Hydruntem: si neutrum erit ἀσφαλές, eodem revertar.*

at last on 17 July he weighed anchor it was from Pompeii,[1] to start
on a voyage that was soon broken off. As we know, he got no
further than Leucopetra, whence on Aug. 6 he gave the order to put
about, returning on the 19th to his starting-point.[2] In four months
he changed his mind fifteen times, and this series of orders and
counter-orders, of aimless agitations and repentances that led to
nothing, forms the case-history of the chronic disease of incapacity
to make decisions—*abulia*, a physician would call it—from which
Cicero suffered.

Rather than accept this diagnosis, Cicero preferred to regard
his disability as the price he had to pay for his intellectual superiority and the profundity of his thought. "Always", he told Atticus,
"the underlying causes of events affect me more than the events
themselves."[3] In another place he declared: "But not to abandon
myself wholly to grief, I have taken certain subjects as theses, so
to speak, which bear on politics and the present times. . . ."[4]
The better to indicate the objectivity of his reflections on these
matters he enumerates them in Greek: "Ought a man to remain in
his country under a tyrant? If so, ought he to strive at all costs to
deliver it from tyranny, even if his methods risk its total destruction? . . . Ought he to use reasoning rather than arms to save his
country? . . . Has a good citizen the right to quit his country in
troubled times and live quietly elsewhere? . . .[5] These are the
questions in which I exercise myself, debating the pros and cons
now in Greek, now in Latin. . . ."[6]

A real statesman would have got to grips with life. Cicero sat
polishing his dissertations, taking care to draw no practical conclusions from them, and pondering over the situation from a
detached and theoretical point of view. Whatever we may think of
his dialectical performances, whether we extol them to the stars or
look on them as a futile schoolboy exercise, they were bound to

[1] *Ad Att.* XVI, 3, 6 (773 T.P.): *Haec ego conscendens e Pompeiano* . . .
[2] *Ad Att.* XVI, 7, 1 (783 T.P.): *VIII Idus Sext(iles) Leucopetra profectus.*
Leucopetra is today the Capo dell'Armi, to the south of Reggio. Cf. Philipp,
P.W. XII, c. 2286.
[3] *Ad Att.* IX, 5, 2 (359 T.P.): *Semper enim me causae eventorum magis movent
quam ipsa eventa.* March 10, 49 B.C.
[4] *Ad Att.* IX, 4, 1 (361 T.P.): *Sed tamen ne me totum aegritudini dedam,
sumpsi mihi quasdam tamquam* θέσεις *quae et* πολιτικαί *sunt et temporum horum*
. . . March 12, 49 B.C.
[5] *Ad Att.* IX, 4, 2 (361 T.P.).
[6] *Ad Att.* IX, 4, 3 (361 T.P.): *In his ego me consultationibus exercens et dis-
serens in utramque partem tum Graece, tum Latine* . . .

weaken his power of decision and at best serve to gain him a little more time. In any case we cannot avoid feeling doubts about their sincerity, and suspecting that everything in them is second-hand and artificial. Cicero was begging in all his letters for the very latest tidings, so that he might bring his attitude up to date, and he was merely using the interval accorded him by the slowing up of events and the absence of news to get on with his philosophisings. In the ordinary way he lay in wait not for the unchanging verities but for the ever-changing news, hoping to detect prophetic glimpses of coming fate. He put off action till tomorrow not in order to bring his conduct into line with his doctrines and his platitudes, but in the hope that "circumstances" would throw some light on his chances.[1] According to the turn events might take, they would dictate his haphazard decision: *utut erit res, casus consilium iudicabit.*[2]

Nothing but disaster could result from such laziness. Following petty occurrences from day to day in a short-term policy without clear aspirations or defined principles, Cicero lost himself in the detail and failed to grasp the significance and the general trend of events. His resolutions were perpetually adjourned or recast, and turned out either to be the very opposite of those he hastily adopted next day or to have been arrived at too late. So it was on that fatal Dec. 7, 43. Not knowing what he wanted, while the choice still lay open to him either to conciliate Octavian or to fly from him, he was overtaken by the assassins of the Second Triumvirate. He was sitting in his litter, into which his retainers had forcibly lifted him, and was on the road leading from his villa at Formiae to the port of embarkation.[3] An hour sooner, and he would probably have been safely aboard.

To sum up: Cicero failed in his ambition to govern the Romans because he was incapable of managing his own life. What a pitiable figure he cuts: a man claiming the right to rule the world who gropes his way through history like a blind man and totters like a victim of locomotor ataxia! What a lesson there is, too, for us in the blunders he committed and the misfortunes which befell him! They were at bottom the fruit of his crude opportunism. Seen

---

[1] *Ad Att.* XIV, 13, 2 (718 T.P.): . . . *et incerto exitu belli* . . . April 26, 44 B.C.

[2] *Ad Att.* XV, 25 (759 T.P.): *Utut erit res, casus consilium nostri itineris iudicabit.* June 25, 44 B.C.

[3] Plut. *Cic.* XLVII and XLVIII.

through the medium of his *Letters*, we seem to see morality aveng-
ing herself on politics, generosity on heartlessness, and sterling
character on the selfish play of mere intelligence.

4. MORBID VANITY

By nature unfitted for action, Cicero's disability was no doubt
increased by those faults which inevitably alienated men's sympathy, and whose unpleasing aspects and fatal consequences are
described in his Correspondence.

The most obvious of these was his vanity, his incorrigible,
monstrous vanity, which even Plutarch recognised as "an ungrateful humour like a disease, always cleaving to him."[1] His biographer
gives no other proof of it than the praise of his own consulship
with which Cicero saturated his conversations, his pleadings, his
speeches to the Senate, his harangues to the people, his books and
his writings of every kind.[2] Amongst many others, this particular
lyric of self-glorification encumbers even his letters, and its high-
pitched note sounds all the more oddly there, since in writing to
friends there was no need for self-advertisement as if playing to
the gallery.[3] It was really unnecessary to refresh Atticus's memory
—as he did with exaggerated bombast—of that famous day of
Dec. 5, 63, in which he won "extraordinary and immortal glory",[4]
or to repeat Pompey's phrase that he had assured "the salvation
of the Empire and of the world".[5] In another place he enlarged
on the extent of his own merit, which, he declared, was incom-
parably superior to Pompey's, since Pompey had only "served"
the State, while he, Cicero, had "preserved" it.[6] There are letters,
too, which record the existence of books, now lost, that he had
consecrated to his own renown: in 60 there was a history of his
consulship in Greek prose,[7] a Latin poem on his consulship,[8]
then another more comprehensive Latin poem not yet completed

---

[1] Plut. *Cic.* XXIV, 1. 　　　　　　　　[2] Plut. *Cic.* XXIV, 1.
[3] Cicero foresaw this criticism, *Ad Att.* I, 16, 8 (22 T.P.): *Non enim mihi
videor insolenter gloriari cum de me apud te loquor.* June or July, 61 B.C.
[4] *Ad Att.* I, 19, 6 (25 T.P.): . . . *semel Nonarum Decembrium eximiam quamdam atque immortalem gloriam consecutus.* March 15, 60 B.C.
[5] *Ad Att.* I, 19, 7 (25 T.P.): . . . *salutem imperii atque orbis terrarum.*
[6] *Ad Att.* II, 1, 6 (27 T.P.): *Sibi enim bene gestae, mihi conservatae reip(ublicae)
dat* [Pompeius] *testimonium.* Mid-June 60 B.C.
[7] *Ad Att.* I, 19, 10 (25 T.P.): *Commentarium consulatus mei Graece compositum
misi ad te . . .*
[8] *Ad Att.* I, 20, 6 (26 T.P.): *De meis scriptis misi ad te Graece perfectum con-
solatum meum.* Mid-May 60 B.C.

The Defects of a Statesman

in 54 which covered his whole previous life under the title *De meis temporibus*.[1] You might think that was enough. Not a bit of it! Cicero was insatiable. He enlisted others to join the chorus: he would fain have seen everyone after and around him blowing the sacred trumpet in his honour. He grew restless in 61 because the poet Archias, whose defence he had undertaken the year before, had not in gratitude written verses in his praise.[2] In 56 he was badgering Lucceius to complete his history of the Social War and the war between Marius and Sulla, by writing the history of the period following, and to put the seal on his literary reputation by a narrative of the years between Cicero's consulship and his return from exile.[3] What better subject could there be? If Lucceius would just give his mind to it he would find it "worthy of his gifts and wealth of language".[4] In this he could use his "knowledge of civil revolutions"[5] and at the same time exercise his eloquence either in proof and praise of "those things which are dear to you" or in pillorying those men who were then practising "perfidy, intrigue and treason" to Cicero's injury.[6] With what eagerness Cicero was prepared to hail the appearance of this work, "for there is pleasure in recalling in security past trials!"[7] This expectation sufficed to "whirl him off to a hope of some immortality".[8] It was, in fact, Lucceius's job to engrave Cicero's features for ever, as Herodotus had immortalised those of Themistocles, Xenophon those of Agesilaus, and—don't let us be too modest—Lysippus and Apelles those of Alexander the Great.[9] At the same time his contemporaries in Rome would learn immediately to know his true worth, and Cicero would be able "to enjoy in his own lifetime his little bit of glory".[10]

---

[1] *Ad Att.* IV, 8B, 3 (118 T.P.): Nov. 56 B.C. On the title see below, p. 251, note 6.
[2] *Ad Att.* I, 16, 15 (22 T.P.): . . . *praesertim cum et Thyillus* (another poet friend of Cicero's) *nos reliquerit et Archias nihil de me scripserit.* June or July 61 B.C.
[3] *Ad Fam.* V, 12, 2 (109 T.P.). June 56 B.C.
[4] *Ad Fam.* V, 12, 3 (109 T.P.): . . . *materies digna facultate et copia tua* . . .
[5] *Ad Fam.* V, 12, 4 (109 T.P.): . . . *poteris uti civilium commutationum scientia.*
[6] *Ad Fam.* V, 12, 4 (109 T.P.): . . . *cum et reprehendes ea quae vituperanda duces et quae placebunt . . . comprobabis et . . . multorum in nos perfidiam, insidias, proditionem notabis.*
[7] *Ad Fam.* V, 12, 4 (109 T.P.): *Habet enim praeteriti doloris secura recordatio delectationem.*
[8] *Ad Fam.* V, 12, 1 (109 T.P.): . . . *ad spem quamdam immortalitatis rapit* . . .
[9] *Ad Fam.* V, 12, 7 (109 T.P.).
[10] *Ad Fam.* V, 12, 9 (109 T.P.): . . . *ceteri viventibus nobis ex libris tuis nos cognoscant et nosmet ipsi vivi gloriola nostra perfruamur.*

The Defects of a Statesman

This letter to Lucceius, gallantly phrased though it is, seems nevertheless to us moderns intolerably presumptuous throughout, and in places absolutely laughable. Cicero, however, saw nothing ridiculous in it, and he valued its elegances so highly that he hoped Atticus would borrow it, get it copied and circulated, for "indeed it is a beautiful letter"—*valde bella est* (*epistola*).[1] The truth is he could find no end to the reasons for admiring himself. He brooded lovingly over his writings and boasted unceasingly about them. He was delighted with his Latin poem and repeated whole passages of it to Atticus. By its nobility it seemed to him to have been dictated to him by the Muse Calliope herself.[2] He was fascinated by his own Greek prose, whose purity might, he thought, be envied by a Greek himself . . . like Atticus,[3] for instance. So completely had Cicero, to his own thinking, "routed the Greeks"[4] that the celebrated Posidonius professed "to be afraid" to attempt anything of the kind himself after having read Cicero's manuscript. Hence the modest author suggested that Atticus should kindly see that copies should be distributed to the libraries of Athens and other Greek towns.[5] Later, Cicero, with equal enthusiasm and a profusion of warm compliments, proudly despatched copies of his verse Memoirs of My Own Times—*De temporibus meis*—to such connoisseurs as Lentulus[6] and Caesar.[7] In between times, he collected his consular speeches for a reason which betrays no excessive modesty: was it not right to follow the example "of your great Athenian Demosthenes"?[8] It is true that he here laid claim to a fame which no one challenges, and anticipated a comparison which, following Plutarch's *Parallels*, has become classic.[9] In this case we may forgive a vanity that springs from justifiable pride. At other times it is simply unpardonable.

---

[1] *Ad Att.* IV, 6, 4 (110 T.P.). June 56 B.C.

[2] *Ad Att.* II, 3, 4 (29 T.P.). Dec. 60 B.C.

[3] *Ad Att.* I, 20, 6 (26 T.P.): . . . *huic autem [puto] Graeco Graecum invidere.* Mid-May 60 B.C.

[4] *Ad Att.* II, 1, 2 (27 T.P.). June 60 B.C.   [5] *Ad Att.* II, 1, 2.

[6] For Lentulus, cf. *Ad Fam.* I, 9, 23 (153 T.P.): . . . *scripsi tres libros de temporibus meis quos . . . curabo ad te perferendos.* Dec. 54 B.C.

[7] *Ad Q. Fr.* II, 15, 5 (147 T.P.): *Scripsit [Caesar] ad me ante, ut neget se ne Graeca quidem meliora legisse.* Aug. 54 B.C.

[8] *Ad Att.* II, 1, 3 (27 T.P.): *Fuit enim mihi commodum, quod in eis orationibus, quae Philippicae nominantur, enituerat tuus ille civis Demosthenes.* June 60 B.C.

[9] This is why I refer the reader to Drumann-Groebe, VI, pp. 543–4, who has patiently collated all the passages in the *Letters* in which Cicero goes into raptures over the perfection of his writings. This literary vanity of Cicero's is a venial sin.

The Defects of a Statesman

When it lured him into boasting of improbable and imaginary exploits, his vanity degenerated into burlesque. Cicero, Proconsul of Cilicia, for instance, dramatised into a heroic siege the commonplace investment of that miserable little hamlet of Pindenissus,[1] and in recording some simple police operations against the brigands of the Amanus mountains he compares them to the marches and camps of Alexander.[2] Still worse. His vanity becomes nauseating when it is rooted in shame, when Cicero, humbled before Mark Antony, pretends to hold his head high, and in an outrageous phrase dares to speak of the dignity of his enslavement: *servivi cum aliqua dignitate*.[3]

In all its forms, whether excusable or not, Cicero's vanity soon became a bore. In his *Letters* it rouses our ironic laughter or our annoyance. It must have frayed still more the nerves of his compatriots who were faced with it in real life. Thanks to his Correspondence we can understand how by puffing himself up he created a void around him and in the end, as Plutarch[4] assures us, overtaxed the public and lost his popularity.

5. BOASTING AND COWARDICE

His lack of courage, besides, necessarily cost him the favour of the masses. His cowardice became so early notorious that, so Plutarch tells us, he hastened the execution of the Catiline conspirators for fear of seeming to be afraid; for, as his biographer phrases it in a neat euphemism: "Cicero enjoyed no great reputation for bravery among his fellow-citizens."[5] The whole course of his later life, as we can gather from his *Letters*, confirms this first impression with innumerable examples. For his own torment,

---

[1] *Ad Fam.* II, 10, 3 (225 T.P.): *Interea cum meis copiis omnibus vexavi Amanienses, hostes sempiternos. Multi occisi, capti, reliqui dissipati: castella munita improviso adventu capta et incensa.* To Caelius, Nov. 51 B.C.; *Ad Att.* V, 20, 1 (228 T.P.): *Isti Pindenissitae qui sunt? inquies, nomen audivi numquam.* No matter!—this miserable little hamlet becomes *oppidum munitissimum* (ibid. 5) which had to be besieged according to all the best rules with *vallum, fossa, agger* and a *turris altissima.* Dec. 19, 51 B.C. It is entertaining to compare these braggart trumpetings with Cicero's precept in the *De Off.* I, 38, 137: *Deforme est de se ipsum praedicare, falsa praesertim, et cum irrisione audientium imitari militem gloriosum.*

[2] *Ad Att.* V, 20, 3 (228 T.P.): *Castra paucos dies habuimus ea ipsa quae contra Dareum habuerat apud Issum Alexander, imperator haud paullo melior quam aut tu aut ego.*

[3] *Ad Att.* XV, 5, 3 (737 T.P.). May 44 B.C.

[4] Plut. *Cic.* XIX, 3.

[5] The same hint recurs in Plut. *Comp. Dem. et Cic.* V, 1 and in *Brut.* XII, 2.

The Defects of a Statesman

Cicero was always torn during his whole career between two in-compatible impulses: a love of power and a horror of responsibility. He could not bear not to be in the forefront of the stage, but yet the moment the play-acting ceased and the real drama began, he forsook his place and took to his heels. We might almost say that he played hide-and-seek with his part. If a ticklish item appeared on the agenda, he arranged not to attend that session of the Senate. We have seen that in 56 he withdrew to Antium so as to keep out of the Gabinius affair.[1] The next year he similarly took refuge in his *villa* at Tusculum to avoid being trapped between the horns of a dilemma which would have compelled him to choose between "defending something he did not approve or deserting someone whom he ought not to leave in the lurch."[2] To the end, his tactics were the same. In May 44, when the allocation of pro-vinces between the competitors threatened to raise storms in the Curia, he was away on his estate in Arpinum, so as not to have to intervene in the matter. He hoped that at the last moment the Senate would give way to the Assembly and his defeat would thus be concealed.[3] He carried this desire not to compromise himself to such a point that often, in retrospect, and merely to justify himself in his own eyes, he threw on to others, and on the advice that they had been so unwise as to give him in response to his repeated requests, the responsibility for things he had done, but whose consequences he now cursed.

In 58 he reproached Atticus and his brother for having per-suaded and encouraged him to go on living. If he had been allowed to commit suicide he would not have had to drain to the dregs the bitter cup of exile.[4] In 47 in face of the dangers to which Pompey's defeat exposed him, he attributed to the disastrous advice of his wife and daughter his inopportune rally to the losing cause, and consequently laid at their door all the misfortunes which might

[1] Cf. above, p. 209.

[2] *Ad Att.* IV, 13, 1 (130 T.P.): . . . *afuisse me in altercationibus, quas in Senatu factas audio, fero non moleste. Nam aut defendissem quod non placeret aut defuissem cui non oporteret.* Between Nov. 14 and 17, 55 B.C.

[3] *Ad Att.* XV, 4, 1 (734 T.P.): *Antonii consilia narras turbulenta atque utinam potius per populum agat quam per Senatum! Quod quidem ita credo.* May 24, 44 B.C.

[4] *Ad Att.* III, 9, 1 (65 T.P.): *In hunc me casum vos vivendi auctores impulistis: itaque mei peccati luo poenas; Ad Q. Fr.* I, 3, 2 (66 T.P.): *Sed testor omnes deos me hac una voce a morte esse revocatum, quod omnes in mea vita partem aliquam tuae vitae repositam esse dicebant: qua in re peccavi scelerateque feci.* Both letters June 13, 58 B.C.

flow from it.[1] No doubt it was in all good faith that he took shelter behind Terentia's and Tullia's skirts. Even after he was reassured about his fate, he could not imagine how he had come to fling himself into the fight. Cicero knew his own temperament well. The moment difficulties arose, his natural instinct was to fly from them. As soon as the spectre of war was seen, he yearned to be neutral. Far from admitting that

> Who wins without danger, he wins without fame,[2]

he would never willingly seek success that excluded repose, just as in Cilicia he felt flattered by achieving the laurels of an *imperator*[3] without having risked a scratch.

His letters about his proconsulship reveal his true feelings and have anything but a warlike ring. During his voyage eastwards, while he hugged the Adriatic coast, he was already anxiously scanning the Asiatic horizon in fear of seeing enemy concentrations which might compel him to embark not on the peaceful military parade he had promised himself, but on a tough and bloody expedition, the prospect of which filled him with terror. Arrived at Actium he was already beginning to fear the possible turbulence of the Parthians: "I only hope the Parthian will stay quiet and fortune will aid us, then we can guarantee our success."[4] In Athens next month he was able to breathe more freely: "There has been no talk of the Parthians. May the Gods look after everything else."[5] Nevertheless, even before he had reached his post, he began protesting against a possible extension of his term of office, and with it of his responsibilities as a commander: he "has only contemplated putting up with it for one year" and the friends who want to safeguard his reputation must "fight, lest if any extension be given, I should

---

[1] *Ad Att.* IX, 6, 4 (360 T.P.): . . . *cum ii ipsi, quorum ego causa timidius me fortunae committebam, uxor, filia, Cicerones pueri me illud sequi mallent, hoc turpe et me indignum putarent.* March 11, 49 B.C. As Tyrrell and Purser say, *illud= cum Pompeio fuisse*; and *hoc=domi mansisse.* Hence in 47 B.C. the clearly expressed grievance—without mention of names—in *Ad Att.* XI, 9, 2 (423 T.P.): *Cessi meis vel potius parui.* Jan. 3, 47 B.C.; and *Ad Fam.* XIII, 29, 7 (457 T.P.): *Hoc mihi velim credas: si quid fecerim hoc ipso bello minus ex Caesaris voluntate . . . id fecisse aliorum consilio, hortatu, auctoritate.* To Plancus, beginning of 46 B.C.

[2] [Corneille, *Le Cid*, II, 3.—E. O. L.]

[3] Cf. his triumphant communiqués, above, p. 252.

[4] *Ad Att.* V, 9, 1 (195 T.P.): *Parthus velim quiescat et fortuna nos iuvet, nostra praestabimus.* June 51 B.C.

[5] *Ad Att.* V, 11, 4 (200 T.P.): *De Parthis erat silentium. Quod superest, di iuvent.* July 51 B.C.

be found disgraced."[1] Six months later, just after the capture of
Pindenissus—which he recorded with such gay enjoyment and
such a blowing of trumpets[2]—he felt no desire for new feats of
arms; they filled him with pride, but he had had enough of war.
Writing to the Consul L. Aemilius Paullus in Jan. 50, he reiterated
the request, which he had already expressed in every possible tone:
"do not let my time be prolonged".[3] For a braggart soldier the best
campaign is a short one, and there is no doubt that when his tour
of duty was over, Cicero left the theatre of his warlike exploits
with a sigh of relief.

During the return voyage in Oct. 50, when he halted for a rest
in Athens, it is true that he was heard regretting Cilicia and
murmuring: "How I should like now to be able to stay on in my
province!"[4] But that was only because ugly rumours had in the
meantime been reaching Greece indicating that the legal clash
between Caesar and the Senate would soon degenerate into a
desperate struggle. By comparison with the civil war rumbling in
the distance, the guerrilla fighting in the Amanus might well seem
harmless fun. To avoid having to take part in a civil war, Cicero
would willingly have resumed his proconsulship to preside over
the mountaineers' boyish games. His fantastic wish was not
granted. Nor were the undeserved honours of a Cilician triumph
granted to him. His military command and his ambition to
secure a triumph, however, served at least one useful purpose, for
to them he owed the fact that he could not re-enter Rome until he
had laid down the *fasces* of a general. This gave him the option of
staying outside as long as he liked and thus remaining aloof from
the fray.[5]

He would by choice have held aloof for ever. For he always
hated the resort to arms. Towards the end of his life he hated it
because war and its hazards were unsuited to his years—*aliena
nostris aetatibus*.[6] At every stage of his existence he hated it,

---

[1] *Ad Att.* V, 11, 5 (200 T.P.): *Sed ego hanc, ut Siculi dicunt, ἀνεξίαν in unum annum meditatus sum. Proinde pugna ne, si quid prorogatum sit, turpis inveniar.*
[2] Cf. the letters of Dec. 51 B.C. quoted above, p. 252, note 1.
[3] *Ad Fam.* XV, 13, 3 (240 T.P.): *In primisque tibi curae sit quod abs te superioribus quoque litteris petivi ne mihi tempus prorogetur.*
[4] *Ad Att.* VII, 1, 5 (284 T.P.): *Ridebis hoc loco fortasse* (and indeed it might well make anyone laugh): *quam vellem etiam nunc in provincia* [*Cilicia*] *morari.*
[5] *Ad Att.* VII, 1, 5 (284 T.P.): *Mihi valde placet de triumpho nos moliri aliquid: extra urbem esse cum iustissima causa.*
[6] *Ad Att.* XIV, 13, 2 (718 T.P.): *Res odiosa et aliena nostris aetatibus est* . . . April 26, 44 B.C. It is true that Cicero adds: *incerto exitu belli.* But what sort of a war is it whose issue is not uncertain beforehand?

because it was repugnant to his temperament. In that century of bloodshed he obstinately looked down on the warlike proceedings of Sulla, Caesar and Octavian with the anachronistic contempt of a Chinese mandarin. To hear him, the only weapons which he would deign to use, and in the handling of which he was a past master, were "wisdom, weight of character, and righteousness". But, as he wrote to Marcellus, when it is a question of "muscles and brute force" the superiority of those spiritual weapons disappears before a morally inferior enemy.[1] If you do not want to be crushed and trampled on, there is nothing to be done but to resign yourself to the inevitable, and give up the struggle, preserving if possible your dignity[2] and living quietly in your own house.[3] Cicero's idea of honour was not ours. He did not ask, like Pascal, that justice should be strong; nor did he fulminate, like Machiavelli, against disarmed prophets.[4] On the contrary, in his letter to Marcellus he seems, rather, to blame prophets who wield a sword they cannot be expected to handle properly, and he implies that justice is incompatible with brutality. Some will perhaps see the gleam of a superhuman ideal in this contrast between force and right. If they read the Correspondence they will forswear their illusions: there was nothing in it beyond an all-too-human attempt of Cicero's to give an air of respectability to his defeatism, and of nobility to his cowardice.

It pains me to use such words: yet they are not too strong. In the humiliating distress of his exile Cicero advertised—too loudly as it proved, since he never carried it out—his intention to commit suicide,[5] and on many later occasions he blazoned abroad a superb indifference to death.[6] It is clear from his letters that his un-

---

1 *Ad Fam.* IV, 7, 2 (486 T.P.): *Non enim in rebus pugnabamus quibus valere poteramus, consilio, auctoritate, causa, quae erant in nobis superiora, sed lacertis et viribus, quibus pares non eramus.* To Marcellus, Sept. 46 B.C. On Aug. 30, 51 B.C., from his camp at Iconium Cicero expressed the same repugnance in a letter to Cato: cf. *Ad Fam.* XV, 3, 2 (212 T.P.): *Mihi ut in eius modi re tantoque bello maximae curae est ut, quae copiis et opibus tenere vix possumus, ea mansuetudine et continentia nostra, sociorum fidelitate teneamus.* We can take the measure of this humanitarianism by referring to his description, five months later, of battles in which the mountaineers of the Amanus were "killed, captured or routed": cf. above, p. 252, note 1.
2 *Ad Fam.* IV, 7, 2 (486 T.P.): *Victi sumus, aut, si vinci dignitas non potest, fracti certe et abiecti* . . .
3 *Ad Fam.* IV, 7, 4 (486 T.P.): *Nonne mavis sine periculo tuae domi esse, quam cum periculo alienae?*
4 See the fine book of A. Renaudet, *Machiavel*, Paris, 1942.
5 Cf. above, pp. 198–9.
6 *Ad Fam.* IV, 7, 4 (486 T.P.): . . . *etiamsi oppetenda mors esset, domi mallem* . . . To Marcellus, 46 B.C.; cf. the slightly earlier letter to L. Mescinius

conquerable aversion from every form of fighting was rooted in dread of fatigue, danger and death, these cheerless accompaniments of war. Hence, his irresistible instinct to retreat and escape as soon as war began. When he foresaw, even afar off, peril, suffering or physical discomfort, he shuddered and his sole thought was how to avoid them. When he was setting out for Greece, news reached him between Formiae and Puteoli that there was a fresh outburst of piracy somewhere along the coasts of Greece, said to be the work of the dispossessed men of Dyme. Immediately he started recasting all his plans.[1] If he had to prepare for a long sea-journey, we find him planning to avoid all conceivable hardships and risks by multiplying his precautions and calculations, and working out with feverish attention to detail dates and ports of call, the tonnage of his transports, the value and the composition of his escort.[2] He was so much in dread of a coming rain of blows that he would take shelter from them even before the shower had begun. A deployment of troops, a suspicious gathering, a popular demonstration, any one of these was enough to send his imagination off the rails, undermine his confidence, and precipitate him into one folly or another.

Dio Cassius and the scholiasts of the *Pro Milone* record how he stammered and botched his pleading[3] when he saw Pompey's legionaries surrounding the Senate House, and his own letters are full of anecdotes which show him panic-stricken, tottering, running away. In the spring of 44, when Mark Antony's veterans were seen prowling in more or less compact groups round the outskirts of the Curia, Cicero either stayed away from the Senate or left the City.[4] When opponents met, fell to abusing each other and finally came to blows in the street, Cicero at the first encounter

Rufus, *Ad Fam.* V, 21, 4 (458 T.P.): . . . *ut mortem quam etiam beati contemnere debebamus, propterea quod nullum sensum esset habitura, nunc sic adfecti non modo contemnere debeamus, sed etiam optare.*

Similarly, in June 44 B.C., *Ad Att.* XV, 20, 2 (752 T.P.): *Ex hac nassa exire constitui . . . ad spem mortis melioris.*

[1] *Ad Att.* XVI, 1, 3 (769 T.P.): *Dymaeos agro pulsos mare infestum habere, nil mirum . . .* July 8, 44 B.C.

[2] *Ad Att.* XVI, 1, 3 (769 T.P.): . . . *sed opinor, minuta navigia*; XV, 26, 3 (763 T.P.): *Ego itinera sic composueram . . . Valde enim festino, ita tamen, ut quantum homo possit, quam cautissime navigem.* July 2, 44 B.C.; X, 7, 1 (388 T.P.): *Ego vero Apuliam et Sipontum probo.* April, 49 B.C.; cf. above, p. 224.

[3] Asconius, *In Mil.*, p. 42 Or.; Dio Cass. XL, 54. 2.

[4] *Ad Fam.* XI, 1, 1 (700 T.P.): . . . *adeo esse militum concitatos animos.* From Decimus Brutus, March 44 B.C.; *Ad Att.* XIV, 5, 2 (707 T.P.): . . . *vides in latere veteranos.* April 11, 44 B.C.; XV, 3, 1 (733 T.P.): *Novi conventus habitatores sane movent.* May 22, 44 B.C.

doubled back and detached himself, as happened in the Forum on Feb. 7, 56: "About three o'clock in the afternoon Clodius's men began spitting at our people. There was an outburst of rage. They began a movement to force us from our ground. Our men charged: his ruffians turned tail. Clodius was pushed off the rostra; then I too made my escape for fear of mischief in the riot."[1]

If he thus lost his nerve in a small scrap, we can easily imagine what a state he got into when a terrible war broke out. Physically he had a horror of fighting, and even when he made a feint of taking a share, his sole object was to evade it. Let us refer to his letters to Atticus of May 49. On the 6th he was determined to rejoin the Senate's army in Epirus. Since Caesar had gone off to Spain, he even thought of undertaking a local war in Italy against the scattered followers of Caesar, the kind of action which a leader of volunteers called Caelius had formerly carried out in Sulla's absence: "I often turn my mind to Caelius, and if I should get a similar opportunity I shall not let it slip."[2] On the 14th exactly such an opportunity presented itself. He immediately turned it down—and how! "I started for my *villa* at Pompeii on May 12, so that I might be there while preparations for my sailing were going on. When I arrived at the *villa* people came to me: 'The centurions of the three cohorts which are at Pompeii want to see you next day'—this is what our friend Ninnius told me—'they want to hand over their forces and the town to you.' Next morning, I can tell you, I was off from my *villa* before dawn, so that they might have no chance at all of seeing me. What did three cohorts amount to? Even if there were more, what equipment had we? I remembered what happened to Caelius."[3] Of course

---

[1] *Ad Q. Fr.* II, 3, 2 (102 T.P.): *Hora fere viiii, quasi signo dato Clodiani nostros consputare coeperunt. Exarsit dolor. Urgere illi, ut loco nos moverent. Factus est a nostris impetus, fuga operarum. Eiectus de rostris Clodius, ac nos quoque tum fugimus, ne quid in turba.*

[2] *Ad Att.* X, 12, 6 (398 T.P.): *De Caelio, saepe mecum agito, nec, si quid habuero tale, dimittam . . . Quo magis efficiendum aliquid est, fortuna velim meliore, animo Caeliano . . .*

[3] *Ad Att.* X, 16, 4 (402 T.P.): *. . . profectus sum in Pompeianum a. d. iiii Idus ut ibi essem, dum quae ad navigandum opus essent pararentur. Cum ad villam venissem ventum est ad me: "centuriones trium cohortium, quae Pompeiis sunt me velle postridie (convenire)"—haec mecum Ninnius noster—"vellé eos mihi se et oppidum tradere". At ego tibi postridie a villa ante lucem, ut me omnino illi ne viderent. Quid enim erat in tribus cohortibus? Quid, si plures? Quo apparatu?—cogitavi equidem illa Caeliana . . .*

he did! The rebel Caelius had been put to death.[1] This recollection at the decisive moment instantaneously froze the braggart's fiery enthusiasm. Cicero acquiesced in war only on condition of not waging it.

We can see this next year in Macedonia. Cicero was on the strength of Pompey's army, but he did not fight. Tradition is unanimous on this point. He was not present in person at the battle of Pharsalia on Aug. 9, 48. Cowardice, says Livy. And Livy's abridgment thus sums up the historian's thought: "Cicero remained that day in camp; no man less born for wars than he."[2] Ever-indulgent Plutarch says that he was ill.[3] But this illness would seem to have been faked, as a deserter fakes himself an alibi, and in any case it has left no trace in his Correspondence. His letters of July 48 to Atticus and to Terentia make no allusion to illness[4]; and on his own showing he landed at Brundisium in good health after the defeat.[5]

Similarly, when war flamed up again in Italy after Caesar's murder, Cicero refused to fight.

A fortnight after the Ides of March he began trembling again, foreseeing—a little late—some violent action by the Consul Mark Antony, of which he would have been one of the first victims. So once again he toyed with the idea of flight. Before expatriating himself to Greece, however—as he planned and re-planned to do— he hid himself in the Italian countryside, changing his hideout at least every second day. From his letters we know that on April 7 he was in a *villa* of Matius in the suburbs of Rome; on the 8th, somewhere between that and Tusculum; on the 9th in Tusculum;

[1] Tyrrell and Purser (T.P. IV, XL, and note IV, p. 193) refer these passages of Cicero to the Caelius (Coelius) whom Plutarch tells of in *Pomp*. VII, 1f. I am not convinced of the accuracy of this identification. I wonder whether this Caelius may not be the luckless defender of Placentia, who after Cinna's victory begged his friend Petronius to plunge his sword through his body. Cf. Val. Max. IV, 7, 5. In the one case we should have an adherent of Marius, in the other an adherent of Sulla. The question of *which* is in this connection of no importance.

[2] Livy, *Per.* CXI: *Cicero in castris remansit, vir nihil minus quam ad bella natus.* Cf. above, p. 18.

[3] Plut. *Cic.* XXXIX, 1.

[4] Cf. *Ad Att.* XI, 4 (413 T.P.) and *Ad Fam.* XIV, 6 (414 T.P.). The first of these is conjecturally dated July 48. The second is definitely dated by Cicero July 15, 48 B.C.

[5] *Ad Fam.* XIV, 12 (415 T.P.): *Quod nos in Italiam salvos venisse gaudes . . .* This letter is dated Nov. 4, 48 B.C., but the news over which Terentia was to rejoice went back much earlier. Cicero's "illness" was obviously over when the discussions arose in which he was threatened with death, a few days immediately after the disaster; see above, p. 226.

on the 10th at Lanuvium; on the 11th at Astura; on the 12th at Formiae; on the 15th at Sinuessa; on the 18th at Puteoli.[1] These zigzaggings only half satisfied him. He would have liked, in addition, to have made himself invisible and intangible. Even in writing to Atticus he was so sure that Antony's spies were on his track and that he must throw them off the scent that he did not dare to name the generous and trusty host who risked taking him on April 7 into his house close to the City's wall.[2] He indicated him at first only by a pseudonym or by periphrases. This was what Cicero called acting "more out of thought for my self-respect than for my danger."[3]

The situation grew more menacing: Cicero took ship.[4] It eased: he disembarked.[5] But he remained on the watch at Puteoli, and he told his friends that as long as things had not completely cleared up, he would not quit the coast.[6] At last the tables were turned. Mark Antony had quarrelled with Octavian and had to abandon Rome to his enemies and carry on hostilities in the north of Italy with forces inferior to those of the opposing coalition. How loudly Cicero then thundered against the scoundrel! With what fury his *Philippics* incited the magistrates, the parties and the legions against Antony! The war round Mutina was *his* war, of which he was the instigator, the harbinger, the herald. But for all that, he will not play the soldier. Firebrand though he was, he had no mind to burn his fingers. It was up to Decimus Brutus to hold out bravely; it was up to the gallantry of the Consuls Hirtius and Pansa to raise the siege and relieve Decimus Brutus. It was up to Cicero eloquently to encourage from Rome their joint efforts, to celebrate in the Curia or from the heights of the rostra their common victories. Each had his own job; each had his part to play. Even after the death on the field of honour of Hirtius and Pansa, it did not occur to Cicero to envy them their lot. In mourning their fate he contented himself with promising Cornificius that he for his part would continue to protect his country in his

---

[1] Cf. the series of letters *Ad Att.* XIV, 1–9 (703–10 and 712 T.P.).
[2] *Ad Att.* XIV, 1, 1 (703 T.P.): *Deverti ad illum, de quo tecum mane*; 5, 1 (707 T.P.): *Calvena* (bald-head) *moleste fert . . .* This refers to Matius; cf. ibid. (703 T.P.) and 4, 1 (706 T.P.).
[3] *Ad Att.* XV, 26, 1 (763 T.P.): *. . . neque id tam periculi mei causa fecerim quam dignitatis.* July 2, 44 B.C.
[4] Cf. above, p. 247, note 1, and below, II, p. 364.
[5] Cf. above, p. 247, note 2, and below, II, p. 367.
[6] *Ad Att.* XVI, 9 (798 T.P.): *Vereor ne valeat Antonius nec a mari discedere ibet.* Nov. 3 or 4, 44 B.C.

own way—*more nostro*—that is to say without risking his life in battle, as they had done.[1] With war raging round him he preferred to forgo the honour of taking part in it, applying to himself—with a slight modification—the orders which in the *Iliad* Zeus gives to Aphrodite:

> My child, the deeds of war are not for you:
> Seek rather thou the witching works of—speech.[2]

When war revealed itself at hand in all its terror, he turned his back on it with the energy of a fanatic and the naïveté of an imbecile: "To arms? Never: rather death a thousand times"—*Ergo et ἰτέον in castra. Millies mori melius.*[3] Logical inconsistency of a flabby soul. Normal reaction of a heart petrified by a fear more terrible in the long run than the danger obsessing it. When confidentially in his *Letters* Cicero confessed his cowardice, it was a cry wrung from the depths of his being. In public he swaggered, he protested that no man lived who was "more prudent or less timorous"[4] than he. In his private letters he had to drop the mask, and admit that "those brave and wise men the Domitii and the Lentuli used to call me fearful—and I was full of fear . . .",[5] to confess that "the king (i.e. Caesar) knew I had no courage",[6] and finally that "if any man is fearful in great and dangerous situations, that man is I."[7]

All the evidence points to the fact that such painful confessions were never meant for the public. In making them available the publishers of the Correspondence were holding up to contempt the man who had signed the *Letters*, and stirring up hatred of Cicero amongst those who in reading his *Letters* suddenly fathomed the depths of his weakness, wickedness and deceit.

[1] *Ad Fam.* XII, 25, 6 (851 T.P.): . . . *quam rempublicam nos si licebit, more nostro tuebimur.* May 43 B.C.

[2] *Ad Att.* XIV, 13, 2 (718 T.P.): . . . *tibi ego possum, mihi tu dicere :*
τέκνον ἐμόν, οὔ τοι δέδοται πολεμήϊα ἔργα,
ἀλλὰ σύγ' ἱμερόεντα μετέρχεο ἔργα λόγοιο.
Homer, *Iliad*, V, 428–9: Cicero has substituted "of speech" for "of wedlock" at the end of the second line.

[3] *Ad Att.* XIV, 22, 2 (729 T.P.). He adds: *huic praesertim aetati.* May 14, 44 B.C., but on May 11 he had omitted this qualifying clause: *Quidvis enim potius quam castra;* cf. *Ad Att.* XIV, 21, 4 (728 T.P.).

[4] Cic. *Phil.* XII, 10, 24: *Nemo me minus timidus, nemo tamen cautior.*

[5] *Ad Fam.* VI, 21, 1 (573 T.P.): *Ego, quem tum fortes illi viri et sapientes, Domitii et Lentuli, timidum esse dicebant—eram plane* . . . April, 45 B.C., to Toranius. Cf. ibid. IV, 14, 2 (535 T.P.), to Plancius, Jan. 45 B.C.

[6] *Ad Att.* XIII, 37, 2 (657 T.P.): . . . *nisi viderem scire regem [Caesarem] me animi nihil habere.* Aug. 2, 45 B.C.

[7] *Ad Fam.* VI, 14, 1 (498 T.P.): *Si quisquam est timidus in magnis periculosisque rebus, is ego sum, et si hoc vitium est eo me non carere confiteor.* To Ligarius, Nov. 26, 46 B.C.

6. MALICE AND DECEIT

We have certainly no need of the Correspondence to suspect his malice. We knew already that he reserved his indulgence for himself and had none over for others. Fantastically witty as he was, he coined epigrams "as easily as others breathe", and from an early date three volumes of his collected sayings were circulating in society circles in Rome, to the wrath of many and the amusement of all.[1] But the Correspondence discloses the cruelty underlying his jesting, which his incense-burning admirers would have wished to conceal.

Plutarch, for instance, draws liberally from the collection and entertains us with the most popular of these stinging repartees.[2] He recognises how much harm they did their author[3]; he attributes them to a quick intelligence and a verbal felicity both equally unusual, and he sees in them only the master-skill of an orator sufficiently gifted to be able "to let fly on the spur of the moment those sharp and biting shafts which disconcert an opponent and nail him to his seat".[4] According to him, Cicero's only fault was that his mighty and irrepressible zest led him all too often to "neglect the decorum and dignity" suited to his vocation.[5] We see from his letters, however, that his brilliant sallies were, on the contrary, barbed with sinister spitefulness. They cannot be excused either by the temptation to disconcert an opponent or the legitimate desire to win a just case. They strike at random, wounding only the absent, and they spare no one: neither people indifferent to him, nor those of his party, nor his friends.

That his flowing pen should insult those who had persecuted him and whom he in return has flayed in public is nothing unnatural. That he should defame his defamers and lash their vices; that he should score off Clodius, who was complaining that his sister would give up only a single foot of the consular seating space she was entitled to in the theatre, by immediately retorting:

---

[1] Quintilian, VI, 3, 5: *Utinam libertus eius Tiro aut alius quisquis fuit, qui tres hac de re libros edidit parcius dictorum numero indulsissent!* Three conclusions can be drawn from this brief sentence of Quintilian's, and they should be borne in mind: (*a*) the compiler of the collection was anonymous; (*b*) it was made early enough to have already been attributed—before Quintilian's day—to Tiro; (*c*) it included in its abundance a number of sayings the crudity or harshness of which embarrassed an admirer like Quintilian. On a preceding collection compiled by Trebonius, see Drumann-Groebe, VI, p. 529.

[2] Plut. *Cic.* V, 4; VI, 4; IX, 2–4; XXV–XXVII; XXVIII–XXXVIII, 2–5.

[3] Plut. *Cic.* XXVII, 1.   [4] Plut. *Cic.* XXVII, 1.   [5] Plut. *Cic.* XXV, 1.

"Don't grumble about one of your sister's feet; you'll get the other too"[1]; we must admit that this is effective fencing. Even if we cannot relish the coarseness of the jest, we cannot deny that it strikes home. Cicero had every right to legitimate self-defence against Clodius and Clodia. But how often his slanderous witticisms seem misdirected! Everyone was subjected to them for no apparent reason, without a shadow of benefit to their author. With delight he scented a whiff of scandal, no matter where it came from, and he was lured by every misadventure or calumny which furnished matter for a witticism. Even if the victims were important people who had in no way offended him, their mere importance, seeming to overshadow his own, was in itself an unconscious cause of offence. His malice even extended to people of the second rank and to quite insignificant figures of the contemporary stage.

In 61 there was young Curio for instance, with whom two years later he was on affectionate terms.[2] The boy had been one of a crowd of young dandies whose demonstration was vexatious to Cicero; he described it cruelly but amusingly in a letter to Atticus as being led by "Curio's little girl".[3] Later he strained his vocal cords with all sorts of imputations and innuendos against the behaviour of the mother and sister of his dear Brutus.[4] Between times, he spitefully scratched three patricians, C. Memmius and the two brothers Lucullus, with whom he had in public been always on excellent terms, by dubbing them "buffoons". Lucius, the elder of the Luculli, had been Consul in 74 and distinguished himself by conquering Mithridates. He was on somewhat cool terms with Memmius, who in 66 had opposed the proposal to grant him a triumph.[5] But Cicero publicly showed him his esteem by dedicating to him in 45 one book of his *Academica*.[6] The younger Lucullus, Marcus, had been Consul in 73[7] and during Caesar's absence had acted for him as Pontifex Maximus. In this capacity he had co-operated in getting Cicero's house on the Palatine restored to its owner, after Clodius had basely tried to alienate the

---

[1] *Ad Att.* II, 1, 5 (27 T.P.): "*Soror quae tantum habeat consularis loci unum mihi solum pedem dat*"—"*Noli,*" inquam, "*de uno pede sororis queri; licet etiam alterum tollas.*" June 60 B.C.
[2] Cf. above, p. 243.
[3] *Ad Att.* I, 14, 5 (20 T.P.): . . . *duce filiola Curionis.* Feb. 13, 61 B.C.
[4] Cf. below, II, p. 349f.
[5] Plut. *Luc.* XXXVII, 1; *Cato Min.* XXIX, 3.
[6] *Ad Att.* XIII, 32, 2 (610 T.P.).
[7] Under his adoptive name of Terentius.

site by having it dedicated to a religious purpose.[1] Cicero expressed his gratitude by associating his name with his brother's in a tribute he paid in the Senate in 56 to "those lights and ornaments of the Republic".[2]

C. Memmius was Aedile in 61 and Praetor in 58. Both in politics and in philosophy he was in touch with Cicero: he opposed Clodius;[3] he was a more or less fervent Epicurean, and as such was honoured by Lucretius, who dedicated to him his master-piece, *De Rerum Natura*, a work which Cicero studied;[4] and it was to him that Cicero addressed one of the finest of his *Ad Familiares*, begging him to see to the preservation of the house in Athens that had once belonged to Epicurus.[5]

Memmius and the Luculli were therefore men whom Cicero might have been expected to spare in his epigrams. But did he? In Jan. 60 the rumour was going round of a guilty love-affair between C. Memmius and the wife of M. Lucullus. What a godsend! Full of pleasant excitement, Cicero brought home the tasty dish red-hot and added seasoning of the best Attic salt: "Now this outrageous year begins. It was inaugurated by the suspension of the annual rites of Iuventas"—over which the family of the Luculli traditionally presided—"for Memmius initiated the wife of M. Lucullus into some rites of his own! Our Menelaus, being annoyed thereat, divorced his wife. But while Paris, the shepherd of Mount Ida, had injured only Menelaus, our Roman Paris played a scurvy trick on Agamemnon too."[6] Thus with ill-concealed glee, Cicero killed two, even three, birds with one stone. So much the worse for them, if his three victims had claims on his respect and gratitude! He could not resist the temptation to fire off his squibs. He would have risked a quarrel with the universe rather than not empty his quiver by shooting at every target in sight.

His jesting frequently took the form of a skilful use of nicknames with which he bespattered his letters, under the pretext that he

---

[1] *Ad Att.* IV, 2, 4 (91 T.P.). Oct. 57 B.C.

[2] Cic. *De Prov. Cons.* IX, 22: *Intueor coram haec lumina atque ornamenta reipublicae, P. Servilium et M. Lucullum. Utinam etiam L. Lucullus illic assideret!*

[3] *Ad Att.* II, 12, 2 (37 T.P.). April 19, 59 B.C. Cf. above, p. 196f, and Schol. Bob., p. 297 Or., and Suet. *Caes.* XX, 4.

[4] *Ad Q. Fr.* II, 9, 4 (132 T.P.). Feb. 54 B.C.   [5] *Ad Fam.* XIII, 1 (199 T.P.).

[6] *Ad Att.* I, 18, 3 (24 T.P.): *Instat hic nunc ille annus egregius. Eius initium eius modi fuit, ut anniversaria sacra Iuventatis non committerentur. Nam M. Luculli uxorem Memmius suis sacris initiavit. Menelaus aegre id passus divortium fecit. Quamquam ille pastor Idaeus Menelaum solum contempserat, hic noster Paris tam Menelaum quam Agamemnonem liberum non putavit.* Jan. 20, 60 B.C.

The Defects of a Statesman

was avoiding the danger of having to take to flight if the letters were intercepted. This happened all too often in those days, for the despatch of letters by courier was risky and uncertain.[1] Instead of mentioning the names of the persons, anecdotes about whom provided matter for his letter-chronicles, he amused himself by inventing pseudonyms for them, which would be Greek to a casual reader, but which his actual correspondent would certainly be able to identify.[2] This precaution was useful in itself, and at the same time it provided a pastime for Cicero—which was also important. In a playful spirit, he proceeded to select these terms which undeniably produced a generally comic effect, but which at the same time were tinged with deadly and corrosive malice. Thus Clodius became Pulchellus—the little darling—a diminutive of his patronymic Pulcher (the Handsome), which carried a flagrant suggestion of his vicious way of living.[3] With such ulterior intention Clodius's sister, the notorious Clodia, was indicated by Cow-eyes—βοῶπις—the Homeric epithet inseparably connected with Hera-Juno, the daughter of Cronos-Saturn, who had married her brother Zeus-Jupiter.[4] In like manner the Consul Afranius, by a sly antiphrasis, was named "Son of Aulus" in allusion to his mother's dubious reputation.[5] Mark Antony's vices, his violence, his love of gaming, his debauchery, his greed, provided a variety of transparent nicknames: the Gladiator,[6] the Dicer,[7] the paramour of Cytheris,[8] the Highway Robber.[9]

Pompey received favoured treatment with a diversity of picturesque descriptive terms supplied in unequal quantities by memories of his Syrian and Palestinian campaigns, and allusions

---

[1] See, in particular, *Ad Att.* I, 13, 1 (19 T.P.); and especially II, 20, 5 (47 T.P.): *Me Laelium faciam, te Atticum [Furium]*. The inconveniences of private letter couriers were ended only when Augustus created an official postal service. See the remarkable monograph by H.-G. Pflaum published anonymously in Oct. 1940 under the title *Essai sur le Cursus Publicus sous le Haut-Empire romain* (*Mémoires présentés par divers savants*, Vol. XIV), p. 22f.

[2] Cf. above, p. 139f., the example of Teucris.

[3] *Ad Att.* I, 16, 6 (22 T.P.); II, 1, 4 (27 T.P.); and II, 22, 1 (49 T.P.).

[4] *Ad Att.* II, 9, 1 (36 T.P.); 12, 2 (37 T.P.); 14, 1 (41 T.P.); 23, 3 (51 T.P.). The double meaning of this Homeric epithet applied to Clodia is unquestionable. Cf. Cic. *Pro Caelio*, XXXII, 78: . . . *eadem mulier cum suo coniuge et fratre* . . .

[5] *Ad Att.* I, 16, 12 (22 T.P.); 18, 5 (24 T.P.); 20, 5 (26 T.P.); II, 3, 1 (29 T.P.). The meaning has been well brought out by L. A. Constans, I, p. 153, note 3.

[6] *Ad Fam.* XII, 2, 1 (790 T.P.): *gladiator*.

[7] *Ad Att.* XIV, 5, 1 (707 T.P.): *aleator*.

[8] *Ad Att.* XV, 22 (755 T.P.) and X, 10, 5 (395 T.P.): *Cytherius*.

[9] *Ad Fam.* X, 5, 3 (810 T.P.); 6, 1 (826 T.P.); XII, 25, 6 (851 T.P.): *latro, latrocinium*.

to his warily arrogant pose of oriental despot: Arabarches,[1] the Jerusalem merchant,[2] Sampsiceramus from the name of the vassal Emir of Coele-Syria,[3] and yet again Epicrates. This last can be interpreted either as the adjective, which in Greek means "the Victorious", or as the proper name of the treacherous bandit whom Antiochus IX of Cyzicus had hired against the Jews.[4] Less important personages were incidentally provided with some nickname or other, neither less witty nor more flattering. By labelling him as either the Tartessian[5] or the Gaditanian,[6] the Spanish origin of Balbus was recalled, and the humble origin of Cn. Octavius by the phrase "a son of Earth".[7] An anonymous suitor for the hand of some relative of Atticus was said to be "better born even than his father"[8]—a discreet certificate of bastardy. Many owed their fictitious names to some ugly feature or to some infirmity. The Consul M. Pupius Piso, who had a somewhat clown-like air, was said to rouse laughter "more by his face than his facetiousness",[9] while the lameness of the Tribune Aufidius Lurco was pilloried as being "of good augury" for the laws he introduced.[10] Cicero made merry over the lisp of Hirrus[11] and over the baldness of Matius[12] and the wen of Vatinius[13]; and other folk were treated with corresponding delicacy.

This flood of uncomplimentary nicknames and remarks, however, recoils on Cicero himself; to us they betoken two unlovely characteristics: a devastating spiritual aridity and an appalling duplicity. If Cicero had had by nature a spark of goodwill towards his fellow-men, he would have refrained from such discourtesies unless when he was obliged to throw the indiscreetly curious off the

[1] *Ad Att.* II, 17, 3 (44 T.P.).　　　　[2] *Ad Att.* II, 9, 1 (36 T.P.).

[3] *Ad Att.* II, 14, 1 (41 T.P.); 16, 2 (43 T.P.); 17, 1 and 2 (44 T.P.); 23, 2 and 3 (50 T.P.).

[4] *Ad Att.* II, 3, 1 (29 T.P.): I do not believe in a confusion with Iphicrates, as Tyrrell and Purser suggest. On the Syrian Epicrates cf. Josephus, *A.J.* XIII, 10, 2–3; *B.J.* I, 2, 7; and Bouché-Leclercq, *Histoire de Séleucides*, I, p. 408.

[5] *Ad Att.* VII, 3, 11 (294 T.P.).　　　　[6] *Ad Att.* VII, 7, 6 (298 T.P.).

[7] *Ad Fam.* VII, 9, 3 (145 T.P.); cf. ibid. 16, 2 (157 T.P.).

[8] *Ad Att.* XIII, 21, 4 (632 T.P.).

[9] *Ad Att.* I, 13, 2 (19 T.P.): . . . *facie magis quam facetiis ridiculus*; 16, 12 (22 T.P.): *Consul ille deterioris histrionis similis.*

[10] *Ad Att.* I, 16, 13 (22 T.P.): . . . *ille legem bono auspicio claudus homo promulgavit.*

[11] *Ad Fam.* II, 10, 1 (225 T.P.).

[12] *Ad Att.* XIV, 2, 2 (704 T.P.); cf. 5, 1 (707 T.P.) and 9, 3 (712 T.P.), 3: Crassus is called *calvus ex Nanneianis*, that is to say "the bald man amongst those sharing out the confiscated property of Nanneius". Cf. *Ad Att.* I, 16, 5 (22 T.P.); the reading of the MS. is here uncertain.

[13] *Ad Att.* II, 9, 2 (36 T.P.); cf. above, p. 207.

scent. In other cases he would have sought characteristic features only in people's misdoings or eccentricities. In fact, he indulged his ugly jesting where there was not the slightest necessity for it, for he often used at the same time in writing to the same correspondent the simple normal name in alternation with these indirect references, and he never employed the nickname or the jesting allusion save in a more or less offensive way. His jokes were aimed by preference at some natural inferiority: obscure origin, foreign or illegitimate birth, or some physical defect, something at any rate for which the unhappy victim was in no way personally responsible.[1] In concentrating on such things, he gives us a low idea of himself and betrays his superficiality of judgment and lack of kindly feeling.

He was so childishly addicted to these things, and so eager to squeeze out the maximum effect from his jests and his witticisms, that he would go out of his way to invent an excuse for committing them. He pretended to take seriously the stammer implied more or less in the proper name of Balbus, and wrote off to Papirius Paetus who had invited Balbus to dine—a fact of which Balbus had boasted: "If you earned his compliments by your conversation, I shall bring you a pair of ears not less appreciative: but if by your menu, I beg you not to think stammerers worth more than men of eloquence."[2] This joke, you may say, if pretty feeble, is innocent enough. But all the same it offends by its lack of kindliness. The ills which afflict the human body, instead of arousing his pity, simply serve to unbridle his wit. He was a vain man, himself good-looking, fit and faultlessly turned out[3]; it did not occur to him to feel for the less fortunate, just as it never crossed his mind to spare a thought of sorrow or sympathy for the acquaintances with whom he rubbed shoulders yesterday in the Senate or the Forum and who today lay dead. His old friend and comrade Diodotus had just died. What then? The sole funeral orison he accorded to a generous benefactor was this to Atticus: "Diodotus is dead: what he left me amounts perhaps to 100,000 sesterces."[4]

Towards the end of May 46 Cicero had a pleasant dinner with

---

[1] See the examples cited above, p. 266.
[2] *Ad Fam.* IX, 19, 2 (478 T.P.): *Hoc si verbis adsecutus es, aures ad te adferam non minus elegantes : sin autem opsonio, peto a te, ne pluris esse balbos quam dissertos putes.* To L. Papirius Paetus, Aug. 46 B.C.
[3] Cf. above, p. 77.
[4] *Ad Att.* II, 20, 6 (47 T.P.): *Diodotus mortuus est ; reliquit nobis HS fortasse $\overline{C}$.* July 59 B.C.; cf. above, p. 102.

Seius.[1] In November Seius was no more: "Hard luck on Seius. But all human happenings must be considered bearable."[2] Hortensius, the glory of the Roman Bar, whose praise is given a place on the first page of Cicero's *History of Latin Eloquence*,[3] Hortensius has passed away: "I am sure you grieve for Hortensius," Cicero wrote briefly to Atticus, "I am heart-broken myself: for I had resolved to live on very intimate terms with him."[4] And that is all. In 48 Pompey was slain in Egypt, Pompey whose flag Cicero had followed and then deserted. To that great shade he devoted two lines of icy comment: "I never doubted how Pompey would end. I cannot help deploring his fate, for I knew him to be a man honest, pure, and high-principled."[5] The phrase is at least decent, while the following, commenting on the death of Pompey's two lieutenants, C. Fannius and L. Lentulus Crus, is simply despicable: "Am I to condole with you about Fannius? He used to talk abominably about your remaining in Rome. L. Lentulus had already promised himself Hortensius's town house."[6] That is how Cicero defamed the two dead soldiers who had been his companions in arms only the day before. We have heard him mocking the infirmities of living men who had a right to believe they were his friends. His Correspondence in giving us these indications of his heartlessness begins to open our eyes to the depths of his hypocrisy.

For when he mocks Matius, who had hidden him in his own house from Antony's assassins,[7] when he jests about Balbus, the Spaniard whose rights to Roman citizenship he had vindicated in a speech we still possess,[8] he reveals himself as an ungrateful cynic, and he disgusts us by a duplicity of which he himself appears to be almost unaware, so easily can he adapt his talk to his inter-

---

[1] *Ad Att.* IX, 7, 1 (462 T.P.).

[2] *Ad Att.* XII, 11, 1 (502 T.P.): *Male de Seio. Sed omnia humana tolerabilia ducenda.*

[3] Cf. the magnificent expansion of this, *ap.* Cic. *Brutus* I, 1–5. 47 B.C.

[4] *Ad Att.* VI, 6, 2 (276 T.P.): *De Hortensio te certo scio dolere. Equidem excrucior. Decreram enim cum eo valde familiariter vivere.* 50 B.C.

[5] *Ad Att.* XI, 6, 5 (418 T.P.): *De Pompeii exitu mihi dubium numquam fuit. Non possum eius casum non dolere: hominem enim integrum et castum et gravem cognovi.* Nov. 27, 48 B.C.

[6] *Ad Att.* XI, 6, 6 (418 T.P.): *De Fannio consoler te? Perniciosa loquebatur de mansione tua. L. vero Lentulus Hortensii domum sibi . . . desponderat.* Nov. 27, 48 B.C. Fannius, as it happens, was not dead; in 35 B.C. he rejoined Mark Antony; cf. *P.W.* VI, c. 1992. We owe this discovery to Münzer (*P.W.* ibid. following Appian, *B.C.* V, 139). If he is not mistaken, and if I myself am right, Fannius had the pleasure of reading this "anthumous" obituary. . . .

[7] See above, p. 259.

[8] The *Pro L. Cornelio Balbo*, 56 B.C.

The Defects of a Statesman

locutor of the moment. In one and the same day he can speak both well and ill of a man, and describe him as a dear friend one minute and an irreconcilable enemy the next.

It is of course permissible to speak in somewhat different terms when talking to a third party on the one hand and to people themselves on the other, when writing for publication or when writing an intimate letter.[1] Politeness imposes a discretion not always compatible with perfect frankness. It is the eternal controversy dramatised by Molière in the *Misanthrope* between Alceste and Philinte. Cicero's admirers, Gaston Boissier for instance,[2] have been tempted to revive it in order to extend indulgence to their hero. In my opinion, however, the shameless discrepancies revealed in his *Letters* transgress by far all the legitimate limits of courtesy and good manners. They introduce us to a perpetual game of "facing both ways". The problem is not one of courtesy but of fundamental morality, and nine times out of ten it puts Cicero in the dock. We shall touch on only a few of the contradictions in question. First, there is one which even Gaston Boissier, in spite of all his sympathy for Cicero, feels bound to indicate. In a letter written at the end of Oct. 50, Cato is spoken of as an excellent friend—*amicissimus*—and his conduct is considered most satisfactory.[3] At the beginning of November he is accused of having been basely malevolent in the very same matter.[4] But, as both letters were addressed to Atticus, Boissier is able to attribute the discrepancy to a changeable and impressionable temperament and not to a hypocritical nature.[5]

The contradictory remarks about Crassus do not lend themselves to any such plausible interpretation. In Nov. 55 Crassus, who was Consul for the second time, did not wait for his term of office to expire before going to take command of the troops which he was to march off to Syria to attack the Parthians. When the propitiatory sacrifice was being offered in the Capitol on the day of their departure, the Tribune C. Ateius Capito, who was hostile

[1] *Ad Fam.* XV, 21, 4 (450 T.P.): *Aliter enim scribimus quod ad eos solos quibus mittimus, aliter quod multos lecturos putamus.* To L. Mescinius Rufus, April 46 B.C.

[2] Cf. below, p. 271, note 2. Tyrrell and Purser, V, pp. xli and xlii, recall the defence put up by Cardinal Vaughan for the discrepancies in Cardinal Manning's letters.

[3] *Ad Att.* VII, 1, 7 (284 T.P.): *Cato ad me iucundissimas litteras misit . . .* 8: *Catoni amicissimo . . .*

[4] *Ad Att.* VII, 2, 7 (293 T.P.): *Cato . . . in me turpiter fuit malevolus.*

[5] G. Boissier, *Cicéron et ses amis*, p. 18.

The Defects of a Statesman

to the expedition, launched out into curses against Crassus "to which the disaster of Carrhae eighteen months later was to give a tragic significance"[1]; Crassus left Rome amid the booing of the populace.[2] When he heard of these demonstrations, Cicero joyously burst out to Atticus: "They say indeed that our friend Crassus started out dressed in his official robes with less dignity than in olden times Aemilius Paullus,[3] who was of the same age as he and also Consul for the second time. Oh, what a bad fellow he is!"[4] Now, the very evening before,[5] to call the Roman people's attention to their pretended reconciliation,[6] Cicero had given Crassus a princely banquet in the gardens which belonged to his son-in-law Crassipes on the banks of the Tiber.[7] And it was from Cicero's hearth, so to speak, that Crassus set out for his province.[8] Further, less than six weeks later, he wrote Crassus a solemn letter of alliance and devotion: "For such a man you are, and such I hope to be. . . . I would fain hope that our union and friendship will redound to the credit of us both. . . .[9] I would have you believe that this letter will have the force of a treaty . . . the defence of your position which in your absence I have undertaken, I will abide by, not only for the sake of our friendship, but also of my own consistency."[10] The discrepancies of these texts are irreconcilable. With Crassus Cicero showed himself not just ridiculously versatile, but odious in his falseness.

In the case of Mark Antony, Cicero's hate was coupled with treachery. When Antony, at Caesar's command, was trying in 49 to keep Cicero in Italy, Cicero wrote to Atticus setting forth the

---

[1] L. A. Constans, III, p. 19.   [2] Dio Cass. XXXIX, 39; Plut. *Crass*. XVI.
[3] In 169 B.C. when leaving for Macedonia and his campaign against Perseus.
[4] *Ad Att*. IV, 13, 2 (130 T.P.): *Crassum quidem nostrum minore dignitate aiunt profectum paludatum quam olim aequalem eius L. Paullum, item iterum consulem. O hominem nequam!* Tusculum, between Nov. 14 and 17, 55 B.C.
[5] I am keeping to the accepted chronology; L. A. Constans, III, p. 19, note 3, is in favour of another, but his arguments are unconvincing. The dates are Nov. 13, dinner with Crassipes; Nov. 14, departure of Crassus for Syria (and of Cicero for Tusculum); Nov. 15 or 16, the letter quoted in the last note.
[6] *Ad Fam*. I, 9, 20 (153 T.P.): . . . *ut quasi testata populo Romano esset nostra gratia*. To Lentulus, Dec. 54 B.C.
[7] Cf. above, p. 158.
[8] *Ad Fam*. I, 9, 20 (153 T.P.): . . . *paene a meis laribus in provinciam [Crassus] est profectus*.
[9] *Ad Fam*. V, 8, 3 (131 T.P.): *Is enim tu vir es et eum me esse cupio, ut . . . coniunctionem amicitiamque nostrum utrique laudi sperem fore*. To Crassus, Jan. 54 B.C.
[10] *Ad Fam*. V, 8, 5 (131 T.P.): *Has litteras velim existimes foederis habituras esse vim; . . . quae a me suscepta defensio est te absente dignitatis tuae, in ea iam ego, non solum amicitiae nostrae, sed etiam constantiae meae causa permanebo.*

The Defects of a Statesman

devices by which he would evade surveillance and veto: "I must of course receive the man. He was to arrive on the evening of May 3. That's today. Perhaps he will come to see me tomorrow. I shall draw him out. I shall listen to him. I shall protest loudly that there is no hurry, that I am sending a message to Caesar. I shall conceal myself somewhere with a very few men. Most assuredly I shall take flight from here."[1] As matters stood, a state of war justified deceit. Later, there was no excuse for it. None; especially in 44, when Cicero made a display both of hate and of courteous attentions towards Antony. Somewhere between April 20 and 26 he received a note from Antony as correct, courteous and temperate as anyone could wish, asking him not to oppose Clodius's recall.[2] We have got Cicero's reply—recopied for Atticus's benefit—and the comments which accompanied it. They are as different as night from day. The reply, which is in the affirmative, opens with a protestation of friendship which positively makes the reader sick[3] and ends with platitudinous assurances of most revolting complaisance.[4] Cicero's remarks on the two letters are simply a diatribe, unjust in proportion as Antony had not pressed his request and violent in proportion as Cicero felt he had been guilty of weakness.[5] Nor was this all.

Cicero was growing uneasy on June 10, 44, about rumours of possible agrarian confiscations of land in Tusculum.[6] Hot on each other's heels two letters were despatched which we can compare: the one on June 21 to Tiro, in which Cicero expresses his wish to preserve Antony's friendship unimpaired[7]; the other on June 22 to Atticus, in which he reports an alleged saying of Antony's, a

---

[1] *Ad Att.* X, 10, 3 (395 T.P.): *Omnino excipiam hominem. Erat autem v Nonas venturus vesperi, id est hodie. Cras igitur ad me fortasse veniet. Temptabo ; audiam ; nihil properare, missurum ad Caesarem me clamabo. Cum paucissimis alicubi occultabor. Certe hinc evolabo.*

[2] *Ad Att.* XIV, 13A (716 T.P.). Letter written by Antony from the south of Italy between April 20 and 26, 44 B.C.

[3] *Ad Att.* XIV, 13B, 1 (717 T.P.): *. . . nam cum te semper amavi, primum tuo studio, post etiam beneficio provocatus, tum his temporibus respublica te mihi commendavit, ut cariorem habeam neminem.* April 26, 44 B.C.

[4] *Ad Att.* XIV, 13B, 5 (717 T.P.): *Illud extremum : Ego quae te velle quaeque ad te pertinere arbitrabor, semper sine ulla dubitatione summo studio faciam. Hoc velim tibi penitus persuadeas.*

[5] *Ad Att.* XIV, 13, 6 (719 T.P.): *Antonius ad me scripsit de restitutione Sex. Clodii—misi tibi exemplum—quam dissolute, quam turpiter, quamque perniciose . . .*

[6] *Ad Att.* XV, 12, 2 (745 T.P.).

[7] *Ad Fam.* XVI, 23, 2 (754 T.P.): *Ego tamen Antonii inveteratam sine ulla offensione amicitiam retinere sane volo, scribamque ad eum, sed non ante quam te videro.* To Tiro.

terrible saying, sufficient to destroy any possible hope of settlement with him: "Cytheris's paramour declares that none save the victors shall live."[1] The double game is obvious. Cicero was thinking only of how to gain time, how to preserve his Tusculan estates intact. On July 11 he was congratulating himself on Atticus's having called on Antony at Tibur to thank him and was rejoicing over the guarantee obtained in this connection: "For certainly we shall part company with our State rather than our fortunes."[2] What pettiness underlies these cunning manœuvres, and if Antony saw through them to the sordid intentions beneath, what good grounds he had for detesting and despising Cicero even more thoroughly!

Cicero's disloyalty was, however, not confined to his enemies. He indulged it even in dealing with men with whom he had no quarrel, with Hirtius and Pansa, for instance, the Consuls-designate for 43. In the spring of 44 he was their neighbour at Puteoli and his relations with them were excellent, on the surface at least: he and Pansa dined with Hirtius,[3] he publicly received their visits; to all appearance there was nothing between them but courtesy and goodwill. At heart, however, he was out of tune with them, he watched them stealthily, and behind their backs he ran them down. On April 22 he wrote to Atticus: "I don't even like these Consuls-designate, who have actually forced me to declaim for them, so that I am not let have peace even by the sea."[4] On May 11 he was still at Puteoli and still continuing to see them, with the concealed intention of drawing them into his political intrigues. As they pretended not to understand, he began running them down again: "I was thinking of dining with Hirtius tomorrow . . . hoping in this way to bring him over to the party of the *optimates*. It is no good. There's not one of that crowd who isn't afraid of peace."[5] Seven months later Hirtius and Pansa, having entered on their office as Consuls, set out against Antony to join the "War of Mutina", and Cicero in writing to Decimus Brutus was placing

---

[1] *Ad Att.* XV, 22 (755 T.P.): *Hic autem noster Cytherius nisi victorem neminem victurum.*

[2] *Ad Att.* XVI, 3, 1 (773 T.P.): . . . *Certe enim . . . deseremur potius a re publica quam a re familiari.*

[3] Cf. above, p. 80.

[4] *Ad Att.* XIV, 12, 2 (715 T.P.): *Haud amo vel hos designatos, qui etiam declamare me coegerunt, ut ne apud aquas quidem acquiescere liceret.* April 22, 44 B.C.

[5] *Ad Att.* XIV, 21, 4 (728 T.P.): *Postridie apud Hirtium cogitabam . . . Sic hominem traducere ad optimates paro.* Λῆρος πολύς. *Nemo est istorum qui otium non timeat.*

all his hopes on these two men,[1] who, as it turned out, were to die on the field of honour.

The publishers of the Correspondence, to prevent our being misled by appearances, contrived to slip in amongst the Letters *Ad Familiares* a letter, not from Marcus Cicero but from his brother Quintus, to Tiro, which was written scarcely a month before that alluded to above, in which he derides the incompetence of the two generals: "I well know them to be full of vices and of the most effeminate weakness of mind. If they do not quit the helm there is the greatest danger of universal shipwreck."[2] Even friends who had rendered him signal service, and who were interested in politics only because of their friendship with politicians, Cicero could not refrain from stabbing in the back. At the end of August 44 he learnt that out of gratitude to Julius Caesar, Matius had undertaken to superintend the games for which Octavian had given permission in honour of his adoptive father. He had not the slightest shame in congratulating Matius on the "pious performance of a humane duty,"[3] though in talking to Atticus he had jeered insultingly at these games, at their organisers and at the preparations for them: "I don't like his arrangement for the games and I don't like Matius and Postumius as his agents: Saserna is a worthy colleague for them."[4] This is a trifling incident, but the contradictions involved are serious. It needed great ingratitude and unscrupulousness on Cicero's part to speak with such vicious contempt of a man to whom he was preparing to hand a bouquet of congratulations, and who only a month before had probably saved his life by sheltering him for a night under his own roof in the suburbs of Rome.[5]

The truth is that Cicero's heart had a short memory. Nothing existed for him—neither duty, nor truth, nor decent feeling—if it was a question of ministering to his own interest or pride or

---

[1] *Ad Fam.* XI, 8, 2 (816 T.P.): . . . *quos spero brevi tempore societate victoriae tecum copulatos fore.* To Decimus Brutus, Jan. 43 B.C.

[2] *Ad Fam.* XVI, 27, 1 (815 T.P.): . . . *quos ego penitus novi libidinum et languoris effeminatissimi animi plenos; qui nisi a gubernaculis recesserint, maximum ab universo naufragio periculum est.* From Quintus to Tiro, end Dec. 44 B.C.

The insertion of this letter from Quintus, independently of the books in which his correspondence was collected, can only have been intentional. The preceding lines suggest that he and his brother had agreed in their opinion of the matter, and that Tiro already knew what that opinion was.

[3] *Ad Fam.* XI, 27, 7 (784 T.P.): . . . *a te pie fieri et humane, ut de curatione ludorum.* Aug. 44 B.C.

[4] *Ad Att.* XV, 2, 3 (732 T.P.): *Ludorumque eius apparatus et Matius ac Postumus mihi procuratores non placent: Saserna collega dignus.* May 18, 44 B.C.

[5] Cf. above, pp. 259 and 268.

curiosity. He went so far as to betray his own brother. In Jan. 47, while he was in retirement in Brundisium, messengers deposited with him a parcel of letters which Quintus was sending to various correspondents. He opened it to see whether there was one for him. There was none. But there were letters for Vatinius and Ligurius, who were living near, and he sent them round to them. As these letters were full of invectives against Cicero, these virtuous busybodies amused themselves by showing them to him. What then? I shall let Cicero tell his own tale in his own words to Atticus: "Having suffered this painful shock, I wanted to know what he had written to the others . . . I found they were in the same strain. I am sending them to you. If you think it to his advantage that they should be delivered, deliver them. It will do me no harm. As for their being unsealed, Pomponia (Quintus's wife, Atticus's sister) has, I think, got his signet. . . ."[1]

This last example of refined treachery is the most damning of all: the breaking of the seals, the diversion of the letters, the suggested resealing with Quintus's signet. It is clear that if Cicero's letters had been collected by faithful admirers they would have omitted this one, in which we catch him in the very act of violating his brother's correspondence. They would have suppressed not only this letter, but all those I have quoted which dim his prestige or cast doubt on his courage or his honesty. Only a mind blindly and passionately hostile could have decided to publish them, and while professing to establish Cicero's literary fame, vented its hate in a way which would destroy all his other glory, not only for the passing moment but for the centuries to come.

For it is his own *Letters* which display in all his nakedness Cicero, the pleader for bad cases, the bad husband and the selfish father, which have exploded his pretensions to statesmanship, which defeat every attempt to rehabilitate him. Who can blame the publishers for having in their turn violated his privacy when he had not the decency to respect his brother's? Who would venture to defend a political career whose worthlessness and inconsistency the collected texts disclose: conduct misguided by blindness and paralysed by fear? Who would try to vindicate after his death a man who lived only for himself, to avenge the murder of

---

[1] *Ad Att.* XI, 9, 2 (423 T.P.): *Hoc ego, dolore accepto, volui scire quid scripsisset ad ceteros . . . Ad te misi. Quas si putabis illi ipsi utile esse reddi, reddes: nil me laedet. Nam quod resignatae sunt, habet, opinor, eius signum Pomponia.* Brundisium, Jan. 3, 47 B.C.

one who until proscribed and assassinated had never ceased lying to others, betraying others, and had callously or mockingly passed by the unhappy and the unfortunate?

The conclusion is inevitable. The portrait of Cicero that emerges from his Correspondence is so full of shadow, so daubed with blackness, that it cannot be the work of clumsy friends. Only hatred could have drawn it for the Romans, and etched it ineffaceably for posterity. Since the publication of the *Letters* dates certainly from the days of the Second Triumvirate,[1] they could not have seen the light without the permission and complicity of the Triumvir at that time in sovereign command of all Italy. It was therefore that Triumvir, Octavian, who inspired the undertaking. On reflection, we see that he thus justified and consummated his work. When in Dec. 43 he allowed Cicero's name to be inscribed on the proscription list, Octavian aimed only at murdering the man. Later, when he caused the *Letters* to be published, he dealt a death-blow at Cicero's honour.

[1] Cf. above, p. 32f.